MW00987723

The Second Conquest of Latin America
Coffee, Henequen, and Oil
during the Export Boom, 1850–1930

iLAS Critical Reflections on Latin America

The Second Conquest of Latin America
Coffee, Henequen, and Oil
during the Export Boom, 1850–1930

Edited by
Steven C. Topik
and
Allen Wells

University of Texas Press, Austin
Institute of Latin American Studies

First Edition, 1998

Requests for permission to reproduce material from this work should be
sent to Permissions, University of Texas Press, P.O. Box 7819, Austin,
Texas 78713-7819

∞ The paper used in this publication meets the minimum requirements
of American National Standard for Information Sciences—Permanence of
Paper for Printed Library Materials, ANSI Z39.48–1984.

Library of Congress Cataloging-in-Publication Data

The second conquest of Latin America : coffee, henequen, and oil
  during the export boom, 1850–1930 / edited by Steven C. Topik and
  Allen Wells.
        p.   cm. — (ILAS critical reflections on Latin America series)
     Includes bibliographical references and index.
     ISBN 0-292-78157-1 (alk. paper). — ISBN 0-292-78153-9 (pbk. : alk.
  paper)
     1. Coffee industry—Latin America—History. 2. Henequen
  industry—Latin America—History. 3. Petroleum industry and
  trade—Latin America—History. 4. Exports—Latin America—
  History. I. Topik, Steven. II. Wells, Allen, 1951- . III. Series:
  Critical reflections on Latin America series.
  HD9199.L382S4 1998
  382'.6'098—dc21   97-32607
                                                                CIP

Contents

Tables

Graphs

Preface

This book began as a conversation. Noting that politicians in Latin America, the United States, and much of the rest of the world have returned to their blind faith in the magic of the market, free trade, and small government, we were struck by the degree to which decision makers are suffering from historical amnesia. Because we had spent decades studying export economies in Mexico and Brazil, we knew that today's new world order was not so new. We had heard many of the arguments, the praise, and the predictions before, and we knew the dead end that export economies had proved to be historically in Latin America.

We responded as academics are wont to do: we organized a panel on the legacy of export economies at the American Historical Association in December 1992. We invited Jonathan Brown—a noted specialist on petroleum—to discuss oil, and two distinguished commentators—Mira Wilkins, pioneering student of the history of multinational corporations and international business in general, and Carlos Marichal, an expert in international finance. The panel generated so much discussion and provoked so many new questions that we knew our work was not done. We then decided to publish a small volume to bring our questions and perspective to the scholarly and general public.

Fortunately, Theresa May, codirector of the University of Texas Press, and Virginia Hagerty of the Institute of Latin American Studies at the University of Texas–Austin, shared our vision. They gave us the space and time to develop our ideas further and we are grateful.

In the years between conversation and text, we incurred numerous intellectual debts, indeed, too many to acknowledge. Intellectual work is by definition teamwork, since we work in communities of knowledge in which our understandings, our questions, our very words are collective actions. We found working together an extremely valuable and enriching experience. Some people stand out, however.

Steven Topik would like to thank Julie Charlip, Elizabeth Dore, Lowell Gudmundson, Catherine LeGrand, Alan Knight, Colin Lewis, Héctor Lindo-Fuentes, Carlos Marichal, Mario Samper, and Rosemary Thorp. He benefited from sharing his ideas on coffee at the Tercer Congreso de Historia Centroamericana, San José, Costa Rica, in July 1996; at the Latin American Export Economies Conference at Lake Atitlán, Guatemala, in December 1996; at the Reinventing Latin American History in the Post–Cold War Conference in Riverside, California, in February 1997; and at the Market Integration Conference in Lund, Sweden, in March 1997. Travel funds from the School of Humanities of the University of California–Irvine made much of this possible.

Allen Wells expresses thanks to Norman Owen, Louis Johnson, and Kenneth Lewellen. Colleagues at the School of Social Sciences at the Institute for Advanced Study, Princeton, New Jersey, especially Albert Hirschman, were helpful in clarifying some of his thinking during his year in residence during 1995–1996. He presented preliminary papers at the Council of Latin American Studies Lecture Series, "Peasants, Democracy and Development," Yale University, in February 1993, and the Conferencia Nacional sobre el Henequén y la Zona Henequenera in Mérida, Yucatán, in October 1992. Jeremy Adelman and Marshall Eakin carefully read the manuscript and offered thoughtful comments and suggestions.

Steven Topik dedicates this volume to Martha Jane Marcy Topik, who greeted him with a fresh cup of coffee in the early morning and patiently listened to him drone on about coffee the rest of the day. Allen Wells dedicates this work to Katherine Conant Wells, who, with seemingly endless patience, perspective, and wry humor, has understood the often tenuous relationship—sometimes dangling by a thread of henequen fiber—between work and family.

—*Steven C. Topik, Irvine, California*
Allen Wells, Brunswick, Maine
April 1997

Map 1. Commodity Distribution of Coffee, Henequen, and Oil in Latin America, 1850–1930

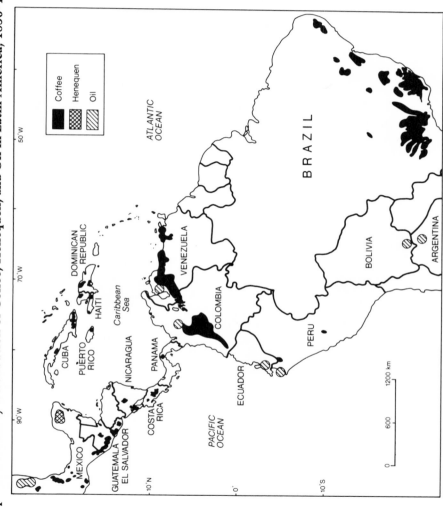

1. Introduction: Latin America's Response to International Markets during the Export Boom

Steven C. Topik
and
Allen Wells

Between 1850 and 1930, closer economic ties among Western Europe, the United States, and Latin America abruptly transformed Latin American societies. In some ways, this encounter was as dramatic as the conquistadors' epic sixteenth-century first encounter with Native American civilizations.

Three hundred years after Cortés and Pizarro, a different kind of battle raged over southern North America and South America. It was known by different names—civilization versus barbarism, progress versus tradition, folk versus modern culture, the transition from feudalism to capitalism—but its essence was always the same.[1]

The agent of change during the late nineteenth and early twentieth centuries was Latin America's integration into the world economy through the export of raw materials. Both foreign investment and liberal ideology sustained this export-led model as Latin American governments not only sought to promote economic development during this era but also encouraged sweeping changes in state building and social engineering. It was clear to nineteenth-century intellectuals and politicians that economic prosperity would pave the road to the creation of a strong nation. The goal of the liberal export regime was to overthrow the previous statist colonial heritage and integrate the countries' far-flung and heterogeneous inhabitants into a citizenry linked not by custom and religion but by the market. Throughout the New World, an emphasis on efficiency, productivity, and international competitiveness replaced protectionism and self-sufficiency as the hemisphere's guiding principles.

In many ways, the means employed in the nineteenth century to tie Latin America more closely to Western Europe and North America resemble the strategies currently in vogue throughout Latin America, as government officials and entrepreneurs seek to develop closer ties to the global economy. There is much to be learned from analyzing the first time that export-led growth and liberalism were embraced by Latin American societies.

This era, which we have labeled with some ambivalence the "Second Conquest," was, after all is said and written, much more a protracted series of negotiated encounters between international investors and Latin American elites than an outright economic victory by foreign entrepreneurs. As this introduction and the ensuing chapters suggest, the variegated character of the export boom, the inconsistent application of the liberal model, Latin America's diverse environmental landscape, and its distinctive cultural and political heritage all ensured that the impact of this encounter would vary greatly throughout Latin America.

The stakes of the Second Conquest were very high. The struggles in the fields, factories, and streets, on the pages, and in the legislatures of Latin America were not just over who held power and wealth, but over the very definitions of power and wealth and the world in which they resided. That world was turned upside down during the export boom, as everything became open to question and subject to power. Even such apparently immutable verities as time and geography were contorted and realigned. The strict discipline and linearity of the clock challenged the more forgiving and circular flow of the natural seasons; the iron rail and the telegraph brought far-flung elites into closer contact with one another than they were with much more physically proximate—but culturally distant—peoples. Standardization of weights, measures, and money—formerly the products of custom and negotiation—were imposed by national capitals, sometimes at gunpoint. Property and markets took on new meanings, indeed, sometimes became fetishes. Land and usufruct became commodities rather than trusts and rights, as before. Attempts were made not only to make the law more uniform, but to ensure the sanctity of private property—by force if necessary. Special groups such as priests, soldiers, and merchants no longer faced separate tribunals or held land communally or in entail. Concepts such as "profit," "interest," "efficiency," "free trade," and "laissez-faire" became talismans for some, while for others they were nothing less than the work of the devil. The boundary between private and public hardened as a civil society gradually emerged; corporate institutions, such as indigenous communities and the Catholic Church, once the bellwethers of the colonial regime, increasingly came under attack. As workers, often reluctantly, became more mobile, gender roles slowly shifted and the family took on new meanings, roles, and forms. Status, class, and race assumed new definitions and configurations as labor relations and labor forms were altered. Ascribed or inherited status slowly gave way, as the notion of social class took on greater importance. Liberal concepts, such as "State," "nation," "individual," "bourgeois," and "commodity," and the institutional baggage they carried with them, wrestled with Iberian patrimonial mercantilist and pre-Columbian communitarian traditions to transform Latin America's social landscape.

This book explores the surge, crash, and din of Latin American economies during the export boom by focusing on the domestic consequences of three key export commodities: coffee, the leading export of many Latin American countries; henequen, Mexico's principal agricultural export at the turn of the century; and petroleum, which would transform the economies of Mexico and Venezuela.

Why study commodities? First, they most palpably link Central and South America to Europe and the United States. As Sidney Mintz has observed, "The integration of the Americas into a European economy . . . was intimately associated with particular substances . . . This bespeaks the organization of capital, effort, technology, and labor force for specific objectives, always taking into account the nature and needs involved in the production of the substances themselves."[2]

Commodities allow us to see the interaction between local geography, resources, and laborers and the forces of the world economy in a most concrete way. The study of export goods reveals more than simply the process of economic development; work in the fields made and transformed cultures and societies. Too often, the current fashion of studying popular culture has concentrated on rituals and representations rather than on material culture; it has emphasized consumption rather than production. Economics has been banished to a marginal "empiricist" purgatory, far from the fields of cultural construction.

This is wrongheaded. It is turning Marx on his head and ignoring the most fundamental elements of daily life. True, workers' consciousness does not predictably flow out of their work experience as milk out of a carton, but, certainly, that laboring experience has a central place in shaping their lives. As Michel-Rolph Trouillot has observed about the Haitian sugar economy:[3]

> Sugar was not simply the major source of revenues. It has acquired a *social culture* [original emphasis]: the socially drawn monopoly to subject to its refraction all other commodities and human beings themselves. Socially selected, socially identified, it became the principle around which human life was organized. Towns were built because of its proximity. Time was marked by its harvest. Status was linked to its possession. In Saint-Domingue [Haiti] there was a . . . ramified *sugar culture* [original emphasis].

Trouillot could have added that sugar created and dispersed families, redefined gender roles, recast and mixed ethnicities, and created nationalities.

The study of export economies helps explain not only the development of economies and the rise of national states, but also the cultures of the societies they formed; it enables us to disaggregate the Latin

American economies from the common generalizations and reifications and to study and compare varying relationships to the international market.

Staple theories suggest that certain commodities are predisposed to certain social consequences. Albert Hirschman, in developing his methodology of linkages, notes that, while specific crops do not force their wills on producers, they do limit the options and make certain outcomes more likely.[4] The notion that some crops are more or less likely to bring progress is embedded in the economic history literature of Latin America and in its folklore. Bananas led to dependent, rural, poor "banana republics." Sugar, it has been argued, led to large plantations and a coerced labor system. Other crops were more ambiguous. Tobacco in Cuba was seen as democratic, but in Colombia it was accused of creating an ephemeral, speculative boom. Coffee was the hero in Colombia, where it led to a national state, and in Costa Rica, where it created a hardy peasantry. In Brazil, however, it only entrenched slavery and a planter elite and in Guatemala it despoiled indigenous peoples.[5]

Interestingly, much has been written about the flow of commodities in the early modern world. Determined to document the evolution of modern capitalism, this literature has emphasized the relationship between primary producers and Western Europe, and the critical role that technology, institutions, and merchant capital played in the growth of what has been called "commodity ecumenes."[6] As we will see, these commodity networks were incresingly liberated from political regulation (mercantilism) after 1800 and left to the "free" play of the marketplace. Mediated by money, these ecumenes were driven by profits and energized by the circulation of goods. Not surprisingly, most contemporary scholars conceive of commodities as objects of economic value that are circulated and exchanged for other things.[7] In fact, the way we think about commodities today is so intimately associated with the growth of capitalism that we rarely think twice about how and why something becomes a "commodity."

Recent scholarship has forced us to reconsider and broaden our understanding of commodities. Cultural anthropologist Arjun Appadurai has emphasized the cultural, rather than the economic, character of commodities and, in the process, has encouraged us to think about the social character of goods—how they acquire and lose value over time, and how societies lay out culturally and legally approved paths for the circulation of such objects. Countervailing tendencies contest these prescribed paths, and the construction and reconstruction of these networks are shaped invariably by the political context. Commodities, Appadurai notes, have life histories or careers, and although the "commodity sphere in the modern capitalist world appears at first glance to be a vast impersonal machine, governed by the large scale movements of prices, complex institutional interests and a totally demystified, bureaucratic and self-regulating character," this belies "complex interactions between local, politically mediated, systems of demand."[8] As we examine the life histories of coffee, henequen, and oil during the Second Conquest, it will become clear that the paths that these primary goods took were anything but inevitable and prescribed.

The study of staples allows us not only to analyze and understand the development of Latin America in its many dimensions, but also to evaluate the nature of Latin America's link to the broader world. Arguably more than any other part of the globe, Latin America was a creation of the world economy. A budding school of analysis, building on the world systems approach, institutional economics, and business history has begun exploring the international complex of articulated layers known as "global commodity chains." These chains include production, transport, processing, financing, and marketing of specific commodities. Production and consumption, the local and the distant, are considered parts of a dynamically interrelated whole.[9] Different staples had different internal and international consequences. Our emphasis on commodities allows us to explore these ramifications.

To place these essays in a proper context, we will first paint with a broad brush the contours of the export boom and then turn to what nineteenth-century contemporaries and modern critics have written about an age that appeared to offer much promise for Latin American societies.

The World Economy

Though the battle was fought on many fronts and with many weapons, it was the market, particularly the international market, that made its heavy hand felt throughout the Western Hemisphere. True, Latin America had been shaped by the Atlantic economy since the beginning of European colonization. Columbus, Cortés, and Pizarro had first sought gold and silver, but the settlements that emerged during the colonial period were limited in scope and development. Owing to Europe's relatively small and poor population and slow, expensive, unreliable trans-Atlantic transportation, few products were shipped abroad from Latin America during the first two hundred years of colonial rule. Sugar was the only important agricultural export, and it was harvested for Europe only in the Caribbean and Brazil. In fact, the vast majority of the population of the Americas remained relatively untouched by European demand and products until the late eighteenth century. Only during the last half-century of colonial rule did Latin America see the development of significant domestic markets. Spanish and Portuguese colonial authorities, bent on creating cash cows to feed their mercantilist systems, instead established relatively self-sufficient settlements.

It would not be until the Industrial Revolution in Europe created a mass consumer market, factories hungry for raw materials, new technologies for production and infrastructure, and, most important, copious amounts of capital for investment that substantial domestic markets would be forged throughout Latin America. We are not engaging in hyperbole when we assert that the world economy was "revolutionized" after 1850. The first forty years of the nineteenth century saw international trade swell 400 percent. But contemporaries would look back at this period as lethargic compared with the headlong burst of world commerce that followed. Between 1850 and 1913, trade ballooned tenfold. (It would grow only half that fast in the next sixty years.) The volume of world trade on the eve of World War I was an astounding forty-four times greater than it had been in 1800![10]

The international market, which had been primarily a fairly marginal, long-distance luxury trade, came to occupy a central place in many economies. Foreign trade grew far faster than total world production and twice as fast as manufacturing. It has been estimated that in 1800 only 3 percent of output was sold internationally; by 1913 international commerce constituted fully one-third of all production.[11] Goods not only became commodities as they were produced with the market in mind, they also became increasingly homogeneous, standardized, and mobile as they flowed to and from many parts of the globe.

World trade experienced a heady expansion, with lower transaction costs and improvements in productive technology providing the impetus. Much is made of today's global capital markets, but capital between 1870 and 1914 was already mobile to a degree not only historically unprecedented, but also unrivaled until recently. Multinational consortia, usually based in London and confident in the value of the pound sterling and the force of European hegemony, placed fabulous sums all over the world. It became easier, cheaper, faster, and safer to sell goods abroad because increased monetarization, the gold standard, London's financial hegemony, and transoceanic telegraphs facilitated an extraordinary increase in commercial credit and lower interest rates. Transportation costs tumbled with the invention of the steamship and the railroad and the construction of the Suez and Panama Canals. And laws and standards became internationally accepted and enforceable as dozens of international conferences met to homogenize the world economy.

All of this became possible because of great capital accumulation in Europe, which led to unprecedented foreign investment. Where around 1850 there was about $2 billion of global foreign investment, in 1900 it stood at $23 billion, and in 1913 it reached the prodigious height of $43 billion, twenty-one times greater than a scant sixty years before.[12] The world had never seen such a dizzying creation of wealth.

Foreign trade and investment meant Western control of much of the world. The era from 1875 to 1914 came to be known as the Age of Empire. During this period, about one-quarter of the earth's land surface was distributed or redistributed among six nations.[13] Many other areas became informal colonies as their fates were controlled by a few countries in Europe and by the United States. Indeed, during the 1850–1914 period, the world's commerce and investment would be concentrated more than at any other time in history. Over three quarters of all international trade was conducted by Europe and the United States. If we include their colonies, Europe and the United States controlled over 90 percent of world trade. They had a similar share of world industrial production. And, by 1914 Western societies were responsible for 95 percent of all foreign investment. Moreover, they also ruled the seas, where nearly all of the vastly expanded merchant marine fleet belonged to the European powers, over half to the British alone.[14]

European dominance derived from capital and industrial might, yet, interestingly, manufactures did not dominate the world market. Raw materials consistently represented about two thirds of trade goods. Tropical exports also remained stable, at least between 1870 and 1913, at around 10 percent of trade.[15] As a formidable supplier of raw materials, Latin America occupied an important niche in the global economy.

Latin America in the World Economy

As the region freest from European colonization, Latin America would be further integrated into the world economy by merchants and investors rather than by colonial officials.[16] Because they were the first European overseas colonies,[17] the recently independent countries of Latin America had legal, economic, and value systems congenial to Europeans. Unlike the Asian elite, the Latin American elite desired European goods and sought to emulate European society and fashion. It was widely believed that all that was necessary was to break down the barriers of Iberian mercantilism, bring political peace, and build roads and rail to get the products of the New World to flow effortlessly to Western Europe.

Between 1850 and 1913, Latin American exports grew 1,000 percent. Entirely primary goods, they took advantage of European hunger for raw materials and exotic foods. Although Latin America's share of world commerce was relatively small—between 5 and 8 percent during this period—it constituted about a third of all tropical exports and most of the exports from the underdeveloped, noncolonial world.[18] And since its population represented only 3 to 4 percent of the world's, its per capita exports were about seven times those of Africa and Asia.[19] Indeed, some Latin American countries surpassed the wealth of some European countries. Chile, Cuba, and Uruguay were certainly better off in terms of per capita exports than Eastern Europe and more prosperous than Portugal, Spain, and Ireland. Brazil was ahead of Japan and about equal to Russia in 1890. And Argentina in 1914 was one of the five richest countries in the world.[20]

European and North American demand for Latin American raw materials (e.g., nitrates, henequen, oil, and rubber) and consumer goods (such as coffee, wheat, sugar, and beef) during the second phase of the Industrial Revolution was the engine that propelled the late-nineteenth-century export boom. Spurred by technological change and the growth of markets in Europe and North America and attracted by the availability of resources and land in the region, developed nations purchased more goods from Latin America and the terms of trade initially favored the producers: it appeared that Latin Americans could buy ever more manufactured goods for the same quantity of exports.

A number of industrial processes were introduced from abroad as new technologies, such as the steamship, Bessemer steel, refrigeration, and barbed-wire fencing, dramatically transformed Latin America's urban and rural landscape. The steamship and the railroad (and its urban counterpart, the tramway) in particular slashed transaction costs and enhanced communication. From 1850 to 1910, some sixty-one thousand miles of railway track effectively tied Latin America's ports to their hinterlands and facilitated the political capitals' control of the countryside.[21]

The new infrastructure and soaring foreign demand for raw materials and consumer items provoked striking changes in land and labor patterns. Land and labor increasingly became commodities subject to the market. In some regions, a dense network of merchants, joint-stock companies, insurance firms, and commercial agencies facilitated the movement of both commodities and imports to market as capital increasingly subjected the population to its demands.

Foreign investment intensified as capital glut in Europe and Latin America's improving credit attracted British, French, German, Belgian, Dutch, Italian, Spanish, and Portuguese capital. Capitalists placed about one fifth of all overseas investment in Latin America, substantially more than went to the much more densely populated African and Asian continents.[22]

In some countries, such as Mexico, foreigners (nationals living abroad as well as immigrants) actually invested more in direct investments, stocks and bonds, and government loans than did nationals. Foreigners helped develop some of the first national banks, enhanced port facilities, and constructed railroads. European and, to a lesser extent, North American capital strengthened capitalist institutions and also bolstered national treasuries, which helped stabilize central governments. This economic transformation went hand in hand with sweeping political changes as generals and local caudillos were ousted from power and formerly cantankerous regions submitted to the national centers.

Latin America's burgeoning cities enabled political authorities to continue the Iberian mastery of the countryside. European immigrants flocked to Argentina and Brazil in a wave exceeded only in the United States between 1881 and 1915. The population influx combined with higher birth rates and longer life expectancies to more than double the number of inhabitants in Argentina and Brazil between 1850 and 1914. In the Southern Cone, urbanization was rapid, and elsewhere some capital cities became very large. By 1895 Buenos Aires was larger than Amsterdam, Brussels, and Hamburg, and Rio was larger than Rome.[23]

Even smaller capitals began to enjoy the blessings of electricity, public lighting, sanitation, and tramways. The internal markets grew as bourgeois property rights appeared in the forms of joint-stock companies, limited liability, stock markets, mortgage and commercial banks, land registries, and greater money supplies. At the same time, a native protobourgeoisie took command of the economies as capital goods and technological inputs from abroad contributed to the growth of textile mills, meat-processing plants, and foundries—to mention a few notable examples.

The Dark Side of the Encounter

Yet for all the dazzling indicators of growth, the export-led boom either exacerbated structural problems inherited from the colonial period or created a host of new contradictions that inhibited the implementation of a productive market economy that could generate linkages to other economic sectors. In the first place, to say that "Latin America" was undergoing an export boom is misleading. The term "Latin America" was coined by a nineteenth-century Frenchman who sought to find a cultural link between imperialist France and the former Iberian New World colonies. It was not a term used by the inhabitants of the countries themselves. More seriously, "Latin America" lumped together as a false monolith twenty countries that had very different relationships with the world economy.

In fact, even though all the countries produced raw materials and were linked to just a few major trade partners, the boom's impact was far from uniform. True, in 1913 thirteen of the twenty Latin American countries had more than half of their exports concentrated in one product, which they exported, in every case, overwhelmingly to Great Britain, the United States, France, and Germany. But the exports were concentrated in just a few countries. Argentina and Brazil alone provided over half of all exports and, together with Chile, Cuba, and Mexico, supplied 80 percent of Latin America's sales abroad.[24] The level of exports per inhabitant also fluctuated wildly. Where Cuba and Argentina in 1912 enjoyed per capita exports of over $60 dollars (20 percent higher than Great Britain's total), Venezuela, Peru, Mexico, and Colombia had levels of $10 or less. As a result, Argentina was one of the richest countries in the world while most of South and Central America still labored in poverty.[25]

Indeed, since three countries with only 15 percent of Latin America's population were responsible for over half of all exports, clearly most people were only indirectly affected by the tightened ties to the international economy. In fact, the impact of the international economy was even more restricted than these statistics imply because of great regional variations within the exporting countries themselves. In Argentina, for example, the Pampa behind Buenos Aires flourished, but more traditional areas farther from the coast, such as Mendoza and Salta, were not touched by European demand. They would benefit only later and indirectly when Argentines began to hunger for their wines and sugar. Brazil's Northeast also failed to take advantage of the burgeoning world market; during this period, it barely shared, even indirectly, in the new export-led prosperity. Similarly, Oaxaca in southern Mexico developed few ties to the international economy.

The timing of export booms and the nature of the products also sharply differed. Some sugar growers in the Caribbean were among the world's most important producers in the eighteenth century. Cuba's rise came in the early nineteenth century. Brazil abandoned sugar exports but turned to coffee, which started to dominate the world economy at mid-century. Costa Rica was also an early coffee exporter, but other coffee producers, such as Colombia, Guatemala, El Salvador, Nicaragua, and Mexico, became important internationally only after the turn of the twentieth century. Chile was successful early with copper and wheat and then late in the nineteenth century with nitrates and copper again. Peru's guano boom provided great wealth beginning in the 1840s but ended by 1880; no other commodity readily replaced the natural fertilizer's primary position in the national economy. Bolivia's silver mines languished until tin and then copper supplanted them in the 1890s. The most prosperous exporters of all, Argentina and Uruguay, found substantial markets for their beef, wool, and wheat only at the end of the nineteenth century. A few countries, such as Paraguay and Honduras, exported very little before World War I.

In some cases, it is questionable whether the exports should be considered "Latin American" at all. Certain commodities required heavy capital investment—well beyond the means of national entrepreneurs—to import new technologies and improve infrastructure and marketing. Foreign capitalists established economic enclaves in mining and commercial agriculture, which frequently entailed the construction of remote "company towns," some at a great distance from national population centers. These mines and plantations resembled foreign islands more than extensions of the national economies. But even when the export sector was more closely integrated into the home economy, foreigners often dominated credit, marketing, transportation, and the sophisticated technologies applied to finishing the product.

This foreign-dominated primary export model carried heavy costs: it exposed the domestic economy to violent shocks brought on by changes in external demand; it exacerbated inequality while ignoring social reform; it often made Latin American nations less self-sufficient, since collaborating elites, who worked hand-in-glove with foreign merchants to move exports, took advantage of reduced shipping rates, railroads, and enlarged urban markets to flood internal markets with foreign grain, foodstuffs, and manufactured goods; and it favored the political dominance of landowner-exporters, who played an increasingly oligopolistic role in regional economies as formerly powerful groups such as urban artisans, merchants, and government officials lost power.

Perhaps the most critical problem was the export sector's vulnerability to price fluctuations on the international market. Periods of high commodity prices were inevitably followed by bust cycles, which spawned a number of complications. First, since capital goods had to be imported on credit (because of the dearth of indigenous capital) to facilitate the expansion of the export sector, a decline in demand or a drop in prices had a debilitating impact not just on the specific export sector, but also on the entire national economy. Second, the scarcity of capital meant that, when prices tumbled, monocultural producers found it difficult to shift to alternative products. Moreover, since few internal markets existed (nor could they be created easily) for these consumer products and raw materials, market fluctuations did not encourage entrepreneurs to diversify, as a self-regulating market mechanism should have. Likewise, the substantial outlays that the export sector required for land, labor, and infrastructure diminished the attractiveness of pursuing new commodities and inhibited the development of new regions. National governments, by and large, were reluctant to take an interventionist stance and prop up specific sectors from a declining market, lest they scare away foreign investors in other areas.[26]

Foreign investment, which largely emanated in London, also oscillated wildly throughout the boom; credit was abundant when commodity prices advanced, but investment diminished when prices contracted. This was precisely the moment when export earnings were reduced, driving many merchants and landowners into bankruptcy courts. Latin American loan booms and debt crises were tied to the expansion and contraction of the international economy. The foreign capital spigot decisively influenced the financial policies implemented by Latin American states during the boom. Carlos Marichal has found that nineteenth-century debt crises were "triggered by a stock market crash in London or at some other financial center, by the collapse of one or more leading international banks, and/or by the news of the imminent default of a given Latin American government." The most severe bust cycle was the so-called Great Depression of 1873–1896, which precipitated the collapse of many large joint-stock companies and the major financial restructuring of other enterprises.[27]

Just as the Second Conquest brought greater economic instability in the wake of rapid growth, so too did it create new social tensions. The region's middle classes and organized labor found the states unresponsive to their growing numbers. In Mexico, where these new groups insisted on greater political participation, they contributed to revolutionary unrest; in many Latin American nations, however, regional and national oligarchical elites found ways to deflect opposition by incorporating or co-opting their rivals through political reform and electoral politics. This created a body of voters for personalistic political machines while replicating and reproducing in form and content the inequalities already present in these societies.[28]

But if politicians wanted to bestow legitimacy on their political institutions by creating a façade of restricted democracy, they also had to be ever-vigilant of the potentially unruly multitude. And if the urban working class or the middle classes refused to cooperate, politicians increasingly called on the military and police to limit dissent and, if necessary, crush unrest.[29]

Urban groups were not the only ones compelled to adapt or face repression. Peasants bore the brunt of the reorganization of the labor markets that the export boom imposed in the countryside. The gradual creation of a rural proletariat and a semiproletariat in some regions meant the loss of Indian lands, the weakening of their community structures and culture, and increasing impoverishment. In some regions, railroads contributed to the seizure of indigenous lands and the importation of foreign grains and foodstuffs, which undercut local production. As Tulio Halperín Donghi relates, landowners preferred a workforce that combined "the docility of a traditional peasantry with the efficiency of a modern proletariat."[30] If landlords were generally successful at exploiting the former, they usually failed at the latter. They were often frustrated with the low productivity of their coerced laborers, who were unwilling to submit to the intense and rigid discipline of capitalism. Peasants often struck an implicit deal in which they pretended to work and the landowners pretended to pay them. But since *hacendados* and plantation owners had the advantage of their ties to the expanding oligarchical state to use as a club in their arguments with their workers, the landed elite usually squeezed out sufficient labor and kept wages very low.

Consequently, the export model often failed to improve the distribution of wealth and reduce poverty. Indeed, they were often exacerbated. As economist John Sheahan soberly notes, "It is very likely that the numbers in absolute poverty increased all through the export boom, and even more likely that these pressures contributed significantly to the increasing violence in the region."[31]

Clearly, the Second Conquest was a mixed blessing for Latin Americans. Some it enriched and empowered, others were impoverished and repressed, still others managed to resist it. Given the often conflicting evidence we have today about the character of the export-led boom, perhaps it is not surprising that modern scholars have offered such divergent interpretations of the period. Interestingly, contemporary observers, who lacked the benefit of hindsight, but who enjoyed the advantages of watching these myriad changes unfold firsthand, shared the same ambivalent feelings, and for many of the same reasons.

The Many Faces of Liberalism

Export economies were inextricably bound up with the ideologies of liberalism, which in their many guises frame the disputes of the first century of nationhood. Politicians and intellectuals in the newly independent countries of early nineteenth-century Latin America had (as do many of today's scholars) a faith in the transformative power of words and ideas—of "discourses" and "imaginations." New liberal constitutions sought to forge a new world. Free trade and laissez-faire state policies were seen then, as now, as universal panaceas that would bring wealth, progress, and stability. The efforts to impose economic liberalism were both applauded as bold attempts to give birth to modern, progressive, democratic nations and decried as slavish imitations of European ideologies, ill-suited to the Iberian realities and indigenous cultures of Latin Americans.

Both sides, however, missed the point. Despite the efforts of some of the most dogmatic ideologues, liberalism in Latin America never succeeded in becoming an intellectual straitjacket. Many strands of liberalisms arose that were applied flexibly and imaginatively, if inconsistently. Given the central role of liberal ideas in the architecture of the export boom, and today's fascination with these two centuries-old ideas, it is worth delving into the ideological terrain of the Second Conquest a little more deeply.

Drawing on the ideas of Adam Smith, who contended that the state often let prurient political interests dictate economic policies that undermined productivity and efficiency, unabashed proponents of free trade called for the unrestricted international exchange of goods and the elimination of protectionist barriers and regulations imposed by the state. Echoing classical economist David Ricardo, free traders also argued that each region or country should produce goods for which it enjoyed a comparative advantage. In Latin America, more often than not, that meant primary products that optimized a region's particular blend of climate, natural resources, land, and labor. Ricardo, in fact, went as far as to argue that the terms of trade would favor nations that produced agricultural goods, since diminishing productivity in the countryside would stimulate higher prices.[32]

Yet theoretical rigor and consistency was, more often than not, forsaken in the interests of political pragmatism in the first decades after independence. Politicians did not find it expedient to act upon *The Wealth of Nations'* stinging critique of monopolies and special interests, nor were they quick to lift internal customs duties, such as the *alcabala* in Mexico, to promote interstate commerce. It was one thing for creole elites to drive Spanish and Portuguese merchants out, but it was quite another to attack vested commercial interests, or to undermine the ability of capital-starved Latin American states to borrow money from abroad even when it came with strings attached. As Paul Gootenberg makes clear in a study of Peru during the guano age, initially, economic liberalism was poorly received and halfheartedly implemented. The economic problems caused by the destructive wars for independence and the unstable political climate that vexed most Latin American states in the first half of the nineteenth century meant that ideological orthodoxy invariably took a backseat to the state's endorsement of what might be euphemistically described as "eclectic" economic policies. Albert Hirschman goes as far as to argue that, so preoccupied were Latin American intellectuals with affairs of state during this period, little time and ink remained to wrestle with substantive economic issues. In fact, Latin American intellectuals favored the writings of the French moral philosopher Jean-Baptiste Say over those of Adam Smith, precisely because the former theorized that economic principles should be divorced from political organization. Conversely, the more sensible Smith was keenly aware (and critical) of the injurious effects of political influence on commerce.[33]

It was not until the onslaught of the export boom that liberalism was, in its economic as well as its political sense, fully accepted throughout Latin America. Simply put, it was transformed from *one* way of looking at the world to *the* way of looking at the world. Indeed, liberalism was recast, in Charles Hale's words, "from an ideology in combat with an inherited set of institutions, social arrangements, and values [the colonial order] into a unifying political myth."[34] Authorities during the late nineteenth and early twentieth centuries repeatedly invoked the precepts of Enlightenment political philosophy and classical economics to justify their willingness to replicate European and North American political traditions and to rationalize Latin America's commercial engagement with the international economy. The United States became the political model to emulate, while Latin American entrepreneurial elites increasingly advocated British free trade and noninterventionist doctrines.

A severe illustration of the latter phenomenon occurred in Chile, when a French economics professor at the University of Chile, Jean Gustave Courcelle-Seneuil, counseled the Chilean minister of finance from 1855 to 1863 to push through a series of libertarian fiscal measures that rewrote the nation's banking, tariff, and fiscal laws. An ardent believer in laissez-faire and free trade, Courcelle-Seneuil (and his zealous Chilean students) helped pen legislation that removed so many government restrictions that the results proved catastrophic for both Chilean banks and national monetary policy. His disciples also would be largely responsible for the surrender of the Tarapacá nitrate mines to private interests after the Chilean victory in the War of the Pacific. Speculators like J. T. North bought up government shares in the mines for a song and then resold them on the London and Paris markets for a huge profit.[35]

Such sweeping changes were the exception, however. Throughout Latin America, although politicians publicly embraced the rhetoric of free trade, pragmatism continued to overrule dogma. Even when liberal policies were implemented, they were imposed gingerly and never without a great deal of debate and conflict. In fact, Paul Gootenberg's study of economic thought in Peru during the liberal century shows that a number of influential intellectuals were surprisingly diffident about the virtues of laissez-faire, and extraordinarily self-critical about their economy's overreliance on international trade and financing during the heyday of the nation's export boom: "They spoke eloquently in terms of harnessing exports to diversify Peru, of bolstering national markets, of extending public protection, of enhancing Peru's global sovereignty, and of engaging the masses in productive, developmental and honorable work." These progressive thinkers were especially taken with the promise of industrialization and envisioned what would later be called an import-substitution regime, made possible through the introduction of modern technology. Yet in the end, in Peru as elsewhere, this alternative perspective could not overcome the marriage of landed wealth and political power, a formidable combination that had cast its lot with the export model.[36]

Government officials throughout Latin America apparently did pay some attention to these perceptive critics, since the contradiction between the liberal ideal and the policies implemented during this period could not have been more striking. The very interventionist role of the state belied the ideology's fundamental principles. As we have noted, national governments during the export boom actively sponsored immigration, courted and facilitated foreign investment (especially for infrastructure), and reduced the economic power of corporate institutions like the church and Indian communities—all policies that satisfied entrepreneurs, but that expressed a characteristic dissonance between ideology and reality. The idiosyncratic blend of liberalism and statism in Latin America spawned variegated economic policies. More often than not, laissez-faire just did not mesh with the realities of political centralization and economic integration.

Not surprisingly, those who benefited the most were the most ardent defenders of free trade and nonintervention. Liberal policies may have been successful in ending the colonial legacy of monopoly, but they certainly did not distribute wealth more equitably. Public land policies in Mexico during the dictatorship of Gen. Porfirio Díaz (the Porfiriato, 1876–1911) and throughout much of Central America, which were designed to stimulate productivity, served only to concentrate land in fewer hands.[37] Political authorities and economic interests congealed—and in certain notable cases they were one and the same—to subordinate liberal doctrine to the more compelling requirement of social control.

A new generation of elites, many of whom were educated abroad, were fascinated with the possibilities of science and technology. The capacity to master nature through investigation and to apply machines to practical problems had tremendous appeal. In a sense, the railroad's multidimensional impact became both tool and symbol of modernization in late nineteenth-century Latin America; it linked peripheral regions more closely to the international market and coupled semiautonomous *patrias chicas* to an evolving nation-state. It also served as a reminder of Western dominance. As Michael Adas has observed, "Steam and trains proclaimed their mastery over time and space and demonstrated their capacity for precision and discipline."[38]

Technocratic elites throughout Latin America encouraged the importation of foreign theories, in addition to capital, technology, and immigration. Positivism, Spencerian social Darwinism, and liberalism were mixed and matched to adapt to Latin American realities. Progress and

modernity were used to rationalize everything from economic development to the inferior treatment of workers. The aggrandizing actions of
regional and national elites were lent credence by intellectuals like
Porfirio Parra of Mexico, who extrapolated from the pseudoscientific
theories of social Darwinism that the contest for control of the corporation had much in common with prehistoric man's struggle to survive
against the elements:[39]

> What occurs among coarse and brutal primitive peoples also
> happens, although in much different form, among modern groups
> in a civilized and refined society. Suppose one had a group of
> shareholders in which a small group excels, a privileged minority
> more capable than the others, and they impose themselves and rule
> the rest, even though, according to the philosophical tenets that
> inspired the Constitution [of 1857], all the shareholders have the
> same right to form the directorship of the company.

In practice, survival of the fittest meant the concentration of wealth
in fewer and fewer hands. Just as significantly, material progress was
impossible, in the minds of these technocrats, without law and order and
respect for private property. "Order and progress," in that order, were the
watchwords of the age.

Yet liberalism and the "scientific" corollaries it generated were met
with considerable skepticism and opposition by Latin Americans of all
social classes. Resistance took many forms. Two superb monographs on
the uneven process of capitalist development in different regions of
nineteenth-century Peru concur that the Peruvian countryside was
engulfed in class struggle throughout the boom, as statist economic
policies were consistently challenged and undermined by peasants,
landowners, and merchants.[40]

Liberalism also meant different things to different social classes.
Wells's research on Yucatán makes it clear that urban workers and rural
peasants conceived of liberalism in ways that differed from each other
and from the version propagated by regional and national elites. Some
elites were most concerned with federalist principles and political
freedoms—more often, it seems, when they were out of power. Others
were concerned with the sanctity of private property and the creation of
institutions and legal sanctions that protected their "rights."
Anticlericalism may have been an essential component of the liberal
tradition for liberal members of the urban middle class; it was anathema
to most campesinos, who on occasion joined in the fight against conservatives throughout the nineteenth century. In fact, rural political bosses
and their clients viewed local autonomy and the protection of commu-

nity rights as the most sacred tenet of the liberal creed. Moreover, an activist current articulated by liberal thinkers like Ignacio Ramírez and Ponciano Arriaga in Mexico, which demanded a more egalitarian society, had little in common with the scientific politics that would become the mainstay of the Porfirian regime. Recent work on community, ethnicity, and nationalism in Mexico shows that each of these factors played key roles in shaping the character and the makeup of liberals in different regions and among different social classes.[41]

In short, there was nothing inevitable, uncomplicated, or orthodox about how contemporaries interpreted and applied liberal doctrine during the export boom.

Interpretations

In the more than half a century since the end of the export boom, many scholars and politicians have looked back at the Second Conquest to draw lessons for their day. Their conclusions have been very much dictated by their ideological perspectives. The collapse of international trade during the Great Depression, for instance, shattered any illusions of consensus about the beneficence of the market and economic liberalism. The confidence of the generation that lived through the Great Depression was seriously shaken as the volume of international trade contracted by half in three years and the steady debilitation of international financial markets cut off the supply of capital to the region.

Three prominent theoretical paths emerged in the aftermath of the depression and the Second World War: (1) the modernization school; (2) the ECLA model; and (3) theories of imperialism. (Some social scientists have conflated the second and third schools. For heuristic purposes, we will treat them separately here.) It would entail another chapter, if not a book, to analyze the complex evolution of these paradigms and the offspring they spawned. Moreover, much already has been written about how different these schools of thought are, how they reflected the distinct visions of the bipolar postwar world, and how they were appropriated by politicians and intellectuals to serve the interests of either the inevitable advance of socialism or the inexorable triumph of capitalism.[42] We will refrain from rehashing these themes because they tell us more about the time in which they were expounded than about the export boom. Instead, we will emphasize the main lines of contention and confluence among these competing theoretical approaches as they relate to the export boom. What becomes clear from an examination of the literature on development since 1945 is that many of the same solutions proffered by contemporaries were, knowingly or unknowingly, reworked and recast by modern theoreticians.

Although all three paradigms lamented the failures of the boom, they prescribed radically different remedies. Given the flawed and compromised character of the boom, it was not difficult for proponents of each school to search for and find "proof" of their perspectives.

The Modernization School

Modernization theorists plausibly argued that the precepts of classical economics had never been strictly adhered to throughout Latin America. Latin American countries lagged ever farther behind the developed countries of Europe and North America, not because of too *much* liberalism, but because of too *little* liberalism. The statist Iberian heritage and the legacy of neofeudal landlords impeded economic development.

Modernization theorists continued to believe in the importance of exports. All economies had to go through a unilinear progression that all economies had to go through from primary exporters to industrial powers—the path followed most notably by England during the Industrial Revolution.[43] Development—what the West had and what Latin America aspired to—continued to frame the conceptual and theoretical debate, just as it had during the boom.

The West's perception of Latin America and other colonial areas implicitly restricted the kinds of questions that scholars asked. When Europeans and North Americans have imagined foreign cultures, they have cast the discussion, in Steve Stern's words, "in terms of dualities—backwardness and enlightenment, tradition and modernization, political innocence and vulnerability to Communism that suffused Western understandings of 'tropical' peoples."[44]

What troubled theorists was the uneven evolution of regional and national economies during the boom. Why had some areas remained relatively untouched, tradition-bound, and oriented toward subsistence? Why was it that some Latin American nations fashioned linkages from their growing export sectors and began the process of industrialization during the boom while others remained committed to staple production? Douglass North and Canadian staples theorists like Harold Innis and Melville Watkins argued that the lesson of the Second Conquest was that nations with vast natural resources should exploit them by exporting raw materials. In some parts of Latin America, exports did generate economic growth through the creation of forward and backward linkages. These linkages transformed subsistence sectors of the economy and created markets.[45]

While staples theory and other free trade models explained the success of Argentina, Cuba, and Uruguay in the pre-1930 period, they were less helpful in explaining why other countries did not share in their prosperity. One also needed to explore how economic interests used their wealth and position to exercise (or influence the exercise of) power and tactics, which oftentimes obstructed the efficient creation of linkages to other sectors of the economy. Development was not just a question of resource allocation and markets; it was fundamentally a political, social, and cultural question.[46]

Modernization theory was attractive, however, for a number of reasons. First and foremost, it emphasized, in a structural sense, an economic journey that could be shared by all nations. The theory's basic tenets had already been articulated by North Americans, Europeans, and like-minded Latin American elites during the export boom. Values harbored by traditional landlords and peasants would, spurred by the growth of the middle class and migration from the countryside to the city, give way to more "modern" attributes. Latin Americans need only follow the same path to progress that Europeans and North Americans had. Michael Adas has argued persuasively that the fundamental assumptions of the modernization paradigm were rooted in Europeans' and North Americans' "civilizing mission ideology" during the age of imperialism. Equal parts humanitarianism, cultural arrogance, and enlightened self-interest camouflaged its true intentions, but the assumption that all people and societies would take advantage of technology and develop along the lines pioneered by the West was consistent with the positivistic ideas advanced during the late nineteenth century. Development jargon obscured the tradition-to-modernity continuum, and words like "underdeveloped" or "emerging" entered the social science vernacular to make the paradigm more, in today's discourse, politically correct.[47] In a sense, the neoclassical and modernization models blame the victim. The poor are poor because they are less industrious, less ingenious. Wealth is the reward for the most efficient, the most productive, the most entrepreneurial. Everyone, modernizationists contend, is playing the economic game by the same rules.

There was substantial debate, however, even among the advocates of the modernization school. Though agreeing on the central importance of foreign trade, external investment, and private property, they frequently disagreed on the proper role of the state in the economy. Purists, foreshadowing the debates of the boom, wanted the market left untouched; interventionists pleaded for a responsible and detached state that would "act on behalf of progress and society,"[48] as the influence of the economic theories of John Maynard Keynes began to be felt. The question was how much social engineering and infrastructure building the state had to do before unassisted market forces could efficiently bring about development.

The ECLA Model

The second current of economic thought, ECLA developmentalism, was clear in its support of responsible state intervention. The United Nations Economic Commission for Latin America (ECLA, or CEPAL in Spanish) shared the neoclassical goal of capitalist industrialization through the wise application of foreign investment. Where it broke with free traders was in its lack of faith in the world market.

Led by Argentine economist Raúl Prebisch, ECLA's model was born of frustration and pessimism. Frustration was directed toward the European and North American states, which in the 1920s and the 1930s turned increasingly inward and autarkic under the pretext of hoarding supplies of essential goods in case of war. The depression only confirmed to Latin American economists that the export model was a vestige of the past and that Latin American states had to create and sustain internal markets and industrialize.

Prebisch and his cohort countered Ricardo's comparative advantage theory by insisting that export-led growth was ephemeral precisely because the terms of trade had turned against primary producers after 1870. Latin America's wealth was siphoned out of the hemisphere because manufactured goods imported to Latin America cost more than the primary products produced there. According to this vision, Latin Americans could not keep up with the development of the industrialized countries because the game was rigged in favor of the rich. The fault of the Second Conquest was not too *much* state interference, but too *little*—not that Latin American countries failed to export enough, but that they failed to pay sufficient attention to the home market and domestic industry.[49]

The polarization precipitated by the cold war and the Cuban Revolution led to full-scale critiques of classical and neoclassical economics and modernization theory. Dependency theorists wedded ECLA's model, various strains of Marxism, and theories of imperialism (see below) to harshly condemn foreign penetration and characterize Latin American capitalism during the boom as dependent. The colonial legacy of exploitation of natural resources, they contended, was transformed in the late nineteenth century by foreign entrepreneurs who, with the assistance of collaborative elites, controlled the export sector to the detriment of society as a whole. Their common refrain was that liberal elites, anxious to participate in the export trade, sold out their nation's economic sovereignty.

The most extreme version of dependency, as articulated by André Gunder Frank, asserted that the capitalist world economy did not permit the raw material–exporting periphery to develop. Because of the great concentration of wealth and power and extensive foreign control, the countries of Latin American actually "underdeveloped" during the Second Conquest.[50] Although at times overwrought and overstated, *dependentistas* did provide a sophisticated framework for studying the evolution of what they called "neocolonial" capitalism throughout Latin America during the nineteenth century.

The dependency approach gave birth to the more systematic world-systems theory, developed first by Immanuel Wallerstein. This is a functionalist approach that emphasizes the role of national economies in the international economy. It has the advantage of a global vision that illustrates the interaction of apparently disparate peoples, resources, and forces. Unfortunately, world-systems analysis often reduces the agency of individual actors, regions, and nation-states. Peripheral actors appear to have had little effect on the system; they are cast merely as victims or collaborators.[51]

A variety of neo-Marxist critiques followed. Marx's discussion of the economic mode of production was used to explain how capitalism grew so unevenly throughout the region. Internecine battles raged among the various theoretical schools and subschools about the definition of capitalism and when and if it finally landed in Latin America, but there is little doubt that the intellectual controversy these debates generated had a salutary effect on subsequent historical analysis of the boom.[52] Modes-of-production analysis, for instance, melds Marxist materialism and the concept of "combined and uneven development" in the periphery with local agency. This approach emphasizes that Latin American countries varied in their ability to resist and shape international forces during the export boom and recognizes the ability of subordinate groups or "subaltern" peoples to turn the forces of economic growth at least partially to their own advantage.[53]

Shared Assumptions

Despite their considerable differences, the dependency school and its offshoots and modernizationists shared some significant assumptions. Both stressed scientific and technological achievement and viewed traditional society as outmoded. Modernity was held to be both inevitable and desirable by both Marxists and modernizationists. In the most dogmatic treatments, haciendas were seen as feudal and archaic and labor as dependent and dependable—both obstinate remnants of the past. Both models shared the conviction that traditional beliefs, customs, and institutions were essentially impediments to the transformation of backward societies. Neo-Marxists were just as positivistic about economic progress and cultural transformations as their ideological enemies.[54]

Informal Imperialism in Latin America

If the Great Depression and the cold war precipitated the debate between the modernization and ECLA paradigms, the roots and the first branches of the "Theories of Imperialism" school can be traced to the first stinging critiques of the rise of industrial capitalism and the creation of colonial empires. Anti-imperialists agreed with ECLA followers that international trade favored the developed countries. But they emphasized at first that the imperialist powers used political control of peripheral countries granted by colonialism rather than by the market mechanisms of international commerce to gain their advantage. Anti-imperialists, who were mostly socialists, tended to be less sanguine about capitalism's potential for prosperity than their ECLA counterparts were.

John Hobson (whose most influential work was published in 1902), Rudolf Hilferding (1911), Vladimir Lenin (1916), and Nikolai Bukharin (1929) were more preoccupied with the causes of imperialism in Europe than with effects of capitalist expansion on Asia, Africa, and Latin America. It was Rosa Luxemburg's contribution to argue that imperialism was the direct result of the expansion of the capitalist mode of production into precapitalist modes of production, which pointed the way for subsequent Marxist (and *dependentista*) analyses of the deleterious impact of imperialism on the colonized.[55]

Conceptually, Latin America represented a different kind of problem for theorists of imperialism, since, with the exception of Cuba and Puerto Rico, all of the former Iberian colonies in the hemisphere had achieved their independence in the first half of the nineteenth century. Political sovereignty and economic autonomy, some contended, were different propositions. In the early 1950s, two non-Marxist historians, John Gallagher and Ronald Robinson, who studied British imperial rule in Africa proposed a controversial model of "informal imperialism," which had significant implications for the study of the export boom in Latin America. Gallagher and Robinson argued in their seminal article "The Imperialism of Free Trade" that economic dominion could flourish outside the confines of colonial rule. In their estimation, the British preference for control during the Age of Empire was captured in the phrase "trade with informal control if possible and trade with rule if necessary." The essential weapons of the Western trader or financier were economic not political, and the nature of imperial control—explicit or implicit—simply reflected need and opportunity.[56]

Robinson refined his ideas when he investigated the mutually beneficial bargain struck between foreign business interests and local exporters. The collaborator matrix, in Robinson's view, did not preclude local landowners, merchants, or political authorities from acting in their own interests. On the contrary, informal imperialism made it possible for like-minded elites to pursue interests that complemented those of foreign entrepreneurs and investors. As Robin Winks has suggested, "where informal empires arose, the relationship between the two [collaborating] elements was initially one stemming from conditions of relative equality." In certain cases, it enabled foreign companies to extract export commodities at a low price without sinking substantial investment in the local or regional economy. Of critical importance to the operation of this arrangement was that collaborators obtained satisfactory profits by expanding production while lowering labor costs. During this era, Robinson adds, indigenous collaboration and resistance together defined the limits of European penetration.[57]

An implicit contract required that national and regional elites honor their financial commitments, pay their debts, and maintain a political regime that was (if we may be permitted the anachronism) "user-friendly" to European and North American investors. If negotiations (sometimes heated and protracted) between the two parties spelled out the specific articles of the contract, there was little doubt who drafted the unwritten arrangement. Moreover, if the ongoing relationship as a whole prospered, an occasional dispute or setback in the negotiations mattered little in the general scheme of things. Indeed, the same range of negotiations went on under colonial rule. As A. G. Hopkins makes clear in a splendid rejoinder to those who have argued that the British did not exercise an informal empire over the Argentine economy during the export boom, "this was not a deal between peers; the parties had joint interests, but not equal power in pursuing them."[58]

The difference in the degree of power should not be underestimated. If, for instance, after 1898 the Cubans had entertained the notion of steering exports away from an imperial power like the United States, the response from Washington no doubt would have been swift and punitive. (One need only talk to Cubans today about such a response.) If, on the other hand, the United States had decided to seek new sources of sugar, the results not only would have been catastrophic for the island economy, but there would have been little that planters and politicians in Havana could have done about it.

Just as important, according to Richard Graham, was that collaborating elites subsumed the ideological and cultural premises of free trade and nonintervention. His reflections on Brazil can be applied more generally to much of Latin America at the turn of the century (and perhaps today):[59]

[T]he force of the imperial power is to be measured not or even primarily by the overt acts of political control but by the degree to which the values, attitudes and institutions of the expansionist state infiltrate and overcome those of the recipient one. In this process the native collaborator or sepoy is indispensable. It is when influential publicists and local politicians become convinced that the way of life of the imperial power is the best one imaginable that the strength of that nation is at its greatest, although the evidence may then be least noticeable. In nineteenth-century Brazil there were both institutional and personal reflections of this mechanism of imperial control.

To be sure, like all theoretical models, the imperialism of free trade doctrine and informal imperialism have been the subject of considerable debate. Economic historians of Latin America like D. C. M. Platt and H. S. Ferns have argued fervently that Gallagher and Robinson have overstated their case, especially when British investment in Latin America is considered. Marxists and neo-Marxists have chimed in to voice their objections. Specialists have joined the debate to demonstrate that the theory does not fit their particular case.[60]

Two recent debates, on the role of the International Harvester Company in Yucatán, Mexico, and on the Amazon rubber boom, highlight conflicting theoretical orientations for why the export trade did not contribute to development. Interestingly, in both cases, the lines are sharply drawn between social scientists—usually economists—who emphasize macroeconomic explanations, especially the vicissitudes of supply and demand—and historians, who stress the social and political forces that shaped relations among foreign capital, collaborating elites, local producers, and coerced labor.[61] In this volume, such a contrast in emphasis is evident in the essays by Brown, Topik, and Wells, who explore the social and political dimensions of export growth, and Wilkins, who stresses market-driven economic decisions.

The sum total of the criticisms make clear that the model cannot be applied uncritically. In certain regions of Latin America, British and North American investments were simply not remunerative and the degree of influence was markedly limited.

The dependency school, relying on Marxist theories of imperialism, would agree with Gallagher and Robinson and their disciples that foreign interests called the tune during the boom.[62] Where they would part company, however, is over the *dependentistas'* obsession with the long-term effects of capitalist expansion. Hopkins argues that Gallagher and Robinson were not concerned with the future economic growth of the periphery. Their goal was more modest: they offered a fresh conceptual point of departure for understanding the variegated nature of imperialism during the late nineteenth and early twentieth centuries. On the other hand, the *dependentistas'* intellectual destination was underdevelopment; therefore, relationships forged between foreign and local interests during the boom were compelling proof of the failings of the export-led model for subsequent Latin American development.[63]

As a commentary and debate on the existence of a British informal empire in Argentina at the turn of the century suggests, the informal imperialism model is still challenging our assumptions about domination and subordination and about accommodation and resistance during the export boom.[64] Given the current fascination with the study of theories of hegemony and patterns of accommodation and resistance, it would appear that the informal imperialism model may well enjoy a new lease on life.

Studying Commodities

As we have seen, there has been substantial disagreement about the consequences of export-led growth, the role of the state and foreign investment, and, indeed, the degree to which a capitalist market–oriented model could bring generalized prosperity and equity. We contend that a most helpful way of threading our way through the labyrinth is by adopting an unusual approach, one centering on studying commodities rather than on examining national or global economic histories. It is clear that the nature of the ties to the world economy was crucial in shaping the consequences of the Second Conquest. The three predominant theoretical schools, however, all emphasize external forces. Variation, as well as Latin American adaptation and resistance, characterized the export boom. Crops were raised and minerals mined in countries with histories and cultures, not on clean slates.

To fully appreciate the dynamics of Latin America's integration into the world economy, we must study, in Cardoso and Faletto's words, "the internalization of the external." To best appreciate the relative roles of foreign markets and capital, domestic resources and geography, culture, socioeconomic relations, and politics, however, we focus on specific commodities and compare their consequences in different national settings. Too often our emphasis on the state has made national boundaries, or at least political boundaries, the preferred category of analysis. To understand export economies, however, the specific commodity that fueled changes in a region or a nation-state is a useful point of departure.

Karl Marx was one of the first to stress what most people have always understood: we are what we work. People's consciousness and their social and political actions are very much dictated by how they earn their living. Too often, however, this insight has been generalized into abstract categories of class, or reductionist dichotomies such as domi-

nant-subordinate. And the histories—the cultures of producing areas—
are forgotten as master theories are concocted. As William Roseberry
notes in his discussion of coffee cultivation, "Despite the frontier
character of much of coffee expansion, however, most of the 'wilder-
nesses' into which coffee farmers moved were already encumbered by
people, overlapping and competing claims to land, conceptions of space,
time, and justice—in short, 'history'. . . and these encumbrances shaped
their respective coffee economies even as the regions were transformed
by the move toward coffee."[65]

We must study the preexisting population, geography, production
techniques, relations to the means of production, and political relations
in local historical settings to understand the impact of the export boom.
Specific commodities limited the range of possibilities of such arrangements, but the variations are as revealing as the generalizations. The
study of commodities enables us to expose the relationship between the
local and the global, between agency and fate. Commodities are congealed in the fields and the factories, just as the economic, social,
political, and cultural are different faces of the same phenomenon.

Why have we chosen coffee, fibers, and oil? First, they cover three
types of commodities. Coffee, an exotic beverage, was typical of the food
crops that dominated the first part of the export boom. Henequen, a hard
fiber used for binding and shipping, was the sort of agricultural product
with industrial applications that became increasingly important toward
the end of the nineteenth century. Oil, a fuel that became the engine of
the third Industrial Revolution, was an extractive mineral.

Because these commodities required different techniques to produce,
they have been viewed differently in the historiography. Henequen,
which grew principally in Mexico, but also in Cuba and Brazil, has been
seen as a backward crop that brought a form of slavery or debt peonage
to the Indians who worked on Yucatán's plantations. The planters have
been cast as a rather traditional elite and the crop as leading to growth
but little development. Coffee, on the other hand, has been viewed as a
backward crop when grown by slaves, yet a progressive one once
immigrants or peasants took to the fields. Coffee planters have been
characterized as a bourgeoisie who took their earnings and invested
them in manufacturing. Oil was the most capitalist of commodities.
Because it employed wage laborers and advanced machinery, it has been
labeled a foreign enclave with few linkages to the national economy.

Of the three, henequen was the most truly indigenous. The hard fiber
was made from a native agave using locally conceived technology and
indigenous workers. But the product was used almost entirely abroad.
Coffee was an African tree. Workers in Brazil and Haiti were Africans;
later European immigrants, local mestizos, and Indians throughout

Latin America harvested the crop. It was grown to satisfy European and North American thirsts. Oil was, of course, indigenous, but the machinery, techniques, and capital necessary to remove it from the ground and refine it were all foreign.

Oil is different from coffee and henequen because the industry was initiated by large-scale foreign industrial firms that first exported into Latin America, then import substituted their products to prevent domestic competition, and finally turned to export. The decisions to drill and refine oil fit into the firms' multinational global logic. Only in oil was the state directly involved in production, although in all three commodities, Latin American governments had a role in marketing. There were no substantial private national oil companies because of the barriers to entry caused by daunting capital and technological demands as well as marketing infrastructure. The state from the outset played a large role in overseeing the industry because of its foreign-enclave character, and, similarly, labor was quicker to organize and more radical as a result.

The next three chapters will examine the costs and benefits for their host societies of the Latin American coffee, henequen, and oil economies. How did they affect property ownership, the distribution of wealth, the nature of labor systems? How did they influence the culture, gender, and ethnic relations of the populations? Did they have a spread effect on the rest of the internal economy either by accelerating the capital accumulation process—by creating a market with their workers—or establishing a transport infrastructure? What were the political effects for the local populations, for the creation of national states, and for the resistance of foreign domination? Were they instances of neocolonialism or mutual development?

In chapter 5, business historian Mira Wilkins offers an alternative approach that emphasizes the importance of international business organization rather than commodities. The final chapter provides a comparative overview of our three case studies and their implications for this interpretive analysis of the Latin American export boom. We conclude with an epilogue that traces the path followed by Latin American policymakers since 1930 and reflections on the similarities and differences between this earlier export-led period of growth and the current fascination with the model.

Notes

1. The nineteenth-century Argentine writer and later the country's president, Domingo Sarmiento, coined the term "civilization versus barbarism" as the subtitle to his novel *Life in the Argentine Republic in the Days of the*

Tyrants, trans. Mrs. Horace Mann (New York: Collier Books, 1961 [1868]). The twentieth-century French social scientist Jacques Lambert, *Le Brésil: Structure social et institutions politiques* (Paris: A. Colin, 1953), introduced "dualism" to distinguish the "modern" from the "traditional." E. Bradford Burns emphasizes the battle between "folk" and "modern" in *The Poverty of Progress: Latin America in the Nineteenth Century* (Berkeley and Los Angeles: University of California Press, 1980), in which he discusses the more traditional historiography. Many Marxist scholars have viewed the export era as a "transition to capitalism." One good example is Jaime Wheelock R., *Imperialismo y dictadura: Crisis de una formación social* (Mexico City: Siglo XXI, 1975).

2. Sidney Mintz, "Comment on Articles by Tomich, McMichael and Roseberry," *Theory and Society* 20:3 (June 1991): 383–392, esp. 383.

3. Michel-Rolph Trouillot, "Motion in the System: Coffee, Color and Slavery in Eighteenth-Century Saint-Domingue," *Review* 5:3 (Winter 1982): 372.

4. Albert Hirschman, "A Generalized Linkage Approach to Development with Special Reference to Staples," *Economic and Cultural Change* 25 (1977): 67–98; Fernando Ortiz Fernández, *Cuban Counterpoint: Tobacco and Sugar* (New York: Knopf, 1947); Luis Eduardo Nieto Arteto, *El café en la sociedad colombiana* (Bogotá: La Soga del Cuello, 1971), 26–27, 34–35; Celso Furtado, *The Economic Growth of Brazil* (Berkeley and Los Angeles: University of California Press, 1965), 123–126; Victor Bulmer-Thomas, *The Political Economy of Central America since 1920* (New York: Cambridge University Press, 1987), 5–6.

5. On bananas, see C. David Kepner and Jay Soothill, *The Banana Empire: A Case Study of Economic Imperialism* (New York: Vanguard, 1967 [1935]). On sugar, see Noel Deerr, *The History of Sugar*, 2 vols. (London: Chapman and Hall, 1949–1950); and Sidney Mintz, *Sweetness and Power: The Place of Sugar in Modern History* (New York: Penguin, 1985). Ortiz Fernández, *Cuban Counterpoint*, emphasizes the democratic qualities of tobacco in Cuba. For a discussion of tobacco in Colombia, see William P. McGreevey, *An Economic History of Colombia, 1945–1930* (New York: Cambridge University Press, 1971). The literature on coffee production in Colombia, Central America, and Brazil is reviewed in chap. 2.

6. For example, see Eric R. Wolf, *Europe and the People without History* (Berkeley and Los Angeles: University of California Press, 1982); Immanuel Wallerstein, *The Modern World System: Capitalist Agriculture and the Origins of the European World-Economy in the Sixteenth Century* (New York: Academic Press, 1974); and Philip D. Curtin, *Cross-Cultural Trade in World History* (New York: Cambridge University Press, 1984).

7. The conception of commodities as products of exchange harkens to Marx and the classical economists. In *Capital* Marx writes: "A commodity is, in the first place, an object outside us, a thing that by its properties satisfies human wants of some sort or another." As society progressed, commodities became intricately tied to money, an impersonal market, and exchange value. Cited in Arjun Appadurai, "Introduction: Commodities and the Politics of Value," in Arjun Appadurai, ed., *The Social Life of Things: Commodities in Cultural Perspective* (New York: Cambridge University Press, 1986), 3–63, quotation on 7.

8. Ibid., quotation on 48. Moreover, knowledge is required for the production, circulation, and consumption of these goods. During the Second Conquest knowledge about commodities became increasingly commoditized. See also in the same volume Igor Kopytoff, "The Cultural Biography of Things: Commoditization as Process," 64–91; and James Ferguson, "Cultural Exchange: New Developments in the Anthropology of Commodities," *Cultural Anthropology* 3:1 (February 1988): 488–513.

9. A good introduction to this approach is Gary Gereffi and Miguel Korzeniewicz, eds., *Commodity Chains and Global Capitalism* (Westport, Conn.: Praeger, 1994).

10. Walt W. Rostow, *The World Economy: History and Prospect* (Austin: University of Texas Press, 1978), 69.

11. A. G. Kenwood and A. L. Lougheed, *The Growth of the International Economy, 1820–1960* (London: Allen and Unwin, 1983), 103.

12. Ibid., 40.

13. Eric Hobsbawm, *The Age of Empire, 1875–1914* (New York: Pantheon Books, 1987), 59.

14. It could reasonably be argued that international trade statistics are biased against continental-sized countries such as Brazil, China, India, Russia, and the United States because in these countries regional commerce covered long distances without crossing national boundaries. But even if we were to take European and North American output as a share of world output as the indicator of concentration rather than of international trade, it would still be true that Europe, its colonies, and the United States produced well over two thirds of world output. See Rostow, *The World Economy*, 52, 70, 71; Kenwood and Lougheed, *The International Economy*, 41; Hobsbawm, *Age of Empire*, 51. According to Paul Bairoch, the carrying capacity of ships worldwide grew twenty-six-fold between 1800 and 1913. See Bairoch, "How and Not Why? Economic Inequalities between 1800 and 1913," in Jean Batou, ed., *Between Development and Underdevelopment, 1800–1870* (Geneva: Librairie Droz, 1991), 17.

15. Kenwood and Lougheed, *The International Economy*, 96. Calculated from Charles C. Stover, "Tropical Exports," in W. Arthur Lewis, ed., *Tropical Development 1880–1913* (Evanston, Ill.: Northwestern University Press, 1970), 49; and Rostow, *The World Economy*, 664.

16. In 1913, according to Hobsbawm, *Age of Empire*, 347, all of Oceania was colonized, as was 96.6 percent of Africa, 68 percent of North America, and 56.8 percent of Asia. Only 7.5 percent of Central and South America was colonized.

17. Technically, Portugal's Atlantic island possessions (e.g., Madeira and São Tome) were the first European colonies overseas.

18. Rostow, *The World Economy*, 5; Stover, "Tropical Exports," 47–48; and Bairoch, "How and Not Why?" 22. The only significant manufactured export was the Mexican peso.

19. According to Bairoch, "How and Not Why?" 19, Latin America's per capita exports in 1910 were $16.60 while Africa's were $2.80 and Asia's, $1.70.

20. Ibid., 33.

21. Kenwood and Lougheed, *The International Economy*, 26.

22. This loan boom, which began after 1850, followed twenty-five years of virtually no foreign lending in Latin America. Wary European investors were reluctant to replicate the 1820s debt crisis, which damaged commercial relations between Latin America and Europe. For a comprehensive analysis of foreign investment in Latin America during this period, see Carlos Marichal, *A Century of Debt Crises in Latin America: From Independence to the Great Depression, 1820–1930* (Princeton, N.J.: Princeton University Press, 1989). For a thoughtful analysis of the forces that precipitated foreign lending, see Eric Hobsbawm, *The Age of Capital, 1848–1875* (New York: Scribner's, 1975), chaps. 2 and 7. Also see Kenwood and Lougheed, *The International Economy*, 42; and M. Barrat Brown, *After Imperialism* (New York: Humanities Press, 1970), 110.

23. Kenwood and Lougheed, *The International Economy*, 60; Michael G. Mulhall, *The Dictionary of Statistics* (London: George Routledge and Sons, 1899), 442; Nicolás Sánchez-Albornoz, *The Population of Latin America: A History*, trans. W. A. R. Richardson (Berkeley and Los Angeles: University of California Press, 1974), 169, 179.

24. Ciro F. S. Cardoso and Héctor Pérez Brignoli, *Historia económica de América Latina*, 2 vols. (Barcelona: Editorial Crítica, 1979), II:136.

25. Calculated in current dollars from Brasil, Diretoria Geral de Estatística, *Anuário Estatístico de 1908/1912*, xi; and W. Arthur Lewis, *Growth and Fluctuations, 1870–1914* (Boston: Allen and Unwin, 1978), 164, 204. See also Carlos Díaz Alejandro, *Essays on the Economic History of the Argentine Republic* (New Haven, Conn.: Yale University Press, 1970), 7, 10, 23.

26. For a thoughtful discussion of these problems, see the introduction by Roberto Cortés Conde and Shane J. Hunt, *The Latin American Economies: Growth and the Export Sector, 1880–1930* (New York: Holmes and Meier, 1985). Two notable exceptions to the commonplace that national governments were reluctant to "protect" commodities were the unsuccessful and short-lived valorization campaigns in support of henequen in Mexico and coffee in Brazil in the first decades of the twentieth century. See Steven Topik, "L'état sur le marché: Approche comparative du café brésilien et du henequen mexicain," *Annales Economies, Sociétés, Civilisations* 46:2 (March–April 1991): 429–458.

27. Marichal, *A Century of Debt Crises*, 7, 100–101; quotation on 7. See also J. T. Walton Newbold, "The Beginnings of the World Crisis, 1873–1896," *Economic History* 2:8 (January 1932), 425–441; Nicolai Kondratiev, *The Long Wave Cycle* (New York: Richardson & Snyder, 1984 [1927]); and Lewis, *Growth and Fluctuations 1870–1914*.

28. Hilda Sábato, "Citizenship, Political Participation, and the Formation of the Public Sphere in Buenos Aires, 1850s–1880s," *Past and Present* 136 (August 1989): 139–163.

29. See, for example, Allen Wells and Gilbert M. Joseph, *Summer of Discontent, Seasons of Upheaval: Elite Politics and Rural Insurgency in Yucatán, 1876–1915* (Stanford, Calif.: Stanford University Press, 1996), esp. chaps. 1, 2.

30. Tulio Halperín Donghi, *The Contemporary History of Latin America*. Edited and translated by John Charles Chasteen (Chapel Hill: University of North Carolina Press, 1993), 120.

31. John Sheahan, *Patterns of Development in Latin America: Poverty,*

Repression, and Economic Strategy (Princeton, N.J.: Princeton University Press, 1987), 79.

32. Topik, "The Economic Role of the State in Liberal Regimes: Brazil and Mexico Compared, 1888–1910," in Joseph L. Love and Nils Jacobsen, eds., Guiding the Invisible Hand: Economic Liberalism and the State in Latin American History (New York: Praeger, 1988), 117–144, esp. 117–119.

33. On eclectic economic policies, see Paul E. Gootenberg, Between Silver and Guano: Commercial Policy and the State in Post-Independence Peru (Princeton, N.J.: Princeton University Press, 1989). Albert Hirschman, "Ideologies of Economic Development in Latin America," in idem, ed., Latin American Issues: Essays and Comments (New York: Twentieth Century Fund, 1961), 4–14. According to Charles Hale, Say's works were more widely disseminated in Spanish America than was The Wealth of Nations: Hale, Mexican Liberalism in the Age of Mora, 1821–1853 (New Haven, Conn.: Yale University Press, 1968), 250.

34. Charles Hale, The Transformation of Liberalism in Late Nineteenth-Century Mexico (Princeton, N.J.: Princeton University Press, 1989), 3.

35. Albert Hirschman, Journeys toward Progress: Studies of Economic Policy-Making in Latin America (Westport, Conn.: Greenwood, 1965), 163–207.

36. Paul Gootenberg, Imagining Development: Economic Ideas in Peru's "Fictitious Prosperity" of Guano, 1840–1880 (Berkeley and Los Angeles: University of California Press, 1993), 203ff., quote on 203; and Richard Weiner, "Discourses of the Market in Porfirian Mexico," Latin American Perspectives, in press. See Joseph Love's characterization of the intellectual community in Latin America in "Structural Change and Conceptual Response in Latin America and Romania, 1860–1950," in Love and Jacobsen, Guiding the Invisible Hand, 5.

37. On the concentration of land ownership in Mexico during the Porfiriato, see Andrés Molina Enríquez, Los grandes problemas nacionales (Mexico City: A. Carranza e Hijos, 1909); Miguel Mejía Fernández, Política agraria en México en el siglo XIX (Mexico City: Siglo XXI, 1979); and Moisés González Navarro, El porfiriato: La vida social, in Historia moderna de México, 8 vols. in 9, Daniel Cosío Villegas, gen. ed. (Mexico City: Editorial Hermes, 1955–1974). For a corrective to the generalization, see Robert H. Holden, Mexico and the Survey of Public Lands: The Management of Modernization, 1876–1911 (DeKalb: Northern Illinois University Press, 1993). On Central America, consult Héctor Pérez Brignoli, A Brief History of Central America, trans. Ricardo B. Sawrey A. and Susana Stettri de Sawrey (Berkeley and Los Angeles: University of California Press, 1989), esp. chaps. 3 and 4.

38. Michael Adas, Machines as the Measure of Men: Science, Technology and Ideologies of Western Dominance (Ithaca, N.Y.: Cornell University Press, 1989), 209. The literature on the impact of railroads in Latin America is formidable. See, for example, Clarence B. Davis and Kenneth E. Wilburn, Jr., with Ronald Robinson, eds., Railway Imperialism (New York: Greenwood Press, 1991); William G. Fleming, Regional Development and Transportation in Argentina: Mendoza and the Gran Oeste Argentino Railroad, 1885–1914 (New York: Garland Press, 1987); Paul B. Goodwin, Jr., "The Central Argentine Railway and the Economic Development of Argentina, 1854–1881," Hispanic American

Historical Review 57:4 (November 1977): 613–632; Arthur Schmidt, *The Social and Economic Effects of the Railroad in Puebla and Veracruz, Mexico, 1867–1911* (New York: Garland Press, 1987); and Allen Wells, "All in the Family: Railroads and Henequen Monoculture in Porfirian Yucatán," *Hispanic American Historical Review* 72:2 (May 1992): 159–209.

39. Quoted in Arnaldo Córdova, *La ideología de la Revolución mexicana: La formación del nuevo régimen* (Mexico City: Ediciones Era, 1973), 64. All translations are ours unless otherwise noted.

40. Florencia Mallon, *The Defense of Community in Peru's Central Highlands: Peasant Struggle and Capitalist Transition, 1860–1940* (Princeton, N.J.: Princeton University Press, 1983); and Nils Jacobsen, *Mirages of Transition: The Peruvian Altiplano, 1780–1930* (Berkeley and Los Angeles: University of California Press, 1993).

41. Wells and Joseph, *Summer of Discontent, Seasons of Upheaval*. On liberalism in Mexico, also see Alan Knight, "El liberalismo mexicano desde la Reforma hasta la Revolución (una interpretación)," *Historia Mexicana* 35:1 (1985): 59–91; and Moisés González Navarro, "Tipología del liberalismo mexicano," *Historia Mexicana* 32:2 (1982): 198–225. On community, ethnicity, and nationalism, see Alan Knight, "The Peculiarities of Mexican History: Mexico Compared to Latin America, 1821–1992," *Journal of Latin American Studies Supplement* 35–53 (1992): 99–144. See also Florencia Mallon, *Peasant and Nation: The Making of Postcolonial Mexico and Peru* (Berkeley and Los Angeles: University of California Press, 1994); and Gilbert M. Joseph and Daniel Nugent, eds., *Everyday Forms of State Formation: Revolution and the Negotiation of Rule in Modern Mexico* (Durham, N.C.: Duke University Press, 1994).

42. Some useful points of departure are Ian Roxborough, *Theories of Underdevelopment* (London: Macmillan, 1991); Cristóbal Kay, *Latin American Theories of Development and Underdevelopment* (London: Routledge, 1989); and Peter F. Klarén and Thomas J. Bossert, eds., *Promise of Development: Theories of Change in Latin America* (Boulder, Colo.: Westview Press, 1986).

43. These economic stages of growth paralleled the sociological contributions of Durkheim, Weber, and Parsons, who argued that all societies evolved along a continuum from tradition to modernity. The British comparison is made in Rostow, *The Stages of Economic Growth* (Cambridge: Cambridge University Press, 1960).

44. Steve J. Stern, "Africa, Latin America, and the Splintering of Historical Knowledge: From Fragmentation to Reverberation," in Frederick Cooper et al., *Confronting Historical Paradigms: Peasants, Labor, and the Capitalist World System in Africa and Latin America* (Madison: University of Wisconsin Press, 1993), 10.

45. Douglass North, "Location Theory and Regional Economic Growth," *Journal of Political Economy* 63:3 (1955): 243–258; Harold A. Innis, *Essays in Canadian Economic History* (Toronto: University of Toronto Press, 1957); and Melville H. Watkins, "A Staple Theory of Economic Growth," *Canadian Journal of Economics and Political Science* 29 (May 1963): 141–158. Some find the theory's dualistic model of a dynamic export-led sector and a traditional subsistence sector too static and reductionist. For a thoughtful discussion of the

model's place in the literature, see Stanley Engarmen, "Douglass C. North's *The Economic Growth of the United States, 1790–1860* Revisited," *Social Science History* 1:2 (1977): 248–257; and Richard Caves, "Export-Led Growth and the New Economic History," in Jagdish Bhagwati et al., eds., *Trade, Balance of Payments and Growth* (Amsterdam: North-Holland, 1971), 403–442.

46. Frederick Cooper, "Africa and the World Economy," in Cooper et al., *Confronting Historical Paradigms*, 86–87.

47. Adas points out some key differences between the civilizing mission ideology of the age of imperialism and modernization theory, most notably, a sensitivity to racism and an opposition to colonialism. See *Machines as the Measure of Men*, chap. 4 and epilogue. See also Dean Tipps, "Modernization Theory and the Comparative Study of Societies: A Critical Perspective," *Comparative Studies in Society and History* 15:2 (1973): 200–211.

48. Cooper, "Africa and the World Economy," 88. A thoughtful discussion of the state's role in capitalist economic development is John Harris, Janet Hunter, and Colin M. Lewis, eds., *The New Institutional Economics and Third World Development* (London: Routledge, 1995).

49. Joseph L. Love, *Crafting the Third World: Theorizing Underdevelopment in Rumania and Brazil* (Stanford, Calif.: Stanford University Press, 1996); and Celso Furtado, *A fantasia organizada* (Rio de Janeiro: Paz e Terra, 1985).

50. André Gunder Frank, *Capitalism and Underdevelopment in Latin America* (New York: Monthly Review Press, 1967); and Ronald Chilcote and Joel Edelstein, eds., *The Struggle with Dependency and Beyond* (New York: John Wiley, 1983).

51. Immanuel Wallerstein, "The Rise and Future Demise of the World Capitalist System: Concepts for Comparative Analysis," *Comparative Studies in Society and History* 15:4 (September 1974): 387–415; and idem, *The Modern World System*. See Steve Stern's suggestive critique of Wallerstein's thesis in "Feudalism, Capitalism, and the World-System in the Perspective of Latin America and the Caribbean," in Cooper et al., *Confronting Historical Paradigms*, 23–83.

52. Roxborough provides a trenchant analysis of these debates in *Theories of Underdevelopment*. Perhaps the most sophisticated *dependentista* analysis is Fernando Henrique Cardoso and Enzo Faletto, *Dependency and Development in Latin America*, trans. Marjory Mattingly Urquidi (Berkeley and Los Angeles: University of California Press, 1979).

53. See John G. Taylor, *From Modernization to Modes of Production: A Critique of the Sociologies of Development and Underdevelopment* (London: Macmillan, 1979); David Goodman and Michael Redclift, *From Peasant to Proletarian: Capitalist Development and Agrarian Transitions* (New York: St. Martin's Press, 1982), chap. 2; Roger Bartra, "Peasants and Political Power in Mexico: A Theoretical Approach," *Latin American Perspectives* 5 (1975): 125–145; Ronald Chilcote and Dale Johnson, eds., *Theories of Development: Modes of Production or Dependency* (Beverly Hills, Calif.: Sage, 1983).

54. One response to the Eurocentric visions of Latin American growth has been the "folk" approach. Sharing much with conservative nationalists who lived during the Second Conquest, advocates of this perspective return to a somewhat romanticized view of life before the export boom. In a widely read

text, E. Bradford Burns has suggested that, under colonialism, Latin America developed corporate, communitarian, and patriarchal principles that were much more generous to the general population than was the individualistic liberalism that prevailed after independence. Interaction with the world economy proved to be an unadulterated ill. Any form of economic growth, whether by means of exports, foreign capital, internal industrialization, or state command economy, damaged the lives of the majority of Latin Americans. This view turns modernization theory on its head, but still does not hold that peasants and workers could work through the challenges of the export boom to defend themselves and better their lives. See Burns, *The Poverty of Progress.*

55. Hobson's and Lenin's original assertions—that (1) colonial expansion was precipitated by European and North American surplus capital badly in need of overseas markets, and that (2) empire generated sizable profits for the colonizer—have largely been discredited. During the boom, investments grew in both the metropolises and the periphery, in colonies as well as independent countries. Scholars have reached a consensus that imperialism had a number of interdependent causes, and most would agree that economic interests, if not as important as once presumed, did play a significant role in shaping political decisions at home and diplomacy abroad. See John A. Hobson, *Imperialism: A Study* (London: Allen and Unwin, 1938 [1902]); Rudolf Hilferding, *Finance Capital: A Study of the Latest Phase of Capitalist Development*, trans. Morris Watnick and Sam Gordon (London: Routledge and Kegan Paul, 1981 [1911]); Vladimir I. Lenin, *Imperialism, the Highest Stage of Capitalism* (Moscow: Progress Publishers, 1966 [1916]); Nikolai Bukharin, *Imperialism and the World Economy* (New York: International Publishers, 1929); and Rosa Luxemburg, *The Accumulation of Capital* (London: Routledge and Kegan Paul, 1951). Critical responses to both Hobson and Lenin are found in Kenneth E. Boulding and Tapan Mukerjee, eds., *Economic Imperialism: A Book of Readings* (Ann Arbor: University of Michigan Press, 1972), esp. the chapter by D. K. Fieldhouse, "'Imperialism': An Historiographical Revision," 95–123.

56. John Gallagher and Ronald Robinson, "The Imperialism of Free Trade," *Economic History Review*, 2nd series, 6:1 (1953): 1–15.

57. Ronald Robinson, "Non-European Foundations of European Imperialism: Sketch for a Theory of Collaboration," in Roger Owen and Bob Sutcliffe, eds., *Studies in the Theory of Imperialism* (London: Longman, 1972), 117–142; Robin Winks, "On Decolonization and Informal Empire," *American Historical Review* 81:3 (1976): 540–556, quotation on 552.

58. A. G. Hopkins, "Informal Empire in Argentina," *Journal of Latin American Studies* 26 (May 1994): 469–484, quotation on 481.

59. Richard Graham, "Sepoys and Imperialists: Techniques of British Power in Nineteenth-Century Brazil," *Inter-American Economic Affairs* 23:2 (Autumn 1969): 23–37, quotation on 24. For other dimensions and mechanisms of U.S. influence in Latin America, see Steven Topik, *Trade and Gunboats: The United States and Brazil in the Age of Imperialism* (Stanford, Calif.: Stanford University Press, 1996); and Gilbert M. Joseph, Catherine C. LeGrand, and Ricardo D. Salvatore, eds., *Close Encounters of the Imperial Kind: Writing the*

Cultural History of U.S.-Latin American Relations (Durham, N.C.: Duke University Press, forthcoming).

60. For an analysis of the debate from a variety of perspectives and reprints of the key theoretical articles by Gallagher and Robinson, see William Roger Louis, ed., *Imperialism: The Robinson and Gallagher Controversy* (New York: New Viewpoints, 1976). An interpretive analysis of the numerous objections is found in William Roger Louis, "Robinson and Gallagher and Their Critics," in ibid., 2–51.

61. On the henequen debate, see Thomas Benjamin, "International Harvester and the Henequen Marketing System in Yucatán, 1898–1915," *Inter-American Economic Affairs* 31 (Winter 1977): 3–19; Gilbert M. Joseph and Allen Wells, "Corporate Control of a Monocrop Economy: International Harvester and Yucatán's Henequen Industry during the Porfiriato," *Latin American Research Review* 17:1 (Spring 1982): 69–99; Jeffery T. Brannon and Eric M. Baklanoff, "Corporate Control of a Monocrop Economy: A Comment," *Latin American Research Review* 18:3 (Fall 1983): 193–196; Fred V. Carstensen and Diane Roazen-Parrillo, "International Harvester, Molina y Compañía, and the Henequen Market: A Comment," *Latin American Research Review* 18:3 (Fall 1983): 197–203; and Joseph and Wells, "Collaboration and Informal Empire: The Case for Political Economy," *Latin American Research Review* 18:3 (Fall 1983): 204–218. Lively discussions on the rubber boom can be found in Barbara Weinstein, *The Amazon Rubber Boom, 1850–1920* (Stanford, Calif.: Stanford University Press, 1983); Warren Dean, *Brazil and the Struggle for Rubber: A Study in Environmental History* (New York: Cambridge University Press, 1987); Bradford L. Barham and Oliver T. Coomes, "Reinterpreting the Amazon Rubber Boom: Investment, the State and Dutch Disease," *Latin American Research Review* 29:2 (1994): 73–109; idem, "Wild Rubber: Organisation and the Microeconomics of Extraction during the Amazon Rubber Boom (1860–1920)," *Journal of Latin American Studies* 26:1 (February 1994): 37–73; and Oliver T. Coomes and Bradford L. Barham, "The Amazon Rubber Boom: Labor Control, Resistance, and Failed Plantation Development Revisited," *Hispanic American Historical Review* 74:2 (May 1994): 231–257.

62. In fact, the dependency school has drawn on the various Marxist theories of imperialism for much of its inspiration. See Roxborough, *Theories of Underdevelopment*, chap. 5.

63. For an example of an empirical study that sought to wed dependency theory and the collaborator matrix, see Joseph and Wells, "Corporate Control."

64. Andrew Thompson, "Informal Empire? An Exploration in the History of Anglo-Argentine Relations, 1810–1914," *Journal of Latin American Studies* 24 (1992): 419–436; see also Hopkins, "Informal Empire in Argentina"; H. S. Ferns, "The Baring Crisis Revisited," *Journal of Latin American Studies* 24 (1992): 241–273; and P. J. Cain and A. G. Hopkins, eds., *British Imperialism: Innovation and Expansion, 1688–1914* (London: Longman, 1993).

65. William Roseberry, "*La falta de brazos*: Land and Labor in the Coffee Economies of Nineteenth-Century Latin America," *Theory and Society* 20:3 (June 1991): 351–381, quotation on 359.

2. Coffee

Steven C. Topik

O coffee, deadly gift of Arabia! How will you compensate the damages you have caused the colonists? The animals we maintained in the woods . . . the materials they [the woods] should have provided all along the centuries . . . the brooks which swelled under their shelter, the people who should have been employed to the most useful tasks, you have devoured them all, indeed destroyed them all.
—French colonist Michel-René Hilliard d'Auberteuil,
Haiti,1779

From radicalism to order, from infancy to middle age, from disorder to stability . . . these are the historical transformations which coffee produces in Colombia. The small producers, the property owners, who have, themselves, cultivated the land, have triumphed. Peace and tranquillity reign in Colombia.
—Colombian historian Luis Eduardo Nieto Arteta,
Bogotá, 1958

Introduction

That cup of coffee you quietly sip tells a long and complicated story. Coffee is the quintessential export crop. One of today's leading internationally traded commodities, it is likely the most valuable agricultural export in history. More than any other crop, strong backs and sweat in poor countries have produced it for the delicate china and refined palates of rich countries.

While it is true that, as the song says, they have a lot of coffee down in Brazil, *Coffea arabica* was a much broader Latin American phenomenon. It became a virtual monopoly. The Americas' share of world coffee production rose from 61 percent in 1880 to 91 percent in 1913, where it remained until 1930. In the nineteenth and early twentieth centuries, coffee was the leading export of nearly half the countries of Latin America and important in a number of others.[1] It was overall the leading export commodity of Latin America, supplying in 1930 about a fifth of all exports. It was, in fact, the one crop in which Latin America retained its world lead throughout the export boom. Latin Americans mastered coffee production; they were the price setters. Coffee, more than any other export crop, allows us to compare the effects of export economies in many Latin American contexts.

Coffee's central role has made it one of the most contradictory and controversial of crops, as the chapter epigraphs hint. It participated in a central way in the construction of cultures. Coffee has tied together the archaic and the bourgeois, the slave and the free, the proletarian and the intellectual, arduous toil and frivolous leisure. As a colonial imposition, it has been accused of destroying societies by perpetuating neocolonialism and underdevelopment. Coffee's champions, on the other hand, have applauded it for its contributions to the creation of independent nations, strong states, and developing economies. Originally a luxury, coffee became a necessity for consumer and producer alike. For some this addiction was a blessing, for others, a vice. It was, in short, a contradictory crop.

In this chapter I have three broad goals. First, I seek to demonstrate the importance of the world economy in setting the scope of possibilities, in broadly directing and defining the nature of coffee's productive process, its internal linkage effects, and its social and political consequences. At the same time, I hope to demonstrate the specificity of coffee cultivation by showing the constraints inherent in coffee's botany and production. Finally, I shall show the variety of forms and consequences of coffee cultivation in Latin America. Not only the world system and biology, but local geographies, histories, cultures, social arrangements, and political institutions created the day-to-day realities faced by growers and workers. Latin Americans had a large hand in shaping the world market for coffee, just as they, in turn, were shaped by it.

I am going to take a less sanguine view than many of coffee's admirers. Coffee required rich land, ample rain, and poor workers. Poverty was much more associated with it than was prosperity. In terms of per capita exports and per capita GNP, coffee-exporting countries were among Latin America's poorest. They also were among the slowest to urbanize, build national markets, and develop redistributive states. I am not arguing that botany predetermined the social and political development of coffee exporters—there was substantial variation among the coffee countries—but coffee did greatly shape producers. Latin America was able to retain dominance of the world coffee market for the century up to 1850 less because of sophisticated production and entrepreneurship than because of cheap labor and virgin lands. Essentially, Latin Americans were exporting part of their surplus value and part of their natural endowments. Still, the peasant nature of production and the income it generated meant that coffee also brought political peace, general social peace, and strengthened national states.

Images of Coffee Growers

Most North Americans who think of coffee think of Juan Valdez, the Colombian peasant who leads his coffee-laden burro down the steep hillsides into your living room. The campesino in clean white cotton *manta* and a sombrero is clearly a simple man of the earth, honest, attentive, worthy. His life is growing coffee. He will not use synthetic fertilizers or modern methods that rush the beans to maturity. Juan brings his crop to market on the back of a burro. No merchant middleman or multinational company intervenes between him and your breakfast table, no chance of adulteration, of additives. The burro also signifies the small scale of his plot. He works the land with his own hands, his own masterly eyes choose the ripe berries. He is an artisan, a skilled craftsman who imbibed his knowledge of cultivation from his mother's breast. He has an intuitive understanding of coffee and pride in producing a fine product. Juan is a yeoman farmer, of modest wealth but proud and happy. Purchasing Colombian coffee does not strengthen a backward rural oligarchy or exploitative multinational plantation owners; coffee (to mix my metaphors) steels the backbone of Colombian society, the rural farmer middle class.

But there is another, perhaps darker, vision of the coffee grower. This is the large-scale planter, particularly prominent in Brazil, who controlled hundreds of slaves and then peons on vast plantations. Since for obvious reasons no ad campaign has created a face for this vision, I will have to invent one: Zé Prado. How different from Juan Valdez would Zé Prado look if we pieced together the parts of the Brazilian coffee myth and packaged them in one composite character? Rather than leading a burro down a winding mountain trail, Zé oversees scores of slaves (and, later, peons) loading coffee onto the train. Or perhaps he strides through his processing plant, where the berries are hulled, dried, skinned, polished, and sorted. He is himself a man of the modern industrial world, an entrepreneur, a businessman, an agro-industrialist. His workers are property or employees, not family members. His plantation stretches over thousands of hectares of rich São Paulo soil, a soil that does not dirty his hands. Yes, he knows coffee, at least, he knows how to oversee it and market it. But Zé knows many other things, too. He is also a banker, an industrialist, a stockholder, perhaps a merchant and a politician. His ties to the outside world are intimate and daily: the price of coffee on the New York market or the political intrigues in the capital affect him personally. He speaks English and French. Zé is an agent of modernization, of industry, of foreign interests. He is taming the frontier, civilizing the backlands, turning nature into money. Zé Prado is dressed in a modern business suit or, perhaps to denote the wealth and leisure of the tropics and the plantation tradition, in a white linen suit.

Coffee has created both Juan and Zé (and many other growers with yet more complicated relations to the means of production) just as it has shaped the societies that grew up around the *cafezales* (coffee lands). Of all tropical export commodities, coffee is the one most often credited with fostering a strong national bourgeoisie, industrialization, and a strong state.[2] Yet coffee is also blamed for glaring inequalities, harsh labor conditions, the subjugation of local interests to those of foreigners, the creation of a monocultural dependent economy, and the despoiling of indigenous peoples.

At the center of the controversy over coffee's consequences for Latin America is a difference of perspective and a difference of emphasis. For many students of the export economy, the key issue is that the commodity was produced overwhelmingly for consumption by other nations. Although there are only spotty and fragmentary data on how much coffee Latin Americans themselves drank, a safe estimate is that at least 80 percent was sent abroad before 1930. According to followers of modernization theory, the aggregate revenue flowing from exports and foreign investment was key to stimulating development. Dependency theory and world-systems advocates, though taking a more negative view of the international connection, also argue that the destination of the crop was fundamental for understanding its internal consequences. The domestic Latin American economy became an extension of the world economy, with locals marching to the beat of a distant drummer.

Other students of the export era, however, stress the importance of the relations of production and culture in the producing lands rather than the ultimate destination of the commodity. Both the staples approach and the modes-of-production approach (a Marxian school that stresses the coexistence of a number of different social relations within the same society) emphasize the variety of consequences that can flow from the production of a given commodity depending on how it is *produced* rather than on where it is *consumed*. Were independent farmers, peasants, wage laborers, renters, sharecroppers, debt peons, or slaves used? Were they "Europeanized" proletarians, fairly self-sufficient peasants, African or European immigrants, or conscripted Indians? Were workers well remunerated? How concentrated was landowning, or was land communally held? How entrepreneurial and capitalist were the growers and what other investments did they make?

Not just economic development is at issue in understanding coffee's consequences. Cultural understandings of societies were shaped and reflected in coffee systems as well. Women, families, communities, ethnicities played new roles and took on new meanings. How people worked—dirtying their hands weeding and straining their backs picking—had much to do with how they thought and acted, how they celebrated and struggled. The creation of a civil society and a body politic were also affected. The relationship between landlord and tenants and the degree to which extraeconomic coercion was applied are crucial to understanding the extent to which democratic institutions prevailed and a civil society sprang up. And the state's capacity, its ability to redirect the economy, was tied to both its international position and the relations of production.[3]

Origins

In the eighteenth century, when coffee left the small plots in the mountains of Yemen where it was first cultivated, it became a colonial product.[4] For its first three hundred years as a commodity, the *arabica* had been an Arab monopoly, produced by independent peasants in Yemen in small irrigated gardens for sale to the Ottoman Empire, Persia, and India. But a growing European taste for the brew caused a revolution in its production. The Dutch transplanted the coffee tree to their colony in Java at the end of the sixteen hundreds. There the Dutch burghers were anything but bourgeois. They forced native Javanese to cultivate coffee and sell it cheaply to colonial administrators. Moving westward, trees from Yemen were planted on the small East African island of Reunion. The island's growers were the first to use African slaves to grow the commodity.

Early in the eighteenth century, the *arabica* crossed the Atlantic as the Dutch brought it to Dutch Guiana (now Suriname). But it was the French who first grew coffee on a large scale in Martinique and then Saint Domingue (today Haiti). Europe's consumption grew tenfold in the fifty years between 1739 and 1789, with French colonies supplying 60 percent of the total. The bourgeois French, engaged in eloquent Enlightenment debates in Parisian salons, at the same time founded the largest slave plantations the world had known in Haiti to grow coffee and sugar. (Clearly, different rules of conduct pertained to the two sides of the Atlantic.) This was an efficient, if cruel, method. In fact, relatively inexpensive Caribbean coffee was already displacing Yemenite beans in the Cairo market. But the *arabica* remained a rather exceptional luxury product under mercantilism. It was treated more as a medicine or a drug than a drink. In 1800 Europeans consumed on average only about one-tenth of a pound a year.[5]

It would be the Industrial Revolution and its transformation of transportation systems and markets together with Latin America's ability and willingness to respond to booming demand and, indeed, stimulate that demand that made coffee the world's third-greatest-traded commodity in terms of value by the end of the nineteenth century. (Today it is often second only to petroleum.)[6] Production grew fifteenfold in the 1800s.

While the Janus-faced beverage helped slake the great bourgeois and proletarian thirst of industrial capitalism in Europe and North America, though, it maintained its archaic guise in the fields of Latin America, where for the first time it was grown on a massive scale. Coffee helped work the machines of the Industrial Revolution in Europe, but in Haiti and then Brazil it resurrected slavery. Just as Eric Williams has observed about sugar, this fragrant bourgeois brew demanded putrid archaic coercion to bring the bean to the breakfast table.[7] Williams may not have been correct when he asserted that slavery supplied the capital that gave birth to the Industrial Revolution, but certainly slave-cultivated coffee—together with tea—helped impose the discipline of industrial time in Europe.

Although slavery had been coffee's handmaiden since its arrival in the Americas, nature had not preordained that the two inevitably would be so bound. Slavery proved itself in Saint Domingue to be not only a vicious and immoral labor form, but also a volatile and dangerous one. A great swelling of the island's slave population in the last decades of the eighteenth century to work the increasingly lucrative coffee plantations and a rapidly growing freedman population of coffee growers led to unbearable tensions. Deciding that they were Frenchmen as well as Africans, first the island's freedmen and then the slaves included themselves in France's 1789 Revolution. Many of the mulatto heads of the insurrection were coffee planters; inadvertently, they led the world's first modern national war of liberation. At a stroke, the former slaves severed the colonial tie, abolished slavery, and set the island's coffee economy into an irreversible decline as the newly freed slaves refused to work in the coffee fields. It would be 150 years before production levels surpassed those of the prerevolutionary years.[8] Coffee's legacy in Haiti was independence and poverty.

But Saint Domingue's bloody disaster did not deter planters from using slaves to cultivate coffee elsewhere. Some Haitian planters fled to Cuba and Puerto Rico, which, together with Jamaica, took the lead in coffee production in the early 1800s. But sugar, with much greater European markets in 1800, and British preference for tea overshadowed coffee throughout the Caribbean.[9] Moreover, none of the islands had the vast natural resources to compete with the last great slave coffee producer: Brazil. Brazil was almost single-handedly responsible for coffee's astounding expansion in the nineteenth century: 80 percent of the new cultivation was in that one country, which by mid-century was producing over half the world's coffee. Because Brazil's singular success shaped the world coffee market, I will devote a disproportionate amount of space to its story.

Brazil

As in the Caribbean and the Indian Ocean, coffee was introduced into Brazil by a European colonial power. This time it was the Portuguese who encouraged the cultivation of coffee in the wake of the collapse of Saint Domingue's economy. The interests of the Portuguese crown together with conditions within Brazil dictated the continued use of slaves.[10] The initial form of labor derived from a combination of the international availability of African bondsmen and the reluctance of European immigrants, a history of social acceptance of slavery, and the lack of a domestic alternative because of internal resistance.

By the time Brazil declared its independence from Portugal in 1822, however, slavery was a waning institution internationally and under question nationally. Brazil's agricultural boom began to fizzle in the early nineteenth century because of a recession in the world economy. The general agricultural downturn made the first four decades of the nineteenth century a time of economic crisis; tradition and slavery were reevaluated. The elite was frightened by Saint Domingue's revolt. Many Brazilians at Rio's court as well as their English allies argued for abolishing slavery in Brazil and reforming land tenure. Indeed, Brazil initially agreed to outlaw the Atlantic slave trade and a modest protective tariff was even briefly erected.[11]

But King Coffee had the last word in this economic debate. A burst of European and North American demand for coffee as their economies recovered from the Napoleonic Wars redoubled Brazil's reliance on the export economy and stimulated its craving for slaves. Plans to substitute slaves with European immigrants, demarcate and divide land, and encourage industry were shelved for half a century. The planter elite once again confidently pronounced that Brazil was an "essentially agricultural country" and, more specifically, that Brazil *was* coffee and coffee meant the slave. The rate at which Africans were landed in Rio and Bahia between 1800 and the abolition of the Atlantic trade in 1850 far surpassed that of any previous place or time. Several hundred thousand slaves labored in the *cafezales*. Brazil would be by far the largest importer of African bondsmen and the last country in the Western world to abolish slavery when emancipation finally arrived in 1888.[12]

The decision to force slaves to till the land and pick the beans had formidable consequences for Brazil. On the one hand, it made Brazil the world's greatest coffee producer. By 1880 it harvested about half of the world's coffee, more than twice as much as the rest of Latin America combined. In aggregate terms, the country prospered. The fear of slave revolt had enabled the Brazilian elite to rally behind their emperor and avoid the crushing civil wars the rest of Latin America experienced in the wake of independence. Rio de Janeiro grew into a major metropolis, larger than Rome or Madrid; the country's GNP was probably greater than that of Eastern Europe or Japan and even its former colonial master, Portugal. And by the time slavery was abolished, Brazil, next to India, had the largest railroad network outside of Western Europe and North America. Not coincidentally, two-thirds of that system was in the coffee-growing provinces.[13]

Yet economists and historians have subsequently emphasized the negative side of the slave economy. Economists such as Celso Furtado, tied to the ECLA think tank and dedicated to import-substitution industrialization, have accused coffee of impeding industry by attracting excessive resources and encouraging imports. Only in times of "adverse shocks," when international crises distanced Brazil from the world economy, did coffee have positive developmental effects.[14]

Other critics, such as André Gunder Frank and Theotonio dos Santos, have developed a more Marxian anti-imperialist approach known as dependency theory. Departing from neoclassical trade theory, they have blamed coffee for Brazil's underdevelopment. The humble bean has been accused of reinforcing slavery, which in turn impeded the development of a domestic bourgeoisie; restricted the internal market; retarded the development of capital markets and banks; concentrated the wealth; discredited manual labor through no or low wages, low educational levels, and backward technology; and created a liberal oligarchic state that sold out national sovereignty. Europeans dominated commerce and finance and set the world price for coffee. Coffee planters were virtual feudal barons uninterested in national progress. They were addicted to routine and a rentier mentality that prevented them from investing in anything but land and chattel. When the rare enlightened entrepreneur, such as the Viscount of Maua, tried to draw back the curtain of ignorance and indolence, planters, through the state, supposedly conspired to bankrupt him. Even progressive technologies such as the railroad were distorted; the Dom Pedro railroad strengthened slavery rather than undermining it.[15] The abolitionist and future ambassador to the United States Joaquim Nabuco most eloquently listed slavery's damaging effects in 1883:[16]

The illusion of wealth, of national development . . . does not fool anyone who examines its shadows. [Our] reality is that of a people who are more slave than master of the vast territory they occupy; a people in whose eyes work has been systematically debased and a people who have been taught that nobility consists of making others work; a people who are strangers to the school; a people indifferent to all those feelings, instincts, desires, and necessities that make the inhabitants of a single country not simply a society, but a nation. When Mr. Silveira Martins told the senate that "Brazil is coffee and coffee is the Negro"—not wishing, of course, to say slave—he defined Brazil as a plantation, a commercial enterprise dominated by a small minority of vested interests, in short, today's slaveholding Brazil.

Brazilian Coffee after Slavery

The abolition of slavery in 1888 created one of the most abrupt and thorough transformations of a labor system in history, particularly in the state of São Paulo, by then the world's foremost coffee producer. Paulistas, rather than employ their freedmen and attract other free Brazilians, as was done in other former slave societies, instead attracted almost a million Italian, Portuguese, and Spanish immigrants to their *fazendas* (plantations) by 1914. This was the only instance in history in which massive numbers of Europeans crossed the Atlantic to work on semitropical plantations.[17] The transformation was so rapid that slavery's end did not harm the coffee economy at all, a very different result from Haiti's forced abolition. Indeed, Brazilian coffee exports ballooned five-fold in the two decades after the Golden Law of abolition was passed. It turned out that coffee didn't need slaves after all.

As a mass consumption good in the nineteenth century once people in the United States started drinking almost half the crop, coffee required cheap labor to continue to expand its markets. International conditions dictated that European immigrants could provide low-cost workers. In the late 1880s, Mediterranean economies were suffering a crisis that encouraged many of their citizens to look across the Atlantic. At the same time, the United States and Argentina were mired in recession while coffee prices in Brazil were nearing all-time highs. With ample fertile land, the end of labor competition from slaves, and government-subsidized ship passage, Brazil seduced immigrants from these troubled European countries.

But the decision to turn to immigrants also derived from internal struggles within Brazil. Resistance by Brazilian freedmen, who refused to work the long hours demanded of slaves and refused to allow their wives and children into the fields, and by other peasants, who preferred to occupy their own plots rather than working for *fazendeiros*, made the more costly immigration solution necessary. Planter racism, which convinced them that former slaves would work well only under the influence of the lash and not voluntarily as a result of the incentives of the market, also contributed to the switch to European field hands.[18]

Many scholars argue that, once the slaves were emancipated in 1888, coffee became a more benign force; its former malevolent effects were not so much the fault of Brazil's reliance on exports, or on coffee itself, as of slavery. Yes, these scholars agree, slave cultivation of the *cafezales* in the Paraíba Valley (parts of Minas Gerais, Rio de Janeiro State, and São Paulo State) was guilty of the pernicious consequences for which it has been so roundly condemned—but not in western São Paulo, where, rather than addicting the country to retrograde human bondage, coffee stimulated capitalist development.

Brazilian Planters as Industrialists

The heroic version of the Paulista success story goes something like this. In the western part of the state of São Paulo slavery was not yet entrenched. When emancipation became inevitable, planters turned to immigrant labor. Zé Prado became an agro-industrialist on a scale previously unknown in coffee cultivation. Indeed, he and fellow Paulistas established some of the largest plantations ever built anywhere, any time. The Cambuhy Estate spread out over 250,000 acres and grew almost 3 million trees, tied together by 60 kilometers of private railroad track and 300 kilometers of roads.[19] Many other plantations spread over tens of thousands of acres. Zé directed some of his agricultural capital not only to urban real estate, public works, and government bonds, but also to railroads, banks, and even factories. Moreover, unlike his Paraíba Valley brethren, Zé and other Paulista agriculturalists were not the captives of urban coffee factors and their parasitic merchant mentality.

Many Paulistas like to believe that the *fazendeiro* was transformed from rentier to capitalist, from coffee baron to entrepreneur. Prominent coffee families diversified into industry, banking, and transportation once their capital was no longer tied up in slaves. They became the leading partners in what is generally acknowledged as the most progressive national bourgeoisie in Latin America and, indeed, one of the most entrepreneurial in the entire Third World. They industrialized São Paulo.[20]

Albert Hirschman has suggested that coffee had special advantages that encouraged the development of a national bourgeoisie and industrialization. He argues that, ironically, the relative lack of forward and backward linkages (other products and services needed to produce coffee that could be made out of coffee) and the simple technology sufficient

to grow and process coffee may have stimulated entrepreneurial initiative. That is because without great capital requirements or "strange"
forward processes, foreigners did not much engage in coffee production
itself. They restricted their participation to the areas in which their
comparative advantages lay: commerce, finance, and transportation.
Unlike the production in Latin America of petroleum, copper, or even
sugar, which was dominated by foreign firms, production and processing
of coffee (except roasting and grinding) were done overwhelmingly by
Brazilians and immigrants. Hirschman argues that production profits
remained in Brazil, which often led to the growth of the internal market
and industry.[21]

The exact role of coffee *fazendeiros* in turning coffee into factories has
been disputed more recently, however. While it is true that there were
certainly plenty of incidents of direct planter investments in factories,
these paled in comparison with the industrial initiatives of merchants,
artisans, and bankers. Jacob Gorender has argued pointedly that "the
'vanguardism' of Paulista planters, whose charm so fascinates authors,
is no more than a myth."[22]

In fact, *fazendeiros* after abolition were not heroic capitalists. Indeed,
because they no longer needed to purchase labor in advance, as they had
under slavery (slaves often accounted for over half the investment in a
plantation), planters may have become less dependent on capital in
agriculture after 1888.[23] Most planters invested little in tools, machinery, warehouses, or irrigation. An informed estimate in 1897 attributed
80 percent of the cost of establishing a plantation to purchasing the land
(20 percent) and replacing the native forests with coffee orchards (60
percent). Money payments were minimized. *Fazendeiros* were loath to
study agronomy, instead sending their children off to become lawyers
and politicians. They attacked the land with predatory savageness and
eschewed contour plowing, shade trees, and fertilizers. Franz Dafert, a
Prussian agronomist hired by São Paulo's state government to increase
productivity, complained that the "indolent" growers "accustomed to
the easy and unworried life of the rich domain of torrid lands, have not
the least idea of the hard work of the great European crops."[24] Planters
were alchemists in reverse, turning fertile virgin forest into desert
within three or four decades. Indeed, Zé Prado and many other Brazilian
fazendeiros more resembled miners rapaciously hauling wealth out of
the soil than agronomists with a reverence for the land. They left in their
wake denuded hills and a hollow frontier. These were no Juan Valdezes
who in Colombia as well as Central America truly did work the same
land generation after generation and carefully maintained its fertility.
Nor did Brazilian planters act in a particularly bourgeois fashion. Their
robber mentality led them to fight against the surveying of land bound-

aries and registration of titles, against mortgage registries and legal foreclosures. They thereby inhibited both land and financial markets. *Fazendeiros* wanted to invest as little as necessary, pay as few taxes as possible, and move on. They acted more as land speculators and merchants than as farmers or agro-industrialists. As we will see later, their commercial advantage came much more from access to capital and the ability to coerce cheap labor than from mastery of technology or ownership of land.

São Paulo's economic revolution has increasingly been seen as a structural response to the capital accumulation and consumption linkages of coffee. That is, coffee exports did enrich São Paulo, but coffee planters were not heroic entrepreneurs. They prepared the ground for industrialization, but they did not sew and cultivate the seeds. Yes, industry grew faster than exports during the last three or four decades of the Second Conquest; by 1930 Brazilian factories provided virtually all of the country's needs in cloth, clothes, shoes, and food and built the foundation for heavy industry. The actual architects of development, however, were merchants, bankers, industrialists, and artisans, not *fazendeiros*.[25]

The *"Colono"* Labor System

Indeed, one can dispute how capitalist Paulista *fazendeiros* were, even after slavery's demise. The *"colono"* system that replaced slavery in São Paulo was a heterogeneous form that included aspects of peasant production and wage labor. The central work unit was the family. Planters were reluctant to take on single immigrants. Social reproduction costs were undertaken by the household, which grew and cooked the food, made the clothes, and reared the children. Under slavery many of these duties had fallen on the master. Now, only the head of household was paid. Most of the year he was occupied in taking care of two thousand to twenty-five hundred trees, and a family might tend five thousand trees (about fifteen acres).[26] There was little specialization or integration. Tending the planter's trees provided the *colono* about 40 percent of his monetary income (often paid in scrip redeemable only at the overpriced company store). During harvest season and occasionally at other times, he was paid for day work, which provided about one-fourth of his monetary income.

But most of his total income came from work as a peasant, not as a coffee worker. *Colonos* by the 1890s received housing, subsistence plots, and pasturage privileges free. Subsistence, according to an estimate by Thomas Holloway, may have constituted 70 percent of the *colono*'s remuneration. And the *colono* sold some of his own corn and beans and livestock, which yielded one-third to 40 percent of his milreis earnings. Consequently, 80 percent of his total income did not come from his work in the coffee groves.[27]

Indeed, coffee was an evil that was borne in order to gain access to cornfields. For the *colono*, says Holloway, "Coffee was dependence, subservience, the source of justified but disagreeable conflicts, mistrust and disciplinary measures; corn was freedom of action and economic autonomy." This is how Brazilian *fazendeiros* obtained sufficient labor to grow coffee, even while paying very little for coffee work. Paulista *fazenda* production in general more resembled a collection of peasants than a factory in the fields. Or in Wolf and Mintz's famous model, it more resembled a hacienda than a plantation.[28] In fact, actual coffee workers in Brazil had far more in common with Juan Valdez than with Zé Prado.

Pay was low. According to one estimate, a worker could harvest one hundred pounds of cherries a day, which yielded twenty pounds of coffee beans. Since the average Santos FOB price in the 1900–1930 period was seven or eight cents a pound and harvest costs were calculated at 15 to 18 percent of the cost of delivering beans to Santos, workers earned in money for their coffee work one cent a pound, or twenty cents a day (and these were probably the highest coffee wages in the world). Verena Stolcke has estimated that not more than 8 percent of the first generation of *colonos* who arrived in the *cafezales* were able to save enough money to buy their own land by 1910. Thomas Holloway and Warren Dean are more sanguine about immigrant opportunities, which probably did improve appreciably after World War I, when coffee prices and urban opportunities increased.[29]

By hiring families, planters such as Zé Prado reduced their direct control over individual workers and relied instead on the patriarchal power of the heads of households. This won the allegiance of the relatively empowered man of the house and lowered planter costs for overseeing workers. Zé obtained a flexible labor force that could be tapped during the harvest season, when more hands were needed. Whereas coffee cultivation under slavery had broken up families and depended primarily on male workers (far more men than women were imported from Africa), the family was the backbone of the *colono* system.

By deciding to appeal to European immigrants, who, after all, had a choice about whether to come to Brazil, planters had to make work conditions sufficiently attractive. Consequently, unlike many other coffee economies, extraeconomic state coercion was limited. The state did not play a large role in keeping *colonos* on the *fazenda* nor was debt peonage applied. There was an active labor market. Verena Stolcke notes the contradictory nature of the system: "It is true that *fazendeiros* used coercion and violence to keep workers on the plantations and to extract profit, but in general they came to treat the problem of reducing labor costs by increasing the supply [of workers]. Extraeconomic coercion, which sometimes was considerable, served essentially to improve the bargaining position of *fazendeiros* in the labor market."[30]

Colonos could and did move about. A French visitor, Pierre Denis, complained that "not being property owners, Italian colonos are imperfectly tied to the soil . . . they only work when they are offered attractive conditions. Colonos are passionate about their independence and refuse all contracts of over one year." It has been estimated that 40 to 60 percent of *colonos*, seeking better lands for their subsistence crops and better treatment, switched plantations every year. Workers also used the weapon of the strike frequently. Between 1913 and 1930, there were over one hundred strikes, usually of limited scope, in São Paulo's coffee groves alone.[31]

And they had the ultimate choice of leaving Brazil altogether. Between 1902 and 1913, 65 percent of Italian immigrants left. This freedom of movement meant that many *colonos* were better off than smallholding Juan Valdezes, whose property rights often forced them to eke out an existence on marginal lands. But landowning was not merely an economic decision. *Colonos* often bought land to increase their independence. As will be discussed later, Brazilian coffee workers' ability to find individual solutions, such as movement or land purchase, reduced their inclination to take collective political action.

The Development of the Brazilian Coffee System: The Defense of Coffee Program

Even if it is true, however, that planters did not adopt full-blown capitalist methods and were not the direct agents of industrialization, coffee at least indirectly stimulated development; that, in turn, subverted the reigning social system. By 1930 land had become less concentrated as immigrant urban dwellers and fieldworkers purchased plots. Slavery was, of course, long gone, but even sharecropping declined, replaced by wage labor and family production. As aged coffee trees became less productive, planters sold them to smallholders. This trend became particularly noticeable after World War I, when the booming economy offered *fazendeiros* many lucrative options to landholding. By 1934 foreigners, overwhelmingly immigrants, owned almost half of the rural holdings in São Paulo. According to Mircea Buescu, by 1927, 74 percent of holdings were smaller than 62 acres and 94 percent were smaller than 312 acres (though the 6 percent greater than that size produced almost half of all coffee). Zé Prado's political might also declined as new urban and agricultural groups grew in power.[32]

But Zé was still able to secure what was most important to him. Indeed, his search to protect his own interests led to a fundamental transformation of the liberal state and, ultimately, of the world market for coffee. By 1932 J. W. F. Rowe, a keen analyst of world commodity markets, could observe that "Brazilian coffee has been subjected to artificial control of a more thorough, prolonged and deliberate character than any raw material of major importance."[33] Beginning with the 1906 coffee price support program known as "valorization" (one of the few Brazilian words introduced into English), proceeding to the Institute for the Permanent Defense of Coffee in the 1920s, and ending with the Departamento Nacional de Café in 1933, the Brazilian federal and state governments came to finance most of the world's coffee trade and hold most of its visible stocks. In 1940 one of the first international commodity cartels was established with the Inter-American Coffee Agreement. And in 1962, the rest of the world's producers were brought under the umbrella in the International Coffee Agreement, which continued until 1989. Coffee set the precedent that, later, OPEC and other raw materials producers would follow. It also transformed the Brazilian state's role in the domestic economy. By the end of the First Republic, in 1930, the Brazilian state was responsible for much of the finance, warehousing, transportation, and sale of coffee and controlled one of the world's largest commodity markets. Coffee had led Brazil from an archaic slavocratic social formation to state capitalism in half a century.[34]

A brief look at Brazil's coffee valorization program will demonstrate that it owed its success to an unusual combination of characteristics inherent in coffee production, to conditions in the international market, and to political and economic arrangements in Brazil. It was not just by chance that Brazilian coffee was the first commodity in which a state successfully controlled the world market.

Coffee's botany certainly made valorization possible. As a tree crop that takes four to six years to reach maturity, coffee was a relatively expensive and inflexible investment. In Brazil upwards of two-thirds of the labor cost of tending to the coffee trees was in year-round maintenance such as weeding and pruning, independent of the size of the harvest.[35] Consequently, planters could not respond to low prices by reducing costs or lowering production. Planting, maintenance, and harvesting were all done by hand. The technologically primitive means that *fazendeiros* had to reduce costs in response to lower market prices was to *increase* production by moving into fertile virgin lands. There tree yield might be double that of existing plantations and workers could be recompensed with usufruct rights to fertile land rather than with money.[36] (This solution was open only for countries like Brazil, with a vast, fertile frontier with cheap land.) Of course, the added cheaper production would exacerbate the glut and thereby create even greater downward pressure on prices. Rational responses by individual planters to the production problem thus led to collective disaster. Therefore, the response to falling profits had to come from marketing, not reducing production or reducing production costs.

No new markets were readily available. Coffeecake is not made with coffee. Outside of a very few individuals who did eat coffee and a tiny demand for coffee flavoring, the bean had no use but as a beverage. Attempts to make plastics out of coffee and to burn it in power locomotives failed. Although Brazilians were among the world's greatest per capita coffee consumers, Brazil could not respond to falling prices with the Argentine solution for excess beef: consume even more at home. They were already drinking more than almost anyone else in the world. A *New York Times* journalist reported in 1894, "the whole country is perpetually in a state of semi-intoxication on coffee—men, women and children alike . . . At all hours of day and night, in season and out, everybody literally guzzles it. The effect is plainly apparent in trembling hands, twitching eyelids, mummy-hued skins, and a chronic state of nervous excitability worse than that produced by whisky."[37] Ninety percent of the crop was going to have to be exported, so international markets would have to be adjusted to remedy crises.

Fortunately, coffee—unlike many other staples—could be held off the market for years without deteriorating; indeed, some gourmets thought it improved with age. Withdrawing coffee from the market made sense because, in another botanical quirk, large harvest years were generally followed by several smaller years during which the trees rested. Demand could catch up with supply. This biological happenstance was compounded in Brazil by variable climatic conditions; São Paulo was farther from the equator than any other coffee-producing area in the world. The variation in São Paulo's yearly production was three times greater than that in the other coffee-producing areas.[38]

Market conditions, which reflected relative factor endowment and socially constituted consumer taste, also came to coffee's aid. Europe, as Eric Hobsbawm has pointed out, came to demand the exotic. And more than any other commodity, coffee was produced by poor countries for the refreshment of the rich ones. Coffee consumption was growing an average 2 percent a year (see Table 2.1). Because it was somewhat addictive and because it was enjoyed amid great sociability during coffee breaks and in coffeehouses, coffee was not easily substituted by other synthetic or natural beverages; it was fairly price inelastic. Attempts to wean coffee drinkers on grain substitutes, as was done during the Napoleonic blockade of Europe, or to dilute the real thing with chicory met with little success. Coffee did not face competitors in the way that henequen did; that is, rising prices quickly invited substitutes for

Table 2.1. Percentage of World Consumption Supplied by Various Latin American Countries

Year	Brazil	Colombia	Central America	Venezuela	Caribbean	Latin America
1843	40	–	–	30	–	70
1875–1885	50	1	5	3	10	69
1900	64	–	–	–	–	–
1905	67	4	9	4	3	87
1910	64	5	8	5	5	87
1915	82	5	7	–	–	94
1920	62	8	9	–	–	90
1925	62	9	8	–	–	89
1930	61	12	10	–	–	89

Sources: Eduardo M. Hafers, *Relatório apresentado ao Instituto de Café do Estado de São Paulo sobre o Comércio de Café* (São Paulo: 1938), 69; Bureau of American Republics, "Coffee in America" Special Bulletin (October 1893): 4; *The Spice Mill* (January 1912): 32, (October 1912): 860; Robert Williams, *States and Social Evolution* (North Carolina, 1994), 268, 269; Ukers, *All about Coffee*, 500. Brazil, IBGE, *Séries Estatísticas Retrospectivas*, vol. 1 (Rio de Janeiro: IBGE, 1986), 85; Becker, *Kaffee aus Arabian*, 20; Edmar Bacha and Robert Greenhill, *150 anos de Café* (Salamandra, 1992), 327.

henequen and hurt the market for binder machines. Thus a corner on the coffee market would not dampen or divert demand. Cognizant of their safe position, coffee roasters in the United States were much more willing to accept and even help finance price supports as long as supply was predictable and the price fairly stable.[39]

But how to affect that vast international market of dozens of producing and consuming countries? Fortunately, Brazil occupied an unparalleled position in the global coffee market (see Table 2.2). It regularly furnished over half of world production and in some years reached as high as 80 percent. In every other case of one country so dominating a global market, either the commodity was relatively unimportant or, as in the cases of nitrates, guano, cochineal, and rubber, the industrialized countries soon discovered synthetic substitutes. But synthetic coffee could not fool the taste buds in the same way that ersatz rubber could satisfy the fingers or chemical fertilizers could please plants.

No other producer was in a position to challenge Brazilian domination even in the medium run.[40] Brazilian preeminence was due mostly to climatic and geographical factors: vast fertile, rolling hills, substantial rainfall, mild climate, and a relative proximity to ports. Labor was also available first because of the preexisting slave trade, then because of Brazil's ability to take advantage of Europe's large available emigrating populations, who were attracted by low and sometimes subsidized ship fares and fertile available land to be worked on shares.[41] No other coffee-producing land attracted much European immigration; Brazil was the third-largest recipient of European immigrants in the world, behind only the United States and Argentina. The other major coffee producers were

Table 2.2. World Coffee Market, 1893–1930

Year	Production (000) bags[*]	Deliveries (000) bags[*]	Visible Supply (000) bags[*]	Spot Price Rio #7 at NY (U.S. cents)
1893–1894	9,401	10,572	2,146	16.6
1900–1901	15,100	14,330	6,868	6.0
1905–1906	14,792	16,741	9,637	7.9
1910–1911	14,524	18,118	13,732	13.2
1915–1916	20,763	20,687	7,328	9.0
1920–1921	20,283	18,468	8,639	6.4
1925–1926	22,108	21,698	7,324	14.2
1930–1931	24,797	25,148	28,721[a]	7.0

Source: Ukers, *All about Coffee,* 500.
[*] bags of 60 kilos each.
[a] figure includes coffee stocks kept in the interior of Brazil; other supply figures are only port figures.

small, poor, independent countries that could not easily or quickly raise production levels. The few European colonial coffee producers, such as Kenya; Indonesia; Jamaica; Papua, New Guinea; and Angola, either had little appropriate land or produced *robusta* rather than Brazil's more desirable *arabica* coffee. Therefore, Brazilians did not have to fear the sort of colonial efforts that led East Indians to seize Brazil's former rubber monopoly and led African hemp to replace Mexican henequen.

But while botany and market conditions may have conspired to make intervention necessary and possible, capital was still needed to withdraw stocks from the market. Planters, although entrepreneurial, were not sufficiently organized or capitalized to impose a private solution. They would need to borrow abroad. Fortunately, their need for foreign capital corresponded with a tremendous wave of European capital seeking foreign markets. Moreover, the notion of state-coordinated cartels was gaining favor.[42] But financiers and merchants wanted state oversight of any intervention to ensure repayment of loans and the internal discipline necessary for a price support scheme to work. Although the great majority of the Brazilian non-coffee-producing states opposed a state-run solution (Table 2.3 demonstrates that coffee often constituted less than half of Brazil's exports) and even coffee *fazendeiros* were suspicious of state participation, coffee planter hegemony allowed them eventually to accept a public program.

Coffee planters and the state could coordinate efforts because the decentralized nature of the Brazilian state allowed the state of São Paulo a great deal of latitude in borrowing and economic policy. Such relative local autonomy was very important because São Paulo provided more than two-thirds of Brazil's coffee exports and in some years nearly half of the world's production. As a result, *fazendeiros* exercised much greater political power in this state than did planters in any other region of Brazil and more than they did on the national level. Paulista planters were well organized, in part because land was so concentrated that 8 percent of the holdings produced 55 percent of the coffee receipts (and some owners had multiple holdings while over 90 percent of the rural population was landless). And they enjoyed political power because the largest *fazendeiros* were overwhelmingly Brazilian nationals. Indeed, Joseph Love's collective biography of the São Paulo political elite notes an enormous share of coffee men, far more than in neighboring Minas Gerais. The overlap he found between the economic elite and the political elite was stronger in São Paulo than in any other country or region where such a study has been done, although it was probably similar in Central American coffee-producing countries.[43]

Whether officeholding really reflected hegemonic power in São Paulo has been questioned by Maurício Font, who argues that by the late 1920s agriculturally diversified immigrants and industrialists challenged the

Table 2.3. Coffee as a Percentage of National Exports

Year	Brazil	Colombia	Costa Rica	El Salvador	Guatemala	Haiti	Mexico	Nicaragua	Venezuela
1900	57	49[#]	76	–	4	–	–	–	–
1905	48	39	78	–	4	–	–	–	–
1912	62	37	35	80	90	64	3[*]	70	52
1920	49	–	–	–	–	–	–	–	–
1925	72	–	45	–	–	–	–	–	–
1930	63	55	58	93[a]	77[a]	4[b]	54[a]	4[b]	–

Source: V. Bulmer-Thomas, *The Economic History of Latin America since Independence* (Cambridge: Cambridge University Press, 1994), 59; idem, *The Political Economy of Central America since 1920* (Cambridge: Cambridge University Press, 1987), 271; Eduardo M. Hafers, *Relatório apresentado ao Instituto de Café do Estado de São Paulo sobre o comércio de café* (São Paulo: Instituto de Café de S.P., 1938), passim; José Antonio Ocampo, *Colombia y la economía mundial, 1830–1910* (Mexico City: Siglo Veintiuno, 1984), 100; Marco Palacios, *El café en Colombia 1850–1970* (Mexico City: El Colegio de México, 1983), 43; IBGE, 89–90; El Colegio de México, *Estadísticas económicas del Porfiriato, Comercio exterior, Menjívar, Acumulación originaria*, p. 50.

Notes: [#] data for 1898.
[*] data for 1910.
[a] data for 1929.
[b] data for 1935.

reign of coffee. I have maintained elsewhere that *fazendeiros'* power within São Paulo did not necessarily translate into control of the federal government. But certainly for more than half a century, planters did predominate in São Paulo. Their role has been likened to the German Junkers, who parlayed landed power into political might in a rapidly developing economy.[44]

Coffee and Industry

How responsible was coffee for the creation of a Junker-like oligarchy and the development of state capitalism? Students of Brazil recognize that coffee production alone did not assure *fazendeiro*-led development. They note that in other areas of the country where coffee predominated, such as Minas Gerais, Espírito Santo, and Paraná, coffee latifundists did not predominate and coffee had limited linkage effects, which therefore translated into little industry. These were noteworthy exceptions; if Brazil had divided into twenty independent countries in 1906, São Paulo would have continued to be the world's greatest coffee exporter, but Minas Gerais would have been second, Rio de Janeiro, third, and even Espírito Santo would have exported almost as much as Colombia. While the *fazendas* of São Paulo led to industry, the states of Rio de Janeiro and Minas Gerais were slow to develop. Rio suffered from the prevailing mode of production during its golden age that depended heavily on slaves and commercial capital; Minas, which continued to be an important coffee producer after emancipation, failed partly because of the dispersion of production. According to one analysis, smallholdings prevented sufficient capital accumulation and entrepreneurship to deliver industry. Minas also suffered because it was landlocked; it became a subject of the port of Rio de Janeiro, which drained off much of its capital and did industrialize.

On the other hand, a study of Espírito Santo argues that, despite relatively large-scale entrepreneurial *fazendeiros,* the absence of urban investment opportunities thwarted their efforts at development. In Paraná, coffee from the beginning was modern capitalist agro-business as an English land development company established the infrastructure and attracted capitalist yeoman farmers. But this sophisticated and successful agro-business did not yield much industry in Paraná, since the state remained a vassal of São Paulo.[45] Certainly, the prevailing relations of production, the stage of the international economy, and forces of internal colonialism greatly affected coffee's economic generative powers.

The same was true for other coffee-growing countries. Industry required not only capital accumulation, but a relatively large, monetarized internal market, which appeared only in areas with relatively large coffee exports, no competing major industrial pole to draw off capital, *and* farmers or wage earners to serve as consumers. Merchants who were nationals rather than foreigners were also an important ingredient for the development of factories. While coffee led to industry in Colombia's state of Antioquia because it expanded the internal market and enriched Colombian merchants, Santander, with its smaller production and sharecropping, was largely left out. El Salvador experienced the greatest industrialization in Central America because of efficient production and dense, proletarianized population and national entrepreneurs. But tiny Costa Rica, poor Nicaragua, and coercive Guatemala—all three with large foreign commercial participation—were slow to convert coffee exports into factories. The principal coffee-growing areas of Mexico—Chiapas, Veracruz, and Oaxaca—enjoyed little industrialization.

Foreign Participation in the Coffee Trade

São Paulo was in at least some ways clearly atypical. It was *the* coffee success story. But can we make some generalizations about coffee's social and economic consequences for all of Latin America? How important was the bean in shaping its producers? During the Second Conquest, 1850–1930, the vast majority of the world's coffee, as much as 95 percent, was produced in Latin America. As Table 2.1 demonstrates, coffee represented an important share of exports and GNP for many countries. Almost all of it was the same species, the *arabica* (though there were various subspecies like "Bourbon" and "Nacional"), and was produced for export.

The market was not entirely homogeneous, however. In the United States, once the Pure Food and Drug Act was enforced after 1907, importers had to sell the beans in specific categories related to the point of origin rather than mixing them as "Moccas" or "Java," as they had before. They were divided between "milds" and "Brazils." Different producers had different preferred customers. Brazilian and Colombian coffee went overwhelmingly to the United States, for instance, while Costa Rican coffee was largely sold in Great Britain and Guatemalan in Germany. Nonetheless, we can generalize that producing countries exported almost all of their crop to Europe and North America.[46]

Since the consumers were in the rich countries, the retailing, wholesaling, roasting, grinding, and packaging were done in the rich countries by North Americans and Europeans. Despite Brazilian factors' efforts to establish roasting companies in Europe and efforts by some Latin Americans, most notably the Venezuelan dictator Guzmán Blanco, to corner the market in Europe, Latin Americans failed to control coffee once it left their ports.[47] They were thus excluded from the most technologically sophisticated aspects of the production of coffee in which the greatest innovations, such as packaging, vacuum sealing, and instant coffee, were invented. That was also where the most forward linkages existed (roasting, grinding, packaging, packing, and advertising) and where at least 40 to 50 percent of the final sales price of coffee was added. (If the coffee was sold by the cup in a cafe rather than by the can in a grocery store, the additional labor cost and markup meant that often 75 to 90 percent of the final value was added in the consuming countries.[48])

These numbers mask the reality that even the wholesale green coffee unloaded in New York embodied substantial foreign participation in the form of the transatlantic shipping costs, insurance, and exporter profits, almost all of which accrued to Europeans and North Americans. Even in Brazil, with its command of the market, its dynamic domestic bourgeoisie, and large state presence, foreign bottoms carried the overwhelming majority of coffee, foreign companies insured the cargo, and foreign exporters exported 60 to 70 percent of the coffee even during the era of the valorization of coffee.[49] These charges often constituted up to one-quarter of the green coffee price in New York or Hamburg. Thus at least two-thirds of the cost of a can of coffee and over 90 percent of a coffeehouse cup of coffee in, say, Chicago went to North Americans and Europeans. The actual cost of cultivating the beans on the *fazenda* was less than 10 percent of the store price. This left little to pay the coffee pickers. The consumer who paid 25 cents a pound for his coffee in San Francisco or Chicago was contributing one cent to the coffee worker.

The coffee boom of the Second Conquest brought with it the largest foreign investment Latin America had ever seen. Only occasionally did foreigners invest directly in plantations—as did Germans in Chiapas, Mexico, Guatemala, Nicaragua, and Brazil; North Americans in Veracruz, Mexico; and British in São Paulo and Paraná. Nowhere in Latin America did they hold a majority of *cafezales*, as they did in their African colonies such as Kenya, Uganda, and Angola. But they sometimes dominated processing, as in Costa Rica and Mexico, and they usually controlled the majority of financing and marketing. North Americans and Europeans came to own or control a majority of the railroad systems that were built to serve coffee exports, although the railroad revolution was not necessarily an innovation *introduced* by foreigners. In many cases, such as in Guatemala, Costa Rica, and Brazil, the first lines were built with large national or state participation. But foreigners often then bought or leased them out. (Internal transportation remained the domain of nationals; but the roads and internal shipping companies were small and in bad condition.) U.S. and European capitalists also invested heavily in public utilities such as power, trams, and lighting for the swelling capitals of the coffee countries and in government bonds. They were slow to participate in industry and production oriented to the internal markets. All major Latin American coffee-exporting countries shared this relationship with the world system.

Coffee as Monoculture

One of the main accusations leveled against coffee is that it led to monocultural dependence on one export. It is true that, for most of the countries, coffee came to dominate national exports at the end of the nineteenth century or early in the twentieth century (see Table 2.3). In 1929 coffee cultivation was responsible for 71 percent of exports in Brazil, 61 percent in Colombia, 77 percent in Guatemala, 77 percent in Haiti, 54 percent in Nicaragua, 67 percent in Costa Rica, and fully 93 percent in El Salvador.[50] Coffee also provided a large share of GDP (see Table 2.4).

This great dependence on coffee exports, however, should not lead us to conclude that coffee was necessarily a monocultural crop, as is usually argued. It is true that, according to official statistics, in the state of Chiapas, Mexico, coffee produced few foodstuffs in the coffee-growing region of Soconusco. And as Guatemala and El Salvador turned ever more to coffee, they had increasingly to import food. On the other hand, overlapping maps of coffee and corn production reveal that they occurred in roughly the same areas in Costa Rica and Honduras. In Colombia, even on coffee haciendas, less than half the land was planted in coffee.[51] Certainly in the greatest coffee-growing area in the world, São Paulo, the *colono* model meant that coffee cultivators also grew large amounts of corn, beans, manioc, and other crops not only for themselves, but also for

Table 2.4. Coffee Exports as a Percentage of GDP

Year	Brazil	Colombia	Costa Rica	El Salvador
1912	18	5	12	16
1929	10	–	19	18

Year	Guatemala	Honduras	Nicaragua
1912	9	13.0	11
1929	17	0.5	7

Sources: Calculated from V. Bulmer-Thomas, *The Political Economy of Central America since 1920*, 34, 271; idem, *The Economic History of Latin America*, 59, 439; and Steven Topik, "The State's Contribution to the Development of Brazil's Internal Economy, 1889–1930," *Hispanic American Historical Review* 65(2) (1985): 214.

the internal market. Only a small share of land was actually dedicated to coffee, leaving the possibility of a healthy subsistence sector that fed the state's cities and, increasingly, other states as well. São Paulo's secretary of agriculture estimated in 1904–1905, during the height of the export boom, that only 12 percent of the state was under cultivation. Of that small amount, 40 percent was in crops other than coffee (and even coffee plantations had other crops planted between the trees).[52] Diversified agriculture was the rule in most coffee-growing areas.

Coffee as Plantation Crop

Did coffee in these areas lead to the same concentration of land and wealth in the form of the latifundium as it did in Brazil? Was coffee a plantation crop? Certainly not when it was first cultivated in Yemen. There it was grown on small farms in broken up, river-fed mountain valleys. So it was in most of Java, with its dense population and lack of frontier lands. Only in the eighteenth century were coffee, plantations, and slavery combined in Martinique, then in Haiti and later in Cuba and Puerto Rico. A colonial planter class created by sugar growing and extermination of the native population and a preexisting thriving Atlantic slave trade explain this arrangement more than any inherent demands of coffee. Even so, in the Caribbean, coffee holdings were much smaller than sugar plantations, often one-fifth the size. Coffee offered opportunities to agriculturalists of modest means while the rich turned to sugar.

It was in Brazil that *large* plantations such as Zé Prado's first became associated with coffee. Bigness was not, however, a result of any economies of scale in the production process. Clearing the soil, preparing the ground, raising and planting seedlings, pruning, weeding, and even harvesting were all done by hand. Because of the enormity of the virgin and fertile Brazilian frontier, land was cheap and readily accessible. An estimate in 1897 put the cost of land at only 20 percent of the total cost of establishing a *fazenda*. Preparing the land and planting trees, on the other hand, consumed 60 percent of the cost.[53]

It should be noted that land in Brazil was cheap because the frontier was socially and politically defined. The forests of São Paulo were populated by native Kaingang and other peoples, but they were seminomadic people, few in number; they enjoyed no protection or rights from the Brazilian government. Moving into the frontier was as much a military campaign as an agricultural enterprise.

The major capital investments were housing (the lack of rural villages in the coffee-growing areas meant that year-round laborers lived on the plantation), drying grounds, and, most of all, hulling and washing machinery. But even the last in Brazil was relatively cheap, constituting

only 12 percent of the cost of a *fazenda*, because Brazilian coffee, though
cultivated in an artisanal manner, was approached with an industrial
mentality: quantity and productivity were valued over quality.[54] Brazilians used the "dry" method of treating the cherry, which required far less
machinery than the "wet" method. The dry method allowed all berries
on a branch to be harvested at the same time, regardless of their stage of
ripeness or size, and to be processed at the same time. This was a labor-
intensive solution that reduced machinery and labor costs.[55]

Brazilian methods lowered the quality of coffee but, by creating
abundant, relatively cheap quantities, stimulated popular demand abroad.
Brazil did not simply respond to world demand but helped create it by
producing enough coffee cheaply enough to make it affordable for
members of North America's and Europe's working classes. Brazil's
ability and willingness to plant millions of trees in the Paraíba Valley and
western São Paulo, together with improved transportation and marketing systems and growing prosperity in Western Europe and the United
States, transformed coffee from a luxury drug to a commonplace drink,
indeed, a necessity.[56]

Processing was relatively simple. First the cherries were sun dried.
Then the outer husks and the internal film were removed at the same
time either by threshing and pounding on a mortar or with specially
constructed hulling machines. There were some economies of scale if
the planter built a sophisticated hulling plant, but this did not improve
quality much. Certainly, the imperative for a large supply of raw
material to feed the voracious machines, as Moreno Fraginals explains
was the case with the sugar central, did not exist on the coffee *fazenda*.[57]
Until the railroad reached into the Paraíba Valley in the 1860s and
decades later into other places, transportation was on mule back, again
lessening the advantages of bigness because freight rates were very high.
(Even with the railroad, in 1907 transportation was calculated at 25 to 30
percent of production expenses, twice the cost of harvesting; before the
railroad the figure was no doubt even higher.)[58]

While capital requirements for coffee plantations such as Zé Prado's
were substantial because of trees' lengthy maturation period, coffee
could be successfully grown on a virtual self-sufficient peasant scale by
people like Juan Valdez. He could process it with mortar and pestle. Even
in Brazil, by the 1920s, two-thirds of all coffee holdings were under fifty
acres (although they owned only 18 percent of the trees).[59]

Brazil's land concentration was caused more by the colonial heritage
of land tenure and labor arrangements and the contour of the land than
by the exigencies of coffee growing. Brazil had been founded as an export
agricultural colony and had imported far more slaves than anywhere else
to grow sugar. Some land had been granted by the state in great latifundia

known as "*sesmarias*." So coffee's large-scale holdings had a slave-based export orientation to call upon. This legacy was especially important because many coffee growers in the Southeast had formerly been sugar planters.

Political realities as well as cultural traditions pointed to the latifundia. In the virgin forests of the frontier, where coffee grew most profitably, land titles were unclear. In the colonial period, vast tracts were given out in return for service to the state. Even after independence, when *sesmarias* were abolished, planters with good connections or with bands of hired thugs appropriated public lands, which were little patrolled by the state. Often, planters waited until smaller-scale squatters cleared and tilled frontier land and fought the Indians, then the planters moved in and seized it. Under these conditions, small-scale growers had little incentive to plant trees that took four or five years to become commercially viable.

Given the sparse free population and the abundance of open land, which protected their independence (open, that is from other Brazilians; native peoples still roamed and fiercely defended their customary hunting grounds), planters turned to slaves. Slaves in Brazil were especially cheap because of the proximity of Africa, the volume of the trade, and the size of the existing Brazilian slave population. But the Zé Prados needed either capital or credit to make sufficient slave purchases. Brazil's financial system was underfunded, rudimentary, and poorly institutionalized. Property rights were ill-defined and poorly policed. Poor institutionalization of credit and property, combined with the clan-based and personalistic nature of Brazilian society, caused personal contacts, not some abstract entrepreneurship, to be the basis for acquiring the factors of production. And they dictated that in the early stages only a limited number of people would enjoy such access. Some individuals, such as Zé, then, had government acquiescence to their boundary lines, violence to protect and expand their lands, personal relationships with the merchants in the ports, and bankers who extended credit. These advantages grew as their holdings and reputation grew. Thus success was a self-fulfilling prophecy. Although planters like Prado introduced few technical or agronomic innovations besides hulling machines, their ability to move into adjoining virgin lands with their much greater productivity greatly increased their chances of success.

Once the railroad forged into the interior, plantations enjoyed the added advantage of lower transport costs. Important planters often were large stockholders in the coffee railroads and had the political influence to ensure that their railway received government monopoly concessions. They thus made sure that the line passed through or near their properties.[60] This allowed them to build private lines to bring their crop to the train station. Since the cost of transport to Rio or Santos even with the railroad often exceeded the cost of gathering the harvest, economies here could greatly increase profits.[61] (Of course, once the rail network became dense in the coffee lands by 1910, special connections became less important as access became easy for everyone.)

Terrain also influenced the size of the unit of production. Mountainsides were steep and valleys narrow in the Paraíba Valley, so plantations there were never enormous. It was too difficult to bring coffee from outlying lands to the central drying grounds and hulling machinery. (Facility of transport within the plantation was important because the newly picked cherries weighed five times more than the beans that were hulled from them.)[62] But in western São Paulo, with much more gentle terrain, individual plantations were far larger.

In other coffee-producing lands, however, large-scale plantations were unusual. Even in Colombia and Venezuela, where there had been a tradition of slave labor and haciendas, the smaller production of the Juan Valdezes eventually prevailed. The colonial legacy did encourage Venezuelan cacao planters to move up the hillsides of central Venezuela and plant coffee on haciendas. Here, it is argued, coffee reinforced latifundia. But in the Andes, where much of Venezuela's coffee was grown, production was almost entirely in smallholdings.[63] Similarly, in Colombia, despite important regional differences, Juan Valdez predominated. The East had a strong colonial tradition of peasants with no slaves or latifundia while the West had both. In the former coffee was mostly grown on shares; demesne production was unable to compete with the sharecroppers. Only in Antioquia were haciendas important social units. Even there, there were many small growers like Juan Valdez. Nationally, by 1932, 87 percent of all coffee farms had fewer than five thousand trees (farmers usually planted five hundred to eight hundred trees per acre) and 74 percent of all production was on farms of fewer than twenty thousand trees (fewer than fifty acres).[64]

Most of Central America also grew coffee mostly on small and middle-sized farms. Instead of *fazendas* or haciendas, they cultivated *fincas*. Although Costa Rica was far from a rural democracy (71 percent of the peasantry was landless by 1883) and land was concentrated, the scale was small. As Ciro Cardoso points out, "even the biggest coffee plantations often remained discontinuous, fragmented into a number of small or medium-sized lots sometimes several kilometers apart."[65] Even the "great estates" in Costa Rica are defined as anything over 76 acres, which in Brazil would scarcely be considered a middle-sized holding. The largest *finca* in Costa Rica, belonging to the Rohrmosen family, reached only 1,320 acres. In fact, the entire country's coffee growing area in 1935 amounted to only one-fourth the land of the Cambuhy plantation in São Paulo.[66]

Elsewhere in Central America coffee estates were somewhat larger than in Costa Rica. Nicaragua did have some coffee haciendas, but they were neither numerous nor extensive. El Salvador, the most dependent of all countries on coffee, had a dynamic agrarian bourgeoisie with extremely efficient and concentrated production, but, again, no large estates. Eugenio Aguilar was considered a wealthy planter with two *fincas* that held 230,000 trees on fewer than three hundred acres. Ownership of multiple medium-sized *fincas* was commonplace, however, leading to a considerable concentration of land.

Guatemala and southern Mexico, with larger frontier areas, had substantially larger holdings. Many in Guatemala were over five thousand acres, and Tehuantepec had several coffee estates with 1.5 million trees on twenty thousand acres. In the Soconusco district of Mexico's southern state of Chiapas there were fifty plantations that averaged three thousand acres each. In Mexico's state of Veracruz, however, the principal coffee exporter for most of the period, holdings tended to be much smaller.[67]

Coffee in Spanish America

Coffee estates in general were smaller in Colombia and Central America than in Brazil because of terrain and transportation problems, shortage of capital and labor, and the relative absence of a frontier and the presence of people with preexisting land claims. Aside from eastern Colombia and parts of Mexico, none of the coffee-growing areas had easy access to the Atlantic. Before the Panama Canal, this was a serious impediment. Costa Rica built a rail line to the Atlantic, but the other areas went through more costly Pacific ports. Moreover, coffee grew in the highlands, distant from ports. In the case of Colombia and, to a lesser degree, Costa Rica, the terrain was rugged and transportation difficult overland. Transportation added considerably to production costs. In Colombia, Brazil's main competitor, there were fewer than four hundred miles of railroad track in the whole country in 1900 (one-sixth the rail that São Paulo alone had at the time), and most of the coffee areas were not well served by rivers. In the 1940s, 80 percent of all Colombian coffee still traveled at least partway on muleback. Transportation from the *finca* to the coast cost eight times as much as the trans-Atlantic fare.[68] Because of late entry into the coffee market and relative prior poverty, credit was short, causing high finance costs. The only way that Colombian or Central American producers could compete with Brazil under these conditions was to produce better coffee and therefore receive a higher price for it while keeping labor costs low. And indeed, their fine mild coffees usually received about one-fifth more than Brazil's coffee.

Higher-quality coffee required more labor-intensive harvesting. Shade trees had to be planted and the berries picked individually just as they ripened rather than stripping entire branches, as done in Brazil. Workers would sometimes have to pass the same tree six or seven times during the harvest rather than once, as in Brazil, and in some places there were two annual harvests. Better quality also demanded the more sophisticated and expensive "wet" method of treating the berry. Inspecting this method in Costa Rica, the Brazilian planter Jorge Dumont Villares marveled that the preparation of coffee was a "true science" there. The berries were picked, hulled, then left twenty-four to forty hours to ferment. Next they were washed to remove the outer membrane and dried for one or two days. From the drying grounds the beans were taken to dryers, where they were left for twenty-five to thirty-five hours drying at fifty to eighty degrees. The parchment film was then removed mechanically and the beans sorted by size, quality, and color. Finally, the beans were polished.[69] Producing high-quality coffee, then, demanded substantial capital and technical expertise as well as abundant cheap labor.

None of these countries enjoyed much capital, available labor, or even large stretches of available land to create competitive coffee latifundia. Costa Rica, the first Central American producer, resolved its problems by using peasants like Juan Valdez. Smallholders were able to compete because they used family labor and grew their own subsistence crops between the rows of *arabica* seedlings or on neighboring plots, as Brazilian *colonos* did. Their overhead and investments were minimal. With the country's small population and limited amount of appropriate land, wages and land prices rose rapidly, making the purchase of largeholdings more difficult. The elite found it more profitable to concentrate on the industrial and commercial ends of the trade than on production. Peasants took their berries to central processing mills that were capitalized by credit from English export merchants. Profit was concentrated by the owners of the 250 *beneficios* (coffee mills).[70]

Colombia, El Salvador, Nicaragua, Guatemala, and Mexico, which became active in coffee growing a half century after Costa Rica, faced somewhat different market conditions than had Costa Rica. Domestically, there was a larger potential labor pool, more capital had been accumulated to permit larger landholdings (at independence Costa Rica had been by far the poorest of these countries), and foreign capital was more available. In fact, in Guatemala, Nicaragua, and parts of Mexico, Germans owned many of the most efficient *fincas* and dominated commerce.[71]

But even in these countries, plantations were impeded by populations already settled on potential coffee lands who were reluctant to work for planters.[72] Since coffee grew up after the abolition of slavery and none of the Central American and Andean countries attracted Europeans as workers, they had to rely on their own populations for laborers. In Costa Rica and Colombia, the indigenous population had either died out or had been forced out of potential coffee-growing areas. The laborers were for the most part Hispanized peasants without traditional claims to the land.[73] These people either competed for land and established small-holdings, or worked as renters, sharecroppers, or day workers.

In El Salvador, Nicaragua, Guatemala, and Chiapas, Mexico, how-ever, the pre-Columbian populations held much of the most fertile lands as communal property. Moreover, in the cases of Guatemala and Chiapas, the indigenous peoples had sufficient land to be uninterested in working on coffee *fincas*. In response, supposedly liberal governments turned land into a commodity through a series of liberal reforms in the last three decades of the 1800s; these went as far in El Salvador as to abolish communal land. This was the law in Mexico as well, but the state was slower to enforce it. In Guatemala the native population held on more firmly to their lands because most of them lived in the Northeast, which was unsuited for coffee.[74] Church, public, and town lands were also privatized. Although there were apparently serious efforts to sell the land in small plots to encourage a farmer class in Colombia, Costa Rica, Guatemala, Chiapas, and Nicaragua, the economic and political power of the elite allowed them disproportionately to take advantage of land sales and concentrate ownership.

Labor Systems

Labor continued to be a problem. A thought-provoking debate between Laird Bergad and Tom Brass on coffee's effect on labor forms in Puerto Rico is relevant. Bergad noted that coffee's eclipse of sugar caused the move away from slavery to less-coercive labor forms. Brass responded that where there was difficulty in procuring workers, either because they refused to work on the coffee lands or because of competition between growers for workers, there was a tendency to use coercive labor forms to fix the workers on the *finca*. Brass was thinking of the British Caribbean, where vagrancy and apprenticeship laws passed in the 1830s after the abolition of slavery, but he applied his rule to all of Latin America.[75]

In reality, the relationship between labor form and coffee varied from country to country and changed over time. As already noted, coffee reinforced slavery in the Caribbean and in Brazil but was little used elsewhere in Latin America. Other extra-economic coercive forms such as the *repartimiento*, the *mandamiento*, debt peonage, and vagrancy laws were applied. These had the longest lives and were the most widely enforced in countries with the strongest pre-Columbian traditions. Where the village remained strong, traditional rights and lands were best defended and coercion was most used to procure labor. Indeed, David McCreery has argued that coercion was a sign of a healthy and somewhat autonomous indigenous sector. Thus the country which had the least Ladinoization and where indigenous lands were remote from coffee estates, Guatemala, only abolished forced labor in 1944. El Salvador and Nicaragua also applied vagrancy laws but to a smaller extent since market forces (and state division of communal land, protection of private property, and repression of labor unions and strikes) usually sufficed to attract workers. Debt peonage, under which workers were forced to labor until they paid off debts, was extensive in Chiapas and Tehuantepec and existed on a limited scale in Colombia in the more backward coffee producing areas. However, at least in Chiapas this might well have reflected worker power to secure advances (essentially loans) as well as owner power to entrap workers. Costa Rica used no coercive labor forms because of the extent of the peasantry and the landless class.[76]

Ethnic Relations

Just as the coffee boom transformed labor and land relations, it also had striking consequences for ethnic relations. Haiti and Brazil were Africanized as millions of slaves were imported. The former became a black republic, but Brazil undertook a policy of "whitening." In São Paulo, European immigrants took the farm jobs from freedmen after abolition. Only in the less successful coffee states such as Minas Gerais and Rio de Janeiro did people of color continue to predominate in the *cafezales* in the period after 1888.

Mestizos, a combination of indigenous and Caucasian genes or lifestyles, prevailed in Colombia, Venezuela, and most of Central America. They became "Ladinoized" or "westernized" as coffee turned their attention to the larger market and they came under the political sway of forces farther away than their village or local *hacendado*.

Although indigenous peoples had grown coffee on communal lands early on (there are records of Indian coffee production in Chiapas as early as the 1820s), rarely would they be able to maintain their indigenous identity and village life while growing coffee.[77] The permanence of this tree crop, which could produce for thirty to fifty years before needing to be replaced, clashed with Mayan traditions of rotating crops, leaving land fallow for years, and redistributing it among village members. Coffee tended to commodify land. Although indigenous people in Oaxaca did sometimes grow coffee (on private rather than communal land) for their own consumption and local sales, even Maya who worked three months a year on the harvest in Chiapas and Guatemala had little interest in growing it on their own land. They were thus forced off of the best coffee lands to marginal subsistence plots or into landlessness. As "semiproletarians" they worked part time on neighboring *fincas* but retained their indigenous identities.

Coffee not only introduced racial groups and intermixed them, but it helped redefine ethnicities. Carol Smith has argued that "the coffee economy reorganized the regional and class patterning of ethnicity in Guatemala." Instead of the white-colored dichotomy that had existed between the Spanish and all people of color, coffee created a dichotomy between Indians and mestizos: "Guatemala's capitalist state created two noncapitalist classes in western Guatemala: that of coerced labor (Indian) and that of labor-coercer (Ladino). These noncapitalist relations were stronger in 1944 than they were in 1844."[78] The same process occurred in El Salvador with a different outcome. In the first decades of the twentieth century, the country's large Indian population in coffee areas was defined out of existence by government officials. Officially, independent mestizos replaced Indian villagers. A similar situation occurred in Nicaragua.[79]

Coffee and Gender

The coffee economy also affected families and gender roles, though probably less than it changed ethnic and class relations. As already noted, in Brazil slave-produced coffee demanded a disproportionate number of male Africans and weakened families, as each slave was an individual possession of the master, who was free to dispose of the slave as he or she wished. The immigrant *colono* system that replaced slavery emphasized the family as the unit of work and strengthened and exploited the traditional patriarchal power of the father. Elsewhere, the peasant family was also the main labor unit for permanent farmers, sharecroppers, renters, or resident laborers. The extent to which women owned or worked land as heads of households is only now beginning to be studied. Pathbreaking work for the states of Oaxaca and Veracruz find women, particularly widows, often owning and working land. The breakup of communal lands and the creation of *fincas* expanded this phenomenon. In more peripheral areas, it seems that women were more able to assert their independence. According to imperfect Mexican data, in 1910 one-third of all of Veracruz's farmers and one-fourth of its agrarian laborers were women. In Colombia, it has been argued, patriarchy was reduced on the frontier, since women often migrated there alone or with their brothers.[80]

Even when males headed households, there was a division of labor by gender. Although this varied over time and by area, generally, men were responsible for clearing new land, tending seedlings, pruning, drying, and transporting the beans. Both men and women picked coffee and weeded, though women and children probably predominated in the latter and men in the former. Processing in the mills was largely women's work.

Although coffee depended on campesino family labor, it also often relied on seasonal workers (*jornaleros*), who sometimes came long distances to work for several months. When the trek was long, as in Chiapas, where workers walked more than a week to arrive in the *cafezales*, *jornaleros* were overwhelmingly men. This probably increased the power of the women, who headed their households a quarter of the year. (Indeed, women's independence grew even when sharecropper men had to work at a distance for weeks at a time to fulfill their service contracts.) On the other hand, when *fincas* drew seasonal workers from dense neighboring populations, women and children also took temporary jobs. Pay usually went to the male head of the family, but women were also sometimes directly paid.

Coffee mills provide the clearest example of proletarianized labor and segregation by sex. Many of those located in towns and cities were essentially factories staffed by women. This sometimes gave rise to a new consciousness. In November 1925, the female workers of Guatemala's La Moderna mill successfully struck for better wages and working conditions. It was the first strike in the history of the Guatemalan workers movement to be led by women.[81]

Coffee Planters

The discussion so far has tried to explain why the plantation was not the norm for coffee, to demonstrate the variety of contexts and problems coffee planters encountered, and to enumerate the diverse consequences for coffee workers. Coffee culture helped form national, ethnic, and gender relations. Neither botany nor the world market strictly dictated labor forms, though both defined the limits of the possible. Internal conditions were primary.

We have seen not only that coffee, plantations, and slavery were not necessarily linked, but also that coffee did not always yield a strong landlord class, since smallholders were often the rule. In Costa Rica, the predominance of merchants and millers was most obvious because of the smallholding pattern. But elsewhere merchants were also the dominant class. In Colombia, most of the progressive planters were initially merchants. Only in areas such as Cundinamarca were traditional landlords the coffee growers. Many Nicaraguan *finqueros* were urban based. El Salvador's coffee-grower class largely comprised merchants and other urban-based capitalists who invested in land in the 1880s and 1890s as coffee prices rose. German merchants in Guatemala and Chiapas followed the same path. In relatively few cases was there much continuity between the colonial landed elite and the coffee bourgeoisie. In fact, many members of the coffee elite were nineteenth-century immigrants. It is a mistake to refer to the coffee growers of Central America and Colombia as Junkers or to discuss "landlord capitalism."[82] Coffee was developed by a new capitalist group that was not reluctant to invest in other sectors of the economy as well.

State Building

Coffee planters have often been credited not only with being profit seekers interested in developing economies, but also with being bourgeois, interested in creating national states and "modern" individual liberties. They are seen as creating both revenues and transportation networks and banks and land registries. Coffee provided tax revenues, transportation infrastructure, domestic capital accumulation, and foreign investment. It broke down local disputes and created national concerns. In Cuba, in 1868 and again in 1895, coffee growers led the fight for independence. Nieto Arteta maintains that coffee's prosperity in Colombia forced politicians to become more concerned with economic policy than with quarreling over politics; civil war ended with the "disappearance of the boundaries between the old political parties."[83] Even a Marxist such as Sandinista Jaime Wheelock praises the role of coffee in his country: "The consolidation of the export structure based on coffee . . . signified the ascension to power of Nicaragua's landowning bourgeoisie and the defeat of the traditional oligarchy."[84] But the independent national states that coffee men constructed were, in fact, oligarchic regimes that narrowly restricted citizenship. The areas that were most successful in coffee production were those most reluctant to democratize.

Certainly there was resistance to the rule of coffee. In Guatemala, villagers frequently destroyed coffee *fincas*; they did not want to be incorporated into the coffee republic. As the villagers of San Felipe wrote to Guatemala's president in 1864:[85]

Those gentlemen and ourselves have the sacred links which make us members of one nation, ruled by one Government and by one set of laws. Could it be that they want to use this factor and historic precedent against us because we lack large sums of capital . . . or that they want to take our only element of vitality from us, throw us out of our homes and off our land and turn us and future generations into a nomadic and wandering people?

Many villagers did become strangers in their own land. (The situation was very different in Africa, where, in Uganda, for instance, coffee actually strengthened village structures.) In western El Salvador, coffee initially was a progressive force that occupied vacant lands in the mountains. But in the twentieth century that "monster began to descend the mountains and swallow up the plains."[86] Then it attacked peasant lands. The peasants, in collaboration with the Communist Party and its leader, Farabundo Martí, responded by attempting to overthrow the government in 1932. The result was at least seventeen thousand peasants dead in the gruesome massacre known simply as La Matanza (The Massacre).

The willingness of coffee growers to use violence has often allowed them to maintain the essence of their rule while changing its appearance. Colombia never had a truly populist ruler; the traditional liberals and conservatives still share power. El Salvador and Guatemala have had the most ferocious and brutal regimes in Central America, still overseen by descendants of the coffee elite. São Paulo was the last state to hold out against populist leader Getúlio Vargas, even waging civil war against him in 1932.

Coffee tended to become more democratic only after it lost its hegemony. The first Brazilian state to seriously undertake restructuring and the creation of smallholdings was Rio de Janeiro at the turn of the century, once its export sector went into decline. São Paulo became the center of radical labor movements only in the 1970s, long after coffee ceased fueling the economy. Costa Rica had its democratic revolution in 1948, after coffee lost its dominant position in the national economy. Nicaragua experienced one of only two socialist revolutions in the Western Hemisphere's history. But here again, the weakness of the coffee economy and the concomitant lack of a strong bourgeoisie explained the possibility of radical restructuring.

Coffee's marriage of convenience to the oligarchy in Latin America derived from the concentration of wealth and power enjoyed by the economy's principal actors—merchants, bankers, processors, and, to a lesser extent, landowners—and from the divisions among coffee workers. They were divided into landowning semiproletarian (and sometimes Indian) peasants, plantation residents, medium-scale farmers, sharecroppers, renters, and landless day workers. They were divided by relations to the land, capital, and markets, and by ethnicity. (Only more

recently, with the rise of Protestantism, has religion divided them.]
Charles Bergquist points out the central issue in coffee: workers often
owned their own land or at least had access to their own plots: "In
winning the battle for the land, these workers in coffee production thus
lost the struggle to transform the exploitative capitalist society in which
they labored . . . Coffee workers won greater control over the work
process and the means of production, only to be exploited more efficiently and easily through capitalist control over coffee commerce."[87]

Even in areas where peasants worked on plantations, such as in
Chiapas, paternalistic relations kept them from revolting.[88] None of the
coffee areas of Mexico, Chiapas, Veracruz, or Oaxaca participated to any
extent in the Mexican Revolution. The Revolution was imported from
outside and came late. Even where a strong agrarian movement later
arose, as in Veracruz, coffee growers and workers seem to have been
marginal to the movement. In El Salvador, the guerrilla resistance that
exploded in the 1970s was always weak in the coffee-cultivating western
part of the country. Labor militancy in Costa Rica and Colombia was
much more associated with banana workers than with coffee growers.
Only in more marginal areas, where small-scale farmers resented market
conditions rather than the power of large planters, have coffee growers
revolted, as in Chiapas since 1994.[89]

Conclusion

Coffee cultivation and culture had enormous effects on much of Latin
America during the era of export-led growth. The *arabica* was the
umbilical cord that tied much of Latin America to the world economy.
European and North American thirst set millions of Latin Americans to
growing coffee. And European and North American capital financed the
trade and in many places built the transportation and processing infrastructure. Certainly, most of the profits in the coffee business accrued to
British, German, French, and U.S. merchants, roasters, and purveyors.
Yet foreigners and the world system did not single-mindedly command
the destiny of Latin Americans.

The botanical demands of the tree crop also set the limits of the
possible in coffee culture. Coffee's long gestation period, the relative
permanence of the trees, low technological but high labor demands, and
climatic requirements shaped labor and land tenure systems, dictated
linkages to other economic activities, and constrained the nature of state
intervention. Coffee was a master that was willing to cede land to
competing crops, however. It was not a monoculture and not an iron
dictator.

The history of coffee is a history of diversity and a history of possibility. The world economy and the demands of botany may have called the tune and rented the dancehall, but producers, to a considerable extent, were free to choose which steps they wished to dance and with which partner(s). Coffee workers, standing in the shadows watching and waiting to clean up, had much less choice.

The preexisting geographic conditions, settlement patterns, social organization, and local resistance combined with differing state policies, transportation possibilities, and evolving world demand to create a plethora of production systems and diverse social, cultural, and economic results. It is as if the same paint were applied to different surfaces at different temperatures and humidities to produce quite distinct colors. The different hues reflected not only who owned the land, who worked it and how, but the place of women and the family in the fields and even the color of workers' skins.

Thus the export boom saw the frontier fall to the ax, railroads crisscross the countryside, cities swell, and, in some places, factories rise. A new elite who married commerce and landowning, preached liberalism, and steadied the national state trooped out of the coffee fields. Yet the façade of lovely plazas in the capitals, inspiring railroad stations, and full bank vaults could not hide the despoiling of indigenous villages, the exploitation of slaves and debt peons, and the abuse of the enormous numbers of landless peoples in the countryside. The coffee republic was an oligarchy ruled by coffee barons and foreign merchants. They managed to bring peace, as Nieto Arteta lyrically notes in the epigraph, but not justice.

Of all tropical export commodities, coffee is the one most often credited with fostering a strong national bourgeoisie, industrialization, and a strong state. Was there in fact something inherently heroic about the brown bean? It appears both in the national mythologies and in historical studies that Zé Prado and Juan Valdez were parts of very different coffee-cultivating systems, but closer scrutiny demonstrates their fundamental similarities. What made coffee heroic was not its ability to transform societies, but, on the contrary, its ability to adapt to them. Both Zé Prado and Juan Valdez articulated archaic production methods with the enormous demand of the industrialized countries where coffee both regulated industrial time and entertained bourgeois leisure. Coffee growers, for a very long time, succeeded in bringing modernization to the countryside without true progress. Coffee brought wealth for some, a few swelling cities, nascent industries, and a greater transportation infrastructure, but was slow to bring full-fledged development. The peasant form hindered the speed of the movement toward full-blown capitalist relations and retarded the emergence of democracy.

The nature of both international demand and Latin American power arrangements meant that coffee's success always rested primarily on rich lands and poor workers.

Notes

1. At one time or another, coffee was the leading export of Brazil, Colombia, Costa Rica, El Salvador, Guatemala, Haiti, Jamaica, Martinique, Nicaragua, Puerto Rico, Suriname (then Dutch Guiana), and Venezuela. It was also important in Cuba, the Dominican Republic, Ecuador, Honduras, and Mexico.

2. Perhaps the most sophisticated debate over the effects of the leading staples is in Canada. For a thoughtful overview, see John Richards, "The Staple Debates," in Cameron Duncan, ed., *Explorations in Canadian Economic History: Essays in Honour of Irene Spry* (Ottawa: University of Ottowa Press, 1985), 45–72. On coffee's fostering of a strong national bourgeoisie, see Fernando Ortiz Fernández, *Cuban Counterpoint: Tobacco and Sugar* (New York: Knopf, 1947); Luis Eduardo Nieto Arteta, *El café en la sociedad colombiana* (Bogotá: Ediciones La Soga al Cuello, 1971), 26–27, 34–35; Celso Furtado, *The Economic Growth of Brazil*, 123–126; and Victor Bulmer-Thomas, *The Political Economy of Central America since 1920* (New York: Cambridge University Press, 1987), 5–6.

3. Barrington Moore, Jr., in *Social Origins of Dictatorship and Democracy, Lord and Peasant in the Making of the Modern World* (Boston: Beacon Press, 1966), inspired Dietrich Rueschemeyer, Evelyne Huber Stephens, and John D. Stephens, *Capitalist Development and Democracy* (Cambridge, Mass.: Polity, 1992), 6–8; Evelyne Huber and Frank Safford, eds., *Agrarian Structure and Political Power: Landlord and Peasant in the Making of Latin America* (Pittsburgh, Penn.: University of Pittsburgh Press, 1995); and Michael D. Shafer, *Winners and Losers: How Sectors Shape the Developmental Prospects of States* (Ithaca, N.Y.: Cornell University Press, 1994).

4. According to André Raymond, *Artisans et commerçants au Caire au XVIII siècle* (Damas: Institute Français de Damas, 1973–1974), 133, Yemen exported about 200,000 quintales a year at the beginning of the eighteenth century, or about 44 million pounds. Brazil would be producing about fifty times as much at the end of the nineteenth century. Yemen's number seems high, since, according to Francis B. Thurber, *Coffee: From Plantation to Cup* (New York: American Grocer Publishing Association, 1886), 242, Yemen produced about 16 million pounds in 1854.

5. Fernand Braudel, *The Structures of Everyday Life: The Limits of the Possible* (London: Collins, 1981), I:259; José Teixeira de Oliveira, *Historia do café no Brasil e no mundo* (Rio de Janeiro: Livraria Kosmos, 1984), 76; Paul Butel, "Les Amériques et l'Europe," in *Histoire économique et sociale du monde*, vol. 3, ed. Pierre Léon (Paris: A. Colin, 1978).

6. M. Mulhall, in *The Dictionary of Statistics*, 4th ed. (London: G. Routledge and Sons, 1899), 130, shows that in the 1890s of all commodities shipped internationally only grains and sugar surpassed coffee in terms of value; each was about 20 percent greater than coffee. See also Randal G. Stewart, *Coffee: The*

Political Economy of an Export Industry in Papua New Guinea (Boulder, Colo.: Westview, 1992), 1; Richard L. Lucier, The International Political Economy of Coffee: From Juan Valdez to Yank's Diner (New York: Praeger, 1988), xvii; Food and Agriculture Organization of the United Nations, Trade: 1990, FAO Statistics Series no. 102 (Rome: FAO, 1991), passim.

7. Eric Williams, Slavery and Capitalism (New York: Capricorn Books, 1966), 52.

8. Michel-René Hilliard D'Auberteure, Betrachtungen über den gegen-wartigen Zustand der Französischen Colonie zu San Domingo (Leipzig: Johann Friedrich Junius, 1779), 54, 55, 62; Michel-Rolph Trouillot, "Motion in the System: Coffee, Color, and Slavery in Eighteenth-Century Saint-Domingue," Review 5:3 (Winter 1982): 331, 351, 354; Carolyn E. Fick, The Making of Haiti: The Saint Domingue Revolution from Below (Knoxville: University of Tennessee Press, 1990), 19, 22, 123, 128.

9. Hans Becker, Volker Höhfeld, and Horst Kopp, Kaffee aus Arabien: Der Bedeutungswandel eines welt-wirtshaftsgutes und seine siedlungsgeographische Konsequenz an der Trockengrenze der Okumere (Wiesbaden: Franz Steiner, 1979), 20. Emília Viotti da Costa shows British Guyana's shift from coffee to sugar and its bloody consequences in Crowns of Glory, Tears of Blood (New York: Oxford University Press, 1994).

10. Brazil's relatively late entry into the coffee market was due to bad timing. When the Portuguese dominated the Persian Gulf trade in the sixteenth century, Europeans were not interested in coffee, so the Portuguese did not disseminate it—as they did sugar—to their colonies. And the twenty years of Dutch control of Pernambuco, Brazil, came a half century before they were able to raise and transship coffee seedlings. Fernando Novais, Portugal e Brasil na crises do antigo sistema colonial, 1777–1808 (São Paulo: Editora HUCITEC, 1979), argues that the Portuguese crown favored African slavery because it was an easily taxable resource and allowed Portuguese slavers in Angola to reap some of Brazil's profit.

11. José Jobson de A. Arruda, O Brasil no comércio colonial (São Paulo: Editora Ática, 1980), 332–337, 612–631; Leslie Bethell, The Abolition of the Brazilian Slave Trade: Britain, Brazil and the Slave Trade (Cambridge: Cambridge University Press, 1970), chap. 1.

12. Philip Curtin, The Atlantic Slave Trade: A Census (Madison: University of Wisconsin Press, 1969), 234. On the eve of the abolition of slavery, Brazil still had roughly 750,000 slaves, probably a third of whom worked directly on coffee plantations. See Verena Stolcke, Cafeicultura, homens, mulheres e capital (1850–1980), trans. Denise Bottmann and João R. Martins Filho (São Paulo: Brasiliense, 1986), 42, and Hildete Pereira de Melo, "O café e a economia fluminense: 1889–1920," paper presented at the First Brazilian Conference of International Economic History, São Paulo, 1993.

13. Instituto Brasileiro de Geografia e Estatística, Estatísticas históricas do Brasil (Rio de Janeiro: IBGE, 1987), 412.

14. Celso Furtado, The Economic Growth of Brazil: A Survey from Colonial to Modern Times, trans. Ricardo Aguiar and Eric Drysdale (Berkeley and Los Angeles: University of California Press, 1971), 197.

15. André Gunder Frank, Capitalism and Underdevelopment in Latin America

(New York: Monthly Review Press, 1969); Theotonio dos Santos, "Brazil, the Origins of a Crisis," in Ronald Chilcote and Joel Edelstein, eds., *Latin America: The Struggle with Dependency and Beyond* (New York: John Wiley & Sons, 1974), 409–490. Numerous historians have provided accounts that, while not always inspired by dependency theory, have lent support to the theory. See, for instance, Anyda Marchant, *Viscount Maua and the Empire of Brazil* (Berkeley and Los Angeles: University of California Press, 1965); Almir Chaiban El-Kareh, *Filha branca de mae preta: A Companhia de Estrada de Ferro Dom Pedro II* (Petrópolis: Editora Vozes, 1980), 25, 28; Stanley Stein, *Vassouras: A Brazilian Coffee County* (Cambridge, Mass.: Harvard University Press, 1956); Luiz Carlos Soares, "A manufatura na sociedade escravista: O surto manufatureiro no Rio de Janeiro e nas suas circunvizinhanças (1840–1870)," in Frédéric Mauro, ed., *La Préindustrialization du Brésil: Essais sur une économie en transition, 1830/50– 1930/50* (Paris: Éditions de Centre National du Recherche Scientifique, 1984), 47; José Roberto do Amaral Lapa, *A economia cafeeira* (São Paulo: Brasiliense, 1983), 29–30.

16. Joaquim Nabuco, *O abolicionismo* (London: Kingdon, 1883), 167. All translations are mine unless otherwise noted.

17. See Rebecca Scott, "Defining the Boundaries of Freedom in the World of Cane: Cuba, Brazil and Louisiana after Emancipation," *American Historical Review* 99:1 (February 1994): 70–102. The future United States had used indentured servants on a smaller scale around the Chesapeake in the colonial era, but they were replaced by slaves once planters became sufficiently prosperous. See Edmund G. Morgan, *American Slavery, American Freedom: The Ordeal of Colonial Virginia* (New York: Norton, 1975).

18. See George Reid Andrews, *Blacks and Whites in São Paulo, Brazil, 1888– 1988* (Madison: University of Wisconsin Press, 1991), on the bias against freedmen in São Paulo, and Sam Adamo, "Race and Povo," in Michael L. Conniff and Frank D. McCann, eds., *Modern Brazil: Elites and Masses in Historical Perspective* (Lincoln: University of Nebraska Press, 1989), 192–208, on their fate in Rio. Thomas Holloway, *Immigrants on the Land: Coffee and Society in São Paulo, 1886–1934* (Chapel Hill: University of North Carolina Press, 1980), is the best study of immigration to São Paulo.

19. *Wileman's Brazilian Review* (19 November 1924): 1550.

20. Zélia Maria Cardoso de Mello, *O metamorfose da riqueza: São Paulo, 1845–1895* (São Paulo: HUCITEC and Prefeitura do Município de São Paulo, Secretaria Municipal de Cultura, 1985), 150; Darrel Levy, *The Prados of Brazil* (Athens: University of Georgia Press, 1987), 83; Eul-Soo Pang, *In Pursuit of Honor and Power: Noblemen of the Southern Cross in the Nineteenth Century in Brazil* (Tuscaloosa: University of Alabama Press, 1988), 120, 250; Sérgio Silva, *Expansão cafeeira e origens da indústria no Brasil* (São Paulo: Editora Alfa-Omega, 1981); Wilson Cano, *Raizes da concentração industrial em São Paulo* (São Paulo: DIFEL, 1977); João Manuel Cardoso de Mello, *O capitalismo tardio: Contribuição à revisão crítica da formação e do desenvolvimento da economia brasileira* (São Paulo: Editora Brasiliense, 1982); Warren Dean, *The Industrial-ization of São Paulo, 1880–1945* (Austin: University of Texas Press, 1969).

21. Albert Hirschman, "A Generalized Linkage Approach to Development,

with Special Reference to Staples," *Economic Development and Cultural Change* 25 (1977), supplement: 67–98. Thomas Holloway, "Migration and Mobility: Immigrants as Laborers and Landowners in the Coffee Zone of São Paulo, Brazil, 1886–1934," Ph.D. diss., University of Wisconsin (1974), 412. The commercial factors, the *comissários*, were originally almost entirely nationals and immigrants, too, although over time the European and the North American houses that dominated exports came to control factorage as well. See Joseph Sweigart, *Coffee Factorage and the Emergence of a Brazilian Capital Market* (New York: Garland Press, 1987).

22. Jacob Gorender, *A burguesia brasileira* (São Paulo: Brasiliense, 1981), 38.

23. Jacob Gorender, *O escravismo colonial* (São Paulo: Editora Ática, 1978).

24. Franz Dafert, *Über die Gegenwartige Lage des Kaffeebaus in Brasilien* (Amsterdam: J. H. de Bussy, 1898), 49. In fairness to Brazilian growers, irrigation was unnecessary and mechanization was difficult. According to Stewart, *Coffee: The Political Economy*, 47, 48, fully modern Australian capitalist planters in the 1960s were unable to mechanize coffee production much in Papua, New Guinea; they could not outcompete the local subsistence farmers who grew a few hundred coffee trees. Quotation from Franz Dafert, *Principes de culture rationnelle du café au Brasil; Étude sur les engrais à employer* (Paris: Augustin Challanuel, 1900), 41.

25. Dafert, *Principes*, 29, 32, 34; Warren Dean, "The Green Wave of Coffee: Beginnings of Tropical Agricultural Research in Brazil (1885–1900)," *Hispanic American Historical Review* 69:1 (February 1989): 91–116. Eduardo Silva, *Baroes e escravidão* (Rio de Janeiro: Editora Nova Fronteira, 1984), shows that there was some concern with studying agriculture, and the government did create the Sociedade Nacional Auxiliadora, but these were few and small voices in a chorus of ignorance. See also Nathaniel H. Leff, *Underdevelopment and Development in Brazil*, 2 vols. (London: George Allen and Unwin, 1982); Steven Topik, *The Political Economy of the Brazilian State, 1889–1930* (Austin: University of Texas Press, 1987), chap. 5.

26. Stolcke, *Cafeicultura*, 35. This number is for the period after 1890; earlier, *colonos* tended only 566 to 813 trees. Thomaz Davatz, *Memórias de un colono no Brasil (1850)*, trans. S. Buarque de Holanda (São Paulo: Editora Itatiaia and USP, 1980), 111, reported that his family oversaw first 5,400 trees, then, when a child left because of marriage, 3,400 trees. Holloway, *Immigrants on the Land*, 84, cites a report of the São Paulo secretary of agriculture, who calculated 5,000 trees as the average for a *colono* family.

27. Calculated from Holloway, *Immigrants on the Land*, 80, 85, 86. Max Leclerc, *Cartas do Brasil* (São Paulo: Companhia Editora Nacional, 1942 [1891]), 83–86, noted that fifty-two of the eighty families working on the Paulista Santa Verediana plantation he visited in 1889 were kept on the plantation by the debts they owed the company store.

28. Quotation from Holloway, *Immigrants on the Land*, 89. See also Eric Wolf and Sidney Mintz, "Haciendas and Plantations in Middle America and the Antilles," *Social and Economic Studies* 6:3 (September 1957): 380–422. On the plantations studied by Michael Jiménez, "Traveling Far in Grandfather's Car: The Life Cycle of Central Colombian Coffee Estates. The Case of Viotá,

Cundinamarca (1904–1930)," *Hispanic American Historical* Review 69:2 (May 1989): 185–219, only 21 percent of the land was dedicated to coffee. Almost all the rest was set aside for the workers' own use or left as forest.

29. Wages calculated from Brazil, *Censo industrial, 1907*, vol. 2, p. 90. See also Dafert, *Gegenwartige Lage Kaffeebaus*, 49; V. D. Wickizer, *Coffee, Tea and Cocoa* (Stanford, Calif.: Food Research Center, 1959), 49; Bulmer-Thomas, *The Political Economy of Central America*, 60, cites thirty cents a day as an average wage where subsistence also was supplied. Stolcke, *Cafeicultura*, 81; Holloway, *Immigrants on the Land*, 150–156; Warren Dean, *Rio Claro: A Brazilian Plantation System, 1820–1920* (Stanford, Calif.: Stanford University Press, 1976), 105–107.

30. Stolcke, *Cafeicultura*, 43.

31. Pierre Denis, *Brazil* (London: T. F. Unwin, 1911), 217; Stolcke, *Cafeicultura*, 72, 75.

32. According to Lucier, *The Political Economy of Coffee*, 29, today Brazil's coffee has become so deconcentrated that the average farm has nine hectares and large producers are responsible for less than 3 percent of total production. See also Dean, *Rio Claro*. Mircea Buescu, *Evolução econômica do Brasil* (Rio de Janeiro: APEC, 1974), 126; Maurício Font, "Coffee Planters, Politics and Development in Brazil," *Latin American Research Review* 22:3 (1987): 69–90.

33. J. W. F. Rowe, *Studies in the Artificial Control of Raw Material Supplies: Brazilian Coffee* (London: London and Cambridge Economic Service, 1932), 5.

34. See Topik, *Political Economy of the Brazilian State*, chap. 3, and idem, "L'État sur le marché: Approche comparative du café brésilien et du henequen mexicain," *Annales, Economies, Sociétés, Civilisations* 46:2 (March–April 1991): 429–458, for more on the Defense of Coffee program. The large state role in Brazil was exceptional for coffee countries, however. Before 1930 little was done by other coffee states besides selling public and communal land, sometimes aiding in coercing labor, and, on rare occasion, investing in transportation.

35. M. G. McCreery and Mary L. Bynum, *The Coffee Industry in Brazil* (Washington, D.C.: U.S. Department of Commerce, Report no. 92, 1930), 97.

36. Wickizer, *Coffee, Tea and Cocoa*, 29, 36–39, 463; Holloway, "Migration and Mobility: Immigrants as Laborers and Landowners in the Coffee Zone of São Paulo, Brazil, 1886–1934," 88–98; Affonso de Escragnolle Taunay, *História do café no Brasil*, vol. XIII (Rio de Janeiro: Departamento Nacional de Café, 1943), 227; Brazil, Departamento Nacional de Café, *Defesa do café no Brasil* (Rio de Janeiro: Departamento Nacional de Café, 1935), I:155.

37. In fact, in the 1930s, for lack of other applications, the Brazilian government would have to burn more than 50 million bags of coffee—the equivalent of several years' of world consumption, which, stacked up sixteen bags wide, would create a pile higher than Mount Everest. A large and growing share of Argentina's meat and wheat were consumed domestically. William H. Ukers, *All about Coffee* (New York: The Tea and Coffee Trade Journal, 1935), 519, reports that an unofficial marketing survey in 1934 put Brazil's per capita consumption 25 percent ahead Sweden's, then the world's official leader. Waldyr Niemeyer, *Brasil e seu comércio interno* (Rio de Janeiro: A. Coelho Branco, 1948), 97, reported that for 1941–1942, Brazil had the second-largest total market for coffee

80 The Second Conquest of Latin America

in the world, trailing only the United States. Quotation in *New York Times* (17 July 1894): 6.2.

38. Wickizer, *Coffee, Tea and Cocoa*, 22–24.

39. Oliveira, *História do café*, 121; Rowe, *Studies in the Artificial Control of Raw Material Supplies*, 20.

40. This was the conclusion drawn by Brazilians commissioned to tour the coffee lands of competing countries. See F. Ferreira Ramos, *The Valorization of Coffee in Brazil* (Antwerp: J. E. Buschmann, 1907), 38, and Jorge Dumont Villares, *O café e sua produção e exportação* (São Paulo: Instituto de Café do Estado de São Paulo, 1927), ii, iii.

41. W. Arthur Lewis, *Growth and Fluctuations* (London: G. Allen and Unwin, 1978), 181.

42. João Cardoso de Mello and Maria de Conceição Tavares, "The Capitalist Export Economy in Brazil 1884–1930," in *The Latin American Economies*, Roberto Cortés Conde and Shane J. Hunt, eds. (New York: Holmes and Meier, 1985), 84, argue that the correspondence of Brazil's coffee boom with the rise of finance capital was responsible for coffee's positive developmental consequences at the end of the nineteenth century. On political elites, see Joseph Love and Bert J. Barickman, "Rulers and Owners: A Brazilian Case Study in Comparative Perspective," *Hispanic American Historical Review* 66:4 (1986): 743–765.

43. Joseph Love, *São Paulo in the Brazilian Federation, 1889–1937* (Stanford, Calif.: Stanford University Press, 1980), 17. In 1925 only 8 percent of São Paulo's coffee trees belonged to foreign investors (immigrants owned another 8 percent). See Robert Greenhill, "The Brazilian Coffee Trade," in D. C. M. Platt, ed., *Business Imperialism* (Oxford: Oxford University Press, 1977), 208–214; and Siegfried Zimmerman, *Theodor Wille* (Hamburg: N.p., 1969).

44. Maurício Font, "Coffee Planters, Politics and Development in Brazil," *Latin American Research Review* 22:3 (1987): 69–90; Topik, *The Political Economy of the Brazilian State*. Winston Fritsch, *External Constraints on Economic Policy in Brazil, 1889–1930* (Pittsburgh, Penn.: University of Pittsburgh Press, 1988), shares my position. Stephen Hahn, "Class and State in Postemancipation Societies—Southern Planters in Comparative Perspective," *American Historical Review* 95:1 (February 1990): 75–98, suggests that Brazilian planters and German Junkers were both much more successful in exercising national power than were the plantation owners of the U.S. South.

45. João Heraldo Lima, *Café e indústria em Minas Gerais, 1870–1920* (Petrópolis: Editora Vozes, 1981); Gabriel Bittencourt, "O esforço industrializante na República do café: O caso de Espírito Santo 1889–1930," 228–229, and Elisabeth Cattapan-Renter, "L'industrie à l'époque de 'l'Encilhamento (1890–1892)," 64, and Soares, in *Le Préindustrialization du Brésil*, 47. See also Oliveira, *História do café*, 297–298.

46. Ukers, *All about Coffee*, 404–405. It is true that Venezuela by the 1930s was consuming almost all its domestic production, but that was because by then coffee, once the country's main export, had fallen into decline and no longer had more than a local social or economic impact. See William Roseberry, *Coffee and Capitalism in the Venezuelan Andes* (Austin: University of Texas Press, 1983), 121.

47. Ukers, *All about Coffee*, 457; Brazil, Câmara dos Deputados, *Anais 1905*,

VII:34, 35; Padua Rezende, *Defesa do Café: Exposição de 1922 e Frigoríficos* (Rio de Janeiro: Imprensa Nacional, 1927), 31, 32.

48. Ukers, *All about Coffee*, 144. The estimate of final value assumes that a retail cup of coffee costs at least twice what a homemade cup costs.

49. Calculated from *Wileman's Brazilian Review* (25 August 1920): 1227–1230; (13 April 1921): 582–584; (21 November 1923): 1547–1549; (22 October 1924): 1416–1419.

50. V. D. Wickizer, *The World Coffee Economy with Special Reference to Control Schemes* (Stanford, Calif.: Food Research Center, 1943), 22; Brazil, Diretoria Geral de Estatística, *Anuário estatístico, 1930/40* (Rio de Janeiro: Imprensa Nacional, 1940), 1378; Bulmer-Thomas, *Political Economy of Central America*, 34.

51. Robert G. Williams, *States and Social Evolution: Coffee and the Rise of National Governments in Central America* (Chapel Hill: University of North Carolina Press, 1994), 125, 130, 142; Marco Palacios, *El café en Colombia 1850–1970* (Mexico City: El Colegio de México, 1983), 209; Robert Wasserstrom, *Class and Society in Central Chiapas* (Berkeley and Los Angeles: University of California Press, 1983), 117.

52. Stolcke, *Cafeicultura*, 84.

53. Dafert, *Über die Gegenwartige Lage des Kaffeebaus in Brasilien*, 49.

54. Dafert, *Gegenwartige Lage*, 49.

55. Ukers, *All about Coffee*, 145.

56. See Wolfgang Schivelbusch, *Tastes of Paradise: A Social History of Spices, Stimulants, and Intoxicants*, trans. D. Jacobson (New York: Vintage Books, 1993), 15–85; Ukers, *All about Coffee*, passim; and Steven C. Topik, "Coffee," in *The Cambridge History and Culture of Food and Nutrition* (forthcoming).

57. Manuel Moreno Fraginals, *El ingenio: Complejo económico social cubano del azúcar*, 3 vols. (Havana: Editorial Ciencias Sociales, 1978).

58. Centro Industrial do Brasil, *O Brasil: Suas riquezas naturais, suas indústrias*, vol. 2 (Rio de Janeiro: Imp. Orosco e Cia., 1908), 91.

59. Even on the plantations, workers grew their own food between the rows of seedlings or on the plot that was set aside for their use. See R. G. Hannicotte, *La vérité sur le Brésil* (Paris: Imp. Encyclopédie Nationale, 1909), 60–61; Dafert, *Culture rationelle*, 29

60. The Paulista railroad, of which Antonio Prado was a major shareholder, ran for six miles through his Santa Verediana plantation: Leclerc, *Cartas do Brasil*, 80.

61. Centro Industrial do Brasil, *Censo industrial do Brasil, 1907*, vol. II.

62. Stein, *Vassouras*, 5.

63. Roseberry, *Coffee and Capitalism in the Venezuelan Andes*, 82, 83.

64. Marco Palacios, *Coffee in Colombia 1850–1970: An Economic, Social and Political History* (New York: Cambridge University Press, 1980), 13, 17, 22; Robert Carlyle Beyer, *The Colombian Coffee Industry: Origins and Major Trends, 1740–1940* (Minneapolis: University of Minnesota Press, 1947), 291; Nieto Arteta, *El café en la sociedad colombiana*, 48, 58, 59; Francie R. Chassen de López, *Café y capitalismo: El proceso de transición en Colombia, 1880–1930* (Mexico City: UNAM, 1982), 44, 55; Malcolm Deas, "A Colombian Coffee Estate: Santa Bárbara, Cundinamarca, 1870–1912," in Kenneth Duncan and Ian

Rutledge, eds., *Land and Labour in Latin America: Essays on the Development of Agrarian Capitalism in the Nineteenth and Twentieth Centuries* (New York: Cambridge University Press, 1977), 269–298; Jiménez, "Traveling Far in Grandfather's Car."

65. Mitchell A. Seligson, *Peasants of Costa Rica and the Development of Agrarian Capitalism* (Madison: University of Wisconsin Press, 1980), 23; Ciro F. S. Cardoso, "The Formation of the Coffee Estate in Nineteenth-Century Costa Rica," in Duncan and Rutledge, eds., *Land and Labour in Latin America*, 175, 176.

66. Cardoso, "Formation of the Coffee Estate," 177.

67. David Radell, *Coffee and Transportation in Nicaragua* (Berkeley and Los Angeles: University of California Press, 1964), 2, 14; Héctor Lindo-Fuentes, *Weak Foundations: The Economy of El Salvador in the Nineteenth Century, 1821–1898* (Berkeley and Los Angeles: University of California Press, 1990), 185; idem, "La economía de Centroamérica de las reformas borbónicas a las reformas liberales," unpublished, 59; J. C. Cambranes, *Coffee and Peasants in Guatemala: The Origins of the Modern Plantation Economy in Guatemala 1853–1897* (Stockholm: Institute of Latin American Studies, 1985), 145; Bulmer-Thomas, *Political Economy*, p. 338; *Mexican Herald* (Mexico City, 29 June 1897) 5, (7 July 1897), 5; Daniela Spenser, "Soconusco: The Formation of a Coffee Economy in Chiapas," in Thomas Benjamin and William McNellie, eds., *Other Mexicos: Essays on Regional Mexican History, 1876–1911* (Albuquerque: University of New Mexico Press, 1984), 137; John Reginald Southworth, *El estado de Veracruz-Llave* (Liverpool: Blake & MacKenzie, 1900), 38–39; Heather Fowler-Salamini, "Gender, Work, and Coffee in Córdoba, Veracruz, 1850–1910," in Heather Fowler-Salamini and Mary Kay Vaughan, eds., *Women of the Mexican Countryside, 1850–1990: Creating Spaces, Shaping Transitions* (Tucson: University of Arizona Press, 1994), 51–73.

68. James J. Parsons, *Antioqueño Colonization in Western Colombia* (Berkeley and Los Angeles: University of California Press, 1949), 142; Jorge Dumont Villares, *O café*, 166, 177.

69. Villares, *O café*, 125; Ukers, *All about Coffee*, 157–158.

70. Villares, *O café*, 123, 129.

71. The extent to which these Germans constituted immigrants or foreign investors is a difficult question. They sometimes brought capital or credit with them, remained for generations but continued to have business and emotional allegiances to the homeland. According to Bulmer-Thomas, *Political Economy*, 338, Germans produced one-third of Guatemala's coffee in 1913. Augusto Ramos, *A crise do café: Parecer apresentado à Sociedade Rural Brasileira* (São Paulo: Revista dos Tribunais, 1930), 331, claims that two-thirds of Nicaragua's producers were foreigners, especially Germans. Graciela de Garay and María Esther Pérez-Salas C., "El café en el Soconusco: Un comercio regional," in Virginia Guedea and Jaime Rodríguez O., eds., *Five Centuries of Mexican History*, vol. 2 (Mexico City: Instituto José María Luis Mora, 1992), 168–192, and Spenser, "Soconusco," 136, say that Germans "monopolized" coffee exports and may have been responsible for 75 percent of the *fincas* in Soconusco.

72. William Roseberry, "La Falta de Brazos: Land and Labor in the Coffee

Economies of Twentieth-Century Latin America," *Theory and Society* 20: 3 (June 1991): 351–382, points to the importance of existing settled populations, as, in another context, does Clifford Geertz, *Agricultural Involution: The Process of Agricultural Change in Indochina* (Berkeley and Los Angeles: University of California Press, 1971).

73. Colombia is complicated because in Santander peasants with communal property still existed while in the dynamic Antioquia-Caldas area there was an unoccupied frontier.

74. Cambranes, *Coffee and Peasants,* 61–96; Lindo-Fuentes, *Weak Foundations,* 125–151; David Browning, *El Salvador, Landscape and Society* (Oxford: Clarendon Press of Oxford University Press, 1971), 174–221.

75. Laird Bergad, "Coffee and Rural Proletarianization in Puerto Rico, 1840–1898," *Journal of Latin American Studies* 15: 1 (May 1983): 83–100; idem, "On Comparative History: A Reply to Tom Brass," *Journal of Latin American Studies* 16: 1 (May 1984): 153–156; Tom Brass, "Coffee and Rural Proletarianization: A Comment," *Journal of Latin American Studies* 16: 1 (May 1984): 143–152.

76. Cambranes, *Coffee and Peasants,* 99, 130–131; Bulmer-Thomas, *Political Economy,* 339; Villar, *O café,* 123; Ciro Cardoso, "História económica del café en Centroamérica," *Estudios Sociales Centroamericanos* 10: 3 (1975): 9–55. Karl Kaerger, *Landwirtschaft und Kolonisation in Spanischen Amerika,* vol. 2 (Leipzig: Duncker & Humblot, 1901), 545–547, gave a more sanguine account of labor in Soconusco than does Jan Rus, "The 'Comunidad Revolucionaria Institucional': The Subversion of Native Government in Highland Chiapas, 1936–1938," in Gilbert M. Joseph and Daniel Nugent, eds., *Everyday Forms of State Formation: Revolution and the Negotiation of Rule in Modern Mexico* (Durham, N.C.: Duke University Press, 1994), 268–269. See also David McCreery, "Wage Labor, Free Labor and Vagrancy Laws: The Transition to Capitalism in Guatemala, 1920–1945," in William Roseberry, Lowell Gudmundson, and Mario Samper Kutschbach, eds., *Coffee, Society, and Power in Latin America* (Baltimore, Md.: Johns Hopkins University Press, 1995), 206–231.

77. Browning, *El Salvador,* 182, and personal correspondence with Janine Gasco.

78. Carol Smith, "Origins of the National Question in Guatemala: A Hypothesis," in Carol Smith, ed., *Guatemalan Indians and the State, 1540 to 1988* (Austin: University of Texas Press, 1990), 89–90.

79. Héctor Pérez Brignoli, "Indians, Communists, and Peasants: The 1932 Rebellion in El Salvador," in Roseberry, Gudmundson, and Samper Kutschbach, eds., *Coffee, Society, and Power,* 249–251; Jeffrey Gould, "El café, el trabajo, y la comunidad indígena de Matagalpa, 1880–1925," in Héctor Pérez Brignoli and Mario Samper, eds., *Tierra, café y sociedad* (San José, Costa Rica: FLACSO, 1994), 279–376.

80. Francie R. Chassen-López, "'Cheaper Than Machines': Women and Agriculture in Porfirian Oaxaca, 1880–1911," 27–50; Fowler-Salamini, "Gender, Work, and Coffee in Córdoba, Veracruz, 1850–1910," 51–73; and Verena Stolcke, "The Labors of Coffee in Latin America: The Hidden Charm of Family Labor and Self-provisioning," in Roseberry, Gudmundson, and Samper Kutschbach, eds., *Coffee, Society, and Power,* 65–94. Regarding Colombia, see Michael F. Jiménez,

84   *The Second Conquest of Latin America*

"Class, Gender and Peasant Resistance in Central Colombia, 1900–1930," in Forrest D. Colburn, ed., *Everyday Forms of Peasant Resistance* (Armonk, N.Y.: M. E. Sharp, 1989), 135.

81. Ana Lorena Carrillo Padilla, "Sufridas hijas del pueblo: La huelga de las escogedores de café de 1925 en Guatemala y Centro América," *Mesoamérica* 15: 27 (June 1994): 157–173.

82. Palacios, *Coffee in Colombia*, 48, 78; Cambranes, *Coffee and Peasants*, 49; Radell, *Coffee in Nicaragua*, 2. These nouveau riche planters did often marry into elite families, which leads Samuel Z. Stone, *The Heritage of the Conquistadors: Ruling Classes in Central America from the Conquest to the Sandinistas* (Lincoln: University of Nebraska Press, 1990), 144, to conclude that the Central American elite can "usually trace their origins back to the conquistadors and the colonial nobility." On landlord capitalism, see Anthony Winson, *Coffee and Democracy in Modern Costa Rica* (London: Macmillan, 1989), 169.

83. Laird Bergad, *Coffee and Growth of Agrarian Capitalism in Nineteenth-Century Puerto Rico* (Princeton, N.J.: Princeton University Press, 1983), 217; Nieto Arteta, *El café en la sociedad colombiana*, 55.

84. Nieto Arteta, *El café en la sociedad colombiana*, 55; Jaime Wheelock, *Imperialism y dictadura: Crisis de una formación social* (Mexico City: Siglo Ventiuno, 1975), 26.

85. Quoted in Cambranes, *Coffee and Peasants*, 75.

86. Stephen Bunker, *Peasants against the State: The Politics of Market Control in Bugisu, Uganda, 1900–1983* (Urbana: University of Illinois Press, 1987); Thomas Anderson, *El Salvador 1932* (San Salvador: Editorial Universitaria Centroamericana, 1982), 20.

87. Charles Bergquist, *Labor in Latin America: Comparative Essays on Chile, Argentina, Venezuela and Colombia* (Stanford, Calif.: Stanford University Press, 1986), 312.

88. Friedrich Katz, "Labor Conditions on Haciendas in Porfirian Mexico: Some Trends and Tendencies," *Hispanic American Historical Review* 54 (February 1974): 1–47, notes that hacienda resident laborers seldom joined the Mexican Revolution anywhere in the country.

89. See George Collier, *Basta: Land and the Zapatista Rebellion in Chiapas* (Boston: Food First, 1995). Jeffery M. Paige, *Agrarian Revolution: Social Movements and Export Agriculture in the Underdeveloped World* (New York: Free Press, 1975), 360–369, theorizes about why migrant-based crops such as coffee usually do not lead to revolt, although smallholders can revolt.

3. Henequen

Allen Wells

We are poor living in the midst of our riches
—Juan Miguel Castro

One of Yucatán's most respected entrepreneurs penned these words in 1876 during the midst of a severe recession triggered by the collapse of henequen fiber prices. Castro, who had earned the admiration of henequen *hacendados* (*henequeneros*) by championing (and contributing financially to) the opening of the port of Progreso on the Gulf of Mexico, was alarmed by the precipitous drop in hard fiber prices.[1] Placing the blame for the downturn on avaricious "New York speculators" and their local agents, Castro, working in tandem with colleague Rodulfo G. Cantón, urged *henequeneros* to form a planters' association and an agricultural bank to combat the evils of "monopoly, intrigues, and speculation."

But Castro and Cantón were well aware that fiber buyers were only part of the problem. If certain "supply-side" aspects of the industry were beyond the control of local producers, the two savvy businessmen contended, *henequeneros* did have room to maneuver to improve their position and defend their interests. In fact, a small planter and merchant committee had recently formed and sent Castro to Europe to aggressively seek new markets to help mitigate chronic fluctuations of the world market price of the region's primary export. Upon his return from the continent, Castro informed his colleagues that they could improve their market share if they addressed one of henequen's chief problems—its lackluster reputation abroad. He chastised *hacendados* for their indiscriminate mixing of clean and inferior fibers in the same bales and their unwillingness to classify their product (henequen's chief competitors, Russian hemp and Philippine abaca [manila] were classified). Castro urged his colleagues to stop sending uncombed, knotted bales; his lemma was "export

higher quality henequen to compete with other fibers." If they followed
his counsel, Yucatecan *henequeneros* would enjoy "abundant markets
at good prices."[2] Cantón added that planters should reduce their production costs to remain competitive.

Although the henequen industry was in its formative stages during
the 1870s, it was obvious from pamphlets published during the
economic downturn that Castro and Cantón and their colleagues
had a thorough appreciation of the means and factors of production
and their commodity's precarious niche in the hard fibers trade. For
three years, an agitated Castro carried on a running debate in the local
press with import-export agents Eusebio Escalante and Manuel Dondé
and their New York fiber factors, the Thebaud Brothers, concerning
the collapse of the fiber market. The debate was joined by local
journalists from *La Revista de Mérida*, who cautioned *henequeneros*
not to become too dependent on North American financiers.[3]

The planters and merchants' committee's actions and the controversy swirling around the decline in fiber prices confirm that *henequeneros* were responsive to the vagaries of the market well before the
invention of the mechanical twine knotter (1878) heightened demand
for raw henequen fiber dramatically. (This remarkable device would
enable North American and European farmers to mechanically bind
sheaves of wheat and other crops; by 1900, 85 percent of "binder" twine
was manufactured from Yucatán's "green gold.") In fact, *hacendados*
and exporters throughout the henequen boom kept abreast of the cordage
and binder twine trades and the latest technology and cultivation
techniques by reading foreign trade publications such as the *Cordage
Trade Journal* and the *Farm Implement News* and regional and national
economic journals like the *Boletín de Estadística*, *El Agricultor*, *El
Henequén*, the *Boletín de la Sociedad Agrícola Mexicana*, and *El
Economista Mexicano*.[4]

Castro's and Cantón's early admonitions conveyed a sense of urgency,
suggesting that these articulate businessmen not only understood the
problems and pitfalls of both the supply and the demand sides of the
henequen equation, but also realized that their fiber's comparative
advantage would not last forever. Interestingly, even though Castro and
Cantón believed the key to success was a strong producers' association,
they stopped short of advocating that *hacendados* withhold production
from the market to improve prices (valorization). Cantón warned that
the forces of supply and demand were not to be taken lightly:[5]

> I do not think it wise to fix a *minimum* price for henequen on
> the American market, because commerce is, by its very nature,
> indispensably free, and the circumstances of a rise or a fall [in

prices] should not depend on the producer's disposition. Consumption is what enforces the law in this matter, following the rules of *supply* and *demand*; that is what produces what is known as exchange value; political economy is an exact science. The equitable flow of commerce necessarily follows these rules and will destroy anyone anywhere who wants to construct a dike to inhibit its course . . . To fix a *minimum* price on Yucatecan fiber would favor the enemy's interests. (Original emphasis)

Not all *henequeneros* shared Cantón's faith in the market, however. Planters repeatedly formed *compañías cooperativas, sociedades,* and *sindicatos* to withhold fiber to enhance their market position throughout the boom (1870s–1930s). Yet, as we shall see, every attempt to act in unison and valorize henequen was a dismal failure. Were Cantón's words prophetic? Was the market too strong to overcome?

How can we appreciate the choices Yucatecan *hacendados* faced as they debated how best to seize the initiative and defend their market position? To unravel the answer requires a thorough examination of the exogenous and endogenous forces that shaped the hard fibers trade. Unfortunately, even with the benefit of hindsight, modern scholars—hindered by the constraints of academic research—have only a passing familiarity with this market. While there are excellent monographs on Russian hemp, Kentucky hemp, the Indian jute industry, Philippine manila, and East African sisal that explicate "their" fiber's ties to the international economy at a concrete historical moment, there has been no systematic effort to explain the evolution of the hard fibers trade over time.[6]

The purpose of this study, then, is twofold. First, I shall paint with a broad brush the history of the hard fibers trade, introducing henequen's chief competitors and illustrating its problematic position within the market. As we shall see, henequen's price and market share throughout the Gilded Age was inextricably tied to its chief rival, manila or abaca, a stronger and costlier fiber that periodically threatened to overtake henequen's share of the binder twine market.

Armed with an appreciation for the fiber trade, we will then turn to an analysis of the interactive relationship that emerged between the forces of supply and demand during the export boom. It was this complex organic partnership that helped define the choices *henequeneros* and local import-export agents made. From marketing arrangements to land tenure patterns, from labor relations to the willingness of local producers to introduce labor-saving processing equipment and infrastructure, *henequeneros* had to mesh the idiosyncrasies of the monocrop with their own social, economic, and political institutions *and* a market constantly in flux. To remain competitive locally and internationally, *hacendados* had to address a number of thorny questions. For instance, was it worth their time, money, and effort to seek alternative applications for their product? Should henequen cultivation be supplemented with corn, beans, and other necessities, or should these primary commodities be imported? What role should the state play in assisting their industry? As will become apparent, there was always ample disagreement; in fact, a healthy tension existed among those entrepreneurs who were content to take what the market gave them at any given moment, the more traditionally oriented, who were more concerned with their social and political position, and those who pursued a more combative or risk-taking approach when they felt their livelihood in jeopardy.

It should be emphasized that no Smithian "invisible hand" was at work here. If the hard fibers market helped shape the choices that buyers and sellers were presented with, it did not preclude them from successfully mobilizing their forces to promote their interests. As we shall see, attempts to manipulate prices, starve demand, and corner the market were as much a reality of the hard fibers trade as was the self-correcting market mechanism. As one historian of the fiber market has noted, "The history of the cordage trade in the United States is a history of an almost uninterrupted series of attempts to restrict competition or prevent it entirely."[7] If merchants and producers were not always successful, that does not mean they did not try to use their political position and economic leverage to influence the global market.

Before we can measure Yucatecan *henequeneros'* full range of responses during the boom, we must first turn our attention to the enigmatic hard fibers market.

The Fickle Ferris Wheel

It may be helpful to conceive of the hard fibers trade as a Ferris wheel that paused periodically to let on new fibers or to let off others. As new fibers were introduced to manufacturers in the nineteenth and twentieth centuries—each with their own strengths, weaknesses, and particular applications—they jockeyed with more established rivals for a choice seat. Sometimes the newcomers successfully replaced the tried and true, at other times, the Ferris wheel never stopped to pick them up as novel experiments turned into costly disasters. Occasionally, a new fiber, after years of trial and error, finally earned a seat as it was adapted to a new industrial or agricultural purpose.

As new uses were pioneered, the market became increasingly more segmented. Some versatile fibers had multiple applications and benefited from the growing complexity of the global market (that is, abaca). Others, like henequen, were confined essentially to a specific submarket.

There were, however, only a limited number of seats on the wheel; in fact, only a few of the more than a thousand American fiber-bearing plants enjoyed a prominent position in the hard fibers market during the nineteenth century.[8] Writing in 1897, Charles Richards Dodge, a Department of Agriculture botanist in charge of fiber investigations, commented on the "built-in" sense of inertia present in the hard fibers trade:

> [T]he present commercial fibers represent in a sense those that have stood the test of experience, and until these are crowded out by new conditions, or through what might be termed evolution in the economic arts, they will have no chance. The only opportunity that may be afforded these secondary forms is in the creation of special uses to which they may be peculiarly adapted, for which the standard forms known to the market price current are not so well fitted.

Dodge added that new fibers had to be first subjected to intense chemical and microscopic scrutiny, followed by controlled cultivation investigations at agricultural experiment stations, before earning a lengthy apprenticeship in the market.[9]

In general, the ride lasted about a century for any given fiber, although in some cases new uses were found or new cultivation or processing techniques were employed to postpone the inevitable. The henequen boom, for instance, lasted only sixty years; abaca, just over a century. Nor did it seem to matter if the fiber was in the hands of a colonial power (abaca, sisal) or an independent nation (Russian and Kentucky hemp, henequen); the Ferris wheel proved very fickle.[10]

Although hard fibers had been used since antiquity for many purposes,[11] it was not until the late sixteenth century, when the British navy and merchant marine industry began to use large quantities of common hemp (*Cannabis sativa*) to outfit their ships. For the next three centuries, the shipping industry grew geometrically to satisfy the demands of the commercial and industrial revolutions. An international specialization of labor led to tremendous improvements in transportation and communication; freight rates dropped more than 75 percent during the nineteenth century. Whalers, clippers, and, eventually, steamships carried manufactured goods, luxury articles, and foodstuffs to Asia, Africa, and Latin America and returned home with a host of primary commodities. Merchant marine tonnage increased from 6.7 million tons a year in 1840 to 43 million by the First World War.[12]

Each ship required a seemingly endless supply of rope for rigging, cable, and towlines. The inveterate sailor and historian Samuel Eliot Morison reminds us of the importance of a ship's ropes: "If you consider the hull as the ship's body and the sails her means of locomotion, the 'lines,' as seamen called the ropes, were her nerves and tendons." The smallest schooner carried a ton of cordage; the frigate *Constitution* used 100 tons. Even the advent of the steamship did not curtail the demand for rope. Although steamships did not require as much rope as sailing vessels, they still used large amounts of cordage for towlines, warps, and auxiliary sails. And even though the steamship displaced sailing ships in the passenger and perishable trades, sailing vessels continued to carry bulk produce on long voyages until the turn of the twentieth century.[13]

First on the Ferris wheel was Russian hemp,[14] which satisfied the needs of the world's merchant marines and navies. The valuable fibers found in hemp stalks are bound by a viscous gum, which must be dissolved before the fiber can be extracted. Using a fermentation process called water-retting, Russian peasants steeped the stalks in a nearby stream or pond, with "weighted frames on top to insure that they would stay completely immersed."[15] This bacterial action softened the tissues of the plant, and the creamy white fiber then was more easily separated from the stalk. Careful attention had to be paid to the retting process; if it continued too long, it caused much of the cementing materials to be destroyed, and the fibers weakened. After three weeks of retting in warm water or five weeks in cold, the hemp was taken out and dried quickly in a kiln or slowly over the long winter, depending on the type of product desired.

Next, the fibers had to be separated from the stalks by hand—a two-stage process called breaking and scutching. The scutched, or scraped, lint that remained was drawn through a wooden comb to unravel the fibers. Alfred Crosby marvels at the patience of Russian farmers: "The Russian processing was so slow and meticulous that much of it didn't reach the Russian ports to await Western European customers until two years after it was sown." By 1800 the United States was importing thirty-four hundred tons a year; the figure climbed to five thousand tons annually in the 1820s and the 1830s.[16]

But Russian hemp had its disadvantages: it had to be saturated with tar to protect it from saltwater, a procedure that not only left the rope heavier and dirtier, but also diminished its flexibility. This was not a problem for standing (or stationary) rigging and shrouds, but was a great disadvantage for cables, sails, and running rigging, especially in colder temperatures, when tar stiffened.[17] Another problem was the uncertainty of its supply; first the Napoleonic Wars and subsequently the Crimean War left cordage manufacturers scrambling for substitutes.

Kentucky hemp farmers tried to crack the lucrative North American cordage market. Utilizing slave labor on small and medium-sized farms in the Bluegrass Region of the state, they supplied ropewalks (cordage factories) in Louisiana, New England, and Kentucky with bales of dark gray fiber. The work was thought to be "very dirty, and so laborious that scarcely any white man will work at it." Henry Clay, who owned several hemp farms, defended the interests of the industry and successfully fought for tariffs on Russian hemp in Congress.[18] Import duties did not sway the shipyards and cordage factories, which preferred to pay more for water-retted hemp. For their part, Kentucky farmers refused to adopt the painstaking, labor-intensive harvesting techniques used in Tsarist Russia. Instead, they dew-retted their hemp. The stalks were spread on the ground and left there for three or four weeks undisturbed, except for an occasional turning. While this process did leach away the glutinous matter, it also weakened the fibers and made for a darker, rougher (and cheaper) product.[19]

Bluegrass farmers were reluctant to adopt water-retting because labor costs were high and water-retting in ponds and streams poisoned fish and any livestock that might drink there. And the steeped water smelled like rotten eggs. Water-retting, Kentucky farmers were quick to point out, also exhausted the soil more quickly than dew-retting, since the latter restored nutrients to the ground while the fiber lay on it. While Kentucky hemp never won the confidence of the maritime trade, it did assist the burgeoning southern cotton industry by providing inexpensive baling rope and bagging.[20]

The hemp industry expanded to the neighboring states of Missouri and Illinois, but entered into a period of decline soon after the Civil War.[21] Some scholars contend that the hemp industry's development was arrested by farmers reluctant to modernize the industry. They cite the growers' unwillingness to mechanize the "breaking" of hemp fibers. Time-consuming hand brakes, which crushed and broke the stalks, continued to be used on hemp farms until the middle of the twentieth century. In 1859 an article published in the *Kentucky Farmer* explained why:[22]

Quite a variety of machinery has been tried for hemp breaking, together with Dutch, Irish and Natives, but a stout negro man, with a good hand brake, a fair task before him, and prompt pay for his overwork, now has a decided preference, if not a complete monopoly. Breaking and cleaning by horsepower machinery is a

possible achievement, but will hardly be profitable in practice
except where there is some other inducement for bringing much
of the hemp in one place, besides to break it.

It is difficult to believe, however, that hemp producers were any
more or any less interested in technological innovation than other
southern planters, many of whom had welcomed the introduction of
labor-saving machinery. The relatively small size of most hemp
farms—"a strong proportion of the [Missouri] farmers grew the
product on less than fifty acres in 1850"[23]—and the availability of a
dependent labor force may better explain why hand brakes continued
to be used on Kentucky and Missouri estates. In any case, the Civil
War hurt the hemp industry as the federal blockade of southern
ports, the embargo on cotton, the Union prohibition on the shipment
of rope and bagging into the South, and the collapse of the postwar
labor market combined to weaken the industry.

Hemp's place was taken in the postwar cotton industry by Indian
jute (*Corchorus capsularis* and *C. olitorius*). Although not as strong,
durable, and elastic as hemp, jute was more plentiful, cheaper to
produce, and easier to manufacture. It soon conquered the bagging
market; by 1880 there was only one hemp bagging factory still in
operation in Kentucky.[24]

Handwoven jute bags produced on looms in the Bengal Delta
Region (present-day Bangladesh) had been an important cottage
industry as early as the sixteenth century. An abundance of "cheap
labor willing to work under disagreeable conditions" in Bengal no
doubt contributed to jute's popularity with fiber buyers.[25] By the mid–
nineteenth century, power-driven jute mills in Dundee, Scotland,
had overtaken the Indian handloom industry. Later, Calcutta bagging
manufacturers would offer serious competition to the Scottish mills.
By 1910 raw jute production in Eastern Bengal had soared to 900,000
tons a year.

Although it was too rough for apparel, jute found a niche in the
fiber trade as a preeminent packaging material. The Dutch government was the first to use the coarse fiber for coffee bags during the
middle of the nineteenth century, and when the Crimean War cut
supplies of Russian hemp and the U.S. Civil War caused a shortage of
cotton bags, the jute industry responded. Three-quarters of manufactured jute was used as burlaps for sandbags, sugar, coffee, rice, wheat,
wool, cocoa, animal feeds, fertilizers, and other chemicals. The jute
industry, like other hard fiber industry, has had its boom-and-bust
cycles, but jute's remarkable versatility has made it difficult to dislodge
it from the Ferris wheel.[26]

While jute and Kentucky hemp vied for control of the bagging market, Philippine manila (abaca, *Musa textilis*) proved to be a more than worthy adversary for Russian hemp in the cordage trade.[27] Manila, a member of the banana family, is extracted from the plant's bark. It is naturally resistant to saltwater so it does not have to be tarred. This clean fiber, introduced and tested by North American cordage manufacturers in 1818, is more durable and 25 percent stronger than tarred hemp. Moreover, it has greater flexibility and elasticity, weighs a third less, and carries a lower price tag. The U.S. consul in Manila may have been exaggerating in 1833 when he gushed that manila was "the article of most importance to the commerce of the United States," but it was obvious the North American merchant marine was quick to appreciate manila's advantages, especially for running rigging. When the Crimean War disrupted Russian hemp supplies, manila's position and price improved. By 1860 it was firmly entrenched in the U.S. maritime market, and consumption by British and other European manufacturers was steadily increasing. Production doubled between 1870 and 1880 alone (see Table 3.1).[28]

The cordage industry's infatuation with manila overshadowed the introduction of a new tropical fiber on the market. Although henequen (*Agave fourcroydes*) had been cultivated in the Yucatán since pre-Columbian times, it was not until the late colonial era that Spanish entrepreneurs began to recognize its commercial potential.[29]

Commonly, but incorrectly, known as sisal, henequen did not garner rave reviews from North American cordage manufacturers at first. It was earmarked for low-end cordage and rigging purposes, since the fiber's low tensile strength failed to sustain heavy-duty usage.

Table 3.1. Philippine Manila Exports, 1850–1890

Year	To Great Britain (piculs)	To United States (piculs)
1850	16,164	100,309
1855	20,669	211,580
1865	79,316	303,044
1870	131,180	343,618
1875	263,974	236,654
1880	356,296	409,134
1890	683,986	262,438

Source: Nicholas P. Cushner, *Spain in the Philippines* (Quezon City, Philippines: Ateneo de Manila University, 1971), 205.
Note: A picul = 63.25 kg, or 1/16 long ton.

Manila is twice as strong, more rot resistant, and smoother than the Yucatecan fiber. The market reflected this qualitative difference, as henequen prices generally were pegged at one to two cents a pound lower than manila. Although some Yucatecan *henequeneros* thought differently, manila certainly merited the higher price it received on the world market, and it remained the fiber of choice in the maritime market. Yet, as an authority on the manila trade has pointed out, with some exceptions, "any fiber could find a market if its price was low enough or if that of its competitors went too high."[30]

Yucatecan import-export agents, wary that higher henequen prices would prompt manufacturers to switch to manila or seek new fibers, counseled *henequeneros* to keep their costs down. Olegario Molina, owner of one of the largest merchant houses in Yucatán, encouraged *henequeneros* to "produce more to sell cheaply." And when a financially pressed *hacendado* came to him with his problems, Don Olegario counseled the man: "Plant more henequen!"[31]

Henequen quickly gained a reputation as an inferior, but inexpensive, substitute for manila. At first, some unscrupulous ropewalks took advantage of the agave's cheaper price and "blended" it with manila without informing their customers. Later, blends were marketed as such and priced midway between the "pure" twines, sisal and manila. To the extent that both fibers catered to the same rope and twine submarkets, henequen would never really shake its reputation as a poor relation. As a result, the prices of these commodities were inextricably bound. An abundance or a shortage of one commodity invariably affected the price of its rival as the fiber division of the International Harvester Company made clear in an internal memo circulated in 1905:[32]

> [T]here is a certain relation existing between manila hemp [abaca] and sisal whereby the price of the former is made a potent factor in regulating the price of the latter. . . . When the difference in price of the two fibers is reduced below a proportionate level it becomes cheaper to use the manila twine than the sisal and while the quantity used of twine made of manila is small when compared to the sisal, the divergence is due entirely to the relatively lower price of sisal. Thus the [North American] farmer benefits by any reduction in the price of hemp through the effect such reduction has in lowering the price of sisal.

Manila's greater versatility, its unquestioned advantages, and its ability to compete with other fibers in different segments of the hard fibers trade meant its stocks usually influenced henequen's price. But, as we shall see, there were key moments when the reverse was true.

Fortunately, demand was assured as technological advancements continued to find new industrial applications for the erstwhile rivals. North American cordage factories, such as the Plymouth Cordage Company (in Plymouth, Massachusetts), were acutely aware of the need to expand their horizons beyond the confines of the maritime market. After the Civil War, the U.S. merchant marine, decimated by Confederate raiders and faced with intense competition from the continent, failed to recover its tonnage from the clipper ship era. Ships were using less cordage than before as wire standing rigging replaced hemp and steel banding supplanted hemp and manila for binding cotton bales.

Necessity *and* technology became the mothers of invention. Tests determined that rope offered the most economical means of conveying power. With new factories springing up overnight throughout North America and Western Europe, manila proved ideally suited for power transmission cables (as multistranded lubricated ropes replaced gears or belts) and the expanding oil drilling industry (for derrick lines, bull ropes, and catline).

The new application of greatest consequence for henequen (and, to a lesser extent, for manila) was binder twine. Labor-intensive hand binding was supplanted in the early 1870s by mechanical wire binders attached to reapers. Harvesting companies at first used soft iron wire to bind wheat, but even after the bundles had been cut at the threshing machines, bits of wire frequently clogged the machinery. Pieces of wire also found their way into the flour mills, animal feed, and hay. The invention of the mechanical twine knotter in the late 1870s substituted biodegradable twine for wire and, in the process, revolutionized the farm implement industry. Now a harvesting machine with two men to pick and shock the sheaf could reap twelve to fourteen acres of wheat a day, effectively doubling the previous output while allowing for a substantial labor savings. The Deering and the McCormick harvesting machine companies realized the importance of the knotting device and built their own twine binder harvesters in 1879 and 1881, respectively.[33]

As promotional literature trumpeted the "emancipation of the American farmer," harvesting machine companies expeditiously adapted the mechanism to other grain crops. Thorstein Veblen did not exaggerate when he characterized the 1880s as "the most remarkable period that has been seen in American wheat growing." Acreage increased from 29 to 41 million, production from 368 to 555 million bushels, and exports from 40 to 150 million bushels. Sales of mechanical grain binders soared in North America and Europe, and by the turn of the century "it was estimated that over one-half the hard fiber imported into the United States was used for this purpose."[34]

Henequen had found its calling. It could be fashioned into a pliable, smooth, single-strand cord, perfect for the binder. The U.S. market purchased more than 90 percent of the total output of Mexican henequen, and "nearly all of it goes into binding twine."[35] Plymouth Cordage found that within a few years binder twine sales matched their rope lines. Henequen and manila production soared to meet the insatiable demand. Since these two fibers competed in the same market, and because prices and profits were ineluctably "intertwined," it will be useful to compare and contrast the two rivals so that we can better understand how these commodities influenced the market and how the hard fibers trade shaped the regional economies of northwestern Yucatán and Kabikolan, Philippines, during the export boom (see Tables 3.1 and 3.2).

Manila versus Henequen

Location theorists, who hold that export staples define the development of regions, might have had southeastern Luzon and northwestern Yucatán in mind when they crafted their hypotheses about the character of regional economic development.[36] This "staples model," first articulated by economic historians seeking to explain Canada's economic growth, theorizes that, when local or regional markets are too small, only significant *external* demand for a commodity can generate the forward and backward linkages and increased division of labor necessary to promote development.

More often than not, in Asia and Latin America, this demand-driven export model has carried heavy costs: it has exposed the domestic economy to violent shocks brought on by changes in external demand; it has exacerbated inequality while ignoring social reform; and it has favored the political dominance of landowner-exporters, who have played an increasingly oligopolistic role in regional economies. Over the course of the "long nineteenth century," Kabikolan and Yucatán reaped both the benefits and the disadvantages of this export-led model, as the requirements of industrial capitalism and the character of their respective commodities helped influence, if not dictate, their economic structures, political institutions, and the everyday lives of their inhabitants.[37]

One way to think about how the late nineteenth-century export model shaped regional economic development is to consider how, in the words of Albert Hirschman, "one thing leads to another." Studying the ways in which an export commodity is linked to other sectors of the economy and to political and social institutions provides the student of economic history with a conceptual framework for evaluating how the most important variables in the fiber equation interacted. Since substantial differences exist between the characteristics and linkages of different staples, care has to be taken when comparisons are made. What

Table 3.2. Henequen Production, 1875–1910

Year	Bales
1875	40,000
1880	113,000
1885	267,000
1890	280,000
1895	383,000
1900	500,000
1905	597,000
1910	619,000

Source: Annual publications of the Cámara Agrícola de Yucatán.
Note: A bale = 350 pounds.

follows is a systematic exploration of the impact of two very different staples on their respective societies.[38]

The development of commercial agriculture in nineteenth-century Latin America and Asia transformed how large landholders and peasants lived off the land. Students of agrarian history agree that the emergence of commercial agriculture was an uneven process that had a variety of effects on preexisting agrarian societies. In addition to ecology, endogenous factors such as demographic patterns, ethnicity, and land tenure all played a role in shaping the evolutionary path that a rural society followed.

Environmental Obstacles

Until the export boom tethered these regions to the international economy, however, Kabikolan and Yucatán were relatively isolated peninsulas.[39] Their lack of mineral resources explains why the Spanish crown, which governed colonies in Mexico and the Philippines, never considered these peripheral backwaters economically valuable enough to be linked to major trade routes. Given the protectionist character of the Spanish empire, commercial opportunities were limited, to say the least. Even though local elites and colonial administrators experimented with a number of crops and products, both native Maya and Bikolanos remained largely oriented toward subsistence agriculture.[40]

Relative isolation may have inhibited economic development, but it did not prevent the assimilation of new modes of thought about people's capability to harness the environment. The coalescence of mechanistic science, transportation and industrial technology, agronomy, education, and the requisites of the expanding international economy transformed the way that Latin American and Asian entrepreneurs perceived their relationship with nature.

If in the past the environment ordained what was, and was not, materially possible, after 1800 nature was viewed increasingly as a resource, destined to be dominated. Carolyn Merchant's perceptive assessment of the ecological transformation of nineteenth-century New England applies equally as well to the tropics: "The animate cosmos, in which nature acted and developed from within, was giving way to a worldview that sanctioned external manipulation and control."[41] Kabikolan's and Yucatán's elites aggressively embraced this modernizing vision by blending technology, human ingenuity, political muscle, and fortuitous timing to overcome their regions' ecological limitations.

Yucatecans, in particular, had to surmount enormous physical and environmental obstacles. Yucatán's physical geography has always strongly limited the location and nature of agricultural production. It is a wonder that, given its ecological impediments, the region has developed at all. The northern and north-central part of the peninsula—what is today largely the state of Yucatán—is a massive limestone rock covered with a thin layer of soil and a dry, rugged scrub forest. Franciscan missionary Diego de Landa described it best: "Yucatán is the country with least earth that I have seen, since all of it is one living rock."[42] This *tierra caliente*, firmly ensconced in the tropics, has no mountains and few hills to deflect the unbearable heat. Large rocks strewn about this thick limestone slab inhibit the use of the plow for cultivation. Porous surface conditions make irrigation ditches impossible as the soil loses its moisture and dries out quickly. Not surprisingly, the thin topsoil quickly becomes exhausted—and in some parts of the northwest, fields must lie fallow for up to twenty years to regenerate.[43]

If these conditions were not debilitating enough, this wretched land and its hardworking inhabitants suffer from a scarcity of water. Surface water is almost entirely lacking. There is little rainfall outside the rainy season (May to September); the parched vegetation has to persevere through many scorching months in succession. The scant rainwater filters quickly through the soil and rock to the water table. The summer rains, which fall in torrential downpours during late afternoons, leach the earth, diminishing the few nutrients there are.

With water at a premium throughout the region, the conquering Spaniards and their descendants used access to water as a powerful tool of social control. Throughout Yucatán, water dictated the location of villages and farms. Relatively speaking, the best soil, water, and climatic conditions for large-scale agriculture in the peninsula are found southeast of Mérida, just north of a set of low hills called the sierra (or, in Maya, the *Puuc*). In these tracts, sugarcane, cotton, and tobacco have been cultivated with some success.[44] Farther to the south and southeast, one encounters a tropical rain forest, where the soil is badly leached. If the forest is cut down for any length of time, the soil rapidly loses its fertility and becomes very hard and unworkable.

Given two poor choices—the arid and rocky Northwest and the jungle environment of the Southeast—the Yucatec Maya and their conquerors opted to populate the dry northern half of the peninsula. The poor soil, the absence of accessible surface water for agriculture, the unpredictability of rainfall throughout the peninsula, and the blistering tropical heat at low elevations all limited the Maya's and the ladino's ability to produce surpluses. No wonder the Spanish crown thought the area such a backwater.

In contrast, Kabikolan was a veritable oasis. The combination of year-round rainfall and the serendipitous juxtaposition of lowland valleys— perfect for wet-rice cultivation—and sloping hills, where yams, tobacco, rattans, bamboo, wax, and honey were cultivated throughout the colonial period, gave the native Bikolanos, Spanish, Chinese, and other ethnic strangers who populated the peninsula a number of viable options. Kabikolan's "offside" location, the vulnerability of its ports to heavy winds, and the infamous Embocadero, or Strait of San Bernardino, at the southern tip of the peninsula, which crushed ships on its rocks, discouraged coastal trade with other islands of the archipelago. While there was modest trade with Manila and Iloilo, the region did not really overcome its isolation until 1938, when a railroad linked the peninsula to Manila. (Yucatán was not linked to the Mexican national railway system until 1950.) A chain of imposing volcanoes and mountains in eastern Bikol also hindered intraregional travel. And Bikolanos found themselves in the heart of the typhoon belt: "Recent studies indicate that 40 percent of all storms with high velocity winds in the Philippines pass through Kabikolan." Taken together, all of these factors have reinforced the inhabitants' self-sufficiency.[45]

Interestingly, at the same moment in history, both regions promoted export staples that took advantage of the peculiarities of their respective environments. Henequen and manila, indigenous to their habitats, fit their ecosystems so well that Yucatán and Kabikolan would earn a Ricardian comparative advantage over their competitors in the hard fibers market, a competitive edge they would not relinquish until after World War I. Yucatán, in fact, had a virtual monopoly on henequen production in Mexico (neighboring Campeche contributed an insignificant amount), while Kabikolan produced anywhere from 30 percent to 80 percent of Philippine annual output during the manila boom.

Yucatán's fibrous agave grows best in tropical climes on soils of partly decomposed limestone, that is, in soils that are too dry and stony for the production of most crops. The northwestern quadrant of the Yucatán affords excellent natural drainage and aeration for the plant's roots. In richer soils (where more rainfall was the norm), the agave's leaves contained too much pulp, and the extracted fiber was inferior in quality and quantity. The Northwest received just enough rain for the hardy agave to survive. While the agave could withstand drought, "the plant nonetheless demanded minimal amounts of rainfall; annual precipitation of under forty inches retarded growth and handicapped separation of the fiber from the leaves."[46] Moreover, the absence of anything but a thin layer of topsoil and loam discourages cultivation of, and hence competition from, maize or beans.

A henequen zone grew up surrounding Mérida (roughly within a radius of seventy to eighty kilometers from the state capital) as *hacendados* increasingly rationalized their land and labor and turned their corn and cattle haciendas into modern fiber estates. *Henequeneros* purchased increasingly greater quantities of basic foodstuffs from abroad to feed their indebted Maya workforce.

Similarly, the indigenous manila plant, which requires rich soil, plentiful moisture, and good drainage, encountered all of these attributes on the volcanic slopes of eastern Bikol. Abundant rainfall was the key, since two to three weeks of dry weather could retard development of the plant. The peninsula's exposure to monsoons and the lack of a prolonged dry spell (precipitation averages over 100 inches a year), enabled manila to flourish there. Typhoons, which periodically hit the peninsula, were manila's most formidable threat, but even when the storms toppled standing plants, the "fiber of the fallen plants could be utilized if stripped within a day or two, and the field would reach full productivity again, without further planting, in a year or two."[47] Since manila cannot grow in standing water yet demands copious rainfall, it must be cultivated on slopes. Fortunately, Bikolanos inhabited lowland valleys in close proximity to the volcanic slopes. As is typical in Southeast Asia, Bikolanos had developed a complementary economic strategy that produced a number of crops that grew well in the highlands and rice in the inundated valleys.

When demand for manila called, the local environment was uniquely qualified to respond. Lowland wet-rice cultivation was never abandoned during the boom, and manila fields were interspersed with plantings of yams, fruit, bamboo, and other "upland" commodities. Clearly, Bikolanos were better able to withstand bust cycles in their primary commodity than were their Yucatecan counterparts.[48]

Large-scale cultivation of these commodities implied that the peculiar characteristics of each plant had to be accommodated to a number of critical variables. Not only did the entire productive process have to be economically rationalized, it also had to fit the economic, political, and social institutions of the society. In some ways, this necessitated major adjustments and, in other ways, it built on the structures present. Inputs like land tenure patterns, labor relations, technological improvements, and marketing and credit practices were either overhauled or fine-tuned in the wake of the boom. It is beyond the scope of this chapter to examine how Kabikolan and Yucatán made all of these adjustments, but we can focus on those variables that had a profound effect on the staples' ability to remain competitive in the hard fibers market.

Land and Labor

It must be emphasized at the outset that both commodities were highly inelastic to price changes in the market. Since landowners had to wait four and seven years in Kabikolan and Yucatán, respectively, to begin harvesting their crops, they invariably based their decision to expand or contract their holdings on their ability to acquire capital. Faced with such a lag between planting and first harvest, landowners could predict neither future prices nor world market demand. As a result, supply in the short run was usually out of phase with demand.[49]

Land tenure patterns and labor relations are a useful point of departure for studying the two regional economies, not only because they helped shape other variables, but also because they present highly differentiated responses to the export regimen. Yucatán's transformation from self-sufficient cattle and maize haciendas to "modern" henequen estates, in particular, illustrates a unique path that rural Latin American society followed on the road to agrarian capitalism. While the henequen estate may have physically resembled a commercial plantation—with modern machinery, narrow-gauge tramways, and land-intensive cultivation of the staple crop—familial ownership, management, and *mentalité* continued to imbue the institution with characteristics of the pre-henequen hacienda. Emblematic of a rural society in the midst of a complex transition, the henequen estate is best viewed as a hybrid that illustrates some of the traits of its predecessor but reflects inevitable adjustments in land, technology, labor, and infrastructure. Moreover, it appears that the emergence of a full-fledged plantation society was inhibited by lingering vestiges of the earlier institution, particularly in the way in which *hacendados* confronted their labor problems.[50]

Just as the syncretic henequen estate combined characteristics of both the traditional hacienda and the commercial plantation, so, too, did its labor relations represent an amalgam of two modes of coercion. To appreciate how obedience to authority was instilled in resident indebted peons by *henequeneros* during the boom, let us briefly focus on "idioms of power," that is, on the ways in which the coercive aspect of domination has been represented to subordinate classes throughout history.[51] In many premodern, traditional societies, force was presented directly, in face-to-face relations and most often transparently. Although this personalistic idiom of power was at times camouflaged by such contrived strategies as fictive kinship, paternalism, and asymmetric gift exchanges, there was little doubt on the part of the superordinate or subordinate elements that domination was the essence of the relationship.

A second materialistic idiom of power later emerged in which the unequal relationship was represented as power over commodities rather than over individuals. As modern capitalism evolved and both parties grew more detached from the commodities they produced, labor-management relations became increasingly depersonalized.

The social relations of henequen monoculture represent something of a halfway point along the continuum joining the personalistic and the materialistic idioms of power. Indeed, many of the constitutive elements of the personalistic idiom found in traditional societies—for example, a thinly veiled paternalism, fictive kinship, and the ever-present agency of human force, exemplified, for instance, in floggings meted out by overseers—were carried over to the new plantation-style society. Underwritten by the assistance of the state political apparatus, three complementary mechanisms of social control—isolation, coercion, and security—allowed *henequeneros* to maintain the disciplined work rhythms of monocrop production. Isolation, coercion, and security worked in unison to cement the structural relationship that not only suited the production requirements of management, but also served the subsistence needs of workers, at least until the eve of the Mexican Revolution.

Designed by *henequeneros* to limit the workers' mobility and autonomy, the three mechanisms were often so mutually reinforcing that it is sometimes difficult to delineate where one began and the other left off. Institutions like the hacienda store, for example, served many functions. On one level, the store gave *henequeneros* a surefire mechanism for raising workers' debts (coercion). On another level, by providing basic foodstuffs and household needs, it diminished the need for resident peons to leave the property to purchase goods, thereby minimizing the chances of potentially disruptive contact between resident peons and neighboring villagers and agitators (isolation). Finally, through the sale of corn, beans, and other staples, it ensured subsistence for resident peons (security). In sum, the hacienda store was a perfect vehicle for appropriating labor in a scarce market, since it facilitated dependency and immobility while conveying a measure of convenience and security to landless peons.

Henequen monoculture's fundamental security of subsistence throughout the boom coupled with the economic demise of nearby village communities enlisted workers for, and harnessed them to, the disciplined work rhythms of fiber production. The *henequeneros'* skillful management of the three complementary mechanisms of social control kept workers very much on the defensive.

Gender relations on henequen estates only reinforced these complementary mechanisms.[52] In fact, masters and peons found common ground in their perceptions of the role Maya women should play on the estates. First and foremost, they agreed on a rigid division of labor. Debt peons toiled in the fields, performing all of the tasks related to planting, harvesting, and processing fiber on the estates. If daughters or wives occasionally worked in the fields to remove the spines from the henequen leaves after cutting (just as they had helped in the past with harvesting corn), they were accompanied by their fathers or husbands and were never paid in scrip for their labors.

Not surprisingly, women on henequen estates were relegated to the domestic sphere. Their tasks centered on rearing the family, cooking, cleaning, retrieving water from the well and firewood from the forest, bringing lunch to their husbands and sons in the fields, and tending the family garden. Ledger books occasionally listed women as domestics who worked in the landlord's "big house" or as hammock and sack makers and corn grinders, but they were not identified as henequen workers. Indeed, it appears that the fiber boom brought little change to the campesinas' regimen, for this strictly observed division of labor on the estates was consistent with preboom patterns. Even at the height of the fiber boom, when planters were desperate for workers, Maya women were not used in the fields.

Why didn't planters, who regularly complained about the scarcity of labor in the henequen zone and who did not shrink from employing coercive strategies when it suited their purposes, employ campesinas in the fields? By permitting the male peon to earn "wages" to provide for his family through access to corn plots and hunting and to exercise power over women in his household, the *hacendado* was securing the "loyalty" and limiting the mobility of his worker. As a consequence, families were rarely separated in the henequen zone, nor does it appear that *hacendados* used the threat of separation to ensure loyalty.

This thin veneer of reciprocity formalized gender relations on the estates. When *henequeneros* arranged weddings for their peons, they provided grooms with a loan—the couple's first debt—to pay for the religious and civil ceremonies and a fiesta. The result was a complicitous arrangement among males on the estate in which the master permitted the peon to preside over his own household as a subordinate patriarch. If this led to cases of domestic violence, more often than not they were handled circumspectly on the estate; rarely did grievances find their way to the local courtroom. Typically, *hacendados* and overseers put gross offenders in the hacienda jail.

Such campesino patriarchy, however, had limits. Often enough, the *henequenero* or his overseer, exercising the humiliating "privilege" of the "right of first night," invaded the peon's hut and violated his spouse or daughter. While such an affront undermined the reciprocal nature of the shared sense of patriarchy, it did provide the peon with one more object lesson in where power ultimately resided on the estate. The servant would seldom take revenge on his boss; more often, we learn of unfortunate cases of misdirected rage, as peons abused their wives to reassert their dominion in the home.

Planters were reluctant to tamper with the peons' patriarchal control of their families because, in the long run, it suited their economic interests. As far as the *hacendado* was concerned, the principal task of Maya women was to procreate and rear the next generation of henequen workers. To permit women to work in the fields would undermine that role and upset social relations on the estate—relations that reflected the acculturated Maya's evolving cultural identity as well as the requirements of fiber production.

If the henequen estate represents a fusion of modernizing influences wrought by the rapidly expanding export trade and the legacy of Yucatán's socioeconomic past, manila production merely acclimated itself, with only minimal adjustments, to prevailing land and labor patterns in the Bikol peninsula. Unlike the prototypical large landed estates found in Yucatán (with sizes varying from 500 to 3,000 hectares), nineteenth-century Kabikolan was a patchwork quilt of small *lates* (plots devoted to manila cultivation). Owen relates that the average landowner possessed fewer than 20 hectares, and in a number of communities the most prominent *principal* held no more than 150 hectares. Even though this proprietary class (the *principalía*) came to acquire more than 50 percent of the cultivated land in the peninsula, most owned a number of scattered plots: "The characteristic Bikol landowner was neither the *hacendero* nor the peasant proprietor, but a member of the local gentry with a few scattered plots worked for him by others."[53] *Principales* coexisted with hundreds of smallholders and squatters who at times worked on their own plots, rented other plots, or hired themselves out to the *principales*.

The consolidation of large landholdings was mitigated in part by the characteristics of manila cultivation (see below) and the existence of an open frontier. In the Yucatán, settlers were hemmed in by a tropical rain forest, which did not lend itself readily to development, and by the jungle's rebellious indigenous inhabitants, the Chan Santa Cruz Indians, who had waged an on-again, off-again "Caste War" against state and federal forces throughout the second half of the nineteenth century.[54] In Kabikolan the frontier remained an open resource until the turn of the century, when population growth curtailed the availability of uncultivated lands.

Principales in the Bikol peninsula fashioned a flexible labor market unlike Yucatán's characteristic structure of domination; at least in theory Kabikolan's labor market offered a degree of mobility and autonomy for manila workers. The personalistic idiom of power prevailed on *lates* as landowners contracted directly with laborers to clear the forest, plant manila, weed fields, and then harvest the crop. Both wage labor and sharecropping were employed by proprietors, who devised a clientelistic relationship in which the worker traded his labor for a wage (or a portion of the crop), credit, and the potential for autonomy.

Sharecropping, or the "beneficiary" system, as it was known, meant that the laborer generally exchanged his labor for half the crop harvested. An arrogant North American observer writing in 1906 felt that share stripping created more problems than it was worth: "When a native cultivator is in urgent need of a few dollars he will often sacrifice unready plants and rush the process of extraction, with the result of injuring the plantation and putting an unnecessarily low-grade article upon the market."[55]

Still, such institutionalized arrangements reflected a paternalistic ethos not present in Yucatán. Owen relates:[56]

> There is no doubt that abaca cultivation did allow more flexibility and mobility to labor (and to those who hired labor) than rice growing did. In abaca there was no connection between those who planted and those who harvested, not even between those who harvested one year and the next. It seems likely, however, that many abaca-strippers lived in the same houses and worked the same fields for the same owners on the same terms year after year, perhaps with some of the same mutual patron-client expectations associated with tenantry elsewhere.

It should be emphasized that labor mobility and autonomous decision-making existed more in the abstract than in reality, because of a system of advances that permeated the entire manila industry. Again, the comparison with henequen monoculture is illustrative. At the outset of the boom in Yucatán, workers were also offered credit, and the clientelistic model was part and parcel of the master-servant relationship. But, as the boom progressed, paternalism on estates waned as work rhythms intensified. Very rarely could Maya henequen workers extricate themselves from debt. The isolation mechanism made certain that workers could not leave the hacienda without written permission of the *hacendado* and that runaways were returned promptly by bounty hunters, district prefects, and the national guard. Moreover, when properties were sold, so were the debts, further diminishing the prospects for mobility. In other words, advances in Yucatán were an essential ingredient of a sophisticated and highly regulated structure of domination.

That kind of overt coercion was not prevalent in Kabikolan. Both landowner and worker were Bikolanos. A common ethnicity and, in certain instances, kinship, no doubt lessened (but did not eliminate) the need for overt violence. Instead, advances underscored the importance of the exchange relationship between patron and client, as Owen makes clear: "In the ideal Western scheme of things each transaction . . . is perceived as complete, with a beginning and an ending, money borrowed and repaid in full, contracts stipulating exactly how much (or how little) each party must do, no loose ends. From an Asian viewpoint, however, the emphasis . . . is on continuity. A given transaction is only one manifestation of an ongoing relationship; the very act of exchange implies a future exchange."[57]

Credit also shifted the risks of manila cultivation to the *principal*. Since payment was in advance, if any problems occurred—for example, natural disaster, or a drop in fiber prices—invariably the loan could not be repaid until times improved. In fact, landowners usually had to give an additional sum to their debtors if they even hoped to recover their original investment, or the debtor might just disappear, something that would have been highly unlikely in Yucatán.

The landholding elite (*principalia*), of course, passed on the costs of this system to middlemen and fiber buyers, who had advanced funds in like manner. Not surprisingly, North American and British fiber buyers in Kabikolan (and Yucatán) abhorred the system of advances. An indignant foreigner observed: "But experience has proved that the natives have not sufficient sense of honour to endeavour to gradually clear off their debts, for, on delivery of the produce, they expect to be again paid the full value and pass over the sums long due . . . the native prefers to live in misery rather than work without payment beforehand."[58]

Gender relations in Kabikolan and Yucatán also differed markedly. Unlike in Yucatán, where the division of labor precluded women from working on the henequen estates, women were actively involved in harvesting manila. Although the male stripped the plant, women and children chopped down plants, cut away the pulp, sliced the plant into ribbons, and hung the stripped fiber up to dry. Women were also actively involved in commerce, as the rise of the manila industry meant a larger and more profitable market for local produce as well. Even the rapid growth of Chinese retailing could not prevent Bikolanas from participating in the retail trade. Although evidence is fragmentary, Owen believes that female participation in the manila industry and retailing undercut traditional weaving and other household tasks. Further research is needed, but it is apparent that female peasants in Kabikolan had options that Yucatecan campesinas could have only dreamed about, but those options meant that traditional norms and expectations were under siege during the fiber boom.

The striking differences in land, labor, and gender patterns are partly explained by landowners' ability to introduce technological improvements and infrastructure. Producers' ability to incorporate these improvements was, in turn, shaped by the particular characteristics of the two plants and environmental considerations.

Despite frequent attempts to mechanize the processing of manila fiber, laborious hand scraping remained the rule throughout the boom. Foreign hemp merchants, many of whom conducted their business from Manila and rarely, if ever, visited Kabikolan, were reluctant to introduce defibering machines. The cultural arrogance of fiber buyers such as Ogden Edwards led them to conclude that "the natives . . . are not civilized enough to use anything so complicated" as a hemp-stripping machine.[59] More to the point, most defibering machines were too cumbersome to be pulled up the narrow paths through the forest to the volcanic slopes where manila was grown. Since the plant yields on average only 2 percent of its total weight in fiber—about ten ounces of fiber per plant—and because it must be processed quickly before it dries out, the cost of carrying manila to the machine was prohibitive. Teams of two or three workers chopped down the plant, cut away the pulp, and stripped the fiber with a knife. Hand stripping was very inefficient, since approximately 30 percent of the fiber was wasted. Productivity also varied greatly, as some teams brought in thirteen pounds while others harvested seventy-five pounds per team per day.

The harvesting of manila fiber gave new meaning to the word "arduous": It was "said to be [the] hardest kind of work that a native can do."[60] So difficult was this task that manila workers had to rest frequently throughout the day and usually worked only half a month. One of the major reasons for the industry's decline in the 1920s was the difficulty the *principalia* had in attracting and keeping workers, who abandoned the manila fields to pursue production of other agricultural commodities.

The use of time-consuming hand scrapers (*toncos* or *pacche*) was also standard operating procedure in the henequen industry until the mid-nineteenth century. Five hundred leaves had to be scraped with these tools to secure one pound of raw fiber. Yucatecans' invention and perfection of a defibering machine during the 1850s, however, enabled the industry to cut production costs and meet rising demand. Defibering machines became an integral part of the estate. By 1860 each rasping machine produced, on the average, a little more than a bale of fiber per day. Improvements in technology continued throughout the fiber boom, however, and with the introduction of steam power to the machine house in 1861, henequen production soared. Motivated by the growing hard fibers trade and by state government attempts to stimulate advances in machine productivity and safety, Yucatecan inventors had defibering machines made to specifications in the United States. By 1900 automatic Prieto machines manufactured in Paterson, New Jersey, cleaned 150,000 leaves in a ten-hour period, a far cry from the first defibering machines.[61]

The combination of powerful defibering machines and a level landscape meant that landowners could take advantage of economies of scale. Throughout the henequen zone, *hacendados*, aided and abetted by state authorities, expanded their holdings by gobbling up adjoining tracts of land owned by smallholders and taking advantage of family heads in nearby villages. Sometimes violence accompanied disputes between property owners and villagers. In general, however, the emergence of the large landed estate met with little resistance during the boom, as *hacendados* utilized state and federal laws to their advantage; small proprietors were powerless to object.

Yucatán's topography also enabled *henequeneros* to make the most of improvements in transportation. In the 1880s *hacendados* began to lay a network of inexpensive, portable Decauville gauge rails, which transported the leaves from field to defibering machine and from processing house to the nearby major railhead. Four railway lines built by and for *henequeneros* fastened outlying villages and estates into a tight orbit around their Mérida hub. From Mérida, fiber was sent to Progreso on the Gulf Coast. This transportation revolution served to reduce transaction costs as it enlarged productive capacities.[62]

The contrast to the Philippines could not have been greater. Owen writes: "From the *lates*, the fiber was carried to the nearest town on the back of the laborer, the collector, or a carabao (water buffalo) if one were available. From the towns it might travel by raft or narrow *baroto* (small boat) down the Bikol river, by small sailing craft along the coast or by carabao cart over one of the colonial roads to one of the major ports, where it would be stored pending shipment to Manila."[63]

The henequen economy's ability to meld technological improvements with its environment, the savings earned from economies of scale, and low labor costs ensured it a seat on the Ferris wheel. Bikol manila, on the other hand, lacked these advantages; yet its acknowledged superiority over henequen and its versatility kept it competitive until the 1920s.

Interestingly, after production in Kabikolan declined, Japanese-owned manila estates were established in Davao Province on the Philippine island of Mindanao. Here we see a more factorylike approach to manila cultivation, replete with decorticating machines, seed selection, fertilization, and irrigation. What is instructive about the comparison with Davao is that Japanese entrepreneurs shoved aside the indigenous population to make room for settlers. In Davao, land was an inexpensive, open resource, unlike in Kabikolan. As a result, Japanese investors could establish factories in the field and invest more in machinery and infrastructure.

Not only were there differences in land and labor patterns and in the willingness of producers to assimilate technological improvements in Kabikolan and Yucatán, but the character of local fiber marketing was also distinct. In Yucatán, as has been well documented, marketing increasingly came under the control of a cohesive oligopoly that limited competition. Social and family connections were utilized to build economic empires and to restrict entry to the market through political connections and the control of capital. Instead of the archetypical enclave, an informal empire evolved between accommodating elites and foreign buyers. The International Harvester Company, the largest farm implement manufacturer in the world and one of the principal purchasers of raw fiber, funneled capital through local agents to regional producers. By the First World War, International Harvester dominated the fiber industry and influenced price trends in the local fiber market. This collaborative matrix had important ramifications for the local economy, because land tenure and ownership of the means of production remained in Yucatecan hands.

In Kabikolan, Bikolano *principales* may have ruled fiber production, but they had little to do with their commodity once it left their estates. A ubiquitous number of middlemen of diverse ethnic origins, including Chinese, Spaniards, and other native Filipinos—but not Bikolanos—purchased the fiber from Bikol landowners and sold it to North American or British import-export houses in Manila. Until manila's denouement in the 1930s, provincial marketing was characterized by ethnic pluralism, limited competition, and the advance system. In contrast to

Yucatán, where at times Harvester and its ally, Henry W. Peabody and Company, controlled over 90 percent of the trade, no foreign concern would ever control more than 40 percent of the market, and the fortunes of merchant houses rose and fell regularly. It must be emphasized that the inability to successfully monoposonize manila production did not mean that foreign merchant houses did not form combinations to restrain trade. Time after time, Manila houses fashioned such "arrangements," but they invariably collapsed. Even the International Harvester Company's 1904 takeover of Macleod and Company, a venerable manila merchant house, apparently did not alter the character of this variegated, vertically integrated marketing system. Perhaps that helps explain why there was little effort made by Bikolano producers to confront foreign buyers and form cooperative societies to withhold production to enhance their market position.[64]

Such was not the case in Yucatán. As the regional economy became increasingly more oligopolistic and world market prices went into a tailspin, producers, feisty under the best of circumstances, turned downright combative. Before analyzing the planters' attempts to organize, an overview of the evolving relationship between fiber buyers, their agents, and local producers during the henequen boom provides context.

The Collaborative Matrix and the Market

All men are liars especially those who deal in Hemp.
        —Ogden Edwards, manila merchant, Peele, Hubbell & Co.

When fiber prices were high, *henequeneros* secured bountiful profits. Yet local *hacendados*—who needed to purchase machinery for processing the fiber, to build tramways, and to clear, plant, and wait seven years for their fiber plants to mature—had to borrow money in advance from import-export merchants (*casas exportadoras*).[65] The *casas*, in turn, were lent capital by banks and buyers in the United States. A small *hacendado* class, numbering between 300 and 400, promised its fiber to the *casas* in exchange for cash advances.

From the 1870s on, local business leaders served as fiber purchasing agents and conduits for foreign loan capital. Thus, North American brokers and manufacturers, such as the Thebaud Brothers and the National Cordage Company, operating during the first decades of the boom, enlisted the services of the large Yucatecan export houses of Eusebio Escalante, Manuel Dondé, and Henry W. Peabody, among others, in their bid to corner the local market. For their own part, these "collaborators," in serving as purchasing agents and financial intermediaries for the North American banks and manufacturers, realized sizable profits usually in the form of commissions and kickbacks, but also by virtue of the usurious loan practice that access to foreign capital enabled them to conduct. Ideally, just as the foreign investor sought to carve out a durable monopoly or "corner" on the trade, so the collaborator wished to enjoy exclusively the benefits that would flow from a monopoly over communication with foreign interests controlling the market.

With these limitations, it was difficult for *henequeneros* to adjust productivity or predict prices. As a result, local landholders were particularly vulnerable to the repeated boom-and-bust cycles that afflicted the hard fibers market. Although henequen provided 85 percent of the fiber for the profitable binder twine industry by the turn of the century, there was enough competition from manila and other hard fibers, as well as occasional attempts by North American buyers to corner the market, to create alternating shortages and gluts. This chronic price instability, coupled with the producers' inability to diversify, meant that Yucatán's regional economy as a whole, and the henequen sector in particular, experienced severe dislocations in the midst of sustained growth. In fact, many *henequeneros* found themselves chronically in debt and bankruptcies were an ever-present fact of life.

If most *henequeneros* found it difficult to negotiate this treacherous monocrop economy, a close-knit elite of thirty families not only survived but flourished. This group dominated the regional economy, controlling land, labor, the import-export trade, and transportation. As the monocrop economy prospered in the last quarter of the nineteenth century, however, competition within this familial elite intensified. By 1902 a much smaller, more cohesive group constituted a hegemonic, oligarchical faction (*camarilla*) in the region. This *camarilla* was based on the Molina-Montes clan. Olegario Molina's faction had homogeneous interests, a relatively closed membership, and—owing in part to its collaboration with the principal buyer of raw fiber, International Harvester Company—so much control over the region's economic and political levers of power that it was able to thwart the opportunities of rival *camarillas*.

Before 1902, a truly exclusive and powerful collaborative mechanism had never characterized the henequen industry. A secret contract consummated between International Harvester and Olegario Molina's *casa exportadora*, Molina y Compañía, in October 1902 dramatically transformed the political economy of Yucatán by weeding out competitors and forcing down the price of fiber. With increasing frequency throughout the rest of the decade, *henequeneros* and merchants became indebted to Molina's *casa* and were forced to advance their product at slightly less than the current market price to cover their obligations. Moreover, the access to foreign capital, and International Harvester's capacity to funnel large amounts of it at critical junctures, enabled Molina and his faction to acquire mortgages, purchase credits outright, and consolidate their hold on regional communications, infrastructure, and banking—all of which guaranteed control of local fiber production and generally worked to depress the price.

The ascendancy of the Molina clan coincided with International Harvester's sudden takeover of the farm implement and binder twine industries. The very establishment of the new "International," a combination of five of the largest harvesting machine companies— McCormick; Deering; Plano; Wardner, Bushnell and Glessner Company; and Milwaukee Harvester—with an initial capitalization of $120 million, eliminated the bulk of existing competition within the U.S. farm implement and twine industries and placed at the manufacturer's disposal organizational and financial resources that hitherto had never existed.

The groundwork for Harvester's rapid rise to prominence in the binder twine industry was laid during the 1890s, when the two largest harvesting machine companies, McCormick and Deering, became increasingly dissatisfied with the practices of cordage companies and their fiber buyers. Twine was an important secondary line for farm implement manufacturers. North American farmers needed a regular supply of twine to operate their binders; if McCormick or Deering could not supply it, sales of their farm machinery would suffer.

To ensure a predictable supply at reasonable prices, harvesting machine companies and cordage companies fashioned pool arrangements. Typically, a committee, composed of board members of prominent cordage manufacturers and buyers, would meet and agree that a certain percentage of the total production of the industry should be assigned to each manufacturer. When a manufacturer's production for a given month exceeded the assigned percentage, that concern paid a penalty to compensate rivals who did not overproduce. These associations were inevitably short-lived, since the agreements were unenforceable—predicated as they were on "gentlemen's honor"—and in a competitive trade like hard fibers, it did not take long before rival suppliers found ways to circumvent the pool.[66]

Since pools proved unsatisfactory to manufacturers and buyers, some elements within the cordage industry aggressively sought to drive competitors out of business and seize control of raw fiber supplies and/ or manufactured output. The classic example of this was the National Cordage Company's ill-fated attempt to monopsonize the hard fibers market during the late 1880s and the early 1890s. The entire hard fibers market was given a Ferris wheel ride as the National Cordage Company trust bought up supplies of henequen and manila, bought out its competitors, used its considerable financial leverage to drive others out of business, and denied their competitors access to cordage machinery. Prices in hard fiber markets at first soared and then collapsed over a period of three years as the industry was riddled by bankruptcies. Producers and merchant houses in Yucatán and Kabikolan were not spared.[67]

Although National Cordage's corner failed miserably, it demonstrated to harvesting machine manufacturers that they had very little control over a vital secondary line. Deering and McCormick took steps to prevent this from happening again. Deering, which had placed orders for millions of pounds of twine from the defunct National Cordage Company, was the first harvesting machine company to build its own twine mill. Construction on its twine works began on 1 October 1894, just a year after National Cordage's bankruptcy. To ensure that farmers would use their line of twine, Deering refused to guarantee their binders if farmers used other twine.

McCormick did not build its own twine mill immediately. First, it bought out a number of cordage mills and fronted $75,000 to one of the largest fiber buyers in Yucatán, Peabody & Company. It worked out similar arrangements with other fiber buyers in the Philippines. Moreover, it decided to act as a silent partner for an intriguing experiment to manufacture binder twine in Yucatán. Olegario Molina and several other Yucatecan *henequeneros* recruited local capital and solicited a loan from McCormick, plus the most up-to-date North American machinery. "La Industrial," if successful, Molina reasoned, would enable Yucatán to reap the value traditionally added by North American cordage manufacturers. McCormick provided technological supervision and influenced the plant's day-to-day operations by dictating production and shipment schedules and standards of quality. It also became La Industrial's largest customer. Such participation suggests the lengths to which McCormick was willing to go to seek an alternative means of supply following National Cordage's attempted corner.

With the outbreak of the Spanish-American War in 1898 and the suspension of manila shipments, henequen prices soared. Interest in twine production waned in Yucatán and plant efficiency deteriorated. Executives at McCormick concluded that La Industrial would not become its principal source of binder twine. By 1899 McCormick was already constructing its own stateside twine mill (which opened in Chicago in 1900) and, by the time of International Harvester's creation in 1902, the trust was committed to providing for most of its twine needs.

Harvester, ever wary of the unpredictable hard fibers market, went to great lengths to diminish its dependence on henequen and manila. The company purchased fiber plantations in Baja California, Mexico, Ecuador, and Cuba and experimented unsuccessfully with flax twine as a homegrown alternative to the two tropical fibers. Despite these efforts to diversify its sources of supply, Harvester continued to work principally with Molina and Montes in Yucatán, and binder twine continued to be manufactured with Yucatecan henequen and Philippine manila until after World War I.

In Defense of Fiber

Planters, merchants, politicians, and journalists openly discussed the role of International Harvester in the industry and its collaboration with the Molina-Montes faction.[68] In the local press, the perception was widely shared that the machinations of *"el trust"* were bringing financial ruin to all but a select few. Harvester became a target in the regional press as the perception of guilt seemed proof enough for many intellectuals and planters, who were disposed to saddle the collaborators with more blame than they probably deserved for the ills of an inherently unstable economy.[69]

Earlier attempts—in 1876, 1887, 1890, 1894–1895, 1902, and 1904—to withhold production and create a shortage of fiber on the market had failed miserably. Invariably, such agricultural associations had lacked the capital to compete with powerful houses with foreign backing. Many *henequeneros* were unable to participate in these cooperatives, since their product was fully or partially promised to Molina and Peabody for advances tendered in years past. Growers might agree in principle, but they lacked the independence to join in such valorization schemes.

Capital-starved planters also had themselves to blame for the failure of these associations. A contentious lot even under favorable market conditions, the planters were hampered from the start by a lack of solidarity. An undercurrent of distrust worked to inhibit these cooperatives. *Henequeneros* prided themselves on their individualism, and when they needed assistance to weather the bust cycles of the fluctuating regional economy, they preferred to rely on extensive kinship networks rather than unite to do battle against the powerful export houses. Generally speaking, planter cooperative societies coalesced only when the price of henequen dropped so low that it cut into the planters' considerable profits. This was precisely the worst time for such a maneuver to succeed, since money was stretched very thin when the price of henequen declined.

The export houses, however, did not take demonstrations of incipient planter solidarity lightly. Playing on the fears and anxieties of the *henequeneros*, the houses and henequen speculators manipulated stocks of fiber and circulated wild rumors of the imminent demise of the market. More times than not, growers, fearing a further drop in price, sold their fiber to speculators, who turned a tidy profit at the expense of the edgy *henequeneros*.

Not until the revolutionary government of Salvador Alvarado committed the resources of the state to a valorization scheme in 1915 did planter solidarity effectively confront the fiber buyers. In a sense, past attempts to organize growers created a collective disposition to confront *el trust* in 1915. Yet, it is instructive that many planters had to be coerced by the state to participate in the valorization campaign. Unlike past attempts to organize, the timing favored the producers. The Comisión Reguladora del Mercado de Henequén (Henequen Market Regulatory Commission) was aided by high fiber prices, as the First World War stimulated demand for cordage and twine. The price rise was short-lived, however; valorization proved to be a temporary solution.

Epilogue

After World War I, henequen and manila found their comfortable niche in the hard fibers trade challenged by a new fiber. Yucatecans were well acquainted with this newcomer. *Yaxci (Agave sisalana)* was indigenous to the peninsula and had long been used by local artisans to make hammocks, bagging, and other products. Although it did not grow well in the rocky henequen zone, scattered cultivation of this crop continued in southeastern Yucatán throughout the boom. This true sisal had been formally identified by the North American consul to Campeche in the 1830s, Henry Perrine, who, after his stay on the peninsula, brought the sisal plant to southern Florida and conducted experiments there. Although sisal did not catch on in the United States, German growers carried the plant from Florida to German East Africa in 1892. By the 1920s, sisal plantations were flourishing in Tanganyika and Kenya. Later, the island of Java in the South Pacific would commit to sisal. Reading about the evolution of the rise of sisal plantation monoculture in East Africa and Java is a familiar story to those acquainted with the history of the hard fibers market.[70]

Sisal proved to be a formidable fiber; it was stronger than henequen and, unlike manila, it lent itself well to defibering machines. Labor costs in these areas were even lower than in Yucatán and the Philippines. By 1927 Asian and African nations accounted for nearly half of world hard fiber production. The Great Depression and the invention of the combine, which did not use twine, also hurt the henequen and manila industries. Production fell drastically; henequen exports reached a low in 1940, when they were less than one-fourth the amount exported during World War I. Although henequen would recover somewhat with the introduction of automatic baling machines, the introduction of low-cost synthetic fibers in the 1960s and the 1970s would devastate the henequen economy. Manila and Kabikolan fared no better.[71]

Appraising the costs and benefits of the two commodities for the economies of Kabikolan and Yucatán is complicated by the environmental, social, and political variables that shaped the evolution of the booms in these two regions. It is clear that, in the short term, the hard fibers boom enriched a small group of foreign investors, merchants, and local elites in both regions. But as we have seen, clear differences existed in just who benefited and why. And if a few profited greatly, the great majority of producers (not to mention the tens of thousands of laborers) found themselves tied to the capricious whims of an unforgiving market.

In Yucatán, the political consequences engendered by the henequen boom were severe, as disgruntled *hacendados* sought to break the Molina faction's stranglehold over the statehouse and the fiber trade. When the Mexican Revolution broke out in 1911, opponents of the Molina faction would even arm some of their henequen workers in a desperate attempt to seize a share of the spoils of the monocrop economy.

Henequen became a political football again in 1915, when the revolutionary government of Venustiano Carranza formed a cartel to push henequen prices higher. In comparison, the political fallout from manila production in the Philippines was noticeably less apparent. Perhaps the Philippines' long-standing, if withering, colonial (and later neocolonial) status meant that the process of nation building was delayed and traditional political arrangements were given an extended lease on life.

Labor arrangements and land tenure patterns also varied for a number of compelling reasons. The idiosyncrasies of the monocrop, the constraints of the environment, preexisting labor relations in the countryside, the potential for economies of scale, the size of landholdings, the relative power of local elites and the state, the existence of communal lands, and the relevance of debt as a means of diminishing labor mobility, all significantly shaped the character of land and labor arrangements in the countryside. The interrelatedness of these complex variables assure us that the commodity's requirements alone do not dictate how coercive or relaxed labor relations are. As we have seen, Yucatán's labor arrangements were much more coercive than Kabikolan's; the reasons for that essential difference are only partly explained by the different qualities and requirements of each fiber.

In both cases, bona fide development proved illusory, as neither industry generated sufficient linkages to prompt future economic growth. Henequen and manila eventually lost their seats on the Ferris wheel. As long as they enjoyed a brief, Ricardian comparative advantage on the hard fibers market during the export boom, those elites that dominated the regional economy prospered. When that short-lived moment passed soon after World War I, Yucatán's and Kabikolan's economies floundered.

Notes

1. Epigraph quotation cited by Rodulfo G. Cantón in an untitled pamphlet dated 15 August 1876, University of Alabama Yucatán Microfilm Collection (hereafter cited as UAYMC), Roll 32. Lyster H. Dewey, formerly the botanist in charge of the Division of Fiber Plant Investigations of the U.S. Department of Agriculture, defined hard fibers as "hard and stiff in texture, extending lengthwise through the pulpy tissues of long leaves or leaf stems of monocotyledonous or endogenous (ingrowing) plants: Henequen, sisal, piteira, fique, yucca, pita, floja, and abaca, and the palm fibers." Dewey identified hemp, cadillo, jute, and ramie as soft, or bast, fibers. These fibers, which had a softer texture, extended "through the inner bark of stems or main stalks of dicotyledonous or exogenous (outgrowing) plants." For the purposes of this chapter, however, I have combined Dewey's classifications, since both hard and soft fibers competed in what was commonly known as the hard fibers trade during the nineteenth and twentieth centuries. Generally, hard fibers are found in tropical zones, whereas soft fibers grow in more temperate climes: *Fiber Production in the Western Hemisphere*, U.S. Department of Agriculture Miscellaneous Publication 518 (Washington, D.C.: U.S. Government Printing Office, 1943), 1.

2. See UAYMC, Roll 32, and Rodulfo G. Cantón, *Proyecto sobre la formación de una sociedad y banco agrícola. Varias indicaciones relativas al henequén* (Mérida: Imprenta de la Librería Meridana de Cantón, 1876); Juan Miguel Castro, *Informe presentado en la sesión del 9 del mayo de 1878, Junta de Hacendados y Comerciantes* (Mérida: Imprenta del Comercio Ignacio L. Mena, 1878), in UAYMC, Roll 34.

3. Juan Miguel Castro, *El henequén de Yucatán y el monopolio* (Mérida: Imprenta del Comercio de Néstor Rubio Alpuche, 1876). For a thorough discussion of the economic depression, the North American panic of 1873, and the ensuing debate between Castro, Cantón, and fiber buyers, see Lawrence J. Remmers, "Henequen, the Caste War and Economy of Yucatán, 1846–1883: The Roots of Dependence in a Mexican Region," 2 vols. Ph.D. diss., UCLA (1981), II:741ff.

4. Excepting the steam engine, by 1890 there was more capital invested in

the manufacture of the twine binder harvester than in any other machine in the world. See Remmers, "Henequen, the Caste War," 824, n87; and U.S. Department of Commerce and Labor, Bureau of Corporations, *The International Harvester Company* (Washington, D.C.: U.S. Government Printing Office, 1913), 44–46. Oftentimes, articles from foreign journals and publications would be reprinted in Mexican trade papers. Yucatecan *henequeneros'* knowledgeable response to the market is another proof that modernizationist theorists' claim of cultural conservatism on the part of landowners and merchants in Latin America (and in other parts of the developing world) is off the mark. See Norman G. Owen, *Prosperity without Progress: Manila Hemp and Material Life in the Colonial Philippines* (Berkeley and Los Angeles: University of California Press, 1984), xv and conclusions.

5. Untitled pamphlet dated 15 August 1876, UAYMC, Roll 32. All translations are mine unless otherwise noted.

6. See, e.g., Alfred W. Crosby, Jr., *America, Russia, Hemp and Napoleon: American Trade with Russia and the Baltic, 1783–1812* (Columbus: Ohio State University Press, 1965); Dianne Bolton, *Nationalization—A Road to Socialism? The Lessons of Tanzania* (London: Zed Books, 1985); John Iliffe, *A Modern History of Tanganyika* (Cambridge: Cambridge University Press, 1979); Rakibuddin Ahmed, *The Progress of the Jute Industry and Trade (1865–1966)* (Dacca: Pakistan Central Jute Committee, 1966); James F. Hopkins, *A History of the Hemp Industry in Kentucky* (Lexington: University of Kentucky Press, 1951); and Owen, *Prosperity without Progress.*

7. Norman G. Owen, "Americans in the Abaca Trade: Peele, Hubbell & Co., 1856–1875," in Peter W. Stanley ed., *Reappraising an Empire: New Perspectives on Philippine-American History* (Cambridge, Mass.: Harvard University Press, 1989), 95–114, quotation on 217.

8. Remmers notes: "Of the more than 26 hard fiber plants producing commercial fibers, henequen was only one of four to achieve a significant position in the marketplace, the others being manila hemp . . . phorium from New Zealand, and *ixtle*, or Tampico fiber, from northeastern Mexico" ("Henequen, the Caste War," 435). See also Dewey, *Fiber Production,* 1–4.

9. Charles Richards Dodge, *A Descriptive Catalogue of Useful Fiber Plants of the World Including the Structural and Economic Classifications of Fibers* (Washington, D.C.: U.S. Government Printing Office, 1897), 18.

10. Jute has proved exceptionally resilient; it found a purpose—for sacks and bags—that no other fiber has yet to match, so its ride continues (Ahmed, *The Progress of the Jute Industry*). Historians refer to these economic cycles as "intercycles." See Owen, *Prosperity without Progress,* xiv.

11. Hemp was cultivated as early as 4000 B.C. in northern China. The first archaeological record dates to the early neolithic period at Yang-shao. See David N. Keightley, ed., *The Origins of Chinese Civilization* (Berkeley and Los Angeles: University of California Press, 1983), 31–32. Flax, a "soft" fiber akin to hemp, was used extensively in ancient Egypt, Phoenecia, and Babylonia for weaving linen and other purposes (Dodge, *Descriptive Catalogue,* 13).

12. Crosby, *America, Russia, Hemp,* 17; and Owen, *Prosperity without Progress,* 42, 44.

13. Samuel E. Morison, *The Ropemakers of Plymouth: A History of the*

Plymouth Cordage Company, 1824–1949 (Boston, Mass.: Houghton Mifflin, 1950), quotation on 6. Morison's technical description of a nineteenth-century sailing vessel's voracious demand for rope deserves to be quoted at length. "Every sail (a full-rigged ship carried at least fifteen, a barque twelve and a brig nine) had to be edged all around with boltrope. The yard to which it was bent—with rope—needed stout lifts or halyards to be raised and lowered. Two tacks and two sheets were required to trim each square sail; two bowlines to keep the leeches taut; two clewlines, two buntlines and two leechlines for clewing it up to the yard for furling; and the sailors needed a footrope to stand on. The several jibs and triangular staysails between the masts, the fore and aft-driver on the main and spanker on the mizzen, and the studdingsails if studdingsails were carried had their own halyards and sheets, topping lifts or brails. Most of this running rigging ran up and down masts that might be 50, 60, or 100 feet tall, and those that did the heaviest work had double or triple purchases at the ends for swaying them taut. In addition, there was the standard rigging, the shrouds and backstays that held up the lower masts, topmasts and topgallant masts, all of heavily tarred rope, neatly wormed and served with small line, together with the rope lanyards that enabled them to be set up or slacked away; for wire rigging did not come into use until after the Civil War. Chain cable was introduced somewhat earlier, but until 1840, at least, every ship needed several heavy rope anchor cables 120 fathoms in length, and these cables consumed an enormous amount of fiber . . ." (5). Even the waste fiber from the manufacturing process was used in caulking the seams of wooden ships (Hopkins, *A History of the Hemp Industry in Kentucky*, 6). On the use of sailing ships until the turn of the century, see Owen, *Prosperity without Progress*, 44.

14. Even though many of the hard fibers came from different botanical families, they were all known as hemp (Russian hemp, Manila hemp, sisal hemp, etc.). Scientifically, only those of the genus *Cannabis* are correctly identified as hemp (Owen, *Prosperity without Progress*, 49).

15. Crosby, *America, Russia, Hemp*, 21.

16. Ibid., 17–20; and Dewey, *Fiber Production*, 66.

17. Standard rigging consists of the chains and ropes used to support the masts. Running rigging moves to set the sails.

18. Despite the use of slaves, hemp farms were not plantations. There was little advantage gained from economies of scale. Bluegrass farmers produced a number of different crops on their estates and employed wage and slave labor. The latter were used almost exclusively to work on hemp (Hopkins, *A History of the Hemp Industry in Kentucky*, 4, quotation on 24; Crosby, *America, Russia, Hemp*, 19–21). Morison notes that hemp enjoyed government bounties and premiums and was even made legal tender for taxes (*The Ropemakers of Plymouth*, 18).

19. Dew-retted hemp was generally two-thirds the price of water-retted (Hopkins, *A History of the Hemp Industry in Kentucky*, 101).

20. One scholarly study of the hemp industry asserts that foreign hemp was superior because growers outside the United States cut the male and female plants at different periods, as the female stalks generally matured six weeks later than the males. Domestic hemp, on the other hand, was all cut at the same time, regardless of plant gender. See Kenneth A. Lewallen, "Economic Inequality

in the Upper South: The Concentration of Wealth in Lafayette County, Missouri, 1850–1960," Ph.D. diss., Kansas State University (1980), 260, n112. The cotton gin opened up a new market for domestic hemp. After cotton was ginned, it had to be compressed into bales and held together with a strong binding material like hemp (Hopkins, *A History of the Hemp Industry in Kentucky*, 21, 81; and Percy Wells Bidwell and John I. Falconer, *History of Agriculture in the Northern United States* [Washington, D.C.: Carnegie Institution, 1925]).

21. By 1859 Missouri had replaced Kentucky as the largest hemp producer (Lewallen, "Economic Inequality in the Upper South," 165).

22. Hopkins, *A History of the Hemp Industry in Kentucky*, 59–60, quotation on 60.

23. Lewallen, "Economic Inequality in the Upper South," 229.

24. Hopkins, *A History of the Hemp Industry in Kentucky*, 191, 201.

25. The cultivation and harvesting of raw jute is just as labor intensive as that of common hemp. Peasants grow it along the banks of the Ganges and the Brahmaputra Rivers and harvest their plants in water that at times may be deeper than the height of a man. Workers dive underwater and cut the plants; an expert can cut eight plants in one dive (Ahmed, *The Progress of the Jute Industry*, 10). Quotation from Dewey, *Fiber Production*, 72.

26. In addition to packaging, it has been used for ropes, twines, baling, roofing fabrics, electric cables, rugs, carpets, blankets, and as a multipurpose war material (for tents, sandbags, camouflage netting, water bags, and tarpaulins); see Ahmed, *The Progress of the Jute Industry*, 21.

27. Abaca carried the name of manila hemp, because the Philippine capital was the principal port for fiber shipments. This nineteenth-century method of naming commodities has been superseded by the use of scientific or indigenous names.

28. Manila resembles the banana plant, but its fruit is not edible (nor are the banana's fibers useful); see Owen, *Prosperity without Progress*, 46–47, quotation on 46. Morison states that manila cost 18 percent more than tarred hemp, but was worth it because it lasted 25 percent longer. Conservative British shipowners, however, doggedly remained faithful to Russian hemp (Morison, *The Ropemakers of Plymouth*, 34). For a discussion of manila's tensile strength, see Dewey, *Fiber Production*, 53–54.

29. Apparently, botanists in the first half of the nineteenth century had mistakenly identified the gray henequen plant as *Agave rigida*; see, e.g., Dodge, *Descriptive Catalogue*, 48–50. Lemaire described the plant in 1865 as *fourcroydes*. See Plymouth Cordage Company papers (hereafter cited as PCC), Baker Library, Harvard University, Topical Files, File 1, Draw 1, Letter, Dewey, Chief of Fibres Investigation, Department of Agriculture, to E. D. Ver Planck, 8 August 1912. A 1766 report to the crown noted that the fiber was used throughout the peninsula for hammocks, mosquito nets, bagging, and rope. Modest amounts of sacks and bags found their way onto Spanish ships. On the early development of the henequen industry, see Howard Cline, "The Henequen Episode in Yucatán," *Inter-American Economic Affairs* 2:2 (1948): 30–51, esp. 31–33.

30. Fiber buyers throughout the boom mistakenly identified it as sisal, naming it after the port the fiber was initially shipped from, located on the Gulf

of Mexico. *Agave sisalana*, or *yaxci*, the true sisal, was described by the North American consul at Campeche, Henry Perrine, in 1837, and, as we shall see, found its way to East Africa and would become a major competitor to henequen after World War I. In fact eight different varieties of henequen—all known locally by their Maya names—had been identified in the peninsula, but only two were grown commercially—*sacci* and *yaxcí. Saccí* was known as *henequén blanco* and was cultivated for export, while, *yaxcí*, or *henequén verde*, was used for hammocks. See Remmers, "Henequen, the Caste War," 431–433. Quotation from Owen, *Prosperity without Progress*, 49.

31. Fernando Benítez, *Kí: El drama de un pueblo y de una planta* (Mexico City: Fondo de Cultura Económica, 1965), 74.

32. International Harvester Company Archives (hereafter cited as IHCA) File #2395, "Manila Hemp and the Export Duty."

33. The wire grain binder was invented in 1873. See *The Story of Twine in Agriculture* (Chicago: International Harvester Company, n.d.), and *Binder Twine Industry* (Chicago: International Harvester Company, 1912).

34. Morton Rothstein, "America in the International Rivalry for the British Wheat Market, 1860–1914," in Harry N. Scheiber, ed., *U.S. Economic History: Selected Readings* (New York: Knopf, 1964), 290–308, esp. 291. Quotation from Owen, *Prosperity without Progress*, 48.

35. Kentucky hemp and jute did not prove up to the task. They either snapped under the fifty-pound pressure exerted by the twine knotters or they jammed the device. At first, twine binders used only manila twine, but after some technical adjustments, cordage factories offered henequen (called sisal), manila, and a blend for sale. Quotation from IHCA, #2395, "Manila Hemp and the Export Duty." It is interesting that efforts by the Department of Agriculture to rekindle interest in hemp as a domestic substitute for henequen proved unsuccessful. See Charles Richards Dodge, *A Report on Flax, Hemp, Ramie, and Jute with Considerations upon Flax and Hemp Culture in Europe*, 2nd ed. (Washington, D.C.: U.S. Government Printing Office, 1892).

36. Unless otherwise noted, this section draws on Owen, *Prosperity without Progress*, and Allen Wells, *Yucatán's Gilded Age: Haciendas, Henequen and International Harvester, 1860–1915* (Albuquerque: University of New Mexico Press, 1985).

37. On location theory and the staples paradigm, see Douglass C. North, "Location Theory and Regional Economic Development," *Journal of Political Economy* 63:3 (1955): 243–258; and Melville H. Watkins, "A Staple Theory of Economic Growth," *Canadian Journal of Economics and Political Science* 29 (May 1963): 141–158. Some find the theory's dualistic model of a dynamic export-led sector and a traditional subsistence sector too static and reductionist. For a thoughtful discussion of the model's place in the literature, see Stanley Engarmen, "Douglass C. North's *The Economic Growth of the United States, 1790–1860* Revisited," *Social Science History* 1:2 (1977): 248–257; and Richard Caves, "Export-Led Growth and the New Economic History," in Jagdish Bhagwati et al., eds., *Trade, Balance of Payments and Growth* (Amsterdam: North-Holland, 1971), 403–442. See also W. Arthur Lewis, *Growth and Fluctuations, 1870–1913* (London: Allen and Unwin, 1978).

38. See Albert Hirschman, "A Generalized Linkage Approach to Develop-

ment, with Special Reference to Staples," in Hirschman, *Essays in Trespassing: Economics to Politics and Beyond* (Cambridge: Cambridge University Press, 1981), 59–97.

39. Kabikolan encompasses the present-day provinces of Camarines Norte, Camarines Sur, Albay, Cantanduanes, and Sorsogon.

40. Colonial rule of the Philippines, of course, lasted much longer than colonial rule of Yucatán; it was given an extended lease on life by U.S. occupation in 1898.

41. Carolyn Merchant, *Ecological Revolutions: Nature, Gender, and Science in New England* (Chapel Hill: University of North Carolina Press, 1989), 260.

42. Diego de Landa, *Relación de las cosas de Yucatán,* Charles P. Bowditch, trans., Alfred M. Tozzer, ed., *Papers of the Peabody Museum of Archeology and Ethnology,* vol. 18 (1941), 186.

43. Some of the more helpful works on Yucatán's environment include Eugene M. Wilson, "Physical Geography of the Yucatán Peninsula," in Edward H. Moseley and Edward D. Terry, eds., *Yucatán: A World Apart* (Tuscaloosa: University of Alabama Press, 1980), 5–40; George C. Shattuck, *The Peninsula of Yucatán: Medical, Biological, Meteorological and Sociological Studies* (Washington, D.C.: Carnegie Institution, 1933); and Cyrus L. Lundell, "Preliminary Sketch of the Phytogeography of the Yucatán Peninsula," in *Contributions in American Archeology* 2:12 (October 1934): 255–321. Robert W. Patch contends that it takes twenty years for some of the soils to regain fertility; Remmers claims ten years to regenerate. See Patch, "A Colonial Regime: Maya and Spaniard in Yucatán," Ph.D. diss., Princeton University (1979), 38; and Remmers, "Henequen," 74.

44. During the first half of the nineteenth century, the southeastern corridor flourished, but the apocalyptic Caste War, which erupted in 1847 and continued on and off for a half century, devastated the subregion. See Cline, "The 'Aurora Yucateca' and the Spirit of Enterprise in Yucatán: 1821–1847," *Hispanic American Historical Review* 27:1 (1947): 30–60; and Remmers, "Henequen," esp. Part One.

45. Owen, *Prosperity without Progress,* 12.

46. Remmers, "Henequen," 436.

47. Owen, *Prosperity without Progress,* 72.

48. See Owen, "Subsistence in the Slump: Agricultural Adjustment in the Provincial Philippines," in Ian Brown, ed., *The Economies of Africa and Asia in the Inter-War Depression* (London and New York: Routledge, 1989), 95–114.

49. Hirschman, "A Generalized Linkage Approach," 82.

50. For an explication of Yucatán's agrarian transformation during the boom, see Allen Wells, "From Hacienda to Plantation: The Transformation of Santo Domingo Xcuyum," in Jeffery T. Brannon and Gilbert M. Joseph, eds., *Land, Labor, and Capital in Modern Yucatán: Essays in Regional History and Political Economy* (Tuscaloosa: University of Alabama Press, 1991), 112–142.

51. For a more nuanced discussion of labor relations in the henequen zone, see Gilbert M. Joseph and Allen Wells, "El monocultivo henequenero y sus

contradicciones: Estructura de dominación y formas de resistencia en las haciendas yucatecas a fines del Porfiriato," *Siglo XIX* 3:6 (1988): 215–277. The discussion of idioms of power draws heavily on Orlando Patterson, *Slavery and Social Death: A Comparative Study* (Cambridge, Mass.: Harvard University Press, 1982), chap. 1.

52. For further analysis of gender in the Yucatecan countryside during the fiber boom, see Allen Wells and Gilbert M. Joseph, *Summer of Discontent, Seasons of Upheaval: Elite Politics and Rural Insurgency in Yucatán, 1876–1915* (Stanford, Calif.: Stanford University Press, 1996), chap. 6; Piedad Peniche Rivero, "Gender, Bridewealth, and Marriage: Social Reproduction of Peons on Henquen Haciendas in Yucatán, 1870–1901," in Heather Fowler-Salamini and Mary Kay Vaughan, eds., *Women of the Mexican Countryside, 1850–1990: Creating Spaces, Shaping Transitions* (Tucson: University of Arizona Press, 1994), 74–89; and Christopher Gill, "Campesino Patriarchy in the Times of Slavery: The Henequen Plantation Society of Yucatán, 1860–1915," Master's thesis, University of Texas–Austin (1991).

53. Owen, *Prosperity without Progress*, 84.

54. On the Caste War, see Nelson Reed, *The Caste War of Yucatán* (Stanford, Calif.: Stanford University Press, 1964).

55. C. H. Forbes-Lindsay, *The Philippines: Under Spanish and American Rule* (Philadelphia, Pa.: John C. Winston, 1906), 292.

56. Owen, *Prosperity without Progress*, 89.

57. Ibid., 91.

58. John Foreman, *The Philippine Islands: A Political, Geographical, Ethnographical, Social and Commercial History of the Philippine Archipelago*, 2nd ed. (New York: Scribner, 1899), 335.

59. Owen, "Americans in the Abaca Trade," 368, n25.

60. From Harry A. Armstrong, "The Manila Fibre Industry," *Cordage Trade Journal* 19 (5 October 1899): 100, cited in Owen, *Prosperity without Progress*, 78.

61. See Renán Irigoyen, "La revolución agrícola-industrial henequenera del siglo XIX," in idem, ed., *Ensayos henequeneros* (Mérida: Ediciones de Cordemex, 1975), 114–128.

62. See Allen Wells, "All in the Family: Railroads and Henequen Monoculture in Porfirian Yucatán," *Hispanic American Historical Review* 72:2 (1992): 159–209.

63. Owen, *Prosperity without Progress*, p. 94.

64. Owen, "Americans in the Abaca Trade." Efforts to reduce competition were the norm in North American business during the Gilded Age. Cf. Gabriel Kolko, *Railroads and Regulation, 1877–1916* (Princeton, N.J.: Princeton University Press, 1965).

65. This section draws on Gilbert M. Joseph and Allen Wells, "Corporate Control of a Monocrop Economy: International Harvester and Yucatán's Henequen Industry during the Porfiriato," *Latin American Research Review* 17:1 (1982): 69–99.

66. On pools and associations, see Arthur S. Dewing, *A History of the National Cordage Company* (Cambridge, Mass.: Harvard University Press, 1913); and Morison, *The Ropemakers of Plymouth*, 71ff.

67. See Dewing, *A History of the National Cordage Company*.

68. This section draws on Wells and Joseph, *Summer of Discontent*.

69. Primary producers, whether they were Yucatecan henequen growers or North American wheat farmers, looked accusingly at those intermediaries and agencies who controlled their access to consumers. In the United States, for instance, wheat growers railed against local grain dealers, terminal elevator owners, grain speculators, and railroads during the last decades of the twentieth century. See Rothstein, "America in the International Rivalry."

70. See Iliffe, *A Modern History of Tanganyika*.

71. Jeffery Brannon and Eric N. Baklanoff, *Agrarian Reform and Public Enterprise in Mexico: The Political Economy of Yucatán's Henequen Industry* (Tuscaloosa: University of Alabama Press, 1987), 42–43, 87–88, 103.

4. Oil

Jonathan C. Brown
and
Peter S. Linder

Two of the world's largest oil companies, Standard Oil of New Jersey and the Royal Dutch–Shell, participated in the Second Conquest by expanding their operations from the North American and Asian economies into Latin America. The questions are how and why and what were the consequences for Latin America? One long-standing view holds that, in the early twentieth century, the modern world had become a battleground in Royal Dutch–Shell's and Standard Oil's war for control of petroleum resources. Each capitalist organization, so the argument went, attempted to monopolize the world's oil resources—not to benefit the host countries, but to be able eventually to strangle the world's consumers with high, monopoly prices. This view had a particular appeal to twentieth-century Latin American intellectuals and politicians; it justified the regulation of foreign interests and the state's eventual nationalization of oil resources.[1] However appealing the viewpoint, it distorts the evidence.

The key to understanding the motivations of the big international oil companies lies in an analysis of how, from 1859 to 1920, the U.S. and world petroleum industry developed from its base in the United States. In a world in which the oil business was booming, development of new competition actually eroded the market dominance of great companies like Standard Oil, which had dominated oil sales in Latin America since the 1880s. Independent companies' opening up of Latin American production threatened, through the process of import-substitution, to eliminate Standard Oil's monopoly. British entrepreneurs began developing the oil fields of Peru's northern coast in the 1890s. In the lucrative market of Argentina, a government drilling crew discovered oil in 1907. Finally, the independent oil producers E. L. Doheny and Sir Weetman Pearson brought in giant oil fields in Mexico in 1910. Latin American production, if not met by Jersey Standard and Royal Dutch–Shell, might have undermined the existing market shares of these refining and sales companies.

Expansion into Latin America was more a question of survival than of domination. The biggest companies had to expand into foreign production or be excluded and absorbed by more aggressive competitors. As Edith Penrose has pointed out, the oil companies found a degree of economic security in vertical integration, that is, in controlling all aspects of the business from production, to transportation, to refining, to marketing, and to sales. Vertical integration assured outlets for crude, and for a steadier and efficient planning of output over time. It made possible more efficient operation of expensive refineries as a result of a secure and managed flow of crude oil. As much as possible, vertical integration also cushioned the disruptive price fluctuations that often raised costs to producers and consumers.[2] For these reasons, neither of the two biggest international oil concerns, Standard Oil of New Jersey and Royal Dutch–Shell, could afford to ignore Latin America. They had to participate in oil production there or be diminished by it.

Nonetheless, the perception was always greater than the reality, and host governments worked assiduously and effectively to undermine the positions of some of the world's most powerful business organizations. The Second Conquest by no means overwhelmed an unprepared polity. Curbing the power of the foreign oil companies came to be one of the few public policies that the elites, the rising middle class, and the working class could agree on.

Foreign oil companies met especially fierce opposition from militant labor unions, which at times worked hand in glove with government officials to secure better working conditions and higher pay. The struggle that ensued between management and labor had significant repercussions for the oil industry and the state throughout the first three decades of the twentieth century. In reality, management, labor, the state, and society were all transformed and reshaped by this process.

Modernization cut both ways; if it brought benefits, it also exacerbated old problems and contributed new ones. Just as the oil industry helped alter the social and political landscape throughout the hemisphere, Latin American society also reshaped capitalism and the manner in which oil companies operated in the region. The second half of this chapter will assess the social impact of the oil industry.

Before we analyze the growth of the oil industry in Latin America, it will be useful to sketch in broad strokes how the oil market evolved from its origins in the United States in the second half of the nineteenth century.

The U.S. Oil Industry and Exports

The modern petroleum industry spread to international markets and production from its base in the United States. In 1859, at Titusville,

Pennsylvania, Col. Edwin Drake discovered that oil, much like water, could be drilled for. Drake's discovery revolutionized American industry. Candles and whale oil had been the primary illuminants of the mid-nineteenth century; wood and coal, the principal sources of fuel. The Drake well was hardly a gusher (25 barrels per day, b/d), but it did prove that oil could be produced in commercial quantities.[3] It was but a matter of time before petroleum illuminants replaced candles and whale oils, first in U.S. markets then in markets elsewhere in the world. Within a half century, petroleum would serve many additional functions, especially as fuel, and be produced in many locations throughout the United States—and Latin America.

Drake's discovery set off an immediate frenzy of oil drilling in western Pennsylvania that soon spread throughout the nation. Following the Civil War, the oil boom spilled over into Ohio and West Virginia. Before the end of the nineteenth century, the search for productive oil fields extended oil production into Indiana, Illinois, Iowa, Kansas, and California. Shortly after the beginning of the twentieth century, oil had also been discovered in Texas, Oklahoma, and Louisiana. The United States became the leading producer of petroleum as well as the major exporter to world markets. Latin America formed an important market for U.S. oil exports.

The Standard Oil Company served as the essential link between this U.S. industrial expansion and Latin America. For a while at least, Standard's rise was closely associated with that of John D. Rockefeller. In 1865 he became a partner in a Cleveland oil refinery. Rockefeller then created the Standard Oil Company (Ohio) in order to combine several specialty oil companies into a multimillion-dollar concern.

Standard next worked to secure a monopoly on oil transport to the eastern seaboard via rail and pipeline. In 1882 Rockefeller's associates organized the first vertically integrated petroleum trust in the nation. The Standard Oil Trust created a business structure in which subsidiary companies carried out different economic functions. As Alfred Chandler writes, the consolidation of committees and departments at Standard's headquarters in New York City "was a natural and rational way to organize a giant integrated consolidation of many small companies." Standard's East Coast refineries soon handled about 90 percent of U.S. petroleum exports.[4] Standard accomplished its expansion into and domination of oil markets in the American Southwest and in Mexico through its affiliate, the Waters-Pierce Oil Company of Saint Louis. It penetrated into South America through another subsidiary company, the West Indian Oil Company (WICO).

The task of developing the markets for petroleum products in the Caribbean and South America fell to WICO. From its refineries at Baltimore, Philadelphia, and Bayonne, Standard Oil exported petroleum products to Latin America as early as the 1860s. Merchant houses in Havana, Veracruz, Rio de Janeiro, and Buenos Aires handled these consignments—mainly kerosene for oil lamps. By the 1880s, however, Standard had established small refineries in Cuba and Puerto Rico to process imported American crude oil into kerosene and later into fuel oil for the sugar mills. Standard's formal marketing subsidiary, the West Indian Oil Company, formed in 1902, pushed U.S. petroleum exports into other parts of Latin America, excluding Mexico. WICO utilized wholesale outlets consisting of established mercantile houses such as W. R. Grace & Co. in Peru. Soon the Standard Oil marketing subsidiary built its own bulk storage branches in San Juan, Managua, Panama City, Caracas, Guayaquil, and Valparaíso. Refineries also went in at Montevideo and Buenos Aires, the latter of which became WICO's most profitable market.[5] By the end of the First World War, the sale of fuel oil for ships and railways had exceeded Standard Oil's sale of kerosene in Latin America.

The WICO agencies, until 1918, were almost exclusively wholesaling concerns. They were generally acquired by buying out commission agencies, the former owner frequently becoming a jobber.[6] WICO sold to large industrial users and serviced large accounts, such as shipping lines and the United States Navy. The native or national merchants to whom WICO sold reached consumers even in remote interior markets.

Kerosene was the main product in the earlier years and continued to be important as an illuminant and as household fuel. WICO sold lamps and stoves in the towns and cities before electricity and gas were developed for such purposes. Lubricants and fuel oils became increasingly in demand for shipping, railroads, and manufacturing, a development that was speeded up during World War I by the practical elimination of British coal from the South American market. Argentina turned to wood and oil when British coal supplies fell off.

While we have no record of actual sales made by the various WICO stations and agencies, accounts receivable at Standard Oil headquarters at the end of each year afford some indication of the relative importance of the various stations. Buenos Aires was by far the most important market from 1912 to 1918; before the end of this period, WICO had a separate lubricating department doing a large business. From 1912 to 1917, profits on WICO's sales to South America increased from $303,428 to $3,569,628, compared with profits from the Caribbean area of $138,885 in 1912 and $317,881 in 1918.[7] South America and the Caribbean were profitable markets for Standard Oil exports, especially during the war years.

Standard exported to Mexico through a second subsidiary, the Waters-Pierce Oil Company, whose business there was actually an extension of its U.S. marketing. In 1878 Henry Clay Pierce sold the majority share of his small Saint Louis distributing company to Standard Oil in order to get capital for expansion. Standard took a 60 percent controlling share of the stock, and Pierce the remaining 40 percent.[8] Waters-Pierce marketed only oil products produced and refined by other Standard Oil subsidiaries and affiliates. In turn, Waters-Pierce expanded as Standard's exclusive agent in the states of Texas, Arkansas, Oklahoma, parts of the states of Missouri and Louisiana, and Mexico. It did not own a single oil well or refinery in the United States. This relationship to Standard Oil made Waters-Pierce a powerful and prosperous company. But the Waters-Pierce company was also vulnerable, because it was not vertically integrated.

Its experience in Texas bears examination, for Waters-Pierce's vulnerability there presaged its later demise as a monopoly firm in Mexico. Before the nineteenth century was out, Waters-Pierce had expanded its sales and competed with a tenacity that gained Henry Clay Pierce and Standard Oil some enemies in Texas. In 1889 and 1895, the state government passed antitrust laws requiring state licensing of all firms that engaged in interstate business. State statutes outlawed any business combination that fixed prices or restricted competition.

Henry Clay Pierce could be an independent—and vicious—competitor. "Stringent methods were usually followed to keep out competition," reported a long-time Waters-Pierce employee, "and wherever a small concern endeavored to invade the territory occupied by the Pierce interests prices were lowered until the smaller concern was driven out of business." In a widely publicized trial, the jury in Austin's district court convicted Waters-Pierce for acting as a "trust" to fix prices, restrain competition, and manipulate prices. Waters-Pierce in 1898 lost its license to operate in Texas.[9] The Texas case represented the continuing efforts of government bodies in the United States to regulate the volatile competition in the petroleum industry and to prevent consumers from getting fleeced—precedents that some Latin American governments would later follow.

Henry Clay Pierce soon recovered his lucrative market, however, by colluding with Standard Oil to reorganize Waters-Pierce. As he later told a Missouri court, he wanted it to appear that he was managing and controlling the company "absolutely free from the dictation and direction of the Standard Oil Company."[10] The stock strategy—and a timely loan to a Texas politician—enabled Pierce to obtain a new Texas license.

In any case, the second license did not restore Waters-Pierce to its monopoly position in Texas for long. Discovery of the Spindletop oil field in 1901, ushered in with Anthony J. Lucas's 100,000 b/d gusher, abruptly transformed the state's petroleum market. Large new consor-

tiums like the Gulf Company and The Texas Company, which combined production, refining, and sales, came to dwarf Waters-Pierce. Just
a few acres at Spindletop in 1902 produced about 20 percent of the
nation's petroleum, and soon the boom spread to other regions of Texas
and to Louisiana and Oklahoma. In 1902 Texas produced more that 18.5
million barrels of oil per year. As other companies expanded refining
capacities along the Texas Gulf Coast from 700 b/d in 1902 to 200,000
b/d in 1905, Waters-Pierce was left out.[11] Its agreement with the Standard
Oil parent company had prevented it from participating in the new oil
boom as a producer and refiner. It soon lost its lucrative Texas market.
Its lack of vertical integration condemned Waters-Pierce to repeat the
same cycle of power and vulnerability in Mexico.

It is unclear exactly when Waters-Pierce began exporting, but American petroleum products had found a small market in Mexico relatively
early. It is certain that Pierce established a permanent and specialized
sales force in Mexico soon after Standard Oil purchased the company. In
1887 Waters-Pierce had three salaried agents, a traveling salesman,
offices in Mexico City and Monterrey, and a small refining operation in
Mexico. Here Pierce managed the business differently from his U.S.
markets. Assisted by Standard Oil, Waters-Pierce built and operated oil
refineries. Beginning in October 1886, when the company completed its
refinery in Mexico City, Waters-Pierce became the monopoly oil company of Mexico for many years. The Tampico plant had a refining
capacity of 450 b/d; Veracruz, 250 b/d; and Mexico City and Monterrey,
100 b/d each.[12] Nowhere else but in Mexico did Waters-Pierce do
anything but sell the refined products of other Standard affiliates.

In Mexico, the refineries processed crude obtained from Standard Oil–
affiliated terminals on the Mid-Atlantic coast. As Pierce himself explained, "we shipped nearly everything that went into the upkeep of
refineries in Mexico from New York, and the tin for the manufacture of
cases went from there and iron for tanks, in fact everything that entered
into the manufacture of oil down there was shipped from New York."
Waters-Pierce exports to Mexico accounted for 60 percent of all Standard's
exports of crude to Latin America and 20 percent of the conglomerate's
total crude exports.[13] His monopoly permitted Pierce to charge higher
prices in Mexico than in its U.S. sales area, where it competed with non–
Standard Oil marketing companies. Its connection to the Standard Oil
Company accounted for the success of Waters-Pierce—and its ultimate
failure, as we will see.

Competitors in South America and Mexico

No doubt, Standard Oil would have been content to continue profiting
by exporting U.S. petroleum products to South America and Mexico.

The company was, in fact, the monopoly exporter of U.S. oil products to Latin America. The problem was that Latin America paid premium prices for North American kerosene, plus the expensive freight and consignment charges. As Latin American economies began to grow in the fourth quarter of the nineteenth century, they created markets for domestically produced, lower-priced illuminants and fuel oils. But Standard Oil was not the pioneer in opening up Latin American production. That role was left to North American and British independent entrepreneurs who engaged in foreign oil production as an extension of their U.S. or of their other foreign business activities, a process described by Mira Wilkins as the "spillover effect."[14]

The British oil pioneers were quite successful on the west coast of South America. American oilmen could not supply the growing mining and transportation facilities before California oil production came on line in the 1890s and before the Panama Canal was completed in 1915. Englishmen opened up Latin America's first oil production in Peru. Thus, they encroached on Standard Oil's import sales monopoly. The British mercantile house of Balfour & Williamson, which had trading interests in Lima, formed a petroleum company to exploit the tar pits on the La Brea y Pariñas desert estate, on the north coast. The Peruvian owners had drilled a well there in 1869, and in the 1870s, several wells went in at nearby Negritos and Talara. Development ceased and the wells sanded up during the War of the Pacific against Chile from 1879 to 1883. Following the war, the Peruvian owner sold the estate to a Scottish engineer, H. W. C. Tweddle, whose father had worked in the Baku oil fields in Russia. He persuaded a London merchant, William Keswick of Balfour, Williamson & Co., to finance a test drilling. The testing having proved successful, Keswick purchased a half-interest in the estate for a consortium of Balfour Williamson and other merchants.[15] Thus was the London & Pacific Petroleum Company, Ltd., organized in 1889.

Facing capital shortages, the British oil entrepreneurs found it convenient to cooperate with the Americans. The London & Pacific had succeeded in producing oil, but the costs of stills, machine shops, living quarters, an ocean water–condensing plant, a wharf, and a lighthouse increased the operating expenses.

Although the London & Pacific's production had increased greatly, to more than 3,000 b/d, it could not expand its production fast enough to supply growing markets. In 1911 Balfour-Williamson, along with the British owners of the Lobitos oil fields, combined with Standard Oil to form the West Coast Oil Fuel Company, Ltd. The company was to carry on trade in petroleum between Peru and California. Both regions were complementary oil producers. California's production was heavier, suitable for the fuel oil demanded by Peruvian and Chilean railways and mining companies. Peru's crude, on the other hand, was light, perfect for supplying the kerosene markets of the West Coast of the United States. Although they shared marketing assets with Standard Oil, the British oilmen nonetheless retained control of Peru's production.

Somewhat the same kind of import substitution also was taking shape in another large national market, Argentina. In the Argentinean case, however, government well drillers found oil deposits before any private firms did. The 1907 discovery of an oil field near Comodoro Rivadavia signaled a scramble for oil leases and concessions on the part of Argentinean and British companies. The government soon established a national reserve at Comodoro Rivadavia but allowed native speculators and foreign companies alike to take out claims to other land in the national territories of the South. Provincial governments likewise offered oil concessions to private entrepreneurs. By 1916 the government had established a refinery in Patagonia and was producing nearly 130,000 cubic meters of crude per year. Although private companies were adding another 8,000 cubic meters, Argentina's vibrant economy at the time consumed more petroleum than both private and public interests could produce domestically.[16] Nonetheless, Standard Oil's growing import sales here were becoming increasingly insecure.

Competition in Mexico, in the meantime, came from two unlikely sources—an American mining prospector and a British engineer. During the 1880s, at the time that Rockefeller was forming the Standard Oil Trust and Pierce was developing the Mexican market, Edward L. Doheny was a mining prospector in New Mexico. After two decades of prospecting, Doheny and his partner, Charles Canfield, arrived in California in 1892 with scarcely $1,000 between them. But they did think to drill for oil near the La Brea tar pits in West Los Angeles. Doheny and Canfield began the Los Angeles oil strike with a 7 b/d, hand-bailed well. They were novice oilmen who sank their first well as a miner sinks a shaft— with picks and shovels. Within five years, experienced well drillers from Pennsylvania moved to Los Angeles, opening up some three hundred wells within a 160-acre area. Well riggings stood "as thick as the holes in a pepper box" among residential homes in the West Lake Park suburb of Los Angeles. To compete with rival oilmen attracted to California, Doheny learned the technology and hired experienced drillers. Soon he had expanded production into the Fullerton, Bakersfield, and Kern River (California) oil fields.[17]

Along with a number of other independent producers who resented the refiners' low prices—for which the producers' overproduction was responsible—Doheny organized the Producers Oil Company and began to build his own marketing apparatus. The new oilman refused to depend entirely on selling his production to existing marketing companies like Union Oil and the growing Standard Oil Company of California. Pressed for markets, Doheny approached the California railway companies. The Southern Pacific Railroad ran its locomotives on coal and wood obtained in the East and the Northwest. The California crude was heavy, suitable especially as fuel oil. He introduced a locomotive fuel system that had been burning petroleum in Peru. That Doheny had known of the Peruvian engine was not unusual, since California at the time was importing light oil products from Peru. He then approached other western railroad men, eventually meeting A. A. Robinson, vice-president of the Atchison, Topeka & Santa Fe Railroad. Coal was more expensive, created much waste, and was expensive to ship. "The Santa Fe does not care a snap about the coal people," Doheny's manager wrote, "but if the oil is cheaper there than coal, they will use it."[18] Increased production and Doheny's contacts among bulk purchasers enabled him to withstand the competition of Standard of California.

His California oil business led Edward L. Doheny directly into Mexico. The Santa Fe Railroad's A. A. Robinson was also builder and vice-president of the Mexican Central Railroad, and he informed Doheny that his line running between San Luis Potosí and Tampico had been depending upon imported Alabama coal of "indifferent quality." Development of oil production in Mexico would also provide revenues for his rail line. Therefore, Robinson asked Doheny to investigate rumors of bubbling tar pits along the railroad's right-of-way. By 1901 Doheny's men opened Mexico's first oil field—at El Ébano. In 1905 Doheny negotiated a fifteen-year contract to sell oil to the Mexican Central Railroad. Railroad engineers found that oil burned cleaner and with less residue than coal; ton per ton, oil saved railway managers 3.02 pesos ($1.50) over coal. In 1910 Doheny's drillers brought in a great well at Casiano, followed by another at Cerro Azul in 1916. He next formed the Huasteca Petroleum Company of Mexico.[19] While Doheny was developing Mexico's markets for fuel oil, a British oil producer was preparing to undermine Waters-Pierce's kerosene sales monopoly.

Sir Weetman Pearson's entry into the Mexican oil business also commenced in 1901, within weeks of the fabulous oil strike at Spindletop, Texas. He learned that prospectors had been attracted to Spindletop by the very same surface indications that his men were finding along the right-of-way of the Tehuantepec Railway—namely, pools of oil. They began immediately to buy and lease land on the Isthmus and in Tabasco. His general manager in Mexico hired several Waters-Pierce executives and engaged drillers who had worked for Doheny at El Ébano. Early exploration on the Isthmus did not prove to be promising, yet expectations remained high.[20] Doheny had already proved that Mexico had oil, and those Pearson wells that did produce on the Isthmus yielded a high grade of crude suitable for fuel oil, lubricants, illuminants, and naphtha.

In 1906 he built a refinery at Minatitlán that would soon turn out domestically produced oil products cheaper than Waters-Pierce's imported products.

The Great Mexican Oil War commenced in 1908. Pearson began buying railroad tank cars and distribution depots in ten of Mexico's largest cities. He offered petroleum products at a 20 percent discount. In April 1909, he formed the Compañía Mexicana de Petróleo "El Águila," S.A. The British firm remained the primary stockholder. On the board of directors, however, sat many prominent members of the Mexican "governing class," including Pres. Porfirio Díaz's son.[21] Registration of the company in Mexico was designed to encourage the assistance of Mexican politicians in Pearson's market struggle with Waters-Pierce, a "foreign" firm. After all, Mexican officials had been seeking for years to have foreign companies incorporate under Mexican laws.

The Great Oil War in Mexico, because it lowered prices, tended simultaneously to widen the consumption of petroleum products throughout the country. El Águila agents noted that nationwide sales of illuminating oil and naphtha had risen from nine million gallons per month in 1906 to twelve million gallons in 1909. In fact, Pierce's imports and volume sales had not decreased. The oil war only diminished the Waters-Pierce sales receipts and eroded Pierce's market domination.[22]

The final decline of the Pierce monopoly came with Pearson's giant oil discovery. In 1910 American geologists and drillers brought in one of the world's greatest wells at Potrero del Llano. Potrero No. 4 produced at the rate of 30,000 b/d.[23] The Mexican oil boom was on. From this point on, Pearson and Doheny converted Mexico from an oil importer to an oil exporter. Waters-Pierce lost its monopoly market in Mexico just as, a decade before, it had succumbed to the Texas oil boom.

Pearson's and Doheny's flush production in Mexico ultimately led them also to create their own multinational business enterprises. While it is true that these independent producers had to sell much of their production to Standard Oil and other large U.S. companies, they also sought the security of vertical integration. Therefore, both built refineries and developed marketing. El Águila opened up an extensive marketing network throughout England. On the east coast of South America, Pearson's company built fuel oil depots in Brazil and Argentina. El Águila already controlled some two-thirds of Mexico's domestic market for petroleum products. Doheny's organization established seven distribution depots on the eastern seaboard from Portland, Maine, to Galveston, Texas. It built a 25,000 b/d refinery in Louisiana. Abroad, the new Doheny interests established additional depots in the Panama Canal Zone, Brazil, Uruguay, and Argentina. Bunker and fuel oil continued to be the principal product sold at these points. The opening of the Panama

Canal in 1915 permitted Doheny to fill contracts with Chilean mining companies for delivery of Mexican fuel oil. As the third decade of the twentieth century began, Huasteca and El Águila were able to sell some 30 million barrels of oil per year.[24] Standard Oil's business in Latin America faced near elimination by the production pioneering of independent oilmen. Moreover, another old competitor was beginning to invest in Latin American production.

Royal Dutch–Shell and Standard Move into Production

The Standard Oil Company of New Jersey and Royal Dutch–Shell felt compelled to respond to the success of new entrants into the world petroleum industry like Pearson, Doheny, and Balfour-Williamson. Neither Jersey Standard nor Royal Dutch–Shell wanted to face elimination in any international market. They either expanded into Latin America or lost markets. It was not a question of the big companies shrinking because of competition; they did not. But while they continued to grow, the industry on a global scale grew more rapidly, diversifying and diffusing control of the world's oil supplies.

The Royal Dutch–Shell had its beginning in oil production in the Dutch East Indies (today Indonesia). By the end of the nineteenth century, the Royal Dutch company had built up markets in the Far East supplied by production and refining in Sumatra. In 1907 the Royal Dutch combined with the British Shell Oil Transport to widen its access to markets in Europe, Great Britain, and the British Empire. Royal Dutch–Shell's interest in Latin America came through its imperial connection. As a half-British, half-Dutch company, it felt able to explore the possibility of producing oil amidst the numerous pitch lakes of the British island colony of Trinidad. Prior to World War I, Royal Dutch–Shell also was selling petroleum products in many of the larger markets of Latin America. According to the "straight-line" theory of the president of Royal Dutch–Shell, Sir Henri Deterding, the expanding company needed to find production close to its new markets: "[Royal Dutch–Shell's] business has been built up primarily on the principle that each market must be supplied with products emanating from the fields which are most favorably situated geographically," Sir Henri explained. "In order, however, to maintain our position in the world market it is not sufficient to be satisfied with the advantages already obtained. We must not be outstripped in this struggle to obtain new territory."[25]

Deterding directed his crews from Trinidad to Venezuela. Royal Dutch–Shell acquired options to several huge but quite neglected Venezuelan oil concessions. The Mexican oil boom having just begun, no Americans were interested in developing any more production farther away from the U.S. market than Mexico—at least, not yet. So Royal Dutch–Shell had a free hand in Venezuela for a decade. By 1912 crews of American geologists had selected drilling sites for Royal Dutch–Shell, its first small production coming in 1916 in the Maracaibo Basin. Here the company built a small refinery whose products soon undersold those imported into the country by Jersey Standard's WICO. Royal Dutch–Shell finally brought in a gusher in 1922, and the Venezuelan oil boom was on.[26] By that time, American oil interests such as Doheny and Standard Oil were shifting their focus from Mexico to Venezuela.

Meanwhile, Royal Dutch–Shell was also moving quickly into Mexico. In 1912, the same year that Royal Dutch–Shell sent geologists to Venezuela, it established its first small subsidiary in Mexico. Royal Dutch–Shell saw its Mexican and, to a lesser extent, its future Venezuelan production as a method of getting into the domestic U.S. market. At the time, Royal Dutch–Shell was setting up marketing outlets in California for its Sumatra production; it could use Mexican and Venezuelan oil for markets on the East Coast of the United States. But its Mexican subsidiary remained a small producer. Therefore, Deterding negotiated to purchase the large independent British company of El Águila. In this way, Deterding was acting upon on another of his business maxims: "Pulling together makes strength." That is to say, the large business enterprises succeed not when they engage in cutthroat competition and price wars, but when they combine new enterprises through alliance and partnership.[27]

Just at the moment that Standard Oil was confronted by the aggressive expansion of several competitors in Latin America, it also found its vertical integration under attack at home. In the culmination of a long domestic antitrust suit against the company, the U.S. Supreme Court in 1911 broke up the Standard Oil group of companies and left Standard Oil of New Jersey, the exporting and refining firm, without any U.S. producing assets. It lost its major producing fields, pipelines, and refineries, except for the Bayonne, New Jersey, plant. Nonetheless, Jersey Standard remained the largest oil company in the world and retained most of its foreign marketing apparatus—except for Waters-Pierce, Jersey Standard's link to the Mexican market. The Supreme Court dissolution also removed Henry Clay Pierce from the Standard orbit.

The irony of the dissolution of Standard Oil is that the petroleum industry worldwide had been expanding so rapidly that the Standard Oil group was becoming each year less of a monopoly.[28] Every oil boom, as in Texas and Mexico, created new rival oil companies and reduced Jersey's market shares. Overseas, where it had always been a dominant exporter of U.S. petroleum, Standard Oil faced aggressive competition from the expansion of foreign production. Thus, the second decade of the twentieth century marked a time of rapid transition for the company. Standard Oil, too, had to expand vigorously into foreign production.

"I feel the real source of power in the oil business is control of production, and it does not seem that our company is sufficiently fortified in this respect," wrote Everitt J. Sadler, an influential Standard executive. "Foreign production is almost exclusively in the hands of our competitors." Sadler became a persuasive proponent of overseas production in several Latin American areas. Moreover, the company's foreign marketing expanded appreciably throughout the second decade of the twentieth century. In 1912 Latin American earnings amounted nearly to $1.5 million, 16.7 percent of Jersey Standard's total overseas sales, but by 1918, the total earnings had risen to more than $7.9 million. Now Latin America constituted 43 percent of all Jersey Standard's international sales.[29] Increased foreign sales dictated a more open policy at Jersey Standard concerning production abroad.

An opportunity presented itself when Balfour-Williamson, faced with a shortage of capital for expansion, offered to sell its Peruvian properties. Jersey Standard's agents investigated and determined that the La Brea y Pariñas oil field would produce quite well if professional oilmen were running the operation. "But the experienced men were not in evidence," the Jersey Standard man reported, "hence the delay in obtaining results, hence the fruitless expenditure for capital and labor for so many years, and the disappointments and heartaches which made the sale of the property necessary—and possible." In 1913 the British group sold the London & Pacific to the Imperial Oil, Ltd., Jersey Standard's Canadian affiliate. The British owners found it more agreeable to sell to a Canadian than to an American company.[30]

Standard Oil also did not want to arouse the nationalist sensibilities of the Peruvian government. Jersey Standard formed a new company in Peru in 1913, the International Petroleum Company (IPC), which soon absorbed other properties near La Brea. In fact, the British government did not become aware that the IPC was now controlled by American capital until 1919. Its embassy in Peru had been lending diplomatic support to the IPC since its formation.[31] The new "Canadian" company, the IPC, began to expand production and increase exports substantially.

In Colombia, Jersey Standard was to follow a course of action much like the one it was undertaking in Peru. It was able to buy and improve production on an existing concession. In 1919 Jersey purchased the De Mares concession in the Magdalena River valley at Barrancabermeja. With the property went Tropical Oil, a Pittsburgh-based company that already had sunk three wildcat wells, of which only one produced. Jersey Standard executives decided to purchase Tropical for the Canadian affiliate, Imperial Oil, Ltd., a strategy calculated to avoid antagonizing

Colombian sensitivity to the active role the United States had taken in 1903 to secure Panama's independence.[32]

Development of production at De Mares was the most difficult that Jersey Standard had yet encountered. Located 560 kilometers up the Magdalena River, the concession was covered with dense tropical growth and lacked roads and living accommodations. Tropical's first five years were employed chiefly in building an infrastructure for its subsequent operations. Varied projects were carried out simultaneously: constructing living quarters, utilities, terminal facilities, a railway, and a refinery at Barrancabermeja; opening trails and roads through the jungle; acquiring river transport; surveying the geology of the concession; clearing well sites in the jungle; and drilling exploratory wells. Even farms had to be established nearby to provide cattle, hogs, cassava, and bananas for employees. The refinery meant to serve the domestic Colombian market was completed within a year at a cost of $1 million. By the end of 1926, workers had completed 141 wells, only 13 of which proved to be dry holes. Tropical's first obligation in marketing, however, was to supply Colombia's domestic needs. WICO withdrew from Colombia, and thereafter Tropical sold its own products through local Colombian merchants. Domestic sales rose from 73,543 barrels in 1922 to 987,853 in 1927, in large measure because Tropical's prices undercut those of imported products. Lower-priced Tropical fuel oil soon replaced wood and imported coal in Colombia's river and coastal vessels.[33] The import-substitution process and the conversion of the economy to petroleum occurred simultaneously, followed by the export of Colombian oil.

Almost as a matter of self-defense, Jersey Standard finally relented and purchased a Mexican producing company, but not Huasteca or El Águila, which were too expensive to acquire. Late in 1917, Jersey Standard bought Transcontinental, a British company with American stockholders. For nearly $2.5 million, Jersey Standard acquired a Mexican charter, valuable leases, permits to construct pipelines and storage tanks, import tax exemptions, one producing oil well, and a small refinery.[34]

Immediately, it began to expand production until, in 1920, it was the third-largest producer and exporter of crude oil in the country. World War I, which greatly curtailed British business in Latin America, did not at all inhibit Standard Oil. As a parent company, Jersey Standard had the ability to draw earnings from many subsidiaries and lend large amounts of capital to designated companies. It had a great reservoir of its own investment capital. In December 1912, Jersey Standard's ledgers recorded loans of $110.8 million to affiliates. The war did not much inhibit these internal capital transfers. At a time when the British-owned oil companies were strapped for capital, Standard Oil of New Jersey poured money into Peru, Mexico, and Colombia.[35]

By the third decade of the twentieth century, both Royal Dutch–Shell and Standard Oil were deeply committed to production in Latin America. In the 1920s, Standard Oil also entered Argentina and Venezuela as an important producer. The 1920s represented the zenith of corporate power in South America. "[T]here can be little doubt," writes George Philip, "that the balance of international power favoured the companies in a way that would never again be fully the case."[36] By 1928 both companies dominated Latin American production, though they hardly excluded other private firms nor the newly formed Argentine state oil company (see Table 4.1). The 1930s, however, would belong more to Standard Oil, which expanded its activities appreciably, and also to the nationalist politicians.

Oil Nationalism

Latin American nationalism had been making itself manifest in the 1920s, but the depression of the 1930s promoted even more hostility toward the Second Conquest. While these nations increasingly restricted all foreign companies, they applied their nationalistic strictures more vigorously to Standard Oil and Royal Dutch–Shell. Few Latin American governments felt comfortable with the size and economic power of these giant oil companies. Like Gen. Enrique Mosconi, first director of Argentina's state oil company, most Latin American politi-

Table 4.1. Royal Dutch–Shell and Jersey Standard Production and Refining in Latin America, 1928

Country	Royal Dutch–Shell		Standard Oil New Jersey	
	Production (b/d)	Refining Capacity (b/d)	Production (b/d)	Refining Capacity (b/d)
Mexico	22,000	195,000	8,500	20,000
Venezuela	125,000	5,000	–	–
Curaçao	–	100,000	–	–
Aruba	–	15,000	–	–
Argentina	400	–	800	3,500
Trinidad	1,000	3,000	–	–
Colombia	–	–	55,000	6,500
Peru	–	–	25,000	15,000
Cuba	–	–	–	2,000
Total	148,000	318,000	89,300	47,000

Sources: The Pipe Line (16 May 1928): 137; Ludwell Denny, *We Fight for Oil* (New York: Knopf, 1928), 283.

cians found differences between the two companies. Royal Dutch–Shell was scientific, prudent, and diplomatic; Standard Oil was crude and audacious. Mosconi compared the British-Dutch company to a silk rope and the American concern to a hemp rope: "Both have served to hang us." From Mexico to Argentina, governments in the 1920s began to restrict the operations of both Royal Dutch–Shell and Standard Oil. Some, like Mexico's, passed restrictive legislation; others, like Argentina's, Uruguay's, and, eventually, Chile's, established official state oil companies to compete against foreign capital.[37]

Argentina

Argentina reserved special animus for Jersey Standard, which ultimately prevented Royal Dutch–Shell, too, from developing to its fullest there. The government of Pres. Marcelo T. de Alvear formed the government oil fields into the first Latin American state oil company, the Yacimientos Petrolíferos Fiscales (YPF). Its director, General Mosconi, felt a moral and nationalistic obligation to break the marketing monopoly of the foreign companies. He built YPF refineries and sales outlets, cut the prices of petroleum products, and used political pressure to prevent the private companies from expanding production. Mosconi's nationalistic views applied to all foreign companies. As he stated, "The great trusts are insatiable organizations, difficult to dominate once they have taken possession of land and once they have been accorded facilities and rights." The Argentinean general accused Royal Dutch–Shell and Standard Oil of attempting to control world petroleum production.[38]

These British and American companies suffered from the government-imposed restrictions of the 1920s, although Jersey Standard had the advantage of a larger market share than Royal Dutch–Shell. President Alvear, prompted by Mosconi, in a 1924 decree, converted the Patagonia territory into a huge state oil reserve. That act restricted all oil companies but YPF from expanding their holdings in the proven Patagonia fields. The decree struck Royal Dutch–Shell harder then Jersey Standard, which was actively exploring provincial oil reserves in the Argentine state of Salta. Mosconi engineered a second assault on the international oil companies in 1929. After having expanded YPF's retailing and refining apparatus, he cut prices by 17 percent and established a uniform price throughout the nation. The private companies were forced to follow suit.[39]

Argentina's burgeoning appetite for petroleum production, the result of economic expansion and the proliferation of automobiles and trucks, saved the foreign companies from an all-out nationalist onslaught.

Mosconi's YPF simply could not handle all the demand. Also, the Alvear government favored British oil investments over Standard Oil, a legacy both of the elite's pro-British sentiments and Standard Oil's international reputation. By 1927 thirteen of the original thirty-seven private oil companies that had operated in Argentina since 1907 were still going. The Royal Dutch–Shell company's Diadema Argentina, S.A. was the country's third largest. Diadema equaled but half of the American investment in Standard Oil of Argentina.

Another mainly British interest, the Compañía Ferrocarrilera, also had production here. The railway company actually was the second-largest producer, but it had no marketing at all beyond delivering fuel to its own locomotives. Together, Royal Dutch–Shell and the Ferrocarrilera accounted for nearly 20 percent of Argentinean production in the 1920s. But Standard Oil was moving up fast.

When Royal Dutch–Shell set up its first production operation in 1922 in Comodoro Rivadavia, Standard Oil of Argentina followed suit. The American company purchased Astra, an independent producer (with British shareholders) that had a refinery in the south. Even with the additional production, though, the two companies could not satisfy the nation's growing need for fossil fuels. Royal Dutch–Shell and its Mexican affiliate still imported fuel oil, and Standard's West Indian Oil Company imported gasoline and kerosene. In addition, Standard was the only private company to produce in the lighter crude oils of Salta Province in northeastern Argentina.[40]

The private firms were also constructing new import facilities. Anglo-Mexican Petroleum Company added a tank farm at Bahía Blanca and a distribution depot at Coronel Suárez in the heart of the pampas. Two new river tankers transported Royal Dutch–Shell's gasoline and kerosene, which were refined from Venezuelan crude at Curaçao, to cities on the Uruguay and Paraná Rivers.[41] Argentina's economic expansion in the 1920s was such that the government could not dispense with the foreign companies.

The national price equalization established by the government in 1929 rendered marketing in the interior cities unprofitable; therefore, Royal Dutch–Shell and Jersey left that market to the YPF, a strategy that weakened the national company in its struggle for Buenos Aires. Royal Dutch–Shell's Diadema, however, had been shut out of much of Argentina's growing market for gasoline because it lacked a refinery. In 1929 Diadema finally obtained permission from the Alvear government to build a refinery at Buenos Aires to compete with both YPF and WICO. But the following year, President Yrigoyen rescinded the permit because a bill to nationalize the oil industry was pending before Congress.

The British ambassador intervened. He promised Yrigoyen that Royal Dutch–Shell would provide on-the-job training at its refinery for students of the new Petroleum Institute of the University of Buenos Aires, and Yrigoyen gave in. With its new refinery, Royal Dutch–Shell gained equal footing with Jersey Standard in the Buenos Aires marketplace. It, too, sold kerosene and gasoline refined from its own Argentinean production and from Mexican and Venezuelan crude.[42] While Royal Dutch–Shell's business grew, its market share continued to decline. Argentina's government action was part of the reason.

YPF's production expanded throughout the 1930s in a way that reduced the importance of oil imports. In 1930 Argentina imported more than 58 percent of its petroleum. Within ten years, that figure had dropped to 37 percent. The private companies retained their position in Argentina only by virtue of their role, dwindling though it may have been, in production. The combined production of Royal Dutch–Shell and Jersey Standard doubled during the 1930s, but YPF's growth as producer was nearly as spectacular (see Table 4.2):[43]

Additional problems arose between YPF and the private companies in 1934. Just as YPF was attempting to expand its marketing in Buenos Aires, the private companies lowered retail prices. A nationalist outcry resulted. Critics accused the international trusts of "dumping" in Argentina in order to destroy YPF. In 1936 the government decreed that YPF henceforward would control all oil imports and distribute them as it saw fit.

But Pres. Juan B. Justo did not wish to antagonize the British, whose home market for imported wheat and beef supported Argentina's economic recovery from the depression. In 1937 the government rescinded the oil import decree and concluded a market sharing agreement among YPF, Royal Dutch–Shell, and Jersey Standard that lasted for a decade. In that agreement, the private companies conceded half the Buenos Aires market to YPF.[44]

Royal Dutch–Shell's experience in Argentina—as elsewhere in South

Table 4.2. YPF's Growth, 1925–1940

Year	Total Production (thousands of cubic meters)	YPF %	Private Companies %
1925	1.0	65.6	34.4
1930	1.4	57.9	42.1
1935	2.3	41.5	58.5
1940	3.3	60.5	39.5

Source: See note 43.

America—was paradoxical. It expanded its business, yet fell behind Standard of New Jersey and, like its American competitors, came under increasing restraint by the state.

While these nations became increasingly restrictive and hostile to all foreign oil companies, they applied their nationalistic strictures more to Standard Oil than to any of the British concerns. Whenever Standard Oil sought reserve sources of supply in foreign countries, wrote two business journalists in the mid-1920s, "it [found] the drilling tackle of more and more rival companies planted in the fields and a strange tendency on the part of foreign governments to grant concessions to anyone rather than to the American 'octopus.'" The Americans often had to "sneak into" Latin America and secretly buy established operations. Colombia is one such case. After discovering Jersey Standard's purchase of the Tropical Oil Company based at Barrancabermeja in the Magdalena River valley, the government at Bogotá agreed to the transfer only after imposing a 10 percent production tax and restricting the oil concession to thirty years.[45]

Peru

In Peru the government refused to approve the sale of the La Brea properties to Jersey Standard. The Peruvian state considered the property to be a concession and increased taxes on it in 1915. The IPC claimed that the oil field was private property, to be transferred freely. It refused to pay the new taxes. Dragging on into 1922, the dispute prevented the IPC from fully developing its Peruvian properties.

Both parties agreed to submit the issue to the World Court at the Hague, which handed down a compromise ruling. The government got a tax hike, and the IPC received more property rights to the oil fields than a full-fledged concession would have allowed. Still, Pres. Augusto B. Leguía would not accept the accord until the IPC paid one million dollars to his government. He even opened negotiations with Royal Dutch–Shell and other British firms for concessions on proven oil lands. Under this pressure, Standard paid up.[46] Thereafter, Peru's production and exports of petroleum rose as Mexico's were declining.

Royal Dutch–Shell acquired some claims held by Peruvians in northern Peru in 1924 but eventually withdrew. Some scholars speculate that this was the result of a secret agreement with Jersey Standard.[47] In reality, Royal Dutch–Shell marketed little on the west coast of South America. Expansion into production here would have been irrational, especially in view of Deterding's straight-line policy of developing crude resources close to Royal Dutch–Shell's markets in Europe and on the East Coast of the United States.

Ecuador

British oilmen continued to compete in Latin America, sometimes with the help of the state, but still lost market share to the North Americans. In Ecuador the government kept Standard Oil at bay while countenancing the operation of a small British firm, the Anglo-Ecuadorian Oilfields Ltd. Oddly, the British company sold its crude to Standard, which still dominated the country's marketing system. The Anglo-Ecuadorian Oilfields Ltd. for a long while managed the only production the country was to have in the early twentieth century, at the Santa Elena oil fields, north of Peru's oil districts. In fact, the merchant company of Balfour Williamson, Peru's oil pioneer, managed this property.

This arrangement typified the major weaknesses of non-U.S. oil concerns. Anglo-Ecuadorian's production was quite modest, 3,500 b/d in 1929. It depended on American drillers, and it sold the bulk of its production to Jersey Standard subsidiaries. In 1929 most of Anglo-Ecuadorian's production was going to Imperial, the Canadian subsidiary of Jersey Standard. Even Anglo-Ecuadorian's refinery sold its 400 b/d production to Jersey Standard's West Indian Oil Company. The latter distributed these products throughout the country from its depot in Guayaquil.[48] Like British oil operations in Peru, the Anglo-Ecuadorian depended on superior American marketing organization.

Mexico

Those oil companies belonging to the Standard Oil and Royal Dutch–Shell groups, like all the others, encountered increasing government supervision in Mexico. Politicians who consolidated their control of the state following the Mexican Revolution (1910–1920) sought to extract larger tax revenues from the only industry that had boomed during the fighting. Furthermore, Mexicans believed that the foreigners' domination of the economy had contributed to revolutionary violence. They thought that uncontrolled capitalist development prior to the Revolution had badly disrupted social relationships and caused the popular classes to rebel.

Article 27 of the 1917 Constitution embodied the nationalist program and mandated state ownership of all subsoil wealth. However, the foreign companies operated on preconstitutional contracts. Their oil leases and fee-simple land ownership were based on private property rights to the oil wealth. Foreign oilmen believed that government infringement of these preconstitutional rights was illegal.[49] The stage was set for confrontation.

Part of the animus between the postrevolutionary regime and the oilmen related to the inevitable involvement of foreign businessmen in domestic politics. Since 1914 various military factions had fought over the oil zone. They had attempted to extract taxes from the booming companies—at gunpoint, if necessary. The companies were forced to pay tribute to the caudillo Gen. Manuel Peláez, who was fighting to bring down the constitutionalist government of Venustiano Carranza. The fact that Peláez's brother was a longtime Mexican attorney for El Águila did little to endear the oil companies to President Carranza. So when the oilmen resisted new drilling taxes levied by Carranza in 1918, government officials took this as a token of the companies' political opposition rather than as defense of their rights.[50] Carranza's fall brought them no respite.

The governments of Presidents Álvaro Obregón and Plutarco Elías Calles not only continued Carranza's tax measures but, in fact, increased them. Public officials utilized their new military command over the oil zones (the Peláez rebellion had fizzled when Carranza fell) to prevent the private companies from drilling wells not registered with the government. Foreign oilmen responded by forming a united front, the Association of Producers of Petroleum in Mexico. Funded and directed by American interests in New York City, the association attempted to mobilize public opinion and engage foreign diplomats in protesting the Mexican actions. In 1919 it orchestrated a boycott of well registration. El Águila resigned from the association in order to obtain drilling concessions and to prevent the government from giving drilling rights on El Águila land to competitors.[51] The British oilmen broke the united front.

El Águila's accommodating attitude became more obvious when the American companies, in 1921, boycotted the export of Mexican oil to protest Obregón's taxation of petroleum exports. Led by Standard Oil, the American companies stopped all oil operations for two months, throwing thousands of Mexican workers out of work. Yet, El Águila paid the higher taxes, albeit under protest, and continued to fill its tankers. Ultimately, the American companies relented and entered into their own negotiations with President Obregón. The so-called Big Five—the presidents of Standard Oil, Huasteca (Doheny), Sinclair, The Texas Company, and Gulf—came to Mexico on two occasions to meet Obregón. Now, the British had cause to worry that they would be excluded from government concessions for which they had been largely responsible.[52] The government was practicing the Mexican tradition of dividing the foreign interests.

So it remained throughout the 1920s. Mexico's government increased the restrictions and multiplied the taxes, and companies fought a rearguard action. Finally, in 1929 the American ambassador, Dwight

Morrow, concluded an agreement with Pres. Plutarco Elías Calles. Morrow conceded Mexico's right to tax the industry and to issue drilling concessions; Calles acknowledged the companies' preconstitutional property rights. The oilmen reluctantly recognized the agreement and continued operating into the 1930s. In a way, El Águila's accommodation had forced the American companies to imitate it.

Venezuela

Venezuela remained the real testing ground of British machismo in South American petroleum. Here in the 1920s, Royal Dutch–Shell expanded from its World War I monopoly but was unable to resist North American encroachment. In line with Deterding's straight-line strategy, the Royal Dutch–Shell group sought production close to its markets. The policy had worked in Asia, where Royal Dutch–Shell had a commanding market share. Royal Dutch–Shell even had production in the United States nearly equal to that of Standard Oil. Worldwide, Royal Dutch–Shell had a production capacity of 344,200 b/d in 1927, compared with Jersey Standard's 214,700 b/d.[53] But in Latin America, Jersey Standard had been the pioneer marketer and, in the 1920s, adopted Deterding's own strategy of starting its own production for those growing markets.

Venezuela was the only country in which the government actively favored the American oil firms over the British in the 1920s. Like other Latin American leaders, President Juan Vicente Gómez was adept at playing off British and American interests against each other to gain a measure of control over the industry and press the British companies to develop their concessions to the fullest extent or lose them to their American rivals. He also moved to assume greater central control over oil development. But in this case, Gómez brought pressure on Royal Dutch–Shell because it had been unable to take advantage of its early start to produce the oil boom Venezuelans had been expecting. In 1920 the government instituted legal proceedings against Royal Dutch–Shell's Colón Company concession, charging nonpayment of taxes. Gómez threatened to break up the giant concession and divide it up among several American companies. When no American companies played that game, however, the government renegotiated with Royal Dutch–Shell's manager, William T. S. Doyle.[54] Yet, lawsuits were also brought against other Royal Dutch–Shell concessions.

Gómez was attempting to force Royal Dutch–Shell to choose its drilling sites and turn the rest of these province-sized concessions back to the government for redistribution. As B. S. McBeth states, "The Shell group of companies, which were the only ones in operation, were seen to be lagging behind in production. There was an urgent need to stimulate production."[55]

Repatriation of the original concessions also enlarged the patronage available to Gómez, his family, and entourage. The concessionaires of the new exploration rights were always political insiders, frequently Gómez's sons and sons-in-law, who grew wealthy selling concessions to the oil companies. The government awarded an average of 323 concessions each year between 1922 and 1935. Nevertheless, the companies were acquiring vast exploration territories relatively cheaply, compared with the numerous smaller leases they had been making during the Mexican oil boom of the 1910s.[56]

Gómez could appear almost obsequious. When the oil companies protested the petroleum law of 1918, he invited them to propose a successor. "You know about oil," he is reported to have said. "You write the laws. We are amateurs in this area."[57] Compared with the virulent nationalism of Mexico, Venezuela seemed to offer the oilmen a welcome business environment in which to operate.

In 1922 Royal Dutch–Shell thought the worst was over. E. C. Clarke informed the Foreign Office that General Gómez had just instructed his ministers "that foreigners are not to be interfered with and that consequently the proposed attack on their concessions will be abandoned." But Gómez was inscrutable: government threats to cancel Royal Dutch–Shell's concessions continued into the mid-1920s.[58] In the end, negotiations and compromises effectively loosened Royal Dutch–Shell's grasp of Venezuelan oil land.

Meanwhile, the British-Dutch interests were beginning to show progress for their efforts. Royal Dutch–Shell's drillers struck Venezuela's first gusher at Barroso No. 2 in 1922. The well shot a column of oil 200 feet into the air, destroying the derrick. The industry recognized the Barroso well, producing at 100,000 b/d, as the world's largest oil strike since Mexico. A second prolific well was drilled in the La Rosa field in 1922. Royal Dutch–Shell's products refined at San Lorenzo were reaching sales agencies throughout Venezuela and undercutting Standard Oil's imported products there. Still, most of Royal Dutch–Shell's production was transported to Curaçao in its fleet of 35 lake tankers. Venezuela's major refining was to be offshore. A twelve-foot sandbar at the entrance of shallow Lake Maracaibo prevented development of a major refining center near the country's oil fields. Steam tankers could not enter the lake's shallow waters. Curaçao had an excellent deepwater harbor, and the Dutch colonial government encouraged Royal Dutch–Shell to build a large refinery there. Full production began in 1922. By the end of the decade, the refinery employed eighty-six hundred persons, many of whom were immigrants from other islands of the Antilles, and processed four-fifths of Royal Dutch–Shell's Venezuelan oil (approximately 140,000 b/d). A fleet of shallow-draft barges delivered crude from Maracaibo day and night.[59]

Gómez actually discouraged the dredging of the sandbar and the building of refineries in the remote Lake Maracaibo region. He feared the separation of western Venezuela—perhaps aided and abetted, Panamanian style, by the gunboats of the United States or British navies. McBeth claims that, although Gómez opposed the dredging of the sandbar at Lake Maracaibo, he sought ways to make the companies build refineries at several bays along the Gulf Coast. But Lago, Doheny's company in Venezuela, built its major refinery at Aruba, a second Dutch island off the Venezuelan coast.[60]

Once Gómez opened the floodgates, American oil interests deluged Venezuela. Royal Dutch–Shell still could congratulate itself in 1928 as the largest producer and refiner in Mexico and Venezuela, but its leadership was vulnerable. The weakness of Royal Dutch–Shell in Venezuela did not relate so much to technology, for the company's operations here were as advanced as in Mexico—and far more advanced than those of the British oil companies in Peru and Ecuador. Other British firms in Venezuela, such as the British Controlled Oilfields, contracted American drilling firms and later sold majority interest to the Americans because their British owners were not "sufficiently equipped technically" to begin production there.[61]

Venezuelans and critics of Standard Oil since have charged that American oilmen bribed Gómez to obtain the lion's share of concessions in the 1920s. This is not the entire story. Royal Dutch–Shell's weakness was palpable: it simply lacked the necessary markets. Jersey Standard had moved vigorously into all of Latin America's major cities, and El Águila and other American firms already supplied most of Mexico's consumption. The American companies, of course, dominated the burgeoning U.S. market, despite Royal Dutch–Shell's expansion in distribution there. Therefore, the Royal Dutch–Shell companies in Venezuela found themselves selling crude oil to competitors that, in any case, preferred to have their own, more secure, sources. American growth resulted. U.S. investments in Venezuela rose from $75 million in 1924 to $161.6 million in 1929. Once again, Standard Oil of New Jersey grew to be the largest oil firm in Venezuela. In 1928 it purchased majority interest in the concessions of the Creole Syndicate, a British company, from which Standard was already buying crude drilled by a Gulf subsidiary.[62] The American oil hegemony in South America was gaining momentum.

Obviously, the foregoing analysis suggests that corporate power in the Latin American oil industry was eroding. While it is true that the giant

international oil firms were engaged in a fiercely competitive struggle in
Latin America, there is little evidence to support the conclusion that
Standard and Royal Dutch–Shell meddled decisively in domestic poli-
tics and fomented war. For example, nationalists have claimed that the
companies bribed the Argentine military to overthrow President Yrigoyen
in 1930. Others charge Jersey Standard with supporting Bolivia and
Royal Dutch–Shell with supporting Paraguay in the 1932–1935 Chaco
War. Supposedly, each aspired to oil concessions in the Chaco region,
which has not proved productive. Others contend that the IPC of Jersey
Standard encouraged Peru in its 1941–1942 war with Ecuador over the
Oriente. Royal Dutch–Shell was supposed to have supported Ecuador.[63]
Scholars have not taken these charges seriously, and no evidence has
emerged to substantiate such claims. One thing is certain, however: the
governments of South America became more assertive in the 1930s.

Brazil and the Southern Cone

In Brazil and the Southern Cone, economic nationalism vis-à-vis the
foreign oil companies reached a crescendo in the 1930s. Neither Jersey
Standard nor Royal Dutch–Shell gained any production at all in Brazil,
Uruguay, and Chile, three vibrant national markets. These governments
tolerated foreign marketing operations but remained wary even of
permitting foreign-owned refineries to operate. Uruguay's state oil
company, Administración Nacional de Combustibles, Álcohol y Portland (ANCAP), had a refinery on line in 1937 in which all foreign
importers, by law, had to process their crude. ANCAP received a quota
of 50 percent of the domestic market and forced the foreign companies
to sell their products at fixed prices. State control of energy resources
commenced in Chile as early as 1927, when the government refused to
grant Royal Dutch–Shell and Jersey Standard certain oil concessions in
Tierra del Fuego. Chile feared a separatist movement in underpopulated
southern Chile, which was already dominated by British and German
ranching interests. Eventually, the government reserved for itself the
right to explore oil resources in the south. Private companies remained
but importers and distributors of oil products throughout this period. In
1935 the state imposed a quota system, allocating 50 percent of the
Chilean market to a state-sponsored marketing firm. It also set the
maximum price for which gasoline could be sold in the country.[64] In
Brazil, as eslewhere in Latin America, market quotas and pricing policies
were a common feature of the Latin American oil landscape in the 1930s.
 Despite its twentieth-century economic performance, Brazil was a
latecomer to oil. It consumed just one-third as much petroleum as did
Argentina in the 1930s. All of it was imported by WICO or by Royal

Dutch–Shell and its affiliate, Anglo-Mexican. No refinery existed, and the tax collectors in 1926 resisted reducing the duty on crude so as to encourage construction. But consumption grew after 1930. Policymakers, therefore, recognized the need for domestic refining and production. Because it was considered a strategic commodity, oil was placed under the aegis of the military. Gen. Júlio Caetano Horta Barbosa became the head of the new state oil agency, the Conselho Nacional de Combustíveis (CNP). In 1939 it drilled in Bahia, discovered oil, and made the area a national reserve.

Brazil followed the nationalist response of other Latin American nations in the 1930s. It made the exploration, refining, and marketing of petroleum a state utility (although not yet a monopoly).[65] After discussions with Uruguayan authorities and with Argentina's Mosconi, Horta Barbosa decided against allowing private firms to build refineries in Brazil. (The CNP under Horta Barbosa, in fact, turned down a proposal of Royal Dutch–Shell's Anglo-Mexican company to build a refinery at Rio de Janeiro.) Brazil in the 1930s established a frankly nationalistic energy policy that favored domestic capital in refining.

Unlike Argentina, as John Wirth points out, Brazil easily nationalized its refining industry because no foreign company had ever established a refinery there to challenge public policy. The country was unable to develop other than a few small private refineries of its own, yet it blocked private companies from entering the refinery business there.[66] Finally, in 1953 the government established Petrobrás as the monopoly producer and refiner, formally restricting the private companies to their evolving, de facto status as import marketers.

Foreign Penetration of Latin America's Oil Industry

The foreign oil companies—Standard Oil in particular—penetrated Latin America in three stages. First, the North American company exported U.S. petroleum products to Latin America, an initial stage lasting roughly from 1880 to 1910. In the second, overlapping, stage, independent entrepreneurs, also foreign except in the case of the Argentine government, began to open up domestic production. This form of import substitution occurred between 1900 and 1916. The final stage began in 1912, when Royal Dutch–Shell and Standard Oil both began to buy small producing companies and expand their production in Latin America. Jersey Standard and Royal Dutch–Shell did not exactly enter Latin America in order to capture all that region's oil production or to strengthen its command of the world's oil resources. Instead, Jersey Standard entered Latin America for the same reasons it ultimately had to enter every major oil boom in the United States from 1859 to 1910: it expanded in order *not* to lose any more market shares than necessary to new companies created by each new boom. If they did not enter Latin American production, Jersey Standard and Royal Dutch–Shell stood to forfeit their lucrative markets to upstarts like Pearson's El Águila, Doheny's Huasteca, and the British in Peru. When oil production in Latin America commenced in the twentieth century, Jersey Standard and Royal Dutch–Shell, too, had to become part of the trend or risk losing valuable markets. They chose participation.

What does this say, finally, about the corporate power of the British oil companies in Latin America? It should call into question the ability of foreign interests to co-opt the governing elites, to dominate the weak state, or to permanently extract profits from Latin America on their own terms. It would be difficult to posit, as some analysts have, that the state in Latin America acted as a surrogate of international capital. While the power of the foreign oilmen was great in Peru, Mexico, and Venezuela, their autonomy was based on immobile—and thus controllable—economic assets rather than on their ability to manipulate domestic politics. Adalberto J. Pinelo also observes that "a government [in Latin America] might be weak in nearly every regard except in its ability to deal with foreign capitalists."[67] The fact is, the oil companies' power tended to dwindle over time. The ability of the government to restrict and regulate correspondingly increased.

The Social Impact of the Modern Oil Industry

Not only did the modern state discover renewed energy to confront the invasion of foreign interests; so, too, did Latin American society rise to meet the challenges of development generated by the massive foreign investment in oil and other export commodities. Here the historian must ask some basic questions. To what degree did this export-led model transform existing social structures in Latin America? In what ways did Latin American society react to foreign investment and actively shape its consequences? The modern industry brought to the region by Royal Dutch–Shell, Standard Oil, and other companies offers an especially appropriate case study in which to answer these questions, because the petroleum industry was one of the wealthiest and most powerful capitalist organizations of the era.

We contend that development of the modern oil industry had a more radical and disruptive impact on Latin American society than it had in the United States, where that industry had its beginnings. Mid-nineteenth-century U.S. society had already been conditioned to continuous economic growth and had proved more amenable to the changes imposed by the modern oil industry. While it is true that Latin America had already begun the process of modernization when the oil industry arrived, that process had not yet sufficiently freed up human and entrepreneurial capital. Neither the railway companies nor the agricultural export industries preceding the oilmen had been able to modify the rigid postcolonial social structure that had subordinated the nonwhite majorities to positions of educational and occupational inferiority.

Not all consequences of foreign oil investments in Latin America were disruptive, however. The oilmen paid their workers more than did native landowners, who remained Latin America's largest employers until the mid-twentieth century. Native-born laborers, therefore, were able to find work in the foreign companies that permitted them access to material comforts and educational facilities for their families. Workers learned new skills they could apply to other occupations.

One difference begs for explanation. In the United States, the oil workers remained fiercely independent, rejecting the formation of labor unions until the mid-1930s—more than a half century after the industry was developed. Latin American oil workers, on the other hand, displayed collective militancy within a decade of the arrival of the foreign companies. Why?

There are two explanations. One concerns the relatively advanced technological level of the industry and the unpreparedness of Latin American society for its introduction. The oil companies could not find trained and experienced workers in the host countries and had to import skilled U.S. and British managers and workers. The presence of foreign workers eventually combined with other problems created by modernization to provoke defensive actions—unionization and strikes—by native-born workers. A second, corollary, explanation has to do with the growth of state institutions and power in the oil-producing countries. Latin American governments slowly discovered mutual advantage in assisting their native-born workers in the struggle against foreign employers. Eventually, the social forces unleashed by modernization coalesced with political reaction to foreign capital to modify and transform the operation of the oil companies—and modern capitalism itself.

The Impact of Oil Booms in the United States

Petroleum production in the United States, which preceded the Latin American oil booms by a half century, also produced some of the same social changes, such as urbanization and labor mobility. But North American society seemed able to manage those transformations, because the oil regions of the United States were more commercially developed than their Latin American counterparts prior to their oil booms. Take western Pennsylvania and the Gulf Coast of Texas as examples. Both had experienced commercial, agricultural, and even industrial florescence. Prior economic growth had prepared the transportation infrastructure, the working population, the commercial and manufacturing sectors, and the financial institutions to manage the oil booms. Cleveland had been connected to New York since the 1840s by the Erie and Welland Canals and to Pittsburgh by the Pennsylvania and Ohio Canals. Completion of the Soo Canal to Lake Superior, opening the route to Minnesota's iron ranges, enhanced Cleveland's strong industrial leadership from iron founding and boilermaking. All this had occurred even before the railroads were built in the 1850s.[68] Owing to its location at the point where the Allegheny and Monongahela Rivers converge to form the Ohio River, Pittsburgh had been for decades the Northeast's gateway to the Mississippi Basin. Commerce in agricultural goods, coal, iron, and glass laid the foundation of Pittsburgh's economy. Iron and steel became the city's growth industry in the 1850s.

The proximity to the coal mines of Pennsylvania accounts for Pittsburgh's industrial leadership in heavy industry. The arrival of the railroads in the 1850s had an additional impact. They widened the market for whale and coal oils, which were to be replaced in the 1860s by kerosene. In 1861 western Pennsylvania and eastern Ohio already had more than thirty-five refineries. River steamers traditionally carried a large amount of agricultural and manufacturing products as far as New Orleans. By 1860 railways connected Pittsburgh to Cleveland and Chicago in one direction, and Philadelphia and New York in the other.[69] To say that Cleveland and Pittsburgh were bustling cities before the oil boom does not exaggerate.

Before the oil boom, society in western Pennsylvania also was fluid, racially homogeneous, and literate enough to spread skills from one industry to another. Workers' and farmers' high level of education facilitated the spread of technology and entrepreneurship that led to the oil boom in the first place. At the time, few racial divisions remained in western Pennsylvania; Anglo Europeans predominated. In Vernango County, where the first oil boom occurred, only 69 of the 25,000 inhabitants were African Americans; there were no longer any Indians at all. Ownership of the land was widespread, and the culturally European farmers produced dairy products, wool, cattle and horses, oats, potatoes, and buckwheat on a commercial scale. Of Pittsburgh's 49,000 residents in the 1870s, only 1,154 were non-Europeans, African American in this case. A mere 800 of Cleveland's 43,417 inhabitants were African American. Since few racial minorities existed in these boomtowns, the mobility provoked by rapid growth certainly did not threaten a rigid social order.[70]

The American oil industry from the very beginning was the exclusive preserve of the white American male. Although no large company had yet been created to bring capital and technology to develop the western Pennsylvania fields, a host of entrepreneurs arrived to do the job—individualistic fortune hunters like Joseph T. Jones and Thomas P. Potts, Civil War veterans from Philadelphia. Like thousands of others, Jones and Potts invested a small grubstake in obtaining a lease, building a derrick, buying a boiler, and beginning to drill. They accomplished this in just sixty days and with their own labor. The oil boom at Titusville soon attracted hundreds of rafters, bargemen, teamsters, water and salt drillers, and blacksmiths—all white. They adapted their skills to the nascent oil industry and spread those skills to the white farmers who joined them in the oil fields.[71] African Americans were accorded little participation in the oil booms.

The only evidence of Pennsylvania's earliest inhabitants—the American Indians—that remained during the oil boom was the name of the product. It was known as "Seneca Oil," for the resident tribe that, a century before, had skimmed petroleum from the waters of Oil Creek for trade with the white settlers at Niagara. Seneca Oil was used as medicine then. But by the mid-nineteenth century, the Seneca Indians had long since disappeared, replaced by a wave of European settlers with whose ancestors they had once traded. Within a few years of the first Pennsylvania oil strikes, all those practicing individual initiative and frontier-style entrepreneurship were white. The lease agents, farmers, distillery and refinery workers, teamsters, boardinghouse operators and hoteliers, cooks, wives, guards, scouts, prostitutes, gamblers, volunteer firefighters, and marching bands—were all white.[72]

It is difficult to conclude that the Pennsylvania oil fields, as capitalistic a venture as one could find in the 1860s and the 1870s, had even created a proletariat. Everyone in the oil fields seemed to work on their own account. The teamsters—"an autocratic gang who charged exorbitantly," as they were remembered by some oilmen—remained fiercely independent. Each of the one thousand teamsters at Pithole owned his own flatboat and team of horses to bring the first crude oil out of the Allegheny valleys on the shallow creeks. Only when these individualistic oil pioneers were replaced by railway tank cars, pipelines, and centralized refineries was the real oil proletariat formed. The individual oil entrepreneurs in the fields then moved on to Ohio, Indiana, Illinois, Iowa, Kansas, California, Texas, Oklahoma . . . and eventually to Latin America. "For oil development was then and forever beyond the next hill," wrote an executive for Sinclair, "and the whole industry literally moved across the countryside from month to month." Boomtowns were created overnight and then abandoned. At the height of the oil production in its area in the 1870s, Rousville, Pennsylvania, grew to a population of nine thousand. By 1880 Rousville had only seven hundred inhabitants; the transient and independent oilmen had moved west.[73]

Similarly, the Texas oil boom initiated by the discovery at Spindletop in 1901 occurred in a Gulf Coast region that had already experienced a thorough commercialization of its transportation, agricultural, and manufacturing base. Railways connected the thriving city of Houston to New Orleans, San Francisco, Saint Louis, Chicago, and New York. Coastal shipping had expanded in order to carry timber and cotton to East Coast markets. Houston's population had reached 44,633 before Spindletop, of whom 12,608 were African American. The population had relatively high levels of education; only 2.1 percent of white adults were illiterate, 11.4 percent of African Americans. Texas even had a nascent manufacturing base that nurtured a skilled white labor force in its sawmills, iron- and brickworks, and railroad repair shops. Spindletop unleashed an economic whirlwind that necessitated imports of labor, materials, and, especially, capital. Nearby Beaumont's population doubled nearly overnight. Local businesses boomed by importing drilling and storage equipment by the ton from Pittsburgh. Observes Joseph Pratt, "Thirty years of gradual development had prepared [Houston] and the surrounding region for continued growth." Even in Texas, a former slave state, the African and Mexican American populations remained minorities. Most economic opportunities were reserved for the more numerous white workers. A former wildcatter explains how the white drillers taught the oil business to the "dumb old boys," who were white also: "They came off the cotton farms, out of the little towns and villages, and away from the sawmill, and cottonseed-oil mills. They came from Texas, Oklahoma, Louisiana, and Arkansas. A few were from other states. From the beginning, [these white boys] favored their own kind, since they spoke the same language and came from the same background."[74]

In a way, even this U.S. regional society, despite its multiracial character, was prepared to manage the fury and disruption of the oil boom. Among its white workers, there remained a fierce sense of independence and mobility, such that there was little union activity until the 1930s.

The Impact of Latin American Oil Booms

In spite—or because—of their potential for distributing wealth, the oil booms had a far more disruptive impact on the rigid societies of Latin America than on those of comparable petroleum zones in the United States. The reason is simple. The lethargic economic development of Latin America prior to the arrival of the oilmen had not conditioned the people's social relationships to change. Latin American society remained ill-prepared for social mobility on a massive scale. Mexico and Venezuela serve as two cases in point.

Mexico

At the turn of the century, economic development in Mexico's future oil zones was quite weak. The overwhelming majority of the population was rural, illiterate, unskilled, and socially differentiated by race and ethnicity. The educated, property-owning commercial class was small. The less-privileged, uneducated, and nonwhite class of rural workers was large, and cities had not yet mobilized a force of commercial and industrial laborers. None of these social groups were quite prepared for the kind of change to which a powerful, technologically modern industry was to subject them.

On the eve of Mexico's oil boom, the future refining cities and oil ports remained small, their inhabitants committed to traditional jobs. In 1900 Tampico had a population of 17,500; Tuxpan, 13,000; and Minatitlán, 6,100. Many of these cities counted agriculturists and fieldworkers among their residents. While 855 *tampiqueños* were in commerce, only 49 worked in industry, even though the railway had arrived a few years before. Nearly two-thirds of the residents could not read or write. Tuxpan was even more rustic. In the entire *cantón* (county) there was but one industrial worker; more than 90 percent of the adult population could not read; only 123 residents had a working knowledge of metals.[75] Mexico's future oil cities lacked any manufacturing base whatsoever.

In the United States, the railways had culminated a transportation revolution in coastal and riverboating, international shipping, and overland freighting. The opposite was true for Latin America. Here the railways began the process of economic modernization. Although the Veracruz–Mexico City railway was complete in 1877, primitive conditions at the port of Veracruz limited traffic on the line. The rail boom during the latter half of the nineteenth century did benefit Mexico's north central plateau. Here, old silver mines were reopened by foreign companies.

Lacking mining resources, the future oil zones on Mexico's Gulf Coast languished in comparison. They served as underpopulated livestock and agricultural frontiers attractive to modest numbers of foreign immigrants and mestizo migrants. Sluggish coastal vessels provided the only link between the port of Veracruz and the future oil towns of Tampico, Tuxpan, and Minatitlán. The eastern sierras effectively prevented large-scale commerce between these places and the more populous cities in the highlands. The Mexican Central Railway completed its construction from San Luis Potosí to Tampico in 1889, but traffic remained light. The Central Railway had to obtain a government concession so that it could spend four million pesos (two million dollars) on port construction and dredging of the river channel at Tampico. All construction projects languished while essential hardware was imported directly from the American steel mills. Soon, Tampico became a center for the distribution of coal throughout the nation. Imported Welsh and West Virginian coal became the king of energy in Mexico, which consumed some 4.5 million tons per year. West Indians were brought in to work in the coal and coke piles at the docks because Mexicans refused to do this work.[76] Expensive coal, which was imported rather than a product of the Mexican economy, would soon yield to domestic petroleum as the chief energy source.

At the beginning of the twentieth century, great variation existed in the landholding patterns and social organization of Latin America's future oil zones. The population lived a dispersed but clearly hierarchical lifestyle. Again, the state of Veracruz serves to illustrate the kind of multiethnic, stratified society that characterized other oil zones. Veracruz society for centuries had blended the descendants of the colonial African slaves with those of the Spaniards and Indians. Except for a narrow elite of mostly white Europeans (many of whom were recent Spanish immigrants), the majority of the population was racially mixed mestizos. Migrants from the highlands, too, were mestizos. The Indian population still predominated in the countryside. In the Tuxpan region, especially to the south, near Furbero and what later would be the Poza Rica oil field, speakers of Indian languages were found in larger numbers. Nearly one-third of the inhabitants of the *cantón* of Tuxpan spoke Huasteco, Mexicano, Totonaco, or Otomí, in that order.[77] The Indians remained isolated from the neighboring mestizo society except to sell their labor. Spanish-speaking, Hispanicized mestizos looked down on those who spoke an Indian dialect and wore Indian clothing.

This rural society did not exist in a state of democratic egalitarianism. By virtue of their family background and economic leverage, the few large landowners exerted a measure of decentralized control over the rural population. Among the *hacendados* of the Veracruz coastal zone were numbers of Spaniards who had immigrated during the late nineteenth century. Despite their recent arrival, Spaniards utilized strong family ties and educational and capital resources (all of which the mestizos lacked) to form a narrow elite. Racially European, religiously Catholic, lingually Spanish, and there to stay, these immigrants easily worked their way into the upper and middle bourgeoisie of a multiethnic society whose historical elites valued these traits. The larger estates of the Spaniards specialized in cattle production as well as agriculture. Here the opportunities of these Spanish immigrants caused resentment among the mestizo lower bourgeoisie and workers. As Andrés Molina Enríquez notes, "Scratch the modern Spaniard and you will discover the ancient conquistador."[78]

Venezuela

In some ways quite different from northeastern Mexico's oil zone, Venezuela's Maracaibo Basin (in the state of Zulia) was equally unprepared for the oil boom. Maracaibo by the mid-nineteenth century had become a center of considerable economic dynamism. The largest city in western Venezuela, it served as the exit port for coffee exports from the Venezuelan Andes and eastern Colombia. It was a growing market for agricultural produce as it was served by an extensive network of waterborne transportation. Maracaibo also had a substantial commercial community. The resident merchants controlled international and regional trade while financing much of the region's agriculture. Nonetheless, the economy and society of the Maracaibo Basin on the eve of the oil boom had some of the limits of their Mexican counterparts.

Essential to the region's economy, commerce remained limited in scope and significantly undercapitalized. The society of the Maracaibo Basin was—like that of northeastern Mexico—diverse, hierarchical, and characterized by conflict and coercion. Much of the region's labor force was but ill-prepared to meet the challenges presented by petroleum production.

Maracaibo had been one of Venezuela's largest cities and busiest ports since the colonial era. In 1873 the population of Maracaibo, Venezuela's second-largest city, and its surrounding territory stood at over 25,000; by 1891 the city alone had a population of 29,180. On the eve of the oil boom, 1920, the city's population totaled 46,706. The rapid growth of the late nineteenth and early twentieth centuries resulted from the Andean coffee boom; all coffee production for western Venezuela and eastern Colombia was funneled through the port of Maracaibo.[79]

The dynamism of Maracaibo's economy and society had, however, quite definite limits. While Maracaibo's population grew in the decades before the oil boom, that growth was much slower in the surrounding rural districts. Towns later famous as centers of the oil industry were, prior to 1920, sparsely populated. Cabimas, which would become an oil center of primary importance, had a population of only 1,940 in 1920. Other sites of future oil camps were, at the turn of the century, uninhabited.[80]

The development of Maracaibo's economy depended on growers' ability to get produce to market and obtain capital to finance their properties. Transportation posed significant difficulties for the agriculturalists of the Maracaibo Basin and delayed the region's complete settlement and the transformation of the economy. The most modern transportation links tied the city to the wider world. Maracaibo was connected by steamship to Europe and the United States via the island of Curaçao. Land transportation between the hinterland and the city of Maracaibo was almost impossible, because the terrain and climate made roads impractical. Most of the region's agricultural and livestock producers relied instead on lake- and riverborne transport to take their products to market.

In the late nineteenth and early twentieth centuries, various attempts were made to improve transportation both on water and land. By the 1880s steamboats were in regular service between Maracaibo and the main ports of the Sur del Lago, and by 1900 several railroads had been built across the region. These improvements remained limited in their effect, however. The railroads were built primarily to facilitate the export of Andean coffee. They connected towns in the Andean piedmont with ports on Lake Maracaibo and its tributary rivers. Though growers in the Sur del Lago Zuliano did make some use of railways, the high freight rates and the limited service area rendered them largely irrelevant. Likewise, the steamboats plying the lake and its tributaries specialized primarily in the shipment of coffee; freight rates were high, service areas were limited, and schedules remained inflexible. As a result, traditional sailing vessels and even poled and paddled canoes successfully competed with steamers and, in fact, carried most of the region's produce to market in Maracaibo.[81] Thus, inefficient and limited transportation significantly delayed the consolidation of the region's economy.

Another economic constraint was the scarcity and cost of credit. In the absence of banking institutions disposed to finance agriculture and other enterprises, those needing capital had to rely on the region's merchants, who charged dearly. As a traveler visiting Maracaibo in 1913 observed, many fell quickly into debt and ultimately lost their properties:[82]

> The poor agriculturalists, the martyred agriculturalists have come to be, with rare exceptions, *mayordomos* . . . on their own haciendas: servitors obligated by a series of gradually ascending commitments that end when the properties, despite being good and properly cared for, are lost because their harvests are insufficient to amortize debts that grow too irresistibly for even the most economical and tenacious workers. With money at one, at two, and at

more than two [percent per month interest] . . . the failure of the grower is not a problem, it is fact.

The scarcity of capital, the high cost of credit, and the constraints placed on transportation and marketing by natural and artificial obstacles limited the size and number of large agricultural properties and help explain the only gradual transformation of the agricultural economy.

Zulia's society had been since the colonial era racially and ethnically divided. A small white elite resided in Maracaibo and dominated large-scale agriculture and commerce, but most of the region's inhabitants were nonwhites. The substantial colonial Indian populations of the zone were by the late eighteenth century undergoing a slow process of assimilation, becoming culturally Hispanic; further, mestizos and mulattos were settled in increasing numbers in formerly Indian communities throughout the nineteenth century. In the southeastern corner of the Maracaibo Basin lived a substantial and distinct black population. They were descendants of slaves introduced in the sixteenth and seventeenth centuries to work church-owned cacao plantations. Since, because of the scourges of malaria and yellow fever, the established population was too sparse to supply agricultural and domestic labor, the larger landowners and well-to-do householders throughout the region imported workers. Some brought in contract workers from the West Indies; most relied on Indians imported from the nearby Guajira Peninsula and held in conditions closely approximating chattel slavery. On the eve of the oil boom of the 1920s, then, the economy and society of the Maracaibo Basin seemed ill-prepared for the transformations about to be wrought.[83]

The scholar should be very wary, therefore, of attributing a kind of "yeoman democracy" to the Mexican Gulf Coast or the Maracaibo Basin at the turn of the century. Although their sparse population and relatively open land provided a measure of economic and social opportunity, the future oil zones displayed many of the social divisions and rigidities that characterized other parts of Latin America. In the absence of egalitarianism, one found sharp social distinctions and hierarchy based on wealth and ethnicity. Although modernizing, societies in these future oil zones were unprepared for the rapid pace of change to which foreign investment subjected them.

The Mexican Revolution and Oil

Beginning in 1911, the foreign oil companies entered a decade in which their Mexican operations benefited from a confluence of several stimuli. Mexican oil production rose spectacularly, international markets were buoyant, prices climbed, the external market gained precedence over the internal, labor remained pliant, and the government was weakened by political disorder and financial need. Several independent foreign entrepreneurs took advantage of the situation to expand their petroleum operations. They even developed significant transportation and marketing assets in the American and European markets heretofore dominated by Royal Dutch–Shell and Standard Oil. Oil prices began to rise gently beginning in 1911 and then steeply with the wartime demand in 1916 (see Graph 4.1). The foreign oil interests in Mexico reaped the benefits.

Although the booming oil industry provided steady work, the Mexican workers were not entirely satisfied with their situation. The Revolution disrupted mining and railroading sufficiently to provide Mexican carpenters, boilermakers, mechanics, blacksmiths, and machinery operators for the oil fields. Unskilled laborers also migrated from agricultural areas suffering revolutionary depredations.[84]

Several problems confronted the worker in the great labor emporium of Tampico. The oil companies did not provide much housing even for the skilled Mexicans, let alone the larger mass of unskilled. Foreign managers and their families inhabited company-built, single-family, hillside residences with window screens and corrugated roofing, but the Mexicans lived in settlements of thatched-roofed *bohíos,* or huts, and

Graph 4.1. Average Yearly Oil Prices in the United States, 1910–1948 ($/bbl)

Source: American Petroleum Institute, *Petroleum Facts and Figures* (New York, 1951), 170.

jerry-built houses on the swamplands surrounding Tampico and the lowlands of oil camps.[85]

Moreover, the American worker in Mexico was not the fittest possible ambassador of the "American way." Principally from Texas and the Old South, the white American workers demanded to live separately. They had their own mess halls, where Chinese cooks prepared the meals. Foreigners made twice as much as Mexicans who worked at similar tasks. Native workers also reserved special resentment toward the Chinese, who kept to themselves and were willing to work for much less than the Mexicans. This is not to say that the Mexicans resented working for foreign companies, at least initially. Relatively high paying positions with some social status, oil jobs were preferable to jobs with Mexican enterprises and haciendas, which paid much less.[86]

One thing more than anything else set the worker against the companies: insecurity. Every worker in the industry worked under individual contract, often informal oral agreements with the employer or contractor for a specific job. Unskilled workers dug foundations, mixed mortar, laid brick, carried building materials, lifted barrels, and cleared vegetation. Working from day to day at unskilled tasks, the peon had no guarantee of steady employment if he wanted it until the pipeline was in or the refinery built.[87] Nevertheless, the Mexican industrial proletarians in the booming oil zone were not overtly dissatisfied—until 1915, when the Revolution disrupted domestic food production and World War I pushed up the prices of imported commodities. As the cost of living and inflation rose, salaries bought them less and less.

Strikes broke out and workers succeeded in shutting down a refinery here and a topping plant there, yet only for short periods. The work stoppages that began in 1915 reached a crescendo in 1917 and continued until 1920. The easing of the economic crisis and the victory of the Constitutionalists (signaled by the 1917 Constitution, which outlined the worker's rights and the employer's responsibilities) encouraged Mexico's oil workers to press hard. The skilled workers organized trade unions; the boiler workers, boatmen, mechanics, and so forth, sought to recover lost purchasing power and, not incidentally, to secure job tenure by pushing for collective contracts to replace individual ones. These craft unions then sought to organize the less-skilled workers in the plants. Some coercion was involved, and scabs and free workers found themselves confronted and threatened by union men. Strikers also demanded that the companies get rid of the Chinese workers. Few strikes lasted because many workers, frightened of losing already insecure jobs, quickly broke ranks. But their militancy did earn the workers some benefits: higher wages to offset inflation, shorter work hours, and extra pay on Sundays and holidays.[88]

The 1920s brought Mexican oil proletarians additional reasons and opportunities to pressure foreign employers. Presidents Obregón and Calles had effected a political alliance with the national labor union, the Confederación Regional Obrera Mexicana (CROM), as a method of centralizing authority over postrevolutionary Mexico. Workers had additional cause for mobilization. The simultaneous exhaustion of the oil fields and the postwar decline in world oil prices late in 1921 had rendered work in the foreign-controlled industry quite insecure. Before that break, the industry had employed nearly fifty thousand Mexicans. The companies reduced wages and let workers go without severance pay. An American oil boycott in 1921 threw an additional seven thousand Mexicans out of work. Royal Dutch–Shell's affiliate, El Águila, likewise reduced labor in order to economize and consolidate its operations. Much of the technological innovation in refining and drilling also worked to lower the employment of Mexicans and preserve the job privileges of skilled foreigners. In the 1920s the private companies turned to temporary contract labor for new drilling and construction projects.[89]

As soon as the crisis stabilized and oil prices recovered slightly, the workers reacted. As the leading employer in Tampico, the Águila refinery could not prevent union militancy. A strike broke out in 1923 among its twelve hundred workers, who seized control of the refinery. As the strike dragged on, the managers of the two principal American companies, Huasteca and Transcontinental, pressured El Águila's executives "to hold out to the limit," so that labor unrest would not spread.

Beset by a number of other problems, El Águila gave in to the workers. It signed a contract recognizing the refinery union, granting the eight-hour day, and providing for wage increases and severance pay.[90] Thereafter, strikes broke out in quick succession at other facilities, as well as at El Águila's other refinery at Minatitlán. Each new strike imitated the success of the Águila workers in Tampico.

Huasteca ended this spasm of labor militancy in 1925 by breaking the strike of its workers, whose loyalties were divided between two rival unions.[91] The oil industry continued its layoffs when another break in oil prices came in 1926 and again in 1930. The strikes of the early 1920s had established a legacy of worker demands to remedy the insecurity of employment. More tangibly, workers had won the right to collective contracts and, especially, to severance pay.

Venezuelan Workers and Oil

Because the oil boom did not commence in Venezuela until the 1920s, the trajectory of Venezuelan oil worker militancy lagged behind Mexico's by a decade. In other words, Venezuelans did not begin their first labor organizing until the mid-1920s. Collective contracts, which some Mexican unions had won in the 1920s, would not be found in the Venezuelan oil industry until the 1930s.

Both labor groups, nonetheless, shared many characteristics. They both worked for industrially advanced foreign companies known for their control of the terms of employment. Both had to contend with privileged American and British supervisors as well as with pliant, lower-paid foreigners. Mexico had its Chinese workers; West Indians came to work in Venezuela. What is remarkable about Venezuela's case is that, although the country experienced no political ferment similar to the Mexican Revolution—military governments with little sympathy for labor ruled the country until 1945—the trajectory of workers' militancy in the Venezuelan oil industry equaled that of Mexico, but ten years later.

In the 1920s British and American oil interests in Venezuela did not have to confront the same kind of labor militancy as in Mexico. The industry was expanding, and first-generation oil workers had little experience with layoffs and reduced income. But there were vexing problems for the native-born workers of this South American country. They received two and three times the wages of agricultural workers, from whose ranks most came. But the cost of living in the oil zones was high. Moreover, as in Mexico, foreign managers and skilled workers held the best positions in the industry and showed little respect for the culture or abilities of those native Venezuelans working under their direction. A double standard existed in all the oil fields, with American and European workers receiving far better living quarters, food, and pay than Venezuelans. In 1925 two American oilmen described the situation at the oil camp in Mene Grande: "The present scope of operation is so extensive that a large supervisory staff, a big crew of imported drillers and expert mechanics, and about 2,000 native laborers are employed. The company has provided living accommodation for this personnel in a very satisfactory manner by the construction of extensive and modernly equipped villages in which the several classes of employees are segregated."[92]

Another sore point for Venezuelan workers reflected their own racial and cultural prejudices. With the start of the oil boom, the foreign companies claimed that insufficient numbers of skilled Venezuelan laborers required the importation of workers from abroad and introduced large numbers of West Indian blacks to work in the oil industry. The local elite despised the West Indians and considered them unfit immigrants; Venezuelan workers resented the West Indians' penchant for identifying with English-speaking Americans rather than with Spanish-speaking natives. Venezuelans sarcastically called the conformist black workers *maifrenes*, from the English "my friend."

Workers also enjoyed no compensation for being incapacitated by accidents. The oil companies hired their itinerant labor through local brokers and contractors, who bore responsibility for the welfare of the workers.

Politics played a role in labor organization as early as the 1920s. The Royal Dutch–Shell refinery at Curaçao employed some fifteen hundred Venezuelans. Many of these, supported by workers, became involved in a movement of political exiles seeking to overthrow the regime of Gen. Juan Vicente Gómez.[93] Under the circumstances, some labor unrest was inevitable.

The largest oil producer in the country, the Royal Dutch–Shell group, felt the first stirrings of Venezuelan workers. The 1925 strike began at Royal Dutch–Shell's Mene Grande camp among workers in the company garage. Some forty of them drafted a letter to the company demanding higher wages, better housing, and medical care at company expense. After a call to local authorities did not result in the suppression of the strike, the company compromised with the garage workers by granting them a wage increase and agreeing to study the other demands.

The success of the striking garage workers led others to emulate them. The strike soon spread to the Lago and Gulf camps and eventually involved twenty-five hundred workers. Strikers demanded a wage increase from six to eight bolívares per day. The companies appealed to the state and national governments, but both indicated they could not spare the troops to protect the oil installations. After a strike of almost two weeks, the companies agreed to raise pay to seven bolívares per day. The state government protected the strikers from being fired, and they returned to work. Another strike the following year in Cabimas failed to duplicate this success.[94]

Spurred by worker unrest, the state became increasingly interested in regulating the conditions under which the oil workers labored. Venezuela's first labor law, passed in 1928, provided for stricter government inspection of the living conditions and safety of Venezuelan workers. Neat concrete-block family units began to replace the communal bachelor barracks, and medical treatment improved; however, many Venezuelans still lived in the nearby oil towns rather than in the company camps. Government inspectors were appalled at the unhealthful conditions of the oil towns and the pollution of the lake. In many places, thick oil slicks and rubbish covered the brackish water of Lake Maracaibo and oil clung to vegetation along the shoreline. Inspectors observed that, despite the strike-induced wage increases, native workers still harbored grievances over the high cost of living and the ill-treatment received from foremen. "It can be seen that there is a great deal of discontentment among the workers," a government official reported, "which encourages disputes and strikes."[95]

Nevertheless, labor militancy in the Venezuelan oil industries during the 1920s did not approximate that of Mexico. Venezuelan workers had not yet experienced massive layoffs. They merely reacted to the negative aspects of their new lives as proletarians: the poor living conditions, the overbearing foreign supervisors, and the competition from low-paid West Indians. The depression would intensify these frustrations. Just as it made the Mexican petroleum workers even more militant, the world-wide economic crisis of 1930 eventually would also give the Venezuelans cause for greater labor organization.

Mexico and Venezuela in Depression

In the long run, the Great Depression further eroded the position of all the foreign companies in the Mexican oil industry, because it fostered an alliance between economic nationalism and militant unionism. The industry consolidated even more, as Jersey Standard absorbed the biggest American company, Huasteca. At the same time, El Águila's drilling program at Poza Rica uncovered the first new oil field since 1920. Several wells were showing promise even as the international price of petroleum plummeted below one dollar per barrel in 1931. Eventually, Poza Rica would contribute one-third of total Mexican production.[96]

The Mexican oil unions were weakened—but only temporarily—by the international depression and by the slide in world prices. At the time, the oil industry was still quite vulnerable to international market conditions, as it exported some 70 percent of its production. Companies responded to sagging prices by laying off workers and cutting wages. At first, workers were disoriented by further decline in the industry, and labor leaders found little support for strikes and work actions. Yet, by 1934 oil prices were recovering, and other Mexican exports and economic activities had resumed. The domestic market for petroleum grew appreciably until, in 1937, Mexicans were consuming more than half of the nation's oil production.[97] As in the United States, gasoline for cars and trucks proved to be the growth market. In 1933, the beginning of this period, the oil firms had parceled out the domestic market for gasoline, as shown on Table 4.3.

This modest resurgence in the demand for oil strengthened the unions, as did the 1934 presidential campaign. A strike in the El Águila

Table 4.3. Foreign Companies' Share of Domestic Mexican Gasoline Market

Company	% of Domestic Market
El Águila (Royal Dutch–Shell)	33.7
Huasteca (Jersey Standard)	24.3
Sinclair-Pierce	21.6
California Standard	20.4

Source: Jesús Silva Herzog, *El petróleo de México*, 46; Philip George, *Oil and Politics in Latin America*, 80.

refinery at Minatitlán, uniting six trade unions, was a crucial test of labor resolve. Pres. Abelardo Rodríguez personally mediated the dispute in 1934 and granted the refinery union coalition a number of critical benefits. The settlement also equalized the pay between refinery and oil field, as workers in the latter always received fewer benefits.

More important, the agreement granted the unions a closed shop. Under the so-called exclusionary clause, labor leaders had the right to nominate workers for all new openings. They could cause veteran workers to lose their jobs merely by expelling them from the union. In the next two years, union after union struck to win the same concessions. When the national labor leadership supported President Cárdenas in his political dispute with former President Calles in 1935, the oil unions finally acquired the power to organize the entire industry. Some twenty oil unions united to form the Sindicato de Trabajadores Petroleros de la República Mexicana (Union of Oil Workers of the Mexican Republic, STPRM).[98] In 1936 STPRM offered the foreign companies a collective contract.

In confronting the demands of the new industrywide union, the British and American companies maintained a united front. They abhorred what they considered the "excessive" demands of labor. The oil workers' union called for wage increases, pay equalization, and administrative powers that would have delivered the industry's personnel management to labor control.[99] President Cárdenas averted an oil workers' walkout by sponsoring labor talks between the companies and the oil union. Intransigence on both sides led to a breakdown of these negotiations in the spring of 1937. The national union then struck the industry for two weeks. Once again, President Cárdenas cajoled the workers back to work by acceding to a union request that a government commission investigate the companies' finances to determine whether they could afford the contract workers sought.

While the commission investigated, there was still much agitation within the oil workers' union. The Poza Rica workers went out on a fifty-seven-day wildcat strike. That action caused much disruption in Mexico City, and Mexicans suddenly became aware of how petroleum-dependent their economy had become. The oil unions had more power now that most of the petroleum was used for domestic consumption rather than export.

Pressure on the government increased to settle the labor dispute. By this time, the workers, too, had became adamant about the wage package: the cost of living in 1937 was increasing.[100] In December the investigative commission decided that the companies could afford the union's administrative demands as well as a twenty-six million peso wage increase.

The administrative impositions rankled the oil executives more than the wage demands did. They decided to compromise on neither. El Águila's management did not believe it could afford the higher wages if it also lost management prerogatives and observed that "the industry is already suffering the consequences of lack of control and discipline."[101] Moreover, a break in oil prices in 1937 signaled a new international recession. The companies appealed to the Mexican Supreme Court, which on 1 March 1938 decided against them.

Still the oil companies resisted. Pres. Lázaro Cárdenas offered them a compromise that would have permitted them to observe the Supreme Court decision. While Cárdenas waited for the companies to respond, the unions pressed for expropriation. Only El Águila's managers wanted to accept the eleventh-hour compromise, but they could not persuade the Standard Oil directors of Huasteca.[102] In the meantime, the oil workers' union threatened a final nationwide strike. They even began seizing oil installations and preventing the companies from exporting and marketing their petroleum.

On 18 March 1938, President Cárdenas nationalized the oil industry, a decision that commanded considerable support from organized labor. Mexican workers did not gain their pay raises with the oil nationalization, but the expropriation greatly consolidated the union's control over the petroleum workplace. That control would, however, result in much corruption and bossism among labor leaders.

Venezuela's oil workers were on a similar trajectory, but continued to lag behind by a decade. By virtue of its later entry into world oil production, Venezuela had escaped the oil glut and low prices of the early 1920s. The 1930s were to be different. As early as 1927, oil prices began to soften. By 1930, when they dropped below one dollar per barrel for the first time since 1916, the world's oilmen knew that they faced another overproduction crisis (see Graph 4.1).

The drop in oil prices was so devastating that the major oil companies colluded to control production. In Venezuela they decided not only to maintain market share but even to cut back production. Royal Dutch–Shell brought in Standard Oil of Indiana (which had purchased Lago) along with Gulf's Mene Grande company and Jersey Standard. They all agreed to shut in about 162,000 b/d of production in the Maracaibo Basin to curtail new drilling by 40 percent.[103] The Venezuelan government lost royalties and export revenues; workers lost their jobs, often in large numbers.

The oil crisis struck Venezuela as early as May 1927, when oil companies cut back their operations in response to overproduction. They immediately discharged some four thousand oil workers, most of them Venezuelans. Further cutbacks in the early 1930s brought new waves of layoffs, totaling perhaps thirteen thousand native and some fourteen hundred foreign workers. Venezuelan workers laid off by the oil companies attempted to reintegrate into the agricultural economy. "Native employees have not been much of a problem," wrote one observer after layoffs in 1931. "Most of those released returned immediately to the ranches or plantations from which they had been drawn at the time of the great demand for peon labor in the rapidly expanding oil industry."[104]

The state government took part in dispersing workers no longer needed by the maturing oil industry. In the wake of layoffs in 1930, the state's governor discussed the problem of unemployment in a memorandum to the minister of internal relations. He noted that many, perhaps most, of the Venezuelan nationals laid off were not from Zulia at all; they had come from other parts of the country. He ordered the district officials in the vicinity of the oil camps to send them back to their places of origin and give them the wherewithal to go: "To the nationals, the majority of whom are workers from adjoining states, I command that the district and municipal executives [*jefes civiles*] order all those who are unemployed to leave and to give them the means to return to their native regions, where they can dedicate themselves to the great work of providing labor for agriculture, which is in such need of them."[105]

The Maracaibo agreements did not survive once Latin America's economies rebounded from the depression. Royal Dutch–Shell's El Águila expanded production in Mexico. In Venezuela Standard Oil bought Lago from Standard of Indiana in 1932, and Gulf purchased additional Venezuelan production. Just to keep up, Royal Dutch–Shell, too, uncapped its Venezuelan wells and resumed drilling (see Graph 4.2).[106] But the American onslaught into what had been a Royal Dutch–Shell domain in the previous decade was astonishing. Although Royal Dutch–Shell had retained some 90 percent of Venezuelan production as

Graph 4.2. Yearly Petroleum Production of Mexico and Venezuela
(1,000 b/d)

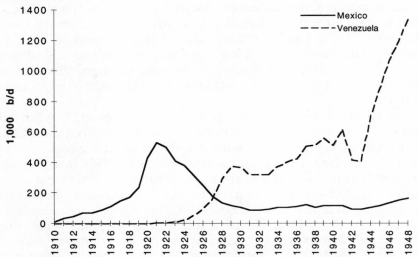

Source: Wirth, ed., *Latin American Oil Companies and the Politics of Energy,*
263–266.

late as 1928, and although its total output had grown twofold, it shared
just one-third of production in 1939. The American firms had grown
prodigiously, as Table 4.4 indicates.

The shock of the depression, however, had spurred the Venezuelan
state, in the meantime, to further regulate the company, and workers
vowed to make up for having been laid off.

Finally, the world oil glut and resultant layoffs in the Venezuelan oil
industry provoked militancy among native workers. Labor in Venezuela
now adopted the main concern of the Mexican oil workers—job security.
But most Venezuelans labored in the oil fields, not in the refineries,
which had been the bedrock of Mexico's labor militancy. After all, three-
quarters of Venezuela's oil was processed in refineries located in Curaçao
and Aruba. Also, Mexico had larger numbers engaged in domestic
marketing, not yet a notable part of Venezuela's export-oriented industry. Moreover, Royal Dutch–Shell and the other companies had been
bringing in workers from the West Indies, which delighted neither the
government nor the Venezuelan workers. Despite the important role
played by Antillean blacks in the Venezuelan economy, the ruling
elite—including General Gómez himself—asked the oil companies to
search for immigrant workers in Spain and Italy rather than the Antilles.

Table 4.4. Production Capacity in Venezuela, 1939

Company	Production Capacity (b/d)
Lago and Creole (Jersey Standard)	250,000
Venezuelan Oil Concession (Royal Dutch–Shell)	175,000
Mene Grande (Gulf)	75,000

Source: The Oil Weekly (18 March 1940): 86.

Note: In 1939 Gulf, Jersey Standard, and Royal Dutch–Shell accounted for all but 1 percent of Venezuela's petroleum production; see Karlsson, *Manufacturing in Venezuela*, 76.

Venezuelans resented the low-wage West Indians, who kept to themselves and spoke only English. West Indians even formed their own cricket teams.[107]

Nevertheless, the Venezuelans experienced a Mexican-style cutback during the Great Depression. In 1928 the foreign companies had employed twenty thousand Venezuelans; the depression had caused the companies to cut back by eight thousand. The layoffs of 1930 allowed the companies to pare some of their large outlays for experienced and expensive American workers. Foreign rig builders, who had been working for $350 per month, with paid vacation, were being replaced by lower-paid native workers. The oil glut of the late 1920s and early 1930s presented the oil companies with the opportunity—nay, the necessity—to reduce this expensive American work force. Between 1929 and 1932, the companies dismissed nearly four of every five of their highly paid foreign employees.[108]

The pay differentials between foreign and native workers caused much bitterness among the latter. Distribution of wages and salaries in the oil industry in 1936 still favored the foreigners. They composed just 13 percent of all personnel, but the foreigners commanded nearly 30 percent of the wage bill. Americans still retained the supervisory and managerial positions. American drillers continued to command long-term contracts, a salary nearly three times that of the highest-paid Venezuelans, paid vacations, the best company housing, stock options, and company savings programs. In the United States, drillers earned half as much and had little job security. Even the American gang pusher, who supervised up to fifty native peons laying twelve-inch pipeline, made nearly twice as much as the Venezuelan foremen.[109]

Venezuelan workers did not indicate overt discontentment when they suffered cutbacks during the depression. Of course, the Gómez government did not approve of strikes, and a 1930 strike in Royal Dutch–

Shell's oil fields lasted only briefly.[110] The oil workers, in any case, were not motivated to organize and push their demands too hard, especially while the companies were laying off.

The layoffs between 1929 and 1933, however, were giving the Venezuelan workers their first taste of job insecurity, an experience on which they would eventually build unions just like the Mexicans'. Those who remained had lost real wages and sought to organize to regain income and prevent future layoffs. Like the Mexicans, they waited until the companies were expanding again and rehiring.

Communist agitators began to organize the oil fields early in the 1930s. In 1933 Rodolfo Quintero and Víctor Vegas, sent by the Communist Party, took part in the founding of the Sociedad de Auxilio Mútuo de Obreros Petroleros (Mutual Aid Society of Oil Workers, SAMOP) in the oil town of Cabimas. Soon the organization was reputed to have five thousand members. It presented the oil companies with a series of demands, including salary increases, an end to racial discrimination, better living quarters, and the firing of "despotic" supervisors. The companies responded by firing SAMOP's leaders. Meanwhile, the Gómez government jailed many of the leaders, including Quintero. The organization disintegrated and the companies ignored its demands.[111]

With Gómez's death in December 1935, however, the changing political climate made possible the organization of openly confrontational labor unions. Communist organizers formed the first oil unions early in 1936. These new organizations received reluctant recognition from the new government, headed by Gen. Eleázar López Contreras, formerly Gómez's minister of war. Labor unrest grew throughout the year. Many strikes broke out in the oil towns of Zulia.[112]

While each union had its own demands, the most common grievances were quite similar from one union to another. Most sought recognition by the companies; an end to racial discrimination; a closed shop; increases in salary, education, and medical care; and better working and living conditions for their members. A few had specific grievances, however. A representative of the Lagunillas union noted a conflict in the Electrical Department of Lago Petroleum, a conflict involving one J. A. Latt, the chief of the department. The workers in the Electrical Department, charging that Latt allowed them no time to eat lunch and demanded twelve hours of work per day, during which he incessantly insulted them in English because he spoke no Spanish, demanded that he be fired. The union representative told the company that the problem with Latt could be resolved by employing Venezuelan supervisors and professionals, currently subject to discrimination and placed in subordinate positions. Other unions voiced similar demands.

The oil companies consistently refused to recognize or negotiate with the unions.[113] The growing militancy of the unions coupled with the intransigence of the companies rendered labor conflict in the oil fields inevitable.

In December 1935 the oil workers went out on a massive strike. The forty-two-day strike defied the companies and challenged López Contreras's new government. Venezuela's economy remained less dependent on modern sources of energy in the 1930s, but the Venezuelan state had come to depend, more than the Mexican government, on oil exports for its income. Obviously, it had to act. The workers offered a pretext: both identified the foreigners as the common enemy.

During the strike, the workers and white-collar employees rallied around the anti-imperialist rhetoric of the Marxist labor leaders. The strikers' demands were in large measure nationalistic, as opposed to purely economic or class-oriented. Oil workers demanded treatment equal to that accorded foreign workers, respect for Venezuela's laws, and recognition of their unions. They denounced the "foreign octopuses" and the privileges enjoyed by foreign workers.

Such nationalist, as opposed to anticapitalist, sentiments generated support among Venezuela's growing urban and bureaucratic middle classes. Like their Mexican brethren, Venezuela's labor leaders sought the closed shop and wished to be able to dismiss unpopular supervisors. They, too, desired to take control of and stabilize the labor market in the oil industry. Labor leaders demanded increases in wages, pay equal to that of foreign workers, and recognition of the unions.[114]

The companies refused labor's demands and denied that the workers had any basis at all for complaint. They declined to enter into a collective contract or even to negotiate with the unions. Company officials, hoping for a Gómez-style crackdown, even turned over the names of labor leaders to the local police.[115]

Instead, the new government in Caracas sought to temporize and create at least the appearance of neutrality. López Contreras promised that the workers would be accorded the guarantees of the law as long as they did not themselves violate the law. Nonetheless, Zulia's governor threatened the workers with jail if they did not return to work, while local officials in other states and regions were allowed to recruit strikebreakers, including some Indians from the nearby Guajiro Peninsula of Colombia.[116]

Such under-the-table aid did not end the strike. As the worker shutdown continued, the government suffered mounting losses of oil revenues. Finally, at the end of January 1937, the López Contreras regime intervened and forced the companies to agree to wage increases and housing allowances for all oil workers. Once the government had settled some of labor's demands, it arrested and deported the most influential labor leaders and members of the opposition; closed the oil workers' newspaper, *Petróleo*; and sought to undermine the unions and distract the membership.[117] Petroleum exports resumed, but the oil companies continued to refuse to recognize the Venezuelan unions, as they had been forced to do in Mexico, nor did they agree to give the workers job security or control over the workplace.

Because it had repressed labor, the López Contreras government lacked the backing of organized oil workers when it attempted, late in the 1930s, to gain fiscal control of Venezuela's petroleum reserves. After the strike of December 1936, the administration sought to resolve a series of its own grievances with the oil companies. These included widespread fraud in royalty payments and the companies' steadfast refusal to establish refineries in Venezuela. Rather than following Cárdenas's lead, López Contreras attempted to resolve these disputes informally or, failing that, in Venezuela's Supreme Court. The companies refused to meet the state's demands and blocked its efforts to establish tighter control over the industry.[118]

Venezuela's futile efforts in the late 1930s were reminiscent of Mexico's inability, in the previous decade, to enforce Article 27. As eventually occurred in Mexico, the Venezuelan government would also have to be assisted—even goaded—by militant and unified oil unions, which had their own agenda.

Conclusions

In the final analysis, it cannot be said that the Second Conquest—the process by which foreign capital invaded Latin America at the end of the nineteenth century—completely overran the political and social structures of the host countries. It would be closer to the evidence to conclude that capitalist enterprises had to adjust as they encountered political and social resistance. Indeed, the foreign oil companies were responsible for setting into motion some of the very forces that eventually emerged to reduce their autonomy. In providing export revenues, the petroleum industry contributed to the growth of the state bureaucracy. As a target at which all domestic political groups aimed, the foreign companies contributed to the state regulations and restrictions that began before the Great Depression and intensified thereafter.

Moreover, the foreign petroleum concerns contributed to their own decline by provoking social opposition to their invasion. The companies had tied Latin America tightly to world markets—capping a process initiated by railways and by the export of crops like coffee and fibers.

This increasingly intimate connection to world markets proved both beneficial and disruptive to Latin America. Petroleum companies introduced modern technological and managerial functions that were, in time, adopted by the commercial and working classes. Moreover, modern fossil fuels contributed to power generation and motor transport, thereby contributing positively to domestic industrialization and commercial exchange. With urbanization and the growth of job opportunities in and around the oil districts, workers found it increasingly possible to escape rural poverty and the tyranny of domestic landowners. Urbanization also expanded workers' access to educational facilities, political processes, and material benefits.

But the kind of modernization brought by the oil companies cut both ways. Workers became dependent on the industrial wage while the state relied on export revenues. Therefore, both the domestic proletariat and the political classes suffered during the periodic recessions and depressions that struck the world's industrial and commercial economy. Following a sharp depression, the politicians' call to regulate the "monopolistic" foreign trusts coincided with renewed union militancy among oil workers. Common ground was not difficult to find. The proletarians appealed deliberately for government assistance against the foreign employer, and the government saw labor unrest as another reason to regulate the foreign companies.

Several factors motivated workers to create the unions. Insecurity in the volatile industrial labor market encouraged collective action to stabilize wages and preserve jobs. Native workers also felt restricted in terms of upward mobility by the privileges of foreign workers and the power of foreign supervisors. In the end, labor militancy and political aggression combined to erode the position of the foreign oil companies within Latin America's economies. The dominance of foreign capital in Latin American petroleum was replaced by government-controlled, para-state companies like YPF, Pemex, and Petrobrás.

Foreign capital, however, ought not to be blamed for a continuation of preexisting social inequities in Latin America. There were definite limits to the social and political impact of the foreign oil companies. They could no more liberate all workers from rural poverty than they could eliminate existing discrimination toward Indians and blacks. (Indeed, many of the foreign supervisors shared these racist prejudices.) The income and benefits of modern capitalist production were not shared equally either before or after the Second Conquest because the host societies resisted rapid change. Capitalism as a historical process may have been rather more limited in the scope of its effects. The oilmen helped increase production and material wealth. They may have decided which workers got what wages, but not how the urban retailers shared increased earnings, nor how peasants and landlords shared the land. Much less did foreign capitalists decide how host governments spent their tax revenues.

To what extent was the experience of the oil industry in Latin America typical of foreign enterprise in other industries in Latin America? Oil companies were perhaps particularly vulnerable to pressure from host governments and their own labor forces. The nature of the industry bound them to specific locations and petroleum deposits. Nonetheless, it is becoming increasingly apparent that the ability of foreign interests to co-opt governing elites, to dominate weak states, to subjugate workers, or to extract profits from Latin America forever on their own terms was more limited than has previously been supposed. Indeed, many foreign concerns in Latin America in the nineteenth and twentieth centuries faced severe difficulties in their dealings with national authorities, made only limited profits, and concentrated in areas of the host economies where local interests were reluctant to invest. It would indeed be difficult to posit, as some analysts have, that the state in Latin American acted as a surrogate of international capital.[119] Over time, the ability of the government to restrict and regulate and the power of the proletariat to demand concessions both increased.

Notes

1. See Jean Meyer, "Los Estados Unidos y el petróleo mexicano: Estado de la cuestión," *Historia Mexicana* 18:1 (1968): 79–96; Anton Mohr, *The Oil Wars* (New York: Harcourt, Brace & Company, 1926); Stanton Hope, *The Battle for Oil* (London: R. Hale, 1958); and Enrique Mosconi, *El petróleo argentino, 1922–1930, y la ruptura de los trusts petrolíferos inglés y norteamericanos* (Buenos Aires: Talleres Gráficos Ferrari Hnos., 1936), among others.

2. Edith T. Penrose, ed., *The Large International Firm in Developing Countries: The International Petroleum Industry* (London: Allen & Unwin, 1968): 46–47.

3. Paul H. Giddens, *The Beginnings of the Petroleum Industry: Sources and Bibliography* (Harrisburg: Pennsylvania Historical Commission, 1941), 5–9; idem, *Early Days of Oil: A Pictorial History of the Beginnings of the Industry in Pennsylvania* (Princeton, N.J.: Princeton University Press, 1948), 10. Also see Harold F. Williamson and Arnold R. Daum, *The American Petroleum Industry*, 2 vols. (Evanston, Ill.: Northwestern University Press, 1959–1965).

4. See Ralph W. Hidy and Muriel E. Hidy, *Pioneering in Big Business, 1882–1911: History of the Standard Oil Company (New Jersey)* (New York: Harper & Row, 1955); Alfred D. Chandler, Jr., *The Visible Hand: The Managerial Revolution in American Business* (Cambridge, Mass.: Belknap Press, 1977), 424.

5. "Reports of W.I.C.O. Co.," Con. Div., Comptroller's Department, Standard Oil Company of New Jersey, New York (hereafter cited as SONJ). All

Standard Oil materials were given to Jonathan C. Brown by the late Henrietta M. Larson.

6. Henrietta Larson interview with W. E. Haley, August 1949, SONJ.

7. "Reports of W.I.C.O. Co."

8. U.S. Supreme Court, Transcript of Record, *The Waters-Pierce Oil Company* vs. *The State of Texas* (October term), 1908, no. 356 (Washington, D.C., 1909), 441.

9. Quotation from "Interview with Mr. S. W. Smith," 11 May 1918, Edward L. Doheny Research Fund Records, Occidental College, Los Angeles (hereafter cited as DRFR); *Waters Pierce Oil Co.* vs. *State* (1898), 44 S.W. Rep 936; 177 US 28.

10. U.S. Supreme Court, *The Waters-Pierce Oil Co.* vs. *The State of Texas* (1908), 442.

11. Marquis James, *The Texaco Story: The First Fifty Years, 1902–1952* (New York: The Texas Company, 1953), 6–8, 11–13, 21–22; Joseph A. Pratt, *The Growth of a Refining Region* (Greenwich, Conn.: Jai Press, 1980), 34–35; Martin V. Melosi, *Coping with Abundance: Energy and Environment in Industrial America* (Philadelphia: Temple University Press, 1985), 40–46.

12. Salary Book A, 1 January 1887, Secy's Dept., SONJ; Hidy and Hidy, *Pioneering in Big Business*, 5; Thomas C. Manning to Mariscal, no. 144, 30 May 1887, National Archives, Washington, D.C., Record Group 59, Despatches of U.S. Ministers to Mexico, 1822–1906; Hidy and Hidy, *Pioneering in Big Business*, 514.

13. U.S. Supreme Court, *The Waters-Pierce Oil Co.* vs. *The State of Texas* (1908), 466.

14. Mira Wilkins, *The Emergence of Multinational Enterprise: American Business Abroad from the Colonial Era to 1914* (Cambridge, Mass.: Harvard University Press, 1970), 123–124.

15. A. H. Clarke, "History of the La Brea y Pariñas Estate-Peru," *Bulletin of the Pan American Union* 18 (1909): 150; César Balestrini C., *La industria petrolera en América Latina* (Caracas: Universidad Central de Venezuela, 1971), 149. On the consortium, see Paul H. Giddens, "Pioneer of Oil Industry in Russia and Peru," in *Oil City Derrick* (7 March 1942).

16. Arturo Frondizi, *Petróleo y política*, 2nd ed. (Buenos Aires: Raigal, 1955), 67.

17. Gerald T. White, *Formative Years in the Far West: A History of Standard Oil Company of California and Predecessors through 1919* (New York: Appleton-Century-Crofts, 1962): 152–153; Edmund Burke to Doheny, Washington, D.C., 18 November 1900, Archive of the Archdiocese of Los Angeles, Mission Hills, California, the Estelle Doheny Collection, Miscellaneous Correspondence, 1900–1913 (hereafter cited as AALA); Frank J. Taylor and Earl M.Welty, *Sign of the 76: The Fabulous Life and Times of the Union Oil Company of California* (Los Angeles: The Company, 1976): 105–106.

18. Burke to Doheny, Washington, D.C., 18 November 1900, AALA.

19. William E. McMahon, *Two Strikes and Out* (Garden City, N.Y.: Country Life Press, 1939), 26–27; U.S. Senate, Committee on Foreign Relations, *Investi-*

gation of Mexican Affairs, 66th Cong., 1st Sess., vol. I:216; and "E. Richards, counsel for H. Clay Pierce, Summary of Correspondence," and J. B. Body to L., 22 August 1908, in "Summary of Correspondence: Negotiations with WPO Co.," Science Museum Library, London, S. Pearson and Son, Ltd., and Associated Companies, Historical Records (hereafter cited as Pearson Records), Box C-44, File 7.

20. Body to Pearson, Mexico, 23 August 1904; Pearson to Body, London, 26 January 1906; Body to Pearson, 23 June 1905; Pearson, "Memo for Mr. J. B. Body," 28 April 1908; B. to P., Coatzacoalcos, 29 May 1903, all in Pearson Records, Box A-4. Despite Pearson's financial ability to hire managerial talent and drilling expertise, his men could not drill deep enough to develop the Tabasco area, which, in the mid-1970s, would become the prolific La Reforma oil fields.

21. P to B, 23 December 1907; Cowdray, "History of the Fight with the Waters Pierce Oil Co.," August 1928; and Cowdray, "Private Memo re. negotiations with Mr. Clay Pierce", 8 March 1909, all in Pearson Records, Box C-44, File 7; Ronald MacLeay to Sir Edmund Gray, 18 June 1909, Public Record Office, London, Foreign Office Records, 368-309/25272; "History: The Mexican Eagle Oil Company, Ltd.," Pearson Records, Box C-43, File 1. F. C. Gerretson, *History of the Royal Dutch*, 4 vols. (Leiden: Brill, 1953–1957), IV:260, claims that El Águila incorporated in 1908.

22. "Extract from letter to Señor Guillermo Landa," 30 July 1909, Pearson Records, Box A-4.

23. Chambers, "Potrero No. 4," 163–164.

24. Lord Cowdray [as Sir Weetman Pearson was known after 1911], "Memorandum re. the Aguila Co.," 13 January 1919, Pearson Records, C-44, File 3. See Pan American Petroleum and Transport Co., *Mexican Petroleum* (New York): 35, 111, 117, 123, 127–168, 180–182; Clarence W. Barron, *The Mexican Problem* (Boston: Houghton Mifflin, 1917).

25. Gerretson, *History of the Royal Dutch*, I:383–386; III:55; quotation from 1920 annual report of the Royal Dutch Company in U.S. Federal Trade Commission, *Foreign Ownership of Petroleum Resources* (Washington, D.C., 1922): 12–13.

26. Gerretson, *History of the Royal Dutch*, III:4, IV:268–272, 276, 278, 280.

27. Ibid., IV:251. "Letter of Undertaking: S. Pearson & Son, Ltd., to the Royal Dutch Company and the "Shell" Transport and Trading Company, Ltd., 26 March 1919, Pearson Records, Box C-44, File 3; American consul general to sec. of state, London, 10 December 1920, National Archives, Department of State Records (hereafter cited as NADS), 812.6363/774; Cowdray, "Memo for Mr. Tanner: The R.D.-Shell Agreement," 21 March 1919, Pearson Records, Box C-44, File 3; R. S. Smith, "Royal Dutch/Shell, an History," unpublished, 174.

28. Hidy and Hidy, *Pioneering in Big Business*, 404, 711–712; Allen Nevins, *John D. Rockefeller: The Heroic Age of American Enterprise* (New York: Scribner, 1940), II:611–612; Bruce Bringhurst, *Antitrust and the Oil Monopoly: The Standard Oil Cases, 1890–1911* (Westport, Conn.: Greenwood, 1979): 134.

29. Sadler to S. B. Hunt, 5 March 1917, Directors' files, Sadler Papers, SONJ; George Sweet Gibb and Evelyn H. Knowlton, *The Resurgent Years, 1911–1927*,

vol. II of *The History of Standard Oil* (New York, 1956), 182, 198–199.

30. J. J. Carter, "Reports on London & Pacific Properties and Lobitos," 22 April, 15 July 1913, Imperial Oil Co., Toronto, file 157; London & Pacific Minute Book, 7 August 1913, IPC. For the subsequent history of the IPC in Peru, see Jonathan C. Brown, "Jersey Standard and the Politics of Latin American Oil Production, 1911–30," in John D. Wirth, ed., *Latin American Oil Companies and the Politics of Energy* (Lincoln: University of Nebraska Press, 1985), 15–22; Adalberto J. Pinelo, *The Multinational Corporation as a Force in Latin American Politics: A Case Study of the International Petroleum Company in Peru* (New York: Praeger, 1973); and Bennett H. Wall, *Growth in a Changing Environment: A History of Standard Oil Company (New Jersey), Exxon Corporation, 1950–1975* (New York: McGraw-Hill, 1988), 431–444.

31. Rosemary Thorp and Geoffrey Bertram, *Peru, 1890–1977: Growth and Policy in an Open Economy* (London: Macmillan, 1978), 374.

32. "Early Development of the Oil Industry in Colombia," 1943, Prod. Dept., administrative files, SONJ; Minister H. Philip to secy. of state, no. 783, Bogotá, 15 December 1921, NADS 821.6363/197; "Colombia . . .," reports on Colombia, 1919, Corwin's Producing files, Prod. Dept., SONJ.

33. "Colombia, General letters of progress . . .," Production Dept., SONJ; A. M. McQueen, "Outline and Developments on Colombia Concession of Tropical Oil Company," as cited in Colombia, Bureau of Information, *Colombia Review* (November 1927), 204–205; "Colombia, Conditions of Operations," 30 June 1921, "Tropical Oil Company Development during 1926," Production Dept., SONJ Production Dept.; "General letters of progress," 1922 and 1927, International Oil Co., Toronto, file 818; Consul E. C. Soule to sec. of state, Cartagena, 16 March 1922, NADS 821.6363/215.

34. Transcontinental Consolidated Oil Co., Ltd., no. 7, 24 August 1917, J. A. Brown to F. D. Asche, 23 June 1917, both in SONJ, Prod. Dept., Transcontinental Contract Files; George Sweet Gibb and Evelyn H. Knowlton, *The Resurgent Years, 1911–1927* (New York: Harper & Row, 1956), 87.

35. Gibb and Knowlton, *The Resurgent Years*, 41; Jonathan C. Brown, "Foreign Investment and Domestic Politics: British Development of Mexican Petroleum during the Porfiriato." *Business History Review* 61 (1987): 387–416.

36. George Philip, *Oil and Politics in Latin America: Nationalist Movements and the State Oil Companies* (New York: Cambridge University Press, 1982), 40. For Jersey Standard's entry into Venezuela, see Mira Wilkins, *The Maturing of Multinational Enterprise: American Business Abroad from 1914 to 1970* (Cambridge, Mass.: Harvard University Press, 1974), 210; Jonathan C. Brown, "Why Foreign Oil Companies Shifted Their Production from Mexico to Venezuela in the 1920s," *American Historical Review* 90:2 (1985): 362–385.

37. Enrique Mosconi, *La batalla del petróleo* (Buenos Aires: Ediciones Problemas Nacionales, 1956), 231; Brown, "Jersey Standard and the Politics of Latin American Oil Production," 30–31. On the relationship between the oil companies and the national governments of South America, see Mira Wilkins, "Multinational Oil Companies in South America in the 1920s," *Business History Review* 48 (1974): 414–446; Carl E. Solberg, "Entrepreneurship in Public

Enterprise: General Enrique Mosconi and the Argentine Petroleum Industry,"
Business History Review 61 (1982): 390–393; Philip, *Oil and Politics in Latin
America*, 169.

38. Mosconi, *La batalla del petróleo*, 214.

39. Solberg, "Entrepreneurship in Public Enterprise," 390–393; Philip, *Oil
and Politics in Latin America*, 169.

40. *The Oil Weekly* (11 October 1929): 73; James E. Buchanan, "Politics and
Petroleum Development in Argentina, 1916–1930," Ph.D. diss., University of
Massachusetts (1973), 182; Frederick A. Hollander "Oligarchy and Politics of
Petroleum in Argentina," Ph.D diss., UCLA (1976), 252, 284, 289, 291, 334–335;
Mosconi, *La batalla del petróleo*, 89–90.

41. *The Pipeline* (3 October 1928, 16 June 1929); Philip, *Oil and Politics in
Latin America*, 182–190.

42. Carl E. Solberg, "YPF: The Formative Years of Latin America's Pioneer
State Oil Company, 1922–39," in Wirth, *Latin American Oil Companies*, 91;
Solberg, *Oil and Nationalism in Argentina: A History* (Stanford, Calif.: Stanford
University Press, 1979), 146–147.

43. Solberg, "Entrepreneurship in Public Enterprise," 389; idem, *Oil and
Nationalism*, 174-175.

44. Solberg, "YPF: The Formative Years," 93.

45. Quotation from E. H. Davenport and Sidney Russell Cooke, *The Oil
Trusts and Anglo-American Relations* (New York: Macmillan, 1924), 87. Brown,
"Jersey Standard and Latin American Oil Production," 30–31.

46. Rory Miller, "British Firms and the Peruvian Government, 1885–1930,"
in D. C. M. Platt, ed., *Business Imperialism, 1840–1930* (Oxford: Oxford Univer-
sity Press, 1977), 378; Mira Wilkins, "Multinational Oil Companies in South
America in the 1920s," *Business History Review* 48:3 (1974): 437–438; Brown,
"Jersey Standard and Latin American Oil Production," 18–21; Thorp and Bertram,
Peru, 1890–1977, 374.

47. Thorp and Bertram, *Peru, 1890–1977*, 101.

48. *The Oil Weekly* (13 December 1929): 42, 44, 147–150.

49. Merrill Rippy, *Oil and the Mexican Revolution* (Leiden: Brill, 1972),
chaps. 1–4; Jonathan C. Brown, *Oil and Revolution in Mexico* (Berkeley and Los
Angeles: University of California Press, 1993), chap. 3; José Colomo, *The
Mexican Petroleum Law: Its Basis and Its Aims* (Mexico City, 1927), 8–10;
Pastor Rouaix, *Génesis de los artículos 27 y 123 de la constitución política de
1917*, 2nd ed. (Mexico City: Biblioteca del Instituto Nacional de Estudios
Históricos de la Revolución Mexicana, 1959), 47.

50. Lorenzo Meyer, *Mexico and the United States in the Oil Controversy,
1916–1942* (Austin: University of Texas Press, 1977), 56; Friedrich Katz, *The
Secret War in Mexico: Europe, the United States, and the Mexican Revolution*
(Chicago: University of Chicago Press, 1981), 326; Alan Knight, *U.S.-Mexican
Relations, 1910–1940: An Interpretation* (San Diego: Center for U.S.-Mexican
Studies, UCSD, 1987), 53–69. On Peláez, see Esperanza Durán de Seade, "Mexico's
Relations with the Powers during the Great War," Ph.D. diss., St. Antony's
College, Oxford University (1980), 283–301; and Brown, *Oil and Revolution*,
chap. 4.

51. H. Walker, "Mexico Memorandum: Action of Principal English Companies," Washington, D.C., 10 December 1920, NADS 812.6363/756; R. C. Craig to R. Seymour, Washington, D.C., 16 December 1920, FO 371-4499/A9015; I. G. Clark to Foreign Office, London, 11 January 1921, FO 371-5580/A278.

52. Tagle, "Informe sobre emigración obrera," Tampico, 23 July 1921, Archivo General de la Nación (hereafter cited as AGN), Mexico City, Department of Trabajo (hereafter cited as DT), caja 329, expediente 30; Andrés Barrientos to Obregón, Tampico, 27 September 1921, AGN, Mexico City, Papeles Presidenciales, Fondo Obregón-Calles (hereafter cited as AGN FOC), 104-H-10, legajo 1; Cowdray and Deterding to Obregón, 16, 17, 23, 24 December 1921, AGN FOC, 104-P1-P-15.

53. Henri Deterding, *An International Oilman*, as told to Stanley Naylor (London: Ivor Nicholson & Watson, 1934), 50–51, 83–84; Ludwell Denny, *We Fight for Oil* (New York: Knopf, 1928), 283.

54. Preston McGoodwin to sec. of state, Caracas, 1 May 1920, 2 May 1921, NASD 831.6363/31, /54; Edwin Lieuwen, *Petroleum in Venezuela: A History* (New York: Russell & Russell, 1967), 33.

55. B. S. McBeth, *Juan Vicente Gómez and the Oil Companies in Venezuela, 1908–1935* (New York: Cambridge University Press, 1983), 25; Lieuwen, *Petroleum in Venezuela*, 33–36.

56. McBeth, *Juan Vicente Gómez*, 17–20, 29, 36, 45, 107.

57. As quoted in Edwin Lieuwen, "The Politics of Energy in Venezuela," cited in Wirth, *Latin American Oil Companies*, 194.

58. E. C. Clarke to Foreign Office, 31 July 1922, FO 371-7325 A4350. See minutes dated 28 June 1922 appended to Anglo-Saxon Petroleum Co., "Memorandum," 21 June 1922, FO 371-7325 A4013. Deterding, *An International Oilman*, 77, claimed that the Shell portion, since 1907, had constituted 40 percent of the combine.

59. Lieuwen, "The Politics of Energy in Venezuela," 195; Weine Karlsson, *Manufacturing in Venezuela: Studies on Development and Location* (Stockholm: Almqvist & Wiksell, 1975), 87–88, 94; Lieuwen, *Petroleum in Venezuela*, 40.

60. McBeth, *Juan Vicente Gómez*, 162; Lieuwen, *Petroleum in Venezuela*, 42, 48.

61. American Consul General to sec. of state, London, 27 June 1922, NASD 831.6363/98; *The Oil Weekly* (18 October 1929): 23.

62. Stephen G. Rabe, *The Road to OPEC: United States Relations with Venezuela, 1919–1976* (Austin: University of Texas Press, 1982), 47; H. M. Wolcott, "The Venezuelan Petroleum Industry," 22 December 1928, NADS 831.6363/415; *The Oil Weekly* (22 April 1930): 76; Larson et al., *New Horizons*, 41–42, 58; Lieuwen, *Petroleum in Venezuela*, 39.

63. Solberg, *Oil and Nationalism*, 154; Jaime Galarza Zavala, *El festín del petróleo*, 2nd ed. (Caracas: Universidad Central de Venezuela, 1974), 91, 107; Philip, *Oil and Politics in Latin America*, 178; Leslie B. Rout, Jr., *Politics of the Chaco Peace Conference, 1935–39* (Austin: University of Texas Press, 1970); Pinelo, *The Multinational Corporation*; Herbert S. Klein, "American Oil Companies in Latin America: The Bolivian Experience," *Inter-American Economic Affairs* 18:2 (Autumn 1964): 47–72.

64. Peter Seaborn Smith, *Oil and Politics in Modern Brazil* (Toronto: Macmillan of Canada, 1976), 2–3, 19; Wilkins, "Multinational Oil Companies in South America," 443; Philip, *Oil and Politics in Latin America*, 193; Peter R. Odell, "The Oil Industry in Latin America," in Penrose, ed., *The Large International Firm*, 276–278.

65. Smith, *Oil and Politics in Modern Brazil*, 37; Philip, *Oil and Politics in Latin America*, 227.

66. John D. Wirth, "Setting the Brazilian Agenda, 1936–53," in Wirth, *Latin American Oil Companies*, 103, 119; idem, *Politics of Brazilian Development, 1930–1954* (Stanford, Calif.: Stanford University Press, 1970), 144–149; idem, "Setting the Agenda," 125; Philip, *Oil and Politics in Latin America*, 230–231.

67. André Gunder Frank, *Dependent Accumulation and Underdevelopment* (London: Macmillan, 1978), 170; Immanuel Wallerstein, "The Rise and Future Demise of the World Capitalist System: Concepts for Comparative Analysis," *Comparative Studies in Society and History* 16 (1974): 403; Nora Hamilton, *The Limits of State Autonomy: Post Revolutionary Mexico* (Princeton, N.J.: Princeton University Press, 1982), 38. Quotation from Pinelo, *The Multinational Corporation*, xiii; see also Philip, *Oil and Politics in Latin America*, 40; Alan Knight, "The Political Economy of Revolutionary Mexico, 1900–1940," in Christopher Abel and Colin M. Lewis, eds., *Latin America, Economic Imperialism, and the State: The Political Economy of the External Connection from Independence to the Present* (London: Athlone, 1985), 309.

68. Elbert Jay Benton, *Cultural Story of an American City: Cleveland*, 3 vols. (Cleveland: Western Reserve Historical Society, 1944–1946): II:12–13, and III:15–18; James Harrison Kennedy, *A History of the City of Cleveland, 1796–1896* (Cleveland: Imperial Press, 1896): 324.

69. Francis G. Couvares, *The Remaking of Pittsburgh: Class and Culture in an Industrializing City, 1877–1919* (Albany: State University of New York Press, 1984), 9–32; Harold F. Williamson et al., *The American Petroleum Industry: The Age of Illumination, 1859–1899* (Evanston, Ill.: Northwestern University Press, 1959), 83–84, 110–111.

70. *Historical Statistics of the United States, Colonial Times to 1970*, part 1 (Washington, D.C., 1975), 382; U.S. Census Office, *Abstract of the Twelfth Census of the United States, 1900* (Washington, D.C., 1902), 115–116.

71. Melodia B. Rowe, *Captain Jones—the Biography of a Builder* (Hamilton, Ohio, 1942), 34, 77. Jones went on to become an independent oilman and railway builder and founded the city of Gulfport, Mississippi. Hildegarde Dolson, *The Great Oildorado: The Gaudy and Turbulent Years of the First Oil Rush, Pennsylvania, 1859–1880* (New York: Random House, 1959): 30–32.

72. See the illustrations in Giddens, *Early Days of Oil*.

73. W. L. Connelly, *The Oil Business as I Saw It: Half a Century with Sinclair* (Norman: University of Oklahoma Press, 1954), 31; Rowe, *Captain Jones*, 32–33, 45; James, *The Texaco Story*, 13.

74. Pratt, *The Growth of a Refining Region*, 30; see also James, *The Texaco Story*, 13. On the size of black population and illiteracy rates, see U.S. Census Office, *Abstract of the Twelfth Census of the United States, 1900* (Washington, D.C., 1902), 113–116; idem, *Twelfth Census of the United States, 1900*, 6 vols.

(Washington, D.C., 1901), VI:681. Wildcatter quotation from Gerald Lynch, *Roughnecks, Drillers, and Tool Pushers: Thirty-Three Years in the Oil Fields* (Austin: University of Texas Press, 1987), 1, 71, 151. Says Lynch of the legendary mobility of the American roughneck, they were "full of quit," rarely staying on the job longer than six months.

75. Mexico, Departamento de la Estadística Nacional, *Resumen del censo general de habitantes de 30 de noviembre de 1921* (Mexico City: Talleres Gráficos de la Nación, 1928), 187–188, 190; Mexico, Secretaría de Economía, Dirección General de Estadística, *Estadísticas sociales del Porfiriato, 1877–1910* (Mexico City, 1956), 11; S. Lief Adleson G., "Historia social de los obreros industriales de Tampico, 1906–1919," Ph.D. diss., El Colegio de México (1982), 4; Mexico, Secretaría de Fomento, *Censo y división territorial del Estado de Tamaulipas verificados en 1900* (Mexico City, 1904).

76. Historically, the port of Veracruz had always dominated Mexico's foreign trade. See Inés Herrera Canales, *Estadística del comercio exterior de México (1821–1875)* (Mexico City: Instituto Nacional de Antropología e Historia, 1980), 237, 245–246, 262, 287–282. On the Mexican Central Railway, see H. S. Gilbert to Magill, 1 October 1902, National Archives, Washington D.C., Record Group 84, The Post Records of the U.S. Consulate at Tampico, Mexico (hereafter cited as Tampico Post Records), Miscellaneous Letters Received, 1905–1906; Daniel Cosío Villegas et al., *Historia moderna de México: El Porfiriato, la vida económica*, 10 vols. (Mexico City: Editorial Hermes, 1965), vol. 7, no. 2:10, 95, 247, 520, 544; Adleson, "Historia social de los obreros," 14–15.

77. Statistical tables of Mexico, Secretaría de Fomento, *Censo y división territorial del Estado de Vera Cruz;* and *Censo . . . de Tamaulipas* (Mexico City, 1904).

78. Powell Clayton to sec. state, 27 May 1898, U.S. Ministers, no. 443; quotation from Andrés Molina Enríquez, *Los grandes problemas nacionales* (Mexico City: Ediciones Era, 1978 [1909]), 158–159.

79. Pablo Perales Frigols, *Geografía económica del estado Zulia*, 2 vols. (Maracaibo: Imprenta del Estado, 1957), II:77. For a concise discussion of the region's rapid growth in the mid-nineteenth century, see Germán Cardozo Galué, "El circuito agroexportador marabino a mediados del siglo XIX," *Boletín Americanista* 33: 42–43 (1992–1993): 367–393. See also Pedro Cunill Grau, *Geografía del poblamiento venezolano en el siglo XIX*, 3 vols. (Caracas: Ediciones de la Presidencia de la República, 1987), II:1115–1148.

80. For example, the oil camps of Mene Grande and Casigua El Cubo were established in virtually unpopulated forest areas: Lieuwen, *Petroleum in Venezuela*, 6; McGoodwin to Secretary of State, Caracas, 26 August 1916, no. 770, 831.6363/13; *Records of the Department of State Relating to the Internal Affairs of Venezuela* (hereafter cited as RDS), microcopy no. M-366, r. 24; Memo, "The Venezuelan Petroleum Industry," Caracas, 7 October 1916, 831.6363/13; RDS, M-366, r. 24; Padre Alfonso Cobos López, *Datos para la historia de Casigua El Cubo* (San Carlos de Zulia: Litografía El Colonés, 1974), 2.

81. For a comprehensive study of the region's transportation system, see Nelson Paredes Huggins, *Vialidad y comercio en el occidente venezolano: Principios del siglo XX* (Caracas: Fondo Editorial Tropykos, 1984); Otto Gerstl,

Memorias e historias, 2nd ed. (Caracas: Ediciones de la Fundación John Boulton, 1977), 65; Benjamin Adam Frankel, "Venezuela and the United States, 1810–1888," Ph.D. diss., University of California–Berkeley (1964), 227; "Navegación por vapor en el Lago Maracbibo [*sic*]," *El Zulia Ilustrado* I:7 (30 June 1889): 58.

82. Juvenal Anzola, *De Caracas a San Cristóbal (1913)*, 2nd ed. (Caracas: Biblioteca de Autores y Temas Tachirenses, 1981), 66–67. All translations are ours unless otherwise noted.

83. On social changes, see, for example, Obispo Mariano Martí, *Documentos relativos a su visita pastoral de la diocesis de Caracas (1771–1784)*, vol. I, *Libro personal* (Caracas: Biblioteca de la Academia Nacional de la Historia, 1969), 130–131, 134–135, 140–141, 146. On the black population, see Federico Brito Figueroa, *La estructura económica de Venezuela colonial*, 2nd ed. (Caracas: Universidad Central de Venezuela, 1983), 103–104; Martí, *Documentos*, I:127, 129. On the culture of Zulia's blacks, see, for example, Juan de Dios Martínez Suárez, *Chimbangueles: Antecedentes y orígenes* (Maracaibo: Colección Afrovenezolana no. 1, 1983); idem, *Las Barbúas: Mitos y leyendas de origen africano presentes en el sur del Lago de Maracaibo* (Maracaibo: Colección Afrovenezolana no. 2, 1986). For a concise analysis of labor recruitment and working conditions in Zulia's agricultural zone, see Peter S. Linder, "Coerced Labor in Venezuela, 1880–1936," *The Historian* 57:1 (Autumn 1994): 43–58.

84. Jesús Silva Herzog, *El petróleo de México* (Mexico City, 1940), 5.

85. Enrique S. Cerdán, "Informe," 9 January 1920, AGN DT, C. 224, E. 24.

86. "Tampico and Minatitlán refinery estimates," 1916, British Science Museum Library, London, Pearson Records, C-45, File 4; Zamora to chief, 19 May 1927, AGN DT, C. 1209, E. 5. These conditions redounded to the benefit of the companies, for morale among the native proletariat remained relatively high. When foreigners momentarily evacuated the oil zone following the 1914 Veracruz invasion and the 1916 Pershing expedition, Mexican workers stayed at their jobs, unpaid, protecting wells and pumping equipment: W. A. Thompson to Robert Lansing, 29 May 1914, NADS 812.6363/85; Hohler to Foreign Office, 26 June 1916, FO, 371-2701, no. 123687.

87. On the rest of the Mexican economy, see John Womack, Jr., "The Mexican Economy during the Revolution, 1910–1920," *Marxist Perspectives* I:4 (1978): 80–123; Alan Knight, *The Mexican Revolution*, 2 vols. (New York: Cambridge University Press, 1986), II:406–419.

88. John M. Hart, *Anarchism and the Working Class in Mexico, 1860–1931* (Austin: University of Texas Press, 1978), 139; Enrique S. Cerdán to chief, Mexico, 29 January 1920, AGN DT, C. 224, E. 23; Inspector to Chief, Minatitlan, 11 July 1920, AGN DT, C. 215, E. 4, Fs. 40-43; J. C. Evans to Thomas H. Bevan, Tampico, 14 June 1915, NADS, Tampico Consulate, 850.4/242. See especially Brown, *Oil and Revolution in Mexico*, chap. 5; S. Lief Adleson G., "The Cultural Roots of the Oil Workers' Unions in Tampico, 1910–1925," in Jonathan C. Brown and Alan Knight, eds., *The Mexican Petroleum Industry in the Twentieth Century* (Austin: University of Texas Press, 1992): 36–62.

89. See Ramón Eduardo Ruiz, *Labor and the Ambivalent Revolutionaries: Mexico, 1911–1923* (Baltimore: Johns Hopkins University Press, 1976); Barry Carr, *El movimiento obrero y la política en México, 1910–1929*, 2 vols. (Mexico

City: Secretaría de Educación Pública, 1976); F. Sánchez Tagle to chief, 21 July 1921, AGN DT, C. 329, E. 30, f. 26; JAA to JB, 24 August 1924, Shell International Petroleum Company, London, Group History, Country Series, Mexico Management (hereafter cited as Shell GHC/MEX), file D29/1/1.

90. Dawson to sec. of state, 20 April 1924, National Archives, Washington, D.C., Record Group 84, Tampico Post Records 850.4.; S. Lief Adleson, "Coyuntura y conciencia: Factores convergentes en la fundación de los sindicatos petroleros de Tampico durante la década de 1920," in Elsa Cecilia Frost et al., eds., *El trabajo y los trabajadores en la historia de México* (Mexico City and Tucson: University of Arizona Press, 1979), 632–660.

91. Araujo to chief, Tampico, 13 May 1925, 30 July 1925, AGN DT, C. 725, E. 2; Bay to sec. of state, Tampico, 26 May 1925, Tampico Post Records, 850.4; Jonathan C. Brown, "Foreign Oil Companies, Oil Workers, and the Mexican Revolutionary State in the 1920s," in Alice Teichova et al., eds., *Multinational Enterprise in Historical Perspective* (New York: Cambridge University Press, 1986), 265–266.

92. Cook to sec. of state, Caracas, 24 April 1925, NADS 831.6363/274, no. 966. Also see Fletcher to sec. of state, La Guaira, 15 March 1922, NADS 831.63/15; Sanders to sec. of state, Maracaibo, 9 December 1922, NADS 831.6363/126.

93. Charles Bergquist, *Labor in Latin America: Comparative Essays on Chile, Argentina, Venezuela, and Colombia* (Stanford, Calif.: Stanford University Press, 1986), 218; McBeth, *Juan Vicente Gómez,* 145, 150–153; Winthrop R. Wright, *Café con leche: Race, Class, and National Image in Venezuela* (Austin: University of Texas Press, 1990), 77–78.

94. Paul Nehru Tennassee, *Venezuela, los obreros petroleros y la lucha por la democracia* (Madrid: Editorial Popular, 1979), 136–137, 143–144.

95. As quoted in McBeth, *Juan Vicente Gómez,* 157. See also Charles Bergquist, *Labor in Latin America,* 225; Lieuwen, *Oil in Venezuela,* 50–51; Celestino Mata, *Historia sindical de Venezuela, 1813–1985* (Caracas: Urbina y Fuentes, 1985), 31–41; Julio Godio, *El movimiento obrero venezolano, 1850–1944* (Caracas: Editorial Ateneo de Caracas, ILDIS, 1980), 74–75.

96. Henrietta M. Larson, Evelyn H. Knowlton, and Charles S. Popple, *New Horizons, 1927–1950: History of Standard Oil Company (New Jersey)* (New York: Harper, 1971), 47; American Petroleum Institute, *Petroleum Facts and Figures, 1950* (New York, 1951), 170; Alberto J. Olvera, "The Rise and Fall of Union Democracy at Poza Rica, 1932–1940," in Brown and Knight, *The Mexican Petroleum Industry,* 63–64.

97. C. E. Macy to sec. of state, 2 September 1931, NADS 812.00-Tamaulipas/ 44; Julio Valdivieso Castillo, *Historia del movimiento sindical petrolero en Minatitlán* (Mexico City, 1963), 59–60. Also see Marcos Tonahtiuh Águila M., "Trends in Registered Mexican Labor Conflicts, 1927–1931," *Economía: Teoría y Práctica,* no. 4 (1995): 85–102; Jonathan C. Brown, "Labor and the State in the Mexican Oil Expropriation," Texas Papers on Mexico, 90-10, Institute of Latin American Studies, University of Texas at Austin, 1990. E. V. K. FitzGerald, "Restructuring through the Depression: The State and Capital Accumulation in Mexico, 1925–40," in Rosemary Thorp, ed., *Latin America in the 1930s: The Role of the Periphery in World Crisis* (New York: St. Martin's Press, 1984), 253–

254; Wirth, *Latin American Oil Companies and the Politics of Energy*, 263.

98. J. Rennow to Luis I. Rodríguez, 15 December 1934, AGN, Papeles Presidenciales, Fondo Lázaro Cárdenas (hereafter cited as AGN FC), C. 432.2/8, E. 1; Hamilton, *The Limits of State Autonomy*, 95; "Extractos," 14 August–3 September 1935, AGN FC, C. 437.1/37; Joe C. Ashby, *Organized Labor and the Mexican Revolution under Lázaro Cárdenas* (Chapel Hill: University of North Carolina Press, 1963), 72–75.

99. Contrato, 1 July 1937, AGN, Archivo Histórico de Hacienda [Records of the Commission of Experts], C. 1844–3, f. 25.

100. James B. Steward to sec. of state, 17 August 1937, NADS, 812.00-Tamaulipas/307; Gallop to Troutbeck, 2 October 1937, FO 371-20636, A7243.

101. *The Mexican Oil Strike of 1937: The Economic Issue*, 2 vols. (Mexico City, n.d.), II:25.

102. On the compromise, see NG to Godber, 7 March 1938, FO 371-21463/A1864; Philip, *Oil and Politics in Latin America*, chap. 10. Lázaro Cárdenas, *Obras*, 3 vols. (Mexico City, 1972), I:389; Godber to the Foreign Office, 17 March 1938, FO 371-20634/A2119.

103. Anthony Sampson, *The Seven Sisters: The Great Oil Companies and the World They Made* (New York: Viking, 1975), 74; John M. Blair, *The Control of Oil* (New York: Pantheon, 1976), 55; Roy Leigh, "Maracaibo Restriction Agreement May Be Extended during 1930," *The Oil Weekly* (17 December 1929): 23, 57. In a way, the 1929 oil glut was a forerunner of the 1982 phenomenon, except that OPEC and other producing countries—not the international companies—now control much of the world's production.

104. On layoffs, see Cook to sec. of state, Caracas, 7 May 1927, NADS 831.6363/357. Quotation from Mokma to sec. of state, Maracaibo, 12 August 1931, National Archives, Washington, D.C., Record Group 84, Post Records for the United States Consulate at Maracaibo, Venezuela (hereafter cited as Maracaibo Post Records), C8.6/850, 1931, vol. 5, no. 850. Also see Walker, "Coffee Report, 1928," Maracaibo, 19 January 1929, no. 333, Maracaibo Post Records, C8.6, 1929, vol. 6, no. 333; Cook to sec. of state, Caracas, 19 September 1927, NADS 831.00/1337, no. 1380; Alex K. Sloan, "The Labor Supply in Maracaibo," Maracaibo, 6 April 1926, Maracaibo Post Records, C.6/850.4, 1926 vol. 5, no. 38; Vincencio Pérez Soto, *Mensaje que Vincencio Pérez Soto, Presidente del Estado Zulia, presenta a la Asamblea Legislativa en su reunión de 1932* (Maracaibo, 1932), 15.

105. Pérez Soto to Ministro de Relaciones Interiores, Maracaibo, 19 July 1930, Acervo Histórico del Estado Zulia, 1930, vol. 7, leg. 5, no. 171.

106. On the breakdown of the agreement, see Williamson and Daum, *The American Petroleum Industry*, II:532. Henrietta Larson has written that, more than any other event, the growth of East Texas production in the 1930s rendered the Achnacarry and other agreements inoperable. Anyway, by 1936, at the age of seventy-eight, Sir Henri Deterding stepped down as managing director of Royal Dutch–Shell. He died in 1939. Walter Teagle retired as the chief executive of Jersey Standard in 1937, staying on as chairman of the board: Larson et al., *New Horizons*, 309–313.

107. *The Pipeline* (2 May 1928): 191; "Venezuelan Annual Report," 1926, FO 371-12063 A1750; Wright, *Café con leche*, 77.

108. Rabe, *The Road to OPEC*, 38, 49; Laura Randall, *The Political Economy of Venezuelan Oil* (New York: Praeger, 1987), 20–21, 64; Tennassee, *Venezuela*, 164; Bergquist, *Labor in Latin America*, 221.

109. McBeth, *Juan Vicente Gómez*, 127; Roy E. Leigh, "Tendency Is toward the Europeanization of South American Oil Operations," *The Oil Weekly* (10 January 1930): 24–25.

110. W. O'Reilly to A. Henderson, Caracas, 19 November 1930, FO 371-14300, A7692.

111. Tennassee, *Venezuela*, 153–154.

112. Ibid., 166–168, 181, 185.

113. Ibid., 200–201, 205–206, 223–228.

114. In the next year, white-collar Venezuelan employees demanded treatment equal to that of the foreign employees. Their association asked for a 30 percent raise and rights to use the same residential areas, clubs, and transport facilities as the foreigners. It rankled the Venezuelan clerks that they had to travel on the lake steamers as second-class passengers, "eating the same food as the crew" (Bergquist, *Labor in Latin America*, 243–244).

115. Luis Vallenilla, *Oil: The Making of a New Economic Order: Venezuelan Oil and OPEC* (New York: McGraw-Hill, 1975), 44; Bergquist, *Labor in Latin America*, 230, 233–234, 238–239; Tennassee, *Venezuela*, 229–231.

116. Tennassee, *Venezuela*, 236, 245, 250–252.

117. Rómulo Betancourt, *Venezuela: Oil and Politics* (Boston, 1979), 56–57; Rabe, *The Road to OPEC*, 49; Bergquist, *Labor in Latin America*, 240–242.

118. Kelvin Singh, "Oil Politics in Venezuela during the López Contreras Administration (1936–1941)," *Journal of Latin American Studies* 21:1 (February 1989): 93, 94–100.

119. See, for example, Nikita Harwich Vallenilla, ed., *Asfalto y revolución: La New York & Bermúdez Company* (Caracas: Monte Ávila Editores, 1992); idem, coord., *Inversiones extranjeras en Venezuela, siglo XIX*, 2 vols. (Caracas: Academia Nacional de Ciencias Económicas, 1992). On the "surrogate" thesis, see Frank, *Dependent Accumulation and Underdevelopment*, 170; Wallerstein, "The Rise and Future Demise of the World Capitalist System," 403; Hamilton, *The Limits of State Autonomy*, 38.

5. An Alternative Approach

Mira Wilkins

In the last few decades, business historians have asked questions about the organization of business activities over time, the nature of what is done within an individual enterprise, and the impact of international business. As business historians, we have not attempted a general theory along the lines of modernization, dependency, or imperialism, but, rather, have aimed to understand how business enterprises perform under changing circumstances and to appraise their role in the world economy. We tend to identify with the modernization argument, accepting that growth is spurred by international interaction, yet, we do not "blame" the victims for lack of responsiveness (or even use the word "victims").

The approach is not normative; rather, it is analytic, seeking to define the place of multinational enterprise in the important economic developments in the nineteenth and twentieth centuries. We argue, for instance, that the vast expansion of international trade from 1870 to 1914, including the great swell in the export of raw materials, did not arise independently of the actors (firms) that made the trade possible. Thus, the conduits that create and bind the integrated world economy have to be studied to aid us in explaining the dynamics of both global and national economies in the last two centuries.[1]

The multinational enterprise—a firm with headquarters in a "home" country and business operations in another or many other "host" countries—is a familiar player today. Yet, the form has a long history. The present book, which covers the years 1850–1930, coincides with the emergence and maturing of the modern multinational enterprise. In this period, their impact was profound.[2] When this volume considers International Harvester, Royal Dutch–Shell, and Standard Oil of New Jersey—now Exxon—the topic is modern multinational enterprise.

Too often, discussions of multinational enterprises have dealt with them as exporters from the home nation and then manufacturers within host nations; this is too limited an approach. We have to ponder the entire range of business activities over borders, along with the effects on the world economy. My definition of a business includes those that produce goods and services; that is, a multinational enterprise is a firm that extends itself to carry on business over borders.[3] Historically, multinational enterprises make both market- and supply-oriented investments, the first to reach a market in the host country and the second to find sources of supply and to export from the host country. An individual multinational enterprise often participates in both activities, sometimes, albeit not necessarily, in the same host country.

Attention to the history of multinational enterprises gives a unique perspective on the integration of the world economy and, specifically, on their influence on Latin America during the "export boom" from 1850 to 1930. Our approach not only looks closely at the business entities, but focuses on the nature and sources of global demand. Businesses do not produce goods and services unless there is a demand for (or a potential demand for) their output.[4] This is crucial, because by the late nineteenth century, worldwide economic change was rapidly accelerating, and the demand for goods and services both expanded and altered substantially. The first Industrial Revolution in Britain (characterized by new technologies in textiles and iron, the rise of the factory, and the application of steam power) was completed by 1850 and its influence was spread globally. Subsequently, the fast-evolving industries in Europe and the United States included those that produced steel, metal products, electrical equipment, oil, chemicals, and processed food. In Europe and the United States, population was growing, urbanization increasing, and real incomes mounting. Productivity in the agricultural and industrial sectors was greatly enhanced as new process technologies multiplied. Demand rose for more and new producer and consumer goods—and for the inputs needed to make them.

In the late nineteenth century, a revolution in transport and communication occurred. Transportation time and costs fell as steamships crossed the Atlantic. The cable also had the effect of cutting time and costs. Shipping, trading, financial, accounting, insurance, and other services facilitated global transactions. The London stock market came of age as an international distributor of financial resources. Separate commodity exchanges took shape. The Chicago Board of Trade, created by Chicago's merchants in 1848, developed in the late 1800s; by 1900 there were grain exchanges in Winnipeg, New York, Buenos Aires, and many European cities. London became the premier metal market. The New York Coffee

Exchange was organized in 1882 (the first modern international coffee market); it was followed by exchanges in Le Havre and Hamburg (1887) and London (1890). Information costs declined sharply. World trade and investment soared with the lower costs of doing international business.[5]

Latin America in the sixteenth century furnished precious metals and thus was very much linked to the world economy. In the eighteenth century, foreign merchants carried sugar from the Caribbean to Europe, but by the late nineteenth century, beet sugar in Europe competed. In the closing decades of the nineteenth century, the United States and Europe had adequate coal and iron resources for their expanding steel industries. Many of the differentiated metal products (from sewing machines to cash registers) did not require inputs from Latin America.

The new electrical industry, however, meant calls for copper, and the response in the early twentieth century was U.S. multinational enterprises' large-scale development of Chilean copper mines. Demand for fertilizers to raise agricultural output had meant collection of guano and its export from Peru and, subsequently, the mining of nitrates in Chile and their export, but by the 1920s, synthetic nitrates were substituting for natural ones. In the case of guano and then nitrates, multinational enterprises played a role. In the late nineteenth and early twentieth centuries, Latin America was a participant in the world economy to a larger extent than ever in history. Argentina, with grain and beef exports, was said to rank among the five richest countries of the world. Mexico during the Porfiriato had very high growth rates.[6]

The surge in demand for the three commodities considered in this volume—coffee, henequen, and oil—must be viewed in the context of swelling world trade and investment during the late nineteenth and early twentieth centuries. The book's focus on these three commodities is important because each contributed to the rise in exports from Latin America. The development of each was in response to a very different demand. The activities in each commodity were, from a business standpoint, differently organized. Each involved multinational enterprises, but in unique ways. Each faced different competition in world markets. And each had a profound impact on the locale(s) where it was produced. Had there not been external demand (demand outside Latin America), none of the developments described in the preceding chapters would have occurred.[7] My argument is that the "boom" in exports from 1850 to 1914 was not a result of a shift from "statist colonial regimes" to "liberal export regimes," or of any *government* policy, for that matter, but, instead, related to the transformation of the world economy and the emergence of key business actors prepared to take advantage of new profit-making opportunities. I will argue that the impact of the exports and the roles of multinational enterprises were not uniform, but that in the producing nations there were, in the cases of all three commodities, fundamental, economic consequences.

The world economy of 1914 was shattered by the First World War. Demand for primary commodities rose rapidly during the war and in its aftermath, only to collapse in 1920–1921. Individual commodities were affected differently in the recovery after 1922. The Latin American export "boom" was more uneven in the 1920s than in the prewar years, and, in many commodities, there was no boom.[8] Then, in the 1930s, all commodity prices were depressed, as worldwide demand evaporated. Problems were global and not confined to Latin America.

Commodity prices in the nineteenth century tended to be set in world markets and to fluctuate sharply. Yet, even then, the prices of certain traded items were set by enterprises that were price makers rather than price takers in world markets; this became more common in the twentieth century. By the early twentieth century, important government interventions in commodity markets took place, from the coffee price support program in Brazil (in 1906) to the henequen valorization plan (in 1915), to the Stevenson Agreement to raise rubber prices (in 1922). These were not "one–shot" arrangements, but were renewed. Brazil, for example, introduced second and third valorization agreements in 1917 and 1923; initially, these were instituted by the São Paulo government, but after 1921 the federal government became involved (on an off-and-on basis); São Paulo state government measures for a "permanent defense of the price of coffee" came into effect in 1925. By 1929 control schemes—by private companies and governments—for many primary products were ubiquitous.[9] When national and colonial governments acted to support prices, this was not the return of "statist colonial regimes," but, instead, an awareness of the special characteristics of commodity trade, for example, the price volatility based on supply and demand conditions.

After 1930 both corporate and governmental interventions into primary commodity markets multiplied. More important, in the decades after 1930, primary products (oil excepted) increasingly became a smaller input in the overall output of goods and services. Food constituted a lower share of consumers' budgets in industrial nations. Synthetic nitrates and, later, synthetic rubber would substitute for the natural product. Synthetic textiles gradually and then dramatically reduced the significance of raw cotton and wool. Coffee continued, however, to have no substitute, and oil demand burgeoned as industrialization, fueled by oil rather than coal, spread globally in the post–World War II era. With oil, new demand spurred new exploration and the opening up of new sources of supply.

I will analyze why the business organizations in the three exported commodities under consideration here were so distinct and will trace how these business structures evolved, their importance, and their economic impacts. I take the view that developments from 1850 to 1930—especially in coffee and oil (and perhaps in henequen)—set the foundation for what would occur in the aftermath of the Second World War.

Coffee

Tea and coffee were imports that transformed European and U.S. existence. Both were introduced into Europe in the early seventeenth century—the first from China, the second from the Arab world. Cargoes of tea are said to have arrived in Amsterdam in 1610. Five years later, coffee reached Venice. During most of the seventeenth century, tea and coffee were expensive. As the volume of trade rose, however, prices fell and over time both moved from luxury to everyday products. Tea was handled by the East India companies and later by private merchants. Tea estates developed in the East. Merchant traders managed the estates. The organization of tea production and markets was entirely different from that of coffee.[10]

Steven Topik documents the spread of coffee cultivation from Yemen. Coffee came to be grown in Java, Ceylon, and in other parts of Asia and then in various African colonies, but it was in Latin America that the raising of coffee triumphed. By 1913 an estimated 91 percent of world coffee production was in Latin America, with the largest output from Brazil. While the British had become fond of tea, Americans and continental Europeans preferred coffee. Tea became a major export from the East because of demand in Britain and, to a far lesser extent, in the United States and continental Europe. Coffee became a key export from Latin America because of the changes occurring in Europe and the United States and escalating consumer demand. Both products came to be sold to consumers in stores and restaurants (and coffeehouses). By the late nineteenth century, both tea and coffee were on occasion sold as packaged brand name products. Where the drinks were served to customers, tea might be sold by brand; coffee almost never was.[11]

Where did multinational enterprises fit into the coffee story? There was little foreign direct investment in coffee growing (although there was some).[12] In certain countries, coffee was a small farm crop; in others, such as Brazil, it was a crop raised, at least in the period under consideration, on large estates principally owned and managed by Brazilians. As with virtually all agricultural products, individual growers did not integrate forward into trade. This seems a general pattern; farmers do not have the ability (or the inclination) to cope with commerce outside the immediate vicinity of the growing area. Yet commodities do not travel over borders without "handlers." This is where multinational enterprise, in the form of traders, figures prominently.

East India companies had moved Arab and Asian coffee in the very early days, but they never diversified to trade in coffee from Latin America. Typically, it was partnerships of foreign merchants (and I include them as multinational enterprises) that provided the conduit for export.[13] By 1880, two-thirds of Brazil's railroad system went through coffee-growing provinces. Many of these railroads seem to have been financed and built with foreign capital. Coffee exports needed to be financed, and a new banking system evolved in Brazil, linked initially with coffee and then to provide credits for other activities. Foreign banks participated.[14]

The end of slavery had no impact on the steady expansion in Brazil's coffee growing; the reason, of course, was the sustained demand for coffee in the ever-larger urban areas of the United States and Western Europe. And then there was the demand for coffee in Brazil itself. There were no substitutes for coffee (tea was not a substitute).

Brazilian capital accumulation was adequate for major Brazilian-owned plantations, which provided wealth to Brazilians. Yet, these developments could not have taken place had there not existed fundamental infrastructure investments, that is, the foreign investment in international trade, finance, and transportation.

Most of the merchants who handled commodities (particularly agricultural ones) after 1850 were involved in family firms, and we are just learning about these enterprises. While some specialized in a particular primary product, others were general trading companies. Robert Greenhill's essay on Brazilian Warrant provides fascinating insights into the structure of the Brazilian international coffee trade. E. Johnston & Co., a British firm, was one of the principal coffee exporters from Brazil and had long been involved in the coffee trade. Its senior partner, Edward Johnston, became president of the London and Brazilian Bank when it began in 1862. This British overseas bank was one of many such. Johnston was also president of the Royal Mail Steampacket Co.[15]

Elsewhere I have written on the British freestanding company, which was a special type of multinational enterprise. Such companies, unlike the "typical" well-studied multinational enterprises, did not start business at home and then pursue business activities abroad based on core competencies established in the home market. Rather, they were set up to undertake business overseas. In the late nineteenth and the early twentieth centuries, there were literally thousands of British freestanding companies headquartered in Britain. Students of Latin American business history have found the concept relevant to their understanding of British investments in Latin America. The British overseas banks have been identified as successful British freestanding companies.[16] One frequent characteristic of freestanding companies was that there was often a loose cluster of companies with overlapping participants, sometimes with a trading company at the center. Johnston's involvement in related trading, banking, and shipping activities seems to fit a pattern.

Greenhill reports that early in the development of the Brazilian coffee trade, relatively few foreign merchants participated, and these were mainly British; by the 1890s, however, numerous German and American traders saw opportunities.[17] After government intervention in the coffee market, however, the prominent German trading house Theodor Wille obtained (in 1908) the government agency. The response in 1909 of British trader E. Johnston & Co. was to launch a new company, Brazilian Warrant, on the London Stock Exchange. The former partners in E. Johnston & Co. obtained a sizable interest in Brazilian Warrant.

Brazilian Warrant's "service" activities in the coffee trade are wonderfully documented by Greenhill, whose research shows how this British multinational enterprise continued to play an important role in the coffee business. By 1919 it owned the largest warehouse company in São Paulo and its profits came from its storage capacity and its mechanized handling of coffee; it was able to mechanically grade, blend, bag, and ship for both foreign and local merchants. It diversified and stored sugar, beans, rice, and cereals, as well as coffee.[18]

Before the First World War, Brazilian Warrant had established wholly owned subsidiaries in New York and New Orleans to sell coffee shipments to importers and roasters, thus internalizing within the firm key facets of its business. The United States was the principal market for Brazilian coffee. Greenhill shows how the "trading company" continued to respond to the enlarged São Paulo government role. Brazilian Warrant integrated backward into coffee plantations and estate management beginning in 1920. (It could take advantage of Brazilian support of coffee prices.) Whereas agricultural companies rarely (if ever) integrated forward, it was not uncommon for trading companies to integrate backward in growing, just as they integrated into a diverse group of related activities. In the mid-1920s, Brazilian Warrant owned the third-largest coffee estate in Brazil. By the late 1920s, it controlled a substantial group of coffee-related companies in Brazil, North America, and the United Kingdom. It was fully integrated, with a presence from growing to selling abroad.[19]

These data on business structures are vital to our understanding of Brazilian economic history. We need more such details on how Brazilian coffee was handled internationally, for they help us discern the attributes of this industry.

We know far less about the role in Brazil of the sellers of coffee within the major consumer markets. Sometimes American exporters from Brazil and importers into the United States were one and the same. Arbuckles, for example, had "up-country buying offices" in Brazil. It was a leading exporter from Brazil and importer into the United States of coffee; it also handled roasting and selling within the United States.[20] In 1907 the son of a Bremen, Germany, coffee merchant, Ludwig Roselius, established a multinational coffee business; one of the group's affiliates was Kaffee Hag Corporation (formed in the United States in March 1914). It marketed a caffeine-free coffee, then called De Kofa and which years later was sold under the name Sanka.[21] By the 1920s, a very few large U.S. food-processing companies—such as General Foods—roasted and packed (in cans) coffee, sold a brand name product, and had integrated backward into purchasing by sending representatives to Colombia and Jamaica, for example.[22] None of the large food-processing companies invested in growing—in Brazil or elsewhere.

If the coffee purchasers in consumer countries had (in general) only a relatively small role in the producing countries, the activities of foreign multinational enterprises in Brazilian banking were significant. These participants, not confined to the London & Brazilian Bank, financed the coffee (and also the rubber) trade. By 1913 sixteen foreign-owned banks operated in Brazil: three were British, three German, five French, two Belgian, two Portuguese, and one Argentinean. They provided numerous linkages within the Brazilian economy. Some established branches at São Paulo's "hinterland coffee plantations." Although a minority in terms of numbers, the British-headquartered banks in Brazil in 1914 were said to control a third of the deposits in the Brazilian banking system. They engaged in both domestic and international banking—as did the other foreign banks.[23]

Brazilian Warrant's return on capital peaked in 1922 (at 14 percent); the firm had a loss in 1926, and in the 1927–1929 period, only modest returns (3.1, 5.9, and 2.1 percent, respectively). The British overseas banks in Brazil had difficulties in the 1920s. The leader, the Bank of

London and South America (which resulted from a 1923 merger), experienced major losses from 1923 to 1927, attributed to bad management.[24] Thus, there was no guarantee that foreign multinational enterprises would flourish.

Earlier, I pointed out that it was rare for growers to integrate forward into trade. Thus, the figures that Topik provides on foreign shippers' handling of Brazilian coffee, foreign companies' insuring of the cargo, and foreign exporters' activities are not surprising. They are even less surprising when put in the context of the time. Ninety-two percent of all U.S. exports moved on foreign flag vessels in 1908; over two-thirds of U.S. cargoes were foreign insured in 1913.[25]

Foreign trading houses also played a role in U.S. agricultural exports, although they in no way dominated this trade. Yet, just as Brazilians complained about the gap between the coffee price at the farm and the price paid by the consumer, so too did farmers the world over complain about "middlemen," domestic and foreign. "Distribution"—the connection between producers and consumers—is not free, whether performed by domestic or foreign business. Yet, distribution is absolutely essential if there is to be a market beyond the locale. There must be profits for the international and domestic distributor, or there would be no market (beyond the nearby one) for the producer's output.

Brazil was by far the world's largest source of coffee exports. While production (ownership, size of plots, nature of the labor force) varied substantially from one producing country to another, the trade, insurance, and financing structures often did not. Foreign merchant firms, insurers, and banks appear to have taken on similar roles in getting the commodity to market. In Central America, German immigrants (not Germans domiciled in Germany) often owned coffee farms, yet in the pre–World War I years there were some plantations, particularly in Guatemala, that were owned by nonresident Germans and, frequently, resident Germans had family back home. The trade, in short, was dominated from Germany. The British trading house Chalmers, Guthrie & Co. was active in the early twentieth century in the El Salvador coffee trade, but British accepting houses had major reservations about financing this firm in 1908, when it "locked up a good deal of money in San Salvador Railways."[26] In some countries, coffee buyers and processors (such as General Foods) had a presence, especially in the 1920s.

Did the differences in coffee production and distribution structures make any systematic differences in the impact on national economic development? Clearly, the network connections by business actors with the outside world made possible the getting of coffee from producer to consumer. The potential demand was there. In each coffee-producing country, foreign businesses linked production and distribution (that is, made contacts beyond borders) in divergent manners. What was universal was the new demand for coffee in the industrial world. Did the contacts between domestic and foreign business leave coffee-growing nations lacking in "true" progress? Were profits "disproportionately" shared? I find an affirmative answer to these questions hard to accept. The new economic activity set the foundation for subsequent economic development, and this was particularly true in the case of the country that dominated the coffee market in this period—Brazil. Brazil's coffee would provide the basis for Brazil's industrialization.[27] Without the initial external demand and the emergence of businesses to connect supply and demand and to facilitate transactions, the linkage effects would have been impossible.

Henequen

The economic impact of henequen in Latin America from 1850 to 1930 was much less significant than that of coffee. The ramifications of henequen exports were regional (within Yucatán), compared with those of coffee exports, which had profound effects on the entire economies of Brazil, Colombia, and several other Latin American countries. As with coffee, the market for henequen was generated by demand outside the producing country. As with coffee, the largest sales were in the United States. And, as with all agricultural commodities, often the rhetoric of the farmer was to blame the "speculator" and the middleman.

As with coffee and other agricultural products, supply and demand conditions meant sharp fluctuations in the price of henequen. There were attempts—first by producer associations and then, more important, by the state government of Yucatán—to stabilize the price. As with coffee in Latin America (in general), foreign buyers of henequen did not become planters, at least in Mexico. The growers in Yucatán were Mexican. (Elsewhere in Latin America and in the Philippines, U.S. purchasers of fibers did invest in plantations.) The decisions Mexican growers made in structuring production (for example, in choosing production methods, hiring labor, and managing the farming) were regional, not foreign imposed.

Yet, in Yucatán, foreign companies' impact was not trivial. Unlike coffee, henequen was a producer good. Demand for it abroad (principally in the United States) was derived, meaning it depended on the demand for cordage and then for twine binder harvesters, which in turn depended on conditions in the market for U.S. grain.[28] Production in Yucatán responded to the new demand for twine binder harvest-ers and increased rapidly as U.S. agricultural output rose and harvester sales increased. The twine binder harvester was introduced in the 1880s and McCormick Harvester (a predecessor of International Harvester) became a major customer for Yucatán output. When International Harvester was formed in 1902, it became a principal buyer of henequen from the Yucatán. The region's success was part of the general economic growth in Porfirian Mexico.

With World War I, the demand in Europe for American foodstuffs rose, as did prices; there was more mechanization in American agriculture, more demand for twine binder harvesters, and prices of henequen accordingly rose. In 1915 the revolutionary government of Venustiano Carranza wanted to capture for Mexico the advantage of the new demand. Yucatán's legislature had established the Comisión Reguladora del Mercado de Henequen (Henequen Market Regulatory Commission, CRMH). It obtained the exclusive right to purchase henequen from the producers. The commission demanded 23 cents per pound from foreign purchasers (compared with the prewar price of roughly 6 cents). The U.S. government sought to push the price down to aid American farmers (and started a campaign to conserve binder twine and suggest substitutes). New York and New Orleans banks, hoping to monopolize the importation and sales of henequen within the United States, extended credit to producers. Henequen was collateral for the loans. The banks assumed the price would stay high; it didn't. Conservation occurred. New supplies came from elsewhere. After the war ended, the price slumped. The CRMH went bankrupt when the price fell to 2.5 cents, and the banks were left with large fiber stocks.

In an effort to recoup, in 1921 a new Mexican corporation for exports, the Comisión Exportadora de Yucatán (Yucatán Export Commission, CEY), was formed. It became, the sole legal purchaser from the producers, and competition disappeared. In November 1921 in the United States, the Sisal Sales Corporation was set up to deal in henequen in that country; it made a contract with the CEY. With the supported prices, the banks sold their accumulated stock.

In 1926 a Yucatecan law restricted production to push up price. The U.S. government, at this point, argued that the interventions in the market constituted a conspiracy—a monopoly—to the disadvantage of the American farmer. The U.S. Supreme Court agreed in 1927.[29]

By the late 1920s, U.S. agriculture was in the doldrums, and things would only get worse for the henequen market. Cheap alternative sources of twine materials (African sisal from British East Africa and sisal from Java) had become available. The largest users of henequen

(International Harvester and Plymouth Cordage) had invested in their own fiber plantations in Cuba and elsewhere. The introduction of combines (which combined harvesting and threshing) began to reduce the demand for twine binders for grain.[30] Demand for Mexican henequen would collapse. The CEY was unable to keep the price high.

How, then, do we evaluate the role of foreign business in the growth of henequen exports and the economic development of Yucatán? Clearly, without an external demand, there would have been no development. Unlike coffee, henequen had many close substitutes. Indeed, the earliest stimulus to Mexican production was from the U.S. cordage companies, which desired an alternative source of supply to the high-priced manila hemp. On their behalf, a New York commodity trader, Thebaud and Sons (later, Thebaud Brothers), had provided financing for Yucatán henequen. Then there came the demand for binder twine and, again, a search for substitutes for manila. Initially, American harvester companies had bought their twine from the cordage companies, then they made it themselves. McCormick Harvester integrated into cordage production and arranged for the Boston-based commodity trader Peabody & Co. to act on its behalf in the Yucatán as a purchaser of henequen. Peabody set up an office in Yucatán to do this.[31]

McCormick provided technical assistance and other aid to Olegario Molina's group, which in 1896 decided to establish a twine manufacturing plant in Yucatán. The timing on this industrial venture is important: to aid the American farmer, the U.S. Congress had sharply reduced the tariff on binder twine in July 1892 and eliminated it entirely as of August 1894 (cordage duties were set at a mere 10 percent ad valorem). Twine imports into the United States rose as American companies bought twine from European mills. The Mexican government—which in the Porfiriato was encouraging industrialization—imposed a tax on the export of unprocessed henequen; twine exports were not taxed. As a consequence, the Molina group had organized La Industrial to make twine in Yucatán. The plant opened in 1898. All sources agree that this did not work out. The mill seems to have ceased twine production in 1903.[32]

While the Mexican plant was being built, McCormick had sought more diversified, cheaper raw material for its existing U.S. facilities. Not long after La Industrial began production, McCormick resolved to build its own large Chicago twine mill, which produced its first twine in 1900. Having its own major plant coped with the two problems of buying twine from outsiders: quality and promptness of delivery. When in 1902 International Harvester was formed, it inherited McCormick's giant Chicago mill (as well as other twine mills of its predecessor companies), along with McCormick's relationship with Molina in Yucatán. Peabody & Co. was purchasing henequen for the large U.S. rope producer, Plymouth Cordage; International Harvester apparently did not want to use the same supplier as its rival.[33]

International Harvester never integrated backward into growing in Yucatán; it continued its association with Molina after La Industrial shut down, but as a purchaser of the raw material. Why didn't International Harvester integrate into henequen production in the Yucatán? Two reasons suggest themselves: there is no evidence that it would have been welcomed as a grower, and it had, moreover, established ties with the Molina group. It was different elsewhere. The firm looked to developing alternatives. As a buyer and a grower of fiber it did not want to be dependent on a single region for a vital raw material. It bought MacLeod & Co., a leading merchant house in the Philippines. Its predecessor, McCormick, had in 1900 acquired 113,217 acres in Baja California, but the land was not suitable, and International Harvester had written off the investment by January 1908. In 1900 McCormick had considered buying a 3,000-acre plantation in Cuba, but turned down the proposition; Molina purchased the land and undertook henequen production there. A decade later International Harvester acquired adjoining land and started producing henequen in Cuba. Elsewhere, International Harvester sought diversified sources of fiber supply, including Ecuador.[34] All the while, International Harvester continued to provide an important market for Yucatecan henequen.

When the price of henequen rose during World War I as a result of both new demand and the 1915 valorization plan, International Harvester followed developments in Yucatán with grave concern. Its stated position was to obtain "sisal hemp at a fair price, so we could sell the twine to the [U.S.] farmer as cheaply as possible."[35] The Sisal Sales Corporation (formed in 1921) was associated with the needs of American banks, and International Harvester watched its formation with anxiety. The company continued to seek more alternative sources of supply.

Before World War I, the Germans had experimented with growing sisal in Tanganyika. The German colony became British after the war, and production rose in both Tanganyika and Kenya. By 1927 African and Asian nations (including the Philippines and the Dutch East Indies) accounted for almost half the world's fiber production. The sisal produced in Africa was cheaper than the Mexican, and multinational enterprises purchase where they can get the cheapest, most satisfactory supplies. International Harvester developed its plantation in Cárdenas, Cuba; by 1929 this was a "huge plantation" with about forty-seven hundred acres. In 1928 International Harvester bought a hemp planta-tion in the Philippines. In 1924 Plymouth Cordage Company also acquired a Cuban plantation.[36]

International Harvester was the defendant in an important antitrust case in the 1920s. It was resolved in 1927, when the U.S. Supreme Court ruled that "the law does not make mere size of a corporation . . . an offense, when unaccompanied by unlawful conduct." During the 1920s, with its possible vulnerability, International Harvester would have been wary about participating in any price-raising activity; as a purchaser of henequen, its interests lay in low but stable prices.[37] Its interests coincided with those of the American farmer. Because foreign users of henequen had no large investments in growing in Yucatán and because local producers "ran the show" (and received the profits from produc-tion), neither International Harvester nor Plymouth Cordage (nor any other user) had a particular commitment to this source of supply. Multinational enterprises never want to be captive to a single source of supply; they fear "foreclosure" (the cutting off of the input). Thus, it was not odd to find International Harvester protecting itself by developing a variety of fiber sources. Plymouth Cordage behaved similarly.

In Yucatán the impact of International Harvester and of the American cordage companies, particularly Plymouth Cordage, was a general one. They needed and wanted a raw material; the specifics of how things were done in Mexico were determined by Mexican producers. Profits from henequen production stayed in Yucatán. It is hard to fault the foreign companies for the problems in the Yucatán region, since the basic development there was Mexican.

Oil

Of the three commodities discussed in this book, the most profound impact on Latin American economic development came as a result of developments in oil. Multinational enterprises participated in all facets of this industry in Latin America. As with coffee and henequen, interna-tional trade in oil greatly expanded between 1859 and 1914 as a result of new demand first for kerosene, and then for gasoline and a range of other products from lubricants to fuel oil. In the early twentieth century, as the British Navy committed itself to oil, it was seen as having particular strategic value. During World War I, oil prices soared and a global fear emerged that supplies would be exhausted. High prices prompted busi-nesses to explore, and governments (particularly those of Britain and France) encouraged their businesses to do so. By 1928, as a consequence, a worldwide oil glut existed. Oil prices, like those of coffee and hene-quen, were based on supply and demand, so they fluctuated. Producers wanted to arrest fluctuation, thus (in the case of oil) companies intervened to stabilize prices.

There are other parallels between oil and coffee and henequen, but these are dwarfed by the differences between them. Oil became fundamental; it was not just "any" commodity. The oil industry required exploration, drilling, refining, transportation, and the creation of an awesome infrastructure. To do this required a willingness to take large risks and to introduce sizable amounts of capital and know-how. Oil demand—if it was to be filled—called for complex logistics. Within producing countries, oil-generated revenues for the state—and linkage effects throughout the economy—would come to overshadow those from coffee or henequen. Since the 1960s, oil has become the basis for the industrialization of Latin America.

The initial involvement of U.S. oil companies in Latin America was in the marketing of U.S.-refined oil. The United States was rich in oil resources, and Standard Oil companies became exporters, setting up marketing outlets in Europe, Canada, Latin America, and Asia.[38] With Mexican duties on refined oil, in the mid-1880s Standard Oil's affiliate Waters-Pierce had built a refinery in Mexico City that processed imported Pennsylvania crude.

The early exploration and some of the production of crude oil in Latin America was by "freestanding companies," that is, individual units, principally from the United Kingdom. Edward L. Doheny (an independent oilman from California) was, in 1901, the first to produce crude oil in Mexico. Sir Weetman Pearson was next to produce (also in 1901). It was not until 1910, however, that Pearson (as of July 1910 Lord Cowdray) found a truly prolific source of oil in Mexico and began to develop an integrated oil business there and abroad. His El Águila (the Mexican Eagle Company) became the largest producer in Mexico.[39]

In 1911, after a U.S. antitrust suit, the Standard Oil group was broken up into thirty-four companies. Of these, only three did business in Latin America: Standard Oil of New Jersey, with a refinery in Cuba (linked with its marketing) and a distribution organization throughout Latin America, except in Mexico; Chesebrough Manufacturing Co., a maker of Vaseline and other specialty products, with sales branches in Latin America; and Waters-Pierce, with its sizable stake in Mexico in marketing, refining, and, by 1911, crude oil production. Subsequent to 1911, other former Standard Oil companies would invest in Latin America. Most important, the 1911 antitrust case had opened the door for the giant Royal Dutch–Shell group to expand both in the United States and Latin America. Shell invested in an integrated oil business in the United States, including the acquisition there of oil-producing properties; it also invested in Venezuela and then in Mexico (it would buy Lord Cowdray's properties in Mexico in 1919). Its activities were global. In 1917 it had built a refinery in Curaçao—a Dutch colony— strategically located to use both Mexican and Venezuelan oil (it eventually handled only the latter).[40]

Standard Oil of New Jersey (the predecessor of Exxon) was the largest spin-off of the Standard Oil group; in 1911–1912 it had a vast marketing organization in Latin America, but no crude oil production.[41] It acquired oil properties in Peru in 1913, in Mexico in 1917, and in Colombia in 1919. The output of these oil lands would be refined and sold through Standard Oil of New Jersey's worldwide marketing organization. During the 1920s, Standard Oil of New Jersey expanded into crude oil production in Argentina and Venezuela (in neither country was it a major producer).

The story of oil in Latin America from the late nineteenth century through the 1920s is complex. Each country was different. Multinational enterprises made market- and supply-oriented investments. They had successes and failures. Governments played differing roles, depending on the period and on the function (marketing, refining, production, exploration) being policed. Numerous foreign companies took part in Latin American developments, even though by 1929 Shell and Standard Oil of New Jersey clearly stood out.[42] In September 1919, 152 American companies were said to have invested in oil exploration in Mexico. In 1918 Mexico had become second only to the United States in terms of oil production. That year it was the world's largest exporter of oil. Oil was responsible for 10 percent of the nation's revenues, more than all the nation's mines produced. Article 27 of the Mexican Constitution, promulgated on 5 February 1917, gave ownership of oil resources to government, albeit foreign companies had continued to invest.[43]

Elsewhere in Latin America, a similarly impressive array of foreign oil companies, including such former Standard Oil companies as Standard Oil of Indiana and Atlantic Refining, such independents as Texas Oil and Gulf Oil, and Anglo-Persian Oil Co. (the predecessor to British Petroleum), participated in developing various facets of the business. Anglo-Persian had its origins in the discovery and development of oil in Iran and wanted diversified sources of supply. In the early 1920s, it explored for oil in Argentina, Bolivia, Brazil, Chile, Ecuador, Guatemala, Honduras, Mexico, Nicaragua, Peru, and Trinidad. It also wanted to invest in Venezuela and Colombia. This British company's historian, R. W. Ferrier, claims that the large British government ownership share in Anglo-Persian precluded the latter's gaining concessions in the 1920s in Venezuela and Colombia—or, for that matter, in Brazil, Chile, Mexico, and Peru. What Ferrier does not realize is that U.S. embassy officials had suggested to host governments in 1921 that they put provisions in their oil legislation to exclude companies dominated by foreign governments. By 1929 only in Argentina did Anglo-Persian have an appreciable presence.[44]

With the new exploration just before, during, and in the aftermath of World War I, oil production in Latin America shot upward, soon led by Venezuela. By 1928 Venezuela had surpassed Russia and Mexico to rank second only to the United States as a producer of oil. Practically all of the oil produced in Venezuela was exported.[45]

The core competencies of the major oil companies proved vital. Individual entrepreneurs and companies set up for that purpose could explore for oil, but beyond that, much more was needed. Thus, Rory Miller notes, when the London & Pacific Petroleum Company in Peru was sold to Standard Oil of New Jersey in 1913, it was in poor shape owing to the inexperience of its entrepreneurs and engineers. Lord Cowdray sold his major oil property in Mexico to Royal Dutch–Shell after realizing that his knowledge of the oil business was inadequate.[46] Everywhere in Latin America except Argentina (where YPF, the state-owned company, had discovered oil in 1907), it was foreign multinationals that made oil properties viable.

Nowhere was the impact of foreign oil companies greater than in Venezuela. In Venezuela, as everywhere, initially there were many foreign companies involved. By 1929, by one estimate, there were still some thirty-nine American companies participating along with British investors. But, just as in Peru and Mexico, the oil industry involved vast expenditures, and the well-integrated oil companies prevailed. Through the 1920s, Shell was the most important oil producer in Venezuela. In 1925 Standard Oil of Indiana acquired from Doheny the Pan American Petroleum and Transport Company, with oil wells and other assets in Venezuela as well as Mexico. An affiliate of this company completed a refinery in 1929 on the Dutch Island of Aruba to process Venezuelan crude for export to the United States. Standard Oil of New Jersey was a relatively minor player in Venezuela until 1932, when it seemed likely the United States would impose duties on oil imports. Standard Oil of Indiana, which had no experience in international marketing, then sold its Latin American properties to Standard Oil of New Jersey (for decades thereafter Standard Oil of New Jersey was a major actor in Venezuela).[47]

The development of Venezuelan oil transformed the country. In 1910 Venezuela had been a poor agricultural nation with little in prospect for the future; by the early 1920s, it was shaping its oil legislation to encourage new U.S. investments. In 1922 the contribution of the oil sector to Venezuelan GDP had been negligible. By 1929 oil contributed 22.6 percent of a greatly enlarged GDP. The entire development was based on the activities of foreign multinational enterprises, which invested in company towns and the required infrastructure.[48] Venezuelan oil became a valuable resource only because foreign companies were prepared and equipped to take risks, to supply large amounts of money, to provide technical knowledge and skills, and to distribute the oil to world markets. In company towns, Venezuelans learned basic industrial skills. When, years later, Venezuela took over its own industry, an entire cadre of Venezuelans had been educated by the foreign multinational enterprises. Economic progress—reflected in longer life spans, increased literacy, a higher standard of living, rising expectations, better jobs, and greater opportunities for the average person—was the outcome.

By 1928, however, a world oil glut existed, to which the large new exports of Venezuelan oil were contributing. Executives of Royal Dutch–Shell, Standard Oil of New Jersey, and Anglo-Persian met at Achnacarry in Scotland in 1928 to attempt to stabilize world oil prices. They were unsuccessful. What is important about the attempt, however, is that, because the oil companies were producers of oil, they had interests identical with those of the Latin American producing and exporting countries, that is, to maintain the price of oil at a stable level, high enough to assure good profits but low enough to encourage the continued expansion of consumption.

Conclusion

Coffee, henequen, and oil were obviously very different primary commodities, and the role of multinational enterprises in their development varied. All three involved exports from Latin America, but it is too simple to equate staple exports and Third World countries. The United States, Canada, and Australia were also important exporters of primary products, for example, raw cotton, grain, and wool.

What is vital to understand is how domestic and foreign companies interact and how domestic business becomes able to build on the newly generated economic activity. While coffee was exported from many Latin American countries, the economic impact differed by country; how the coffee growers' wealth was used differed by country. In the case of henequen, local Yucatán producers flourished, but did not develop the foundations for the economic development of the region. With coffee and henequen, nationals of the particular country dominated as growers of an agricultural product. In the case of oil, by contrast, the impact of foreign companies was deeper. While there were state oil enterprises—

and these would take on ever-greater importance in Latin America as the twentieth century progressed (until very recent times)—nowhere in Latin America did wealthy nationals invest in crude oil production.[49] The wealth generated (and there was wealth generated) and the entrepreneurship generated (and there was entrepreneurship) went into other activities. Developing the oil industry involved modern managerial corporations with sizable resources and the ability to spread risk. On the other hand, the state, by means of public policy and state-owned companies, played a very important role in setting the framework for foreign direct investments. In the 1920s this was already true, and, later, the state's role would become even more pervasive. As state interventions multiplied in subsequent decades, they had major consequences.

In the process of economic change, allocation of rewards between capital and labor, manager and worker, merchant and grower, urban and rural, foreign and domestic is always uneven. It is, however, that unevenness that may well provide incentives for change, for the reallocation of resources, for growth itself. The sharing of rewards in Latin America during the period in question more often than not was altered sharply by government policy. When a multinational enterprise had investments in production within a country, its interests often coincided with those of national producers. When the multinational enterprise did not produce and only purchased commodities, there was a seeming divergence: the producer wanted high prices, the buyer, low ones. This point should not be exaggerated—or taken too far—however, for if the price was too low, producers would exit and buyers would not have continuity or security of supply.

Coffee producers in Brazil, aided by the local government in São Paulo, reallocated their wealth to the industrialization of the state; coffee producers in Colombia did not. Wealthy henequen producers in Yucatán were unable to sustain industrialization attempts. After the Mexican Revolution, the ill-advised and badly planned government efforts to hike prices proved counterproductive (buyers looked to other sources of supply). Oil, which was discovered, produced, processed, introduced into international trade, and carried to the ultimate consumer by international companies, had far profounder impacts on economic development than did any agricultural (or, for that matter, any other internationally traded mineral) product. Oil served as the basis for true national wealth.

I am convinced that multinational enterprises on their own neither aid nor retard a host nation's economic growth and development; what they do is open the possibility for that growth and development. The way they interact with the economic (and political) actors in each nation is critical. Imitation and innovation are the fundamentals for economic development. Multinationals provide the opportunity for both.

Notes

I want to extend special thanks for guidance and wisdom on henequen to Fred Carstensen and Cindy Knight (archivist, McCormick–IHC Collection, State Historical Society of Wisconsin) and on coffee to Maria Willumsen and Tom Schoonover. For oil I have relied heavily on my own research.

1. Sociologists—for example, Gary Gereffi and Miguel Korzeniewicz, *Commodity Chains and Global Capitalism* (New York: Praeger, 1994)—deal with commodity chains in the context of center and periphery. The historian of multinational enterprise focuses directly on the business actors.

2. On occasion, multinational enterprises may have two, or even more, home countries; one home is, however, typical. For a selection of writings on their history, see Mira Wilkins, ed., *The Growth of Multinational Enterprise* (Aldershot, England: E. Elgar, 1991). See idem, *The Emergence of Multinational Enterprise: American Business Abroad from the Colonial Era to 1914* (Cambridge, Mass.: Harvard University Press, 1970); idem, *The Maturing of Multinational Enterprise: American Business Abroad from 1914 to 1970* (Cambridge, Mass.: Harvard University Press, 1974); and Alfred Chandler, *The Visible Hand: The Managerial Revolution in American Business* (Cambridge, Mass.: Harvard University Press, 1977), on U.S. business abroad only. For the more general story, see Geoffrey Jones, *The Evolution of International Business* (London: Routledge, 1996). See also Mira Wilkins, "Multinational Corporations: An Historical Account," in Robert Rowthorn and Richard Kozul-Wright, eds., *Transnational Corporations and the Global Economy* (London: Macmillan, forthcoming).

3. I do not share the literature's "goods production mind-set"; see Richard E. Caves, *Multinational Enterprise and Economic Analysis*, 2nd ed. (Cambridge: Cambridge University Press, 1996), 5n. As in much of the recent literature that now embraces service sector activities, my definition of multinational enterprise includes merchant enterprises that are headquartered in one country and have direct investments (however small) in at least one host country.

4. To be sure, they may produce for a while but, ultimately, if there is no demand, the business will stop producing.

5. On the eighteenth- and early nineteenth-century commodity exchanges for grain, see Stanley Chapman, *Merchant Enterprise in Britain: From the Industrial Revolution to World War I* (Cambridge: Cambridge University Press, 1992). See also Dan Morgan, *Merchants of Grain* (New York: Viking, 1979), 95–97; Charles Harvey and Jon Press, "The City and International Mining, 1870–1914," *Business History* 32 (July 1990): 98–119; Robert Greenhill, "The Brazilian Coffee Trade," in D. C. M. Platt, ed., *Business Imperialism, 1840–1930* (Oxford: Clarendon, 1977), 209.

6. On nitrates, see Robert Greenhill, "The Nitrate and Iodine Trades, 1880–1914," in Platt, *Business Imperialism*, 231–283. The early foreign direct invest-

ments in nitrates were of a freestanding company–type of multinational enterprise (see later in this chapter). See Reinhard Liehr and Mariano E. Torres Bautista, "British Free-Standing Companies in Porfirian Mexico, 1884–1911," in Mira Wilkins and Harm Schröter, *The Free-Standing Company in the World Economy, 1830–1996* (Oxford: Oxford University Press, forthcoming); and Stephen H. Haber, *Industry and Underdevelopment: The Industrialization of Mexico, 1890–1940* (Stanford, Calif.: Stanford University Press, 1989).

7. In the 1950s and the 1960s, economists paid a great deal of attention to commodity exports and their impact on the exporting countries. For a sample of that literature, including discussions of staple theory, see Jorge Salazar-Carrillo, *Oil and Development in Venezuela during the Twentieth Century* (Westport, Conn.: Praeger, 1994), chap. 2. J. W. F. Rowe, *Primary Commodities in International Trade* (Cambridge: Cambridge University Press, 1965) is an extremely useful volume on trade in primary products.

8. Coffee prices were very high from 1927 to 1929, with the São Paulo government holding up the price, which encouraged large plantings; see Celso Furtado, *Obstacles to Development in Latin America* (New York: Anchor Books, 1970), 114. By 1929, however, rubber prices and oil prices, for example, despite support attempts, were relatively low (relative to, say, 1919) as a result of earlier overexpansion. This book's discussion of the Latin American "export boom (1850–1930)" is, in a certain sense, poetic license: throughout the "boom" there were booms and busts.

9. Eugene Staley, *Raw Materials in Peace and War* (New York: Council on Foreign Relations, 1937), is excellent on the government measures taken to support prices. It contains a fine summary of the São Paulo government's "valorization" policies (259–261); on henequen, see 297–298; on rubber, 290–291. While supply and demand considerations were important in these markets, we are always talking, in economists' terms, about " imperfect markets." On control schemes, see Rowe, *Primary Commodities*, 127.

10. Fernand Braudel, *The Structures of Everyday Life* (New York: Harper & Row, 1981), 250, 257. On tea, see Stanley Chapman, "British Free-Standing Companies and Investment Groups in India and the Far East," in Wilkins and Schröter, eds., *The Free-Standing Company*. The organization of tea and coffee production may well be a regional matter. In the East, some trading companies did have coffee estates of consequence (Chapman, *Merchant Enterprise*, 127, 254). Yet the traders in tea, with a few possible exceptions, do not seem to have been identical with those in coffee.

11. Except at proprietary coffeehouses. Hal Morgan, *Symbols of America* (New York: Penguin, 1986), 112, 114, presents pictures of "Javarye Coffee Compound" advertising put out by the Javarye Coffee Co., Portsmouth, Ohio, 1897, and of the Hills Brothers' turbaned figure advertising Java and Mocha (first introduced on packaged coffee in 1897).

12. Greenhill writes that in Brazil in the early twentieth century some "Dutch, Belgian, and German syndicates" purchased coffee plantations; British ownership was uncommon, but he gives as prominent examples the Dumont Coffee Company and the São Paulo Coffee Estates (both set up in 1896),

which firms "introduced model estate management methods," built connecting railways to the main line, and brought in modern machinery to reduce costs and to increase output and quality. There were also cases of foreclosures, when a foreign trader or foreign financial institution temporarily owned and ran coffee farms (such properties would be sold as soon as was possible): Greenhill, "The Brazilian Coffee Trade," 214, 208–209. I will, as this chapter progresses, note a later important foreign owner in Brazil, one that invested to take advantage of the Brazilian government's support of coffee prices.

13. Braudel, *The Structures of Everyday Life*, 260. Since my definition of multinational enterprises includes services, I include these merchant firms under the rubric of multinational enterprises.

14. Steven Topik, in chap. 2 here, writes that North Americans and Europeans came to "own or control" a majority of the railroads built to carry coffee that would be exported from Brazil. Some railroads had been started by private Brazilian planters who received government concessions and subsequently passed into foreign hands. Not until 1910 could the railroad network into coffee lands be described as "dense." See also Maria Bárbara Levy, "The Banking System and Foreign Capital in Brazil," in Rondo Cameron and V. I. Bovykin, eds., *International Banking 1870–1914* (New York: Oxford University Press, 1991), 351–370.

15. Chapman, *Merchant Enterprise*, is an innovative study of family firms; Geoffrey Jones is writing a history of British trading companies. On Brazilian Warrant, see also Robert Greenhill, "Investment Group, Free-Standing Company or Multinational? Brazilian Warrant, 1909–52," *Business History* 37 (January 1995): 86–111. This supplements his earlier splendid article "The Brazilian Coffee Trade." Brazilian Warrant illustrates the way one British firm functioned; we need more such case studies. For the early history of Johnston & Co. and its rank among Brazilian coffee exporters, see Greenhill, "The Brazilian Coffee Trade," 200, 208. On banking, Levy, "The Banking System," 353; and Geoffrey Jones, *British Multinational Banking 1830–1990* (Oxford: Oxford University Press, 1993).

16. Mira Wilkins, "The Free-Standing Company, 1870–1914: An Important Type of British Foreign Direct Investment," *Economic History Review*, 2nd ser., 41 (May 1988): 259–282, and idem, "The Free-Standing Company Revisited," in Wilkins and Schröter, eds., *The Free-Standing Company*, chap. 1. See also Charles Jones, "The Origins of Modern Multinational Corporations: British Firms in Latin America, 1850–1930," in Carlos Marichal, ed., *Foreign Investment in Latin America: Impact on Economic Development, 1850–1930* (Milan: Università Bocconi, 1994), 27–37; Marichal, "Introduction," 7, in ibid.; and Rory Miller, "British Free-Standing Companies on the West Coast of South America," in Wilkins and Schröter, eds., *The Free-Standing Company*. The separately established—albeit few—foreign direct investments in Brazilian coffee growing mentioned above would fit well the definition of freestanding company. On British overseas banks, see Geoffrey Jones, "British Overseas Banks as Free-Standing Companies," in Wilkins and Schröter, eds., *The Free-Standing Company*. These were "free-standing" in that they did not involve the expansion to

foreign markets of a British bank that did business in Britain. These banks were set up to do business in a particular country or region abroad and had a headquarters in the home country.

17. Greenhill, "The Brazilian Coffee Trade," 200, 208. Greenhill lists the major British traders around 1900, which included E. Johnston & Co., Naumann Gepp, Quayle Davidson, Nicholsons, Moore & Co., Norton Megaw, and Edward Ashworth; he also lists the leading coffee exporters from Rio de Janeiro and Santos in the late nineteenth and early twentieth centuries.

18. Greenhill, "Investment Group," 92–96.

19. I am speaking about agricultural commodities in general, not specifically about coffee, although the backward integration strategy did apply to coffee. Greenhill, "Investment Group," tells a fascinating story about the recruitment and training of managers and the organization of the business. Topik, chap. 2 here, and all the literature recognizes the crucial importance of the U.S. market.

20. Greenhill, "The Brazilian Coffee Trade," 207–228.

21. Mira Wilkins, *The History of Foreign Investment in the United States to 1914* (Cambridge, Mass.: Harvard University Press, 1989), 337.

22. In the United States, between 1925 and 1929, a group of companies with brand name food products (including Post Cereal Company; Jell–O Company; Ingleheart Brothers, makers of Swan's Down Flour; Walter Baker, Baker's chocolate; and Cheek–Neal Company, which sold Maxwell House coffee) were amalgamated into the giant General Foods Corporation. This diversified food product firm was copied by Standard Brands, which in a 1929 merger joined Fleischmann's yeast, Royal Baking Powder, and the Chase and Sanborn coffee company. Fleischmann's had a sizable national fleet of delivery trucks to call on grocery stores, bakeries, restaurants, and all the locations where the highly perishable yeast was sold. This was splendid for Chase and Sanborn, a big U.S. importer of Brazilian coffee; Chase and Sanborn could claim the freshness of its coffee, delivered in Standard Brands trucks. This advantage was short-lived, however, owing to technological progress. In the late 1920s or possibly in the early 1930s, General Foods developed the vacuum can, which kept ground coffee fresh; rapid delivery was no longer essential. Vacuum sealing was invented in 1900, but more than two decades would pass before the technology was adopted to any great extent (on the West Coast, in 1905, Hills Brothers had started vacuum canning with a proprietary technology). As early as 1907 Maxwell House coffee was advertised as "Good to the last drop." On General Foods and Standard Brands, see Thomas Horst, *At Home Abroad* (Cambridge, Mass.: Ballinger, 1974), 28–29. On "the complex distributive structure in America through importers, jobbers, roasters, and wholesalers," see Greenhill, "The Brazilian Coffee Trade," 215. On the 1900 date for vacuum sealing, see Steven C. Topik, "Integration of the World Coffee Market," unpublished, 1997. Topik is also my source on Hills Brothers. For Maxwell House advertising, see Morgan, *Symbols of America*, 114.

23. Jones, *British Multinational Banking*, 83. And they engaged in domestic and international banking from a Brazilian base, not long-distance; they needed to be on the spot for information purposes. See also Levy, "The Banking

System," 364–370, citing Topik, *Capital estrangeiro e o estado no sistema bancário brasileiro, 1889–1931* (Rio de Janeiro, 1979); Jones, *British Multinational Banking*, 56.

24. Greenhill, "Investment Group," 103; Jones, *British Multinational Banking*, 144.

25. Wilkins, *The History of Foreign Investment in the United States to 1914*, 519; idem, *The History of Foreign Investment in the United States after 1914*, forthcoming.

26. Sometimes the same foreign merchants, banks, and insurers participated in getting the product to market; other times, different foreign companies were the actors. On German domination, see Regina Wagner, "Actividades empresariales de los alemanes en Guatemala, 1850–1920," *Mesoamérica* 13 (June 1987): esp. 98–107. See also Wilkins, *The History of Foreign Investment in the United States to 1914*, 801 n247. On El Salvador, see Chapman, *Merchant Enterprise*, 209–210, quotation on 217.

27. Warren Dean, *The Industrialization of São Paulo 1880–1914* (Austin: University of Texas Press, 1969).

28. This oversimplifies a very complicated story. Henequen was an input for twine; twine was a complementary product to harvesters (*ceteris paribus*, the more harvesters sold and the more U.S. grain produced, the more twine would be sold and the larger would be the demand for henequen). American-made harvesters were, however, sold domestically and exported; foreign farmers could buy twine that was exported or purchased abroad. Likewise, American farmers could use imported twine or domestically produced twine that was not made with Mexican henequen.

29. U.S. Department of Commerce, *Sisal Production, Prices, and Marketing, Trade Information Bulletin 200* (Washington, D.C.: U.S. Government Printing Office, 1924); *U.S. vs. Sisal Sales Corp.*, 174 U.S. 168 (1927); Staley, *Raw Materials in Peace and War*, 297–298; Kingman Brewster, *Antitrust and American Business Abroad* (New York: McGraw-Hill, 1958), 67, 70, 122–123.

30. The change in technology from twine binders to combines was only beginning in the late 1920s; an undated memorandum in International Harvester files (probably summer of 1937) indicates that, although combines were making some inroads, American harvester companies were still building ten grain binders for every combine: International Harvester Company Records, State Historical Society of Wisconsin, Madison, M95–262, Box 20 (H. L. Boyle Economic Research File, Mexican Binder Twine Committee); hereafter cited as Boyle files, IHC.

31. 1 have found valuable Fred Carstensen and Diane Roazen, "Foreign Markets, Domestic Initiative, and the Emergence of a Monocrop Economy: The Yucatecan Experience, 1825–1903," *Hispanic American Historical Review* 72:4 (1992): 555–592, which provides an excellent complement to chap. 3 here.

32. On the Molina group, see Diane Roazen-Parrillo, "U.S. Business Interests and the Sisal Industry of Yucatan, Mexico, 1876–1926," Ph.D. diss., University of Chicago (1984), esp. chap. 2. On the project's not working out, see Wells, chap. 3 here, and Carstensen and Roazen, "Foreign Markets," 583–

585. After an attempt to use the mill to extract alcohol from the roots of henequen, Molina sold it in 1908 to a Mexican firm, which tried, in vain, to restart twine production. Apparently, not until 1931 did twine output in Mexico resume on any scale. In the late 1930s, the Yucatán government, desiring to encourage twine production, arranged to sell henequen to Mexican twine mills at prices lower than those offered to U.S. manufacturers. Data from 1937–1938 in Boyle files, IHC, reveal the concern of International Harvester and other American makers of twine over the competition from Mexican twine. Whereas in the late nineteenth century, McCormick Harvester had been prepared to aid Mexican industry and buy its output, by the late 1930s, with overcapacity in the United States and with European twine imports, American twine makers resented Mexican competition created by preferential raw material prices.

America was a net exporter of twine through the 1920s. In 1925 U.S. twine exports were 54 million pounds; in 1936 this amount had shrunk to 6 million pounds. In 1925 U.S. twine imports were 12 million pounds (with that from Mexico negligible); in 1936 twine imports were 80 million pounds, of which 23.5 million were from Mexico. Boyle files, IHC, contain a fascinating discussion on the 1937 responses of the harvester and cordage companies to the rise in Mexican twine imports. In terms of value, it is important to note that Mexico's raw material exports still far exceeded its manufactured exports: out of every $100 of income to Mexico in 1936 from fiber and twine exports, $90 was from fiber exports and $10 from twine exports. On these matters, see E. W. Brewster Memorandum, 14 April 1937, and Suggested memorandum from R. A. Gibson, U.S. Department of State to U.S. Ambassador Josephus Daniels, 24 August 1937, Boyle files, IHC.

33. Wells, chap. 3 here; Esko Heikkonen, *Reaping the Bounty: McCormick Harvesting Company Turns Abroad, 1878–1902* (Helsinki: Finnish Historical Society, 1996[?]), 259; Carstensen and Roazen, "Foreign Markets," 585, 589. International Harvester apparently continued to purchase from Peabody until 1905; Roazen-Parrillo, "U.S. Business Interests," 101.

34. Carstensen and Roazen, "Foreign Markets," 589. On the company's continuing relations with Molina, see 585; on MacLeod and Baja California, see 586 n89. It is unclear when Molina bought the land in Cuba and when International Harvester followed; see also Wells, chap. 3 here. International Harvester may have bought the Cuban land after the close of the Porfirian era in Mexico. Mexican newspapers were full of shrill criticisms of American business "exploitation" of Mexico. The change in regime might make International Harvester fear that its source of supply would be in jeopardy.

35. See Cyrus H. McCormick, Memorandum of meeting, 8 November 1915, at Continental and Commercial Bank, Chicago, Cyrus H. McCormick, Jr., Papers, State Historical Society of Wisconsin, Madison, McCormick MSS 2C, Subject Files, Box 38, IHC Correspondence.

36. In 1928 there was still more Mexican henequen produced than African and Javan fiber together, but by 1936, African and Javan fiber production would be double that of Mexico (E. A. Brewster Memorandum, 14 April 1937, Boyle files, IHC). Fred Carstensen has provided me with data from the Plymouth Cordage Company papers (hereafter cited as PCC), Baker's Library,

Harvard Business School, Boston, on International Harvester's Cuban plantation. See also Wilkins, *The Maturing of Multinational Enterprise*, 102, for
International Harvester's Cuban and Philippines plantations.

37. *U.S.* vs. *International Harvester Co.* 174 U.S. 683, 708 (1927). The
evidence indicates that International Harvester purchased more fiber than it
grew. The plantations were intended to protect it against price increases.
Roazen-Parrillo, "U.S. Business Interests," 339–349, is wonderful in showing
International Harvester's and Plymouth Cordage's opposition to the activities of
the Sisal Sales Corporation.

38. Wilkins, *The Emergence of Multinational Enterprise*, 63–64, 82–85, 123;
chap. 4 here.

39. Chap. 4 here, and Wilkins, *The Emergence of Multinational Enterprise*,
123; see also the excellent article by Jonathan Brown, "Domestic Politics and
Foreign Investment: British Development of Mexican Petroleum 1899–
1911," *Business History Review* 61 (Autumn 1987): 387–416, in which he
argues that Cowdray's success was based on his political ties to Porfirio Díaz.

40. Wilkins, *The Emergence of Multinational Enterprise*, 85; idem, *The
History of Foreign Investment in the United States to 1914*, 287–292, and idem,
The History of Foreign Investment in the United States after 1914 (for expansion in the United States); Latin American expansion must be seen in this
context. See also Shell, Annual Reports. When Shell purchased Lord Cowdray's
properties, it already had a small subsidiary in Mexico, established in 1912;
on this, see Geoffrey Jones, *The State and the Emergence of the British Oil
Industry* (London: Macmillan, 1981), 77, 217–218. Mira Wilkins, "Multinational Oil Companies in South America in the 1920s: In Argentina, Bolivia,
Brazil, Chile, Colombia, Ecuador, Peru," *Business History Review* 48 (Autumn 1974): 422 gives the 1917 date; the full commitment to processing
Venezuelan oil came in 1922, after Royal Dutch–Shell's sizable oil discovery
there. This became a huge refinery, which, as Jonathan Brown and Peter Linder
point out in chap. 4 here, by 1929 had eighty-six hundred employees.

41. Wilkins, *The Emergence of Multinational Enterprise*, 85.

42. See chap. 4 here, Table 4.1.

43. See chap. 4 here. In Wilkins, "Multinational Oil Companies in South
America in the 1920s," I looked at such companies by function and found
that the U.S. and host governments' roles varied sharply by function. On
Mexico's rank as an oil producer, see Wilkins, *The Maturing of Multinational
Enterprise*, 36. On Mexico's rank as an oil exporter, see R. W. Ferrier, *The
History of the British Petroleum Company*, vol. I, *The Developing Years, 1901–
1932* (New York: Cambridge University Press, 1982), 542. See also Wilkins,
The Maturing of Multinational Enterprise, 35–36, and chap. 4 here.

44. Ferrier, *The History*, 11, 540, 552–554, 557, 560; see also Wilkins,
"Multinational Oil Companies in South America in the 1920s," 439 n109.

45. Edwin Lieuwen, *Petroleum in Venezuela: A History* (Berkeley and Los
Angeles: University of California Press, 1955). On the switch from Mexico to
Venezuela, see chap. 4 here; Jonathan C. Brown, "Why Foreign Companies
Shifted Their Production from Mexico to Venezuela in the 1920s," *American
Historical Review* 90:2 (1985): 362–385; and Wilkins, *The Maturing of Multina-*

tional Enterprise, 113–116. The reasons for the switch were economic, political, and technological. There were the big discoveries in Venezuela; Venezuela provided a more congenial political environment; and saltwater began to appear in some of the Mexican wells. Mexico had barely surpassed Russia as the world's number two producer in 1917, the year of the Russian Revolution; in 1918 Mexico was clearly number two; Russia's oil output resumed slowly, finally surpassing Mexico's in 1927. In 1929 the world leaders were the United States, which produced one billion barrels of oil; Venezuela, 137 million; Russia, 77 million; Mexico, 45 million; Iran, 42 million; and the Dutch East Indies, 39 million. There were no other important oil-producing countries. See crude oil production figures in American Petroleum Institute, *Petroleum Facts and Figures* (1971), 548–550.

46. Miller, "British Free-Standing Companies on the West Coast of South America." See also Wilkins, *The Emergence of Multinational Enterprise*, 186.

47. Wilkins, *The Emergence of Multinational Enterprise*, 109–210.

48. Salazar-Carrillo, *Oil and Development in Venezuela*, 33, 44–45, 65–68; Wilkins, *The Maturing of Multinational Enterprise*, 115, 122–127.

49. At least, this is the thrust of current research. It would not surprise me to find evidence that wealthy individuals invested in the foreign *companies* that did business in their countries.

6. Retrospect and Prospect:
The Dance of the Commodities

Steven C. Topik
and
Allen Wells

The Second Conquest was neither uniform nor complete. The terrain of the "battlefield" varied enormously, as did the tactics, techniques, and results. These chapters have shown the weaknesses of global generalizations about export economies, foreigners and their corporations, Latin American states, labor systems, and social settings. The nature of the export commodity greatly affected its production system and its social, economic, and political consequences. Still, local histories and geography caused ample variation even within the same commodity. One needs to be specific, and the exports must be understood in their international commodity chain context; that is, we must understand their relation to the organization of the world market and the structure of businesses in it, not just as local products. Viewed in this way, comparative analysis of commodities can reveal patterns hidden in most studies of national economies *grosso modo*.

Export Orientation

Starting at the most fundamental level of similarity, coffee, henequen, and oil were all export products sold primarily in the United States and Europe. But they did not begin as colonial or neocolonial impositions. Oil and henequen were both native to Latin America; however, the demand for oil in Latin America was created by foreign imports while U.S. and North American needs for ship rigging created a market for henequen. In other words, oil began as a domestically consumed but imported good while henequen started as an export crop. Coffee, native to Africa, first came to the Americas as an imported luxury. The first trees in most countries were planted to please coffee addicts at home. In a sense, coffee and oil were the first import-substitution industries that became export oriented.

Coffee-growing methods were imported into the Americas, where they were modestly improved. Henequen cultivation and processing was developed in Mexico by Mexicans. Oil drilling and refining were perfected in the United States, Rumania, and Russia; only later were they transplanted to the Americas. These differing relations with the exterior reflect the fact that the world markets of the three products differed sharply. Coffee, an important international luxury for five centuries, became a mass product in the nineteenth century and a cheap luxury as well as an addictive drug; it faced little competition. Over 90 percent was produced in the Americas and two-thirds or more in one country, Brazil. Latin American growers dominated the large and ever-growing market. Substitutes, either roasted grains or tea and cocoa, could make few incursions into coffee's market share as long as coffee prices remained relatively low.

On the other hand, henequen faced stiff competition from Philippine abaca and, later, African hemp. Its virtue was its cheapness, but it could be easily substituted. Henequen's niche was much smaller than coffee's and it was considerably more subject to the whims of manufacturers and consumers. Consequently, the opportunities for dynamic growth in this sector and for large multiplier effects were quite restricted.

Oil was a truly global commodity. Indeed, the major oil companies moved into Latin America as part of a global strategy. As the fuel of the third Industrial Revolution, with uses ranging from lubrication and illumination to plastics, petroleum has been the success story of the twentieth century. Demand expanded vertiginously both within Latin America and abroad. Unlike coffee and henequen, however, which were produced mostly in poor countries (in the South) for use in rich countries (in the North) oil was produced and consumed in both.

Foreigners' Control of Production

Oil

Oil production's dynamism and complexity as well as the fact that its techniques were first developed in the United States, where capital was relatively cheap but labor was expensive, meant that capital-intensive methods were developed. This, in turn, led to the domination by finance and industrial capitalists, who formed the first true multinational corporations. These companies, headquartered in the United States and Europe, sought to control the world market through vertical integration. They strove to own every step in the production process, including mineral rights and oil wells in Latin America. Oil production would produce cultural and political clashes in the South precisely because it was an advanced capitalist production method implanted in poor and often remote backwaters. The first oil fields, usually located close to the coast, became company towns that initially resembled colonial enclaves with limited ties to the hinterland that surrounded them. Some of the world's richest and most powerful "trusts" dominated every step from the gas station back to the oil wells and even workers' housing and the local company store.

Coffee

Foreign participation was quite different in the coffee economies. Native growers had started most of the coffee groves to sell to their compatriots. European and North American merchants then began selling some of the coffee in their home markets. Over time a small number of merchants came to dominate exports, but different companies imported, roasted, and marketed the product in the consuming countries, and Latin American nationals always dominated production. It is true that in some countries, such as Guatemala and Mexico, Germans became important growers, but they were mostly immigrants rather than agents for German companies.

Vertical integration was slow because consolidation of the coffee-roasting industries in the consuming northern countries proceeded slowly. The technological barrier of retaining the flavor of roasted coffee beans before the invention of vacuum packing as well as cultural preferences in blends deterred centralization and homogenization. Although industrial capital in the form of companies such as Arbuckles (Yuban coffee), General Foods, and A&P began consolidation in the 1920s, these companies were far from controlling the industry in consuming countries and much less vertically integrated on a large scale internationally. Latin Americans continued to own the land, the trees, and the processing mills. In most countries the landowners were peasants; even in countries such as Brazil, where latifundia predominated, the size of holdings diminished over time. Relatively large foreign firms, however, dominated transportation, exports, and the ever more complex roasting, packaging, and marketing aspects of the trade. Thus, rather than being vertically integrated under the control of multinationals, as was petroleum production, coffee growing was a hybrid, a cross between northern industrial capitalist financing, transport, processing, and marketing and southern peasant production. Europeans and North Americans owned the most lucrative parts of the trade. Consequently, it is safe to estimate that over two-thirds of the profits accrued to European and North American firms, even though Latin Americans dominated production.

Henequen

Henequen's experience was a cross of the two organizational systems just discussed. Mexican nationals cultivated the agave using simple, local techniques and rather traditional labor arrangements. Land owner-ship continued in Mexican hands. Until the Mexican Revolution, the size of the fields grew as control became concentrated among a small group of Yucatecan families. The "divine caste" succeeded in widening its grasp because it collaborated with what was virtually a monopsonis-tic buyer: the huge North American International Harvester Company. Because Yucatecan henequen was overwhelmingly exported to the United States, this one company had greater control of the local industry than did the foreign oil companies—even though the oil companies actually owned and operated the oil fields.

The larger size and greater profitability of the world oil and coffee markets created far more competition, which Latin Americans used to play companies off against each other. Not so with henequen. International Harvester's domination was particularly painful for Yucatán because the company made its profits by selling binding machines rather than from twine sales. Hence Harvester and its agents in Yucatán had an interest in keeping down the consumer's price of twine to make its farm implements more attractive (just as automobile manufacturers still depend on cheap oil). In contrast, oil and coffee producers profited from high consumer prices.

Despite the quite marked differences in foreign organization, con-trol, and interests in the three production systems, it is clear that all three export economies faced North American and European control and disproportionate profits from coffee, henequen, and oil.

Developmental Consequences

This is not to say that the Latin American countries that exported these commodities reaped no economic benefits. All three commodities produced some positive developmental consequences. The nature and extent of these consequences varied according to the production pro-cesses themselves, the organization of the world market for the goods and participating businesses, and the power and political will of the participating Latin American states. The most straightforward way of discussing the economic ripple effects of coffee, henequen, and oil is to review their linkages, that is, the other economic activity that they engendered.

Coffee

Coffee, grown mostly with simple, land-extensive, and labor-intensive methods, had few important backward linkages besides transportation improvements in railroads and shipping. Brazil, to widen the domestic market, developed one of the largest rail networks in the Third World, primarily in the coffee area. Other coffee lands, however, such as Colombia, Nicaragua, and Guatemala, were slow to build rail, though the effects were positive for domestic industry once the networks appeared. Coffee's comparative advantage lay in the exploitation of rich soil and poor labor, not sophisticated methods with ample inputs.

In Brazil, "*cafeicultura*" was closer to the mining of natural resources than to the cultivation of agro-industry. Planters earned a "forest rent"; no one calculated the depreciation costs of the slain forests and denuded hills on their balance sheets. In countries with less fertile land, such as Costa Rica and El Salvador, depredations of the soil were less egregious, but cultivation practices were little different. Since the only use for coffee beans was as a beverage, and since companies roasted and packaged the product close to their consumers overseas (who bought close to 90 percent of the coffee grown), forward linkages were also slight within Latin America.

Coffee's main benefit presented itself in what is known as consumption linkages; however, coffee workers unfortunately shared little in the increased consumption of goods in their home markets. They received minimal wages and survived mostly on self-provisioning on their own or *fazenda* land and unremunerated family labor. Those profits that remained in Brazil and Central America concentrated in the cities, where the intermediaries, planters, and processors spent and invested. This exacerbated the gulf in standard of living and lifestyle between the vast countryside and the privileged cities as it widened the divide between the rich and the poor.

The ample profits made by larger landowners, processors, merchants, and bankers (essentially, those who farmed the farmers) were not all frittered away on imported luxuries and palaces, though an excessive share was spent in just that way. The profit-takers also invested in urban improvements such as electricity, lighting, trams, banks, and factories that produced simple manufactured goods such as cloth, shoes, and processed foods. So coffee led to the first stirrings of industrialization, though only São Paulo and Rio de Janeiro were well along that path by 1930.

Henequen

Henequen's trajectory resembled that of coffee, but because it employed a much smaller population in an area that offered few other economic attractions, the economic multiplier effects were muted. Again, the main backward linkage was in transport. But the grid of rail that crisscrossed the henequen fields failed to link important secondary cities or to tie the Yucatecan peninsula to mainland Mexico. This heightened the sense of Yucatán's being an outward-looking island while limiting its consumption linkages.

Although henequen was useful for a number of manufactured products, including rope, hammocks, and sacks, few industrial forward linkages arose, despite efforts to create them. Cheap rail and steam transport made shipping the raw material abroad for industrial processes economical.

Again, the main stimulus to growth was the urban concentration of capital and purchases. Trappings of urban modernity such as the telegraph, sanitation, and electricity followed, but the local economy was too small to seduce much investment in other productive enterprises. Rather than attracting national capital from other parts of the country, as occurred in some coffee centers, Yucatán was a net capital exporter, as *henequeneros* invested in other parts of Mexico and even in Cuba. Henequen growers and merchants, just like large-scale coffee growers, processors, and merchants, were profit-seeking capitalist entrepreneurs.

Unfortunately, because of poor natural resources, geographic remoteness, and an extreme concentration of the wealth that left rural workers almost outside the money economy, henequen's wealthy did not find so many investment opportunities in the land of the agave. Unlike coffee in some countries, henequen grown in the oligarchic Yucatecan model was unable to lead to self-sustaining economic development. This was as much because of the sociopolitical setting and the environment as because of the crop itself or the dominance of International Harvester.

Oil

Because oil production required an advanced industrial process, linkage effects were more substantial. Petroleum required a great many backward linkages in construction to create pipelines, derricks, housing, and ports. Although the most sophisticated machinery was imported, there was still ample room for local materials. Forward linkages were even more impressive, because petroleum had been oriented toward the home market from the beginning. Oil not only illuminated cities initially and lubricated machines, it replaced coal to provide cheap factory and vehicular fuel. Thus oil directly fed the growth of other industries.

Consumption linkages were also important. Oil workers, unlike agricultural peasants, were paid in money, which they used to purchase their needs. In contrast to coffee and henequen workers, who lived with their families and lived off family labor, roughnecks tended to be single men or men living distant from their families. Hence they earned and consumed in the money economy. The economy, however, suffered from great leakage: the foreign-owned oil companies earned and repatriated the vast majority of the profits, and, because the main oil fields in Mexico and Venezuela were close to the coast and distant from population centers, many daily necessities were imported. Over time, however, the petroleum areas became growth poles for cities and industries as people flocked there to take advantage of the relatively high wages paid by the oil companies.

Although linkages are impossible to measure accurately, it is safe to say that oil enjoyed greater linkages than did coffee or henequen. This was in good part because it was an advanced capitalist process that relied on many inputs and operated in the money economy while coffee and henequen continued to exploit peasant forms of production. Nonetheless, because all three sectors were largely foreign controlled, they did not provide sufficient economic multiplier effects to substantially transform the national economies and societies. All three, to different degrees, led to gross inequities in pay and profit.

Exports and State Building

But one cannot gauge the economic and social impact of the export sectors merely by focusing on production processes. Latin American states had the potential of encouraging or discouraging the fruits of exports, the power of foreign companies, and the distribution of wealth for their societies. In all three cases, the exports had ambivalent effects on state building. Postcolonial nineteenth-century Latin American states were weak, fragmented, and broke. They did not enjoy reliable armies and police forces, legitimacy, or financial resources. Although recognized by the international community from early in the century (despite numerous invasions by European and North American imperialists and filibusters), they exercised little control over their own interiors. Indeed, the nineteenth century has been termed a "Second Conquest" with a meaning very different from the one we have employed: the national states' consolidation of their own territories.[1] How were the two sorts of Second Conquest related? Did export economies lead to internal political consolidation, and were stronger states able to wrest more concessions from foreign investors and merchants?

Coffee

Coffee states were all weak and fragmented before coffee, many having suffered serious civil wars and revolts between self-named Conservatives and Liberals during the tumultuous nineteenth century. Although factions calling themselves Liberals often won out, in fact, both protagonists favored coffee exports and were favored by them. And both sought oligarchic, authoritarian regimes. It is difficult to see the coffee boom as a "Liberal Revolution" in anything but name.

Coffee was earliest and most successful in countries in which the national government had appreciable legitimacy with regional elites before the boom, as in Brazil and Costa Rica. In other countries, such as Colombia, Mexico, El Salvador, and Nicaragua, the coffee economies began before national political power was secured. But if the direction of the causal relationship between export boom and state formation is ambiguous, there is no doubt that the two reinforced each other.

In many countries, the largest planter often became president. Still, there was no direct correlation between coffee ownership and national power. Most Brazilian leaders during the era when coffee was king were not major planters, nor were they completely beholden to planters. Brazil had too many economic and regional interests to create a monolithic coffee republic.

The growth of centralized state power should not be confused with the spread of citizenship rights. Suffrage remained extremely limited in coffee countries. Elections were fraudulent, as local boss politics coupled with violence predominated. Local village and town governments, which had previously been the most democratic institutions, often lost authority to landlords, merchants, generals, and federal officials. Even property rights were slow to replace colonial patrimonialism and arbitrary and personalistic impositions by the elite. Indigenous communities and small towns often lost land ownership and use rights with little compensation. In general, a frontier justice continued in most places. Landownership as often came out of the barrel of a gun as from a notary's pen. Where legally sanctioned land rights were most secure was where most of the accumulation of profit came from processing and trading rather than from growing, in other words, where landownership was less important.

Indeed, many people lost control of their own labor as well as their land because first slavery and then government-supported coercive labor schemes played important parts on the *cafezales.* Women in particular often found themselves subject to increasing patriarchal power, though the boom was liberating for some women. In no coffee lands, however, did women gain the vote before 1930.

Coffee states strengthened their grip not through increased popular sovereignty but by gaining control over the new boom-generated resources, especially foreign loans and taxes on international trade. The new funds allowed federal officials to co-opt or suppress local warlords, bring the military and bandits to heel, and hold foreign gunboats at bay. This, in turn, protected wealth and production from arbitrary seizures and the depredations of war. Government spending mounted, but mostly in the cities, where it was spent on civil and military bureaucracies, monuments to modernization such as boulevards and opera houses, and transportation infrastructure for the export economy.

State officials were reluctant to redistribute revenues to the poor through education or health services. Instead, coffee states won legitimacy by purchasing the support of the elite and urban residents. The bulk of the populations living in the countryside benefited mostly from political peace and federal neglect. But since coffee depended on peasant-style agriculture, with families usually retaining access to land use (if not ownership) and multiple relations to the means of production, coffee countries experienced almost no mass rural revolts. Hence the governing elite felt free to ignore coffee workers. Coffee countries were among the last in Latin America to experience populist pressures or unionization in the countryside.

Coffee politicians clearly aided the concentration of wealth; however, they did not support all wealth equally. They often took nationalistic stands against foreigners, especially foreign merchants. Brazil's coffee valorization program and Colombia's Federación Nacional de Café (National Coffee Federation) were the two most notable examples. Far from following the laissez-faire policies that Liberals supposedly so admired, coffee leaders asserted the state's power in the international market and successfully modified the terms of trade. Indeed, coffee was the first commodity in which a less-developed country asserted mastery over a major world commodity market.

The state capitalist model later would be appropriated by other sectors such as banks, railroads, and petroleum. One should be cautioned that, while this clearly was not the action of a neocolonial comprador state, neither was it socialism. States continued to protect private property, private accumulation, and an unequal distribution of wealth. Nor did xenophobia motivate coffee state capitalism. Foreign loans and export revenues fueled valorization. European and North American land ownership was never questioned, and foreign immigrant labor—either southern Europeans in Brazil or Guatemalan Maya in Mexico and El Salvador—continued to play an important role in the labor market. Brazilian leaders wanted to protect and increase the rent they earned from Brazil's near monopoly position in the world market, not distance themselves from it.

Henequen

Henequen's consequences for state building and political organization resembled those of coffee, though at a more local level, since the crop was of only regional importance and never provided more than about 15 percent of Mexico's total exports. State power certainly grew during the boom. The state's relationship to henequen was a good deal closer than in the case of coffee, because there was no contesting base of power in the state. Hacienda ownership, commerce, and political power became intertwined. The interior was conquered not only through a frontier movement felling sparsely populated forests, as was the case with coffee, but as an army of occupation conquering Maya lands and villages. Unlike in the Philippines, where production was done by villagers who used traditional labor systems, in Yucatán Spanish-speaking landlords used state power to break the power of communal villages and coerce Maya to work on haciendas.

Although *henequeneros* professed liberal ideals, they were anything but liberals. They confused state and personal power and aims. By 1910 one man, Olegario Molina, was the largest merchant and landlord and was elected governor. Until the Revolution fought its way into the peninsula, this truly was a henequen republic. As the comparison with the Philippines demonstrates, the patrimonial export state in Yucatán was more the result of local history and social context than it was driven by demands of the export economy per se.

Still, International Harvester's preeminent place in the fiber market and its close links to the commercial house of Henry Peabody and, ultimately, to Governor Molina meant this truly was a comprador state. Before 1910 the Yucatecan state worked to concentrate wealth, facilitate exports, and break worker resistance. During Molina's tenure as governor from 1902 to 1911, the state government operated as an extension of International Harvester, doing the company's bidding.

Since the state in Yucatán was composed of prominent henequen planters and merchants, plantation workers had little hope of improving their working conditions by petitioning state authorities. These indebted peons were arguably some of the most exploited laborers in Latin America. Recognizing that a frontal assault on the planters and the state would have proved futile, workers opted instead for everyday forms of resistance, joining revolts only when other groups in Yucatecan society had made collective resistance possible.

The Mexican Revolution radically changed the basis of state power and the relationship of Yucatán's state government to International Harvester. Because *henequeneros*, unlike some coffee planters, had been unwilling to bend during the ancien régime, the Revolution forced some to break. Revolutionaries outside Yucatán insisted that the state reorder the relations of production, initially valorized production, and later created *ejidos* and a state bank to finance them. This was a much sharper break with the export capitalist system than had occurred in any coffee country. The state also ended its cozy relationship with International Harvester, attempting instead a short-lived price support system. Despite the more radical discourse of Mexican revolutionaries and the meaningful changes in social relations they enacted, they never tried to reduce the Yucatán's dependence on the international economy; they felt that Yucatán simply had no alternatives.

Oil

Oil presents a rather different picture, not only because of the different configuration of its world market, the scale of the participating multinational corporations, and its more sophisticated production process, but also because it burst on the Latin American scene forty to fifty years after coffee and henequen. That half a century made an enormous difference in the nature and form of state power that oilmen confronted. By the 1910s and the 1920s, Latin American states had expanded their popular base to include at least the urban male middle and working classes. Political power was disputed increasingly at the ballot box rather than on the battlefields. State bureaucracies were larger and more able. Oil supplied valuable tax revenues, but also represented an important symbol of national progress, since it was both necessary for the national defense and an internal consumption item. Petroleum simply occupied a much larger position in the national imagination because of its links to industrialization and its domestic applications.

It also was politically volatile because many of the workers were nationals while the management was foreign. Paying good wages, but unfamiliar with the personalistic labor relations prevalent elsewhere in Latin America, Yankee, British, and Dutch managers aroused some of the most militant and best-organized labor organizations. Some politicians saw these vocal, organized workers as a base of support. Consequently, petroleum became the product most subject to nationalist pressures.

At first, the efforts relied mainly on raising taxes to increase government rents. But over time the state's role became more radical: state corporations were established in Argentina, Colombia, and Brazil to search for oil. Finally, Mexico and Venezuela, two of the world's largest petroleum producers, nationalized their oil industries with little compensation. These attacks on foreign capital were a central part of a new state policy that had been developing since the 1920s: import-substitution industrialization. The nationalizations were not intended to represent attacks on capital or private property, but to earn a greater share of the oil profits for the Latin American countries to help them develop other sectors. They were powerful political symbols, intended to make the countries more self-sufficient and less reliant on foreign capital and foreign markets.

The export economies carried within themselves the seeds of their own transformations. They strengthened states, slowly built up internal markets, and gradually led to wider, more mobilized polities. The Latin America that the export boom bequeathed in 1930 was quite different from that of 1850. There were far more miles of railroad track and larger, more glamorous cities. New nationalities were introduced, such as the Italians in São Paulo's *cafezales,* West Indians in Venezuela's oil fields, Chinese in Yucatán. Ethnicities were transformed as coffee turned many Indians into ladinos and Africans into Brazilians (sometimes against their will). The export economies were slow to offer new opportunities to women, though some space for mobility appeared in the cities that exports spawned and on the spreading frontier. The Second Conquest conquered many indigenous groups, severed communal relations, and slaughtered forests. It exacerbated inequalities and, in many instances, only rechanneled violence rather than ending it.

Note

1. Colin Lewis, "The Economics of the Latin American State: Ideology, Policy, and Performance, c. 1820–1945," paper presented at the Conference on State and Sovereignty in the World Economy, Laguna Beach, Calif., 22 February 1997.

Epilogue

Steven C. Topik
and
Allen Wells

Why did Latin American governments turn away from export-led growth in 1930? An examination of the forces that prompted the rise of "inward-looking development" in the wake of the Great Depression and how that eventually led to a return to liberalism and export-oriented growth may help answer that question.

Equipped with the benefit of hindsight, historians readily point to a number of factors that contributed to the demise of the export boom.[1] From the outbreak of the First World War until the onset of the Great Depression, scholars contend, the telltale signs that presaged momentous shifts in the international economic order were there for Latin American elites and foreign investors to see. But those signs were not so patently obvious to contemporaries on either side of the Atlantic. After sixty years of viewing their economic world in a certain way, of focusing primarily on an export-led model rather than gearing production to the domestic market, of consolidating their collective energies in the production of one or two commodities, of emphasizing agricultural or extractive pursuits at the expense of manufacturing, few Latin American elites and politicians were willing to chart bold new paths. Even though World War I would turn commodity markets upside down, provoking considerable price and earnings instability, most observers came to the not-so-unreasonable conclusion that such a sudden shift in the demand curve, which had played havoc with prices, would right itself soon after the war, just as it had during prior cycles. Henequen and oil (along with copper, tin, and nitrates) witnessed soaring market prices and strong demand during the conflict, since they were sought-after strategic materials. On the other hand, coffee and other nonessential raw materials did not fare as well.

Contemporaries should also be excused for drawing the wrong lesson from the worldwide recession of 1920–1921, when prices of many commodities dropped precipitously. Most merchants, businesspeople, and farmers reasoned that the relaxation of wartime price controls by Western Europe and the United States after the war had contributed to a rapid surge in commodity prices. Such price increases triggered an increase in production, which eventually contributed to a glut and a collapse of commodity prices during the recession.[2]

These short-term boom-and-bust cycles were not, after all, uncommon, and, historically, wars have been a principal catalyst of significant market fluctuations. The Spanish American War, we may recall, had disrupted supplies of abaca and precipitated a sudden rise in henequen prices after 1898. But that increase was short-lived, as market forces and the machinations of corporate interests combined not only to bring fiber prices down by 1907, but also to keep them depressed until the outbreak of World War I. Entrepreneurs no doubt believed that such cycles were part and parcel of the export-led model and, given the difficulties posed by diversification—for example, start-up costs, the search for markets and barriers to entry—battening the hatches through the lean years made eminent sense.

The 1920s were very much a roller coaster for export commodities. After the decade began in recession, commodity prices recouped by 1925, only to falter again by 1928. What this particular short-run cycle hid, however, was a secular decline of European and North American demand for primary products, induced by Europe's determination to protect its agricultural sectors and a progressive worsening of the terms of trade for commodity producers. Two additional factors contributed to a general weakening of Latin American commodity markets: (1) a considerable reduction in the natural rate of population increase (coupled with rising income in Europe and the United States), which contributed to a proportionately slower growth in the demand for primary goods; and (2) the creation and production of synthetic substitutes by competitors for a number of key commodities, such as cotton, rubber, and nitrates. Only three of the twenty-two commodities that dominated Latin American exports—oil, cacao, and rubber—grew at annual rates above 5 percent a year between 1913 and 1928; fifteen products had disappointing growth rates below 3 percent a year; and six key commodities witnessed minimal increases of 1 percent a year or less (production or exports in volume terms). Moreover, the cost of importing manufactured goods rose faster than the revenues garnered from exports in the postwar period. Obtaining reliable data about the sudden shifts in the relative values of these imports and exports, however, was exceedingly difficult for contemporary economic analysts. Indeed, economic historians still quarrel about precisely when the terms of trade turned against Latin American and other primary exporting nations. Most agree, however, that by 1929 the terms of trade for primary markets had, with some exceptions, fallen below their 1913 levels.[3]

If it was difficult to read the short-run economic indicators after the First World War, it must have been harder still to step back and gain some perspective on the entire eighty years of export-led growth. With the historian's hindsight, we realize that Latin America's economic growth throughout the boom was predicated on the expansion of land and labor inputs rather than on increases in the productivity of those inputs. Since those inputs were not energized by advancements in technology and improvements in productivity were not forthcoming, output would inevitably suffer. Furthermore, since wealth was extremely concentrated, internal markets were slow to develop.

The far from uniform decline in demand for commodities also made it difficult for businesspeople and politicians to read the economic signs. In fact, certain mineral products—most notably, oil, copper, and tin—were deemed strategically vital by Western governments, and, as we saw in the case of oil, multinational firms were encouraged by their home governments to invest in Latin America during the 1920s. It is instructive that only four countries achieved satisfactory growth rates, and all four produced oil and other "strategic" minerals. Yet even in the commodity sectors where substantive growth occurred, foreign companies—taking advantage of generous concessions from Latin American governments—not indigenous entrepreneurs achieved a preeminent position in their respective markets. And, as Rosemary Thorp relates, "Oils and minerals are precisely the products with relatively low returned value (that part of export proceeds retained locally through taxes, wages, construction or other expenditures) owing to the capital intensive nature of their production process and to foreign ownership."[4]

Efforts to manipulate the market—by buyers and sellers—also served to obscure long-run trends. As chapter 2 illustrates, the revival of the Brazilian valorization campaign in the 1920s held coffee off the market, thereby raising prices for producers in the short run. The scheme, however, encouraged competition to increase cultivation in Colombia and Central America, where no such restraints on exports existed. By 1929 the coffee market was saturated.

Unfortunately, Latin Americans also found that markets, especially in Europe, were not as open as they had been prior to the Great War. By protecting their home agricultural sectors and by making it abundantly clear that they would give preference to commodities from their colonies, Western European nations constructed irksome barriers to trade with Latin America, foreshadowing similar measures that would be adopted during the depression. For its part, the United States continued its protectionist policies, a strategy dating to the Civil War.

Change in Latin America, then, was prompted by technological, demographic, and ideological changes in the United States and Western Europe, not by autonomous decisions by Latin American politicians. But disappointment over restraints of trade was assuaged by growing North American investment in Latin America. Even though Latin Americans found it difficult to break into the North American market, the United States had little difficulty parlaying its newfound clout as the chief capital creditor to the region after World War I into a way of opening new economic doors throughout Latin America for its manufactured goods. In fact, as Thorp has noted, the war years and the ensuing decade saw a bonanza of North American private foreign lending; investment rose from $3.5 billion to $6.4 billion from 1914 to 1919 alone, as the United States eclipsed the British as the preeminent capital exporter to the region. By 1919 New York's National City Bank had established forty-two branches in nine Latin American countries. North American bankers pressed loans on Latin American governments, many of those loans destined to increase the supply of already overproduced commodities and others destined for extravagant and unnecessary projects.[5]

A case in point is Cuba's sugar industry, which increasingly came under North American control after the "Dance of the Millions" (an episode of unrealistically high sugar prices and profligate lending) foundered on the shoals of the 1920–1921 recession. But the influx of North American loans, as wasteful as much of it was, served to reassure producers that the export-led model was worth sustaining.

After the October 1929 stock market crash, commodity prices plummeted as international trade and investment tailed off markedly. Export-led growth had been predicated on an open world economy, but to paraphrase an old aphorism, when the United States (and Europe) caught a cold, Latin America caught pneumonia. All of Latin America was affected, but not, as we should by now expect, uniformly. Initially, falling export prices and volumes plagued the entire region. Nations pursued different policies to overcome this difficult moment. It would not be until the end of 1932 that the Latin American republics would stop the economic hemorrhaging and gradually achieve positive growth rates.

But the depression only reinforced the trend toward protectionism in Europe and the United States. The passage of the Smoot-Hawley tariff in 1930 by the United States and the British creation of a system of imperial preferences at the Ottawa Conference in 1932 were just two examples of this trend. With these barriers erected, Latin Americans responded by gradually encouraging their manufacturing sectors without relinquishing their reliance on commodity exports. In fact, with the exception of Argentina, the rest of Latin America rebounded well from the depression and from 1932 to 1939, commodity export performance was, in Bulmer-Thomas's words, "surprisingly robust."[6]

If the thirties, then, did not alter Latin American reliance on export-led growth, the promotion of industrialization—and here we are, with the exception of Uruguay, referring to the larger nations in the region—did set the table for an inward-looking development model that gained momentum during the 1940s and the 1950s. Manufacturing grew naturally out of the export-led model, as earnings from primary commodities would provide start-up funds, not only for the continued expansion of traditional industries, such as textiles, shoes, and hats, but also for the growth of heavy industry, such as the iron and steel works in Monterrey, Mexico, as well as consumer durables and intermediate goods, most notably in Brazil, Argentina, and Chile. Populist governments took hold throughout the hemisphere during and after the depression and eclectically mixed and matched corporatism, militarism, nationalism, and, in some cases, fascism to suit their needs. These ideologies were consistent with an activist state that both co-opted its workers and sought to bring together heterogeneous groups and classes under the same nationalistic banner. Mexico's nationalization of the oil industry in 1938 was part and parcel of this trend toward greater state intervention into the economic sphere.

It must be emphasized that import-substitution industrialization (ISI)—that is, the process of substituting domestic industrial goods for imported goods—came about gradually; Latin Americans rebuilt their export sectors in the wake of the depression and understandably were reluctant to cut their ties from their economic past. But the foundations for a new model predicated on manufacturing had been laid.

The Second World War, much like the depression and the First World War, destabilized commodity markets. Latin American nations that exported principally to Europe were hurt while those that had shifted their gaze northward to the United States were not as seriously affected. In retrospect it is clear that World War II was the final straw. The cumulative effect of three shocks to the global economy over a span of three decades persuaded the larger countries in the region to embrace ISI more vigorously. Theoretical justification for the shift to an inward-looking model was provided by a young cohort of Latin American economists working for ECLA, which came into existence in 1948. As mentioned in the introduction, Raúl Prebisch, the head of ECLA, argued that Latin American economies responded sluggishly to world market price signals because of "structural rigidities," market imperfections that arose because of Latin America's social and political institutions and values and infrastructural deficiencies. Strong government intervention, protectionism, and monetary controls were required to promote industrialization, to diminish the region's historical reliance on primary exports, and to overcome what they believed to be worsening terms of trade. By the early 1950s, the export-led model had given way to ISI in the larger countries in the region while the smaller and intermediate-sized countries, lacking the wherewithal to reconfigure their economies as dramatically, moved more gradually toward manufacturing.[7]

Pessimism about primary export markets was reinforced by a sluggish 2 percent per annum growth in exports and a 20 percent decline in the terms of trade during the 1950s. Exports bought ever fewer imports. Over the next two decades, ambitious industrialization programs were devised that focused, for the most part, on the home market. Protective tariffs were imposed and state and para-state enterprises were undertaken.

The results were, in some ways, encouraging. Rates of growth of industrial production increased by 4 percent a year during the 1950s and inched over 6 percent from 1965 to 1970. These rates of growth exceeded those of the industrialized countries. But these impressive rates of increase hid the fact that ISI worked against industrial exports while largely confining the growth of manufacturing to the growth rate of domestic demand. To make matters worse for primary producers, state governments imposed steep taxes on exports and used multiple exchange rates to take away income from exporters and subsidize imports of industrial equipment and technology. As John Sheahan relates: "For exporters of primary products, the strategy acted to discourage both production and exports by reducing the real income that could be earned from exporting, and the resources available to them for investment." Inward-looking development represented a reversal of sorts of the principles and policies of the Second Conquest. Sheahan concludes that the ISI model "reflect[ed] a punitive domestic strategy aimed against landowners, a deep-rooted aversion to international trade that worked against promotion of industrial exports as well as primary, and the natural pressures of industrialists seeking both protection in their own interests and low-cost access to imported equipment."[8]

Inward-looking development would begin to unravel in the 1970s, as changes in the international economy and the huge OPEC oil price increases in 1973 and 1979 sharply increased the cost of imports throughout Latin America. Oil exporters deposited funds in commercial banks, which, in turn, lent those "petrodollars" in massive quantities to the private and public sector throughout the hemisphere. But by the beginning of the 1980s, tighter monetary policies in the industrialized countries drove up interest rates and curtailed new international lending. The prices of many raw material exports dropped precipitously. The major debtors faced interest payments equal to 5 percent of their GDP. By 1988 the combined Latin American debt owed to private banks, as well as the World Bank and the International Monetary Fund (IMF), had climbed to more than $400 billion. Latin America was actually decapitalizing as debt payments outpaced inflows of capital. The debt crisis crippled Latin American economies during the 1980s, as GDP declined by almost 10 percent. As countries teetered on the brink of insolvency throughout the decade, the International Monetary Fund lent funds on the condition that Latin American nations accept a stabilization program that rolled back inward-looking development policies and insisted that governments once again embrace an export-led model of development to enable them to pay off foreign bankers.

Has Latin America come full circle or is it on the verge of a brave new world, as proponents of new export-oriented policies maintain? As governments embrace the neoliberal orthodoxy so familiar to students of the Latin American export boom, at first glance the similarities between the two eras appear to be striking. Latin America still needs capital and technology and access to foreign markets, just as it did during the Second Conquest. Governments are once again taking a strong hand in bringing about the conditions conducive for investment and the opening of markets. State promotion of the economy, then as now, does not mean laissez-faire, as local interests still want their share of new businesses and privatization comes to fruition with a great deal of government assistance. Moreover, Latin Americans are still highly ambivalent about the costs and benefits of foreign investment. Even the globalization of the international economy and the ability of multilateral lending agencies such as the World Bank and the IMF to enforce financial discipline, which are often cited as structurally unique to today's world economy, have precedents prior to 1914, when London exercised a similarly preponderant control over capital markets and the gold standard to enforce fiscal order.

Yet, as striking as the similarities are, there are some key differences. The Second Conquest was a time of expanding employment opportunities, attracting, as it did, both immigration and internal labor migration. Economic growth was seen as a crucial element of state- and nation building. Today's neoliberal reforms, on the other hand, are privatizing the economic assets of the state and causing high levels of unemployment and the emigration of labor. Furthermore, to a much greater extent than one hundred years ago, domestic entrepreneurs' reliance on technology transfers has generated a plethora of business consortia involving domestic and foreign interests. Bankers, through their agencies and collective action, exercise economic and political power on a global scale to a degree unthinkable one hundred years ago.

Finally, capitalist ideology is today hegemonic in a way that it would have been impossible to conceive of at the turn of the nineteenth century. With the defeat of communism, the discrediting of socialism, and the incorporation of the peasantry, a consensus has arisen about the sanctity of private property, the autonomy of the individual, and the importance of wage labor.

This anthology has sought to reconceptualize the Latin American export boom on its own merits rather than as a way station on the road to poverty or progress,[9] because, as Alexander Gerschenkron has noted, "No past experience, however rich, and no historical research, however thorough, can save the living generation the creative task of finding their own answers and shaping their own future."[10] As this study of commodities has made abundantly clear, there is no mistaking the infinite variety of social, economic, and political webs of relations spun out by localities, regions, and nations. The diversity of the paths taken, the inherently destabilizing character of commodity markets; the critical role that external capital, technology, and knowledge played; and the fact that Latin America was the only part of the Third World that simultaneously went about the process of state formation as it underwent the transition to capitalism all created a bundle of contradictions that "export boomers" bequeathed to twentieth-century Latin America. Some of these have not yet been satisfactorily resolved. The Second Conquest created wealth but severely concentrated it in a few hands as public lands were privately appropriated. It forged national states, but states often ruled by narrow oligarchies that were commonly dependent on the resources of foreign banks while the indigenous and mestizo peasantry lost control over their lives and their resources. Latin American states during the export boom opened their economies, lowering duties and barriers to private accumulation; but state policy continued to be central to determining winners and losers, rich and poor. The market was never free or natural. Latin America's outward orientation before 1930 certainly made life better for many of its residents, but the world economy also allowed states and social systems to develop and persist without great concern about enacting fundamental reforms that would bring about justice and equality. Unlike the prospering nations of East Asia, which unseated the old elite through land reform and political transformations *before* they began their outward-oriented surge, Latin American nations have viewed exports and foreign capital as an alternative to reform.

While the antistatist rhetoric and export emphasis of the Second Conquest succeeded for more than half a century, it bore the fruits of its own destruction. The social revolution, as in Mexico, or statist popular reform, as in most of the rest of the continent, that brought the Second Conquest to a close was not so much a break with the export model as a natural outgrowth. Today's free traders, who often do not even justify their policies as nation building or the extension of citizenship, as did their liberal precursors before 1930, would do well to consider whether the market has enough magic and trade enough freedom to placate the masses who bear on their backs much of the costs of privatization and of the new export boom, and who endure, but will not endure forever.

Notes

1. This section has benefited from a number of insightful syntheses of twentieth-century Latin American economic history. See especially Victor Bulmer-Thomas, *The Economic History of Latin America since Independence* (New York: Cambridge University Press, 1994); idem, "The Latin American Economies, 1929–1939," in Leslie Bethell, ed., *Cambridge History of Latin America*, vol. VI, pt. 1 (New York: Cambridge University Press, 1994), 65–115; Rosemary Thorp, "The Latin American Economies, 1939–c.1950," in Bethell, *Cambridge History* VI, pt. 1: 117–158; idem, *Latin America in the 1930s: The Role of the Periphery in World Crises* (New York: St. Martin's Press, 1984); Ricardo Ffrench–Davis, Oscar Muñoz, and José Gabriel Palma, "The Latin American Economies, 1950–1990," in *Cambridge History* VI, pt. 1: 159–249; Barbara Stallings, *Banker to the Third World: U.S. Portfolio Investment in Latin America, 1900–1986* (Berkeley and Los Angeles: University of California Press, 1987); Mira Wilkins, *The Maturing Enterprise: American Business Abroad from 1914–1970* (Cambridge, Mass.: Harvard University Press, 1974).

2. Rosemary Thorp, "Latin America and the International Economy from the First World War to the World Depression," in Bethell, *Cambridge History* VI, pt. 1: 57–81.

3. Bulmer-Thomas, *Economic History*, 157–158, 164–165; Thorp, "Latin America and the International Economy," 62.

4. Thorp, "Latin America and the International Economy," 69.

5. Ibid., 59.

6. Bulmer-Thomas, "The Latin American Economies, 1929–1939," 96.

7. See Joseph L. Love, "Economic Ideas and Ideologies in Latin America since 1930," in Bethell, *Cambridge History* VI, pt. 1: 393–460; and idem, *Crafting the Third World: Theorizing Underdevelopment in Rumania and Brazil* (Stanford, Calif.: Stanford University Press, 1996). Central America and smaller nations still clung to commodity exports.

8. John Sheahan, *Patterns of Development in Latin America: Poverty, Repression and Economic Strategy* (Princeton, N.J.: Princeton University Press, 1987), 84, 89, 93.

9. The scholarly obsession with Latin American underdevelopment shows little sign of abating. A recently published anthology entitled *How Latin America Fell Behind* employs the methods of "the new economic history" to analyze economic problems in Latin America during the nineteenth century. Despite the rigorous application of quantitative methods, these case studies cover familiar terrain and offer conclusions that few students of nineteenth-century Latin American history would find surprising; see Stephen Haber, ed., *How Latin America Fell Behind: Essays on the Economic Histories of Brazil and Mexico, 1800–1914* (Stanford, Calif.: Stanford University Press, 1997).

10. Alexander Gerschenkron, "Economic Backwardness in Historical Perspective," in idem, *Economic Backwardness in Historical Perspective: A Book of Essays* (Cambridge, Mass.: Belknap Press of Harvard University Press, 1962), 5–30, quotation on 6.

Bibliography

Adamo, Sam. "Race and Povo." In Michael L. Conniff and Frank D. McCann, eds., *Modern Brazil: Elites and Masses in Historical Perspective*. Lincoln: University of Nebraska Press, 1989, 192–208.

Adas, Michael. *Machines as the Measure of Men: Science, Technology and Ideologies of Western Dominance*. Ithaca, N.Y.: Cornell University Press, 1989.

Adleson G., Lief. "Coyuntura y conciencia: Factores convergentes en la fundación de los sindicatos petroleros de Tampico durante la década de 1920." In Elsa Cecilia Frost et al., eds., *El trabajo y los trabajadores en la historia de México*. Mexico City and Tucson: University of Arizona Press, 1979, 632–660.

———. "The Cultural Roots of the Oil Workers' Unions in Tampico, 1910–1925." In Jonathan C. Brown and Alan Knight, eds., *The Mexican Petroleum Industry in the Twentieth Century*. Austin: University of Texas Press, 1992, 36–62.

———. "Historia social de los obreros industriales de Tampico, 1906–1919." Ph.D. diss., El Colegio de México, 1982.

Águila M., Marcos Tonahtiuh. "Trends in Registered Mexican Labor Conflicts, 1927–1931." *Economía: Teoría y Práctica*, no. 4 (1995): 85–102.

Ahmed, Rakibuddin. *The Progress of the Jute Industry and Trade (1865–1966)*. Dacca: Pakistan Central Jute Committee, 1966.

Anderson, Thomas. *El Salvador 1932*. San Salvador: Editorial Universitaria Centroamericana, 1982.

Andrews, George Reid. *Blacks and Whites in São Paulo, Brazil, 1888–1988*. Madison: University of Wisconsin Press, 1991.

Anzola, Juvenal. *De Caracas a San Cristóbal (1913)*. 2nd ed. Caracas: Biblioteca de Autores y Temas Tachirenses, 1981.

Appadurai, Arjun. "Introduction: Commodities and the Politics of Value." In Arjun Appadurai, ed., *The Social Life of Things: Commodities in Cultural Perspective*. New York: Cambridge University Press, 1986, 3–63.

———, ed. *The Social Life of Things: Commodities in Cultural Perspective* . New York: Cambridge University Press, 1986.

Arruda. José Jobson de A. *O Brasil no comércio colonial*. São Paulo: Editora Ática, 1980.

Ashby, José C. *Organized Labor and the Mexican Revolution under Lázaro Cárdenas*. Chapel Hill: University of North Carolina Press, 1963.

Bairoch, Paul. "How and Not Why? Economic Inequalities between 1800 and 1913." In Jean Batou, ed., *Between Development and Underdevelopment, 1800–1870*. Geneva: Librairie Droz, 1991, 1–42.

Balestrini C., César. *La industria petrolera en América Latina*. Caracas: Universidad Central de Venezuela, 1971.

Barham, Bradford L., and Oliver T. Coomes. "Reinterpreting the Amazon Rubber Boom: Investment, the State and Dutch Disease." *Latin American Research Review* 29:2 (1994): 73–109.

———. "Wild Rubber: Organisation and the Microeconomics of Extraction during the Amazon Rubber Boom (1860–1920)." *Journal of Latin American Studies* 26:1 (February 1994): 37–73.

Barron, Clarence. *The Mexican Problem*. Boston: Houghton Mifflin, 1917.

Bartra, Roger. "Peasants and Political Power in Mexico: A Theoretical Approach." *Latin American Perspectives* 5 (1975): 125–145.

Becker, Hans, Voker Höhfeld, and Horst Kopp. *Kaffee aus Arabien: Der Bedeutungswandel eines welt-wirtshaftsgutes und seine siedlungsgeographische Konsequenz an der Trockengrenze der Okumere*. Wiesbaden: Franz Steiner, 1979.

Benítez, Fernando. *Kí: El drama de un pueblo y de una planta*. Mexico City: Fondo de Cultura Económica, 1965.

Benjamin, Thomas. "International Harvester and the Henequen Marketing System in Yucatán, 1898–1915." *Inter-American Economic Affairs* 31 (Winter 1977): 3–19.

Benton, Elbert Jay. *Cultural Story of an American City: Cleveland*. 3 vols. Cleveland, Ohio: Western Reserve Historical Society, 1943–1946.

Bergad, Laird. "Coffee and Rural Proletarianization in Puerto Rico, 1840–1898." *Journal of Latin American Studies* 15:1 (May 1983): 83–100.

———. *Coffee and the Growth of Agrarian Capitalism in Nineteenth-Century Puerto Rico*. Princeton, N.J.: Princeton University Press, 1983.

———. "On Comparative History: A Reply to Tom Brass." *Journal of Latin American Studies* 16:1 (May 1984): 153–156.

Bergquist, Charles. *Labor in Latin America: Comparative Essays on Chile, Argentina, Venezuela and Colombia*. Stanford, Calif.: Stanford University Press, 1986.

Betancourt, Rómulo. *Venezuela: Oil and Politics*. Trans. Everett Bauman. Boston: Houghton Mifflin, 1979.

Bethell, Leslie. *The Abolition of the Brazilian Slave Trade: Britain, Brazil and the Slave Trade*. Cambridge: Cambridge University Press, 1970.

Beyer, Robert Carlyle. *The Colombian Coffee Industry: Origins and Major Trends, 1740–1940*. Minneapolis: University of Minnesota Press, 1947.

Bidwell, Percy Wells, and John I. Falconer. *History of Agriculture in the Northern United States*. Washington, D.C.: Carnegie Institution, 1925.

Binder Twine Industry. Chicago: International Harvester Company, 1912.

Bittencourt, Gabriel. "O esforço industrializante na república do café: O caso de Espírito Santo, 1889–1930. In Frédéric Mauro, ed., *La preindustrialization du Brésil: Essais sur une economie en transition, 1830/50–1930/50*. Paris: Editions de Centre National du Recherche Scientifique, 1984.

Blair, John M. *The Control of Oil*. New York: Pantheon Books, 1976.

Bolton, Dianne. *Nationalization—A Road to Socialism? The Lessons of Tanzania*. London: Zed Books, 1985.

Boulding, Kenneth E., and Tapan Mukurjee, eds. *Economic Imperialism: A Book of Readings*. Ann Arbor: University of Michigan Press, 1972.

Brannon, Jeffery T., and Eric M. Baklanoff. *Agrarian Reform and Public Enterprise in Mexico: The Political Economy of Yucatán's Henequen Industry*. Tuscaloosa: University of Alabama Press, 1987.

———. "Corporate Control of a Monocrop Economy: A Comment." *Latin American Research Review* 18:3 (Fall 1983): 193–196.

Brass, Tom. "Coffee and Rural Proletarianization: A Comment." *Journal of Latin American Studies* 16:1 (May 1984): 143–152.

Braudel, Fernand. *The Structures of Everyday Life: The Limits of the Possible*. London: Collins, 1981.

Brewster, Kingman. *Antitrust and American Business Abroad*. New York: McGraw-Hill, 1958.

Bringhurst, Bruce. *Antitrust and the Oil Monopoly: The Standard Oil Cases, 1890–1911*. Westport, Conn.: Greenwood Press, 1979.

Brito Figueroa, Federico. *La estructura económica de Venezuela colonial*. 2nd ed. Caracas: Universidad Central de Venezuela, 1983.

Brown, Jonathan C. "Domestic Politics and Foreign Investment: British Development of Mexican Petroleum, 1890–1911." *Business History Review* 61 (Autumn 1987): 387–416.

———. "Foreign Oil Companies, Oil Workers and the Mexican Revolutionary State in the 1920s." In Alice Teichova et al., eds., *Multinational Enterprise in Historical Perspective*. New York: Cambridge University Press, 1986, 257–269.

———. "Jersey Standard and the Politics of Latin American Oil Production, 1911–1930." In John D. Wirth, ed., *Latin American Oil Companies and the Politics of Energy*. Lincoln: University of Nebraska Press, 1985, 1–50.

———. "Labor and the State in the Mexican Oil Expropriation." Texas Papers on Mexico, 90-10, Institute of Latin American Studies, University of Texas at Austin, 1990.

———. *Oil and Revolution in Mexico*. Berkeley and Los Angeles: University of California Press, 1993.

———. "Why Foreign Companies Shifted Their Production from Mexico to Venezuela in the 1920s." *American Historical Review* 90:2 (1985): 362–385.

Brown, M. Barrat. *After Imperialism*. New York: Humanities Press, 1970.

Browning, David. *El Salvador: Landscape and Society*. Oxford: Clarendon Press of Oxford University Press, 1971.

Buchanan, James E. "Politics and Petroleum Development in Argentina,

1916–1930." Ph.D diss., University of Massachusetts, 1973.

Buescu, Mircea. *Evolução econômica do Brasil.* Rio de Janeiro: APEC, 1974.

Bukharin, Nikolai. *Imperialism and the World Economy.* New York: International Publishers, 1929.

Bulmer-Thomas, Victor. *The Economic History of Latin America since Independence.* New York: Cambridge University Press, 1993.

———. "The Latin American Economies, 1929–1939." In Leslie Bethell, ed., *Cambridge History of Latin America,* vol. VI, pt 1. New York: Cambridge University Press, 1994: 65–115.

———. *The Political Economy of Central America since 1920.* New York: Cambridge University Press, 1987.

Bunker, Stephen. *Peasants against the State: The Politics of Market Control in Bugisu, Uganda, 1900–1983.* Urbana: University of Illinois Press, 1987.

Burns, E. Bradford. *The Poverty of Progress: Latin America in the Nineteenth Century.* Berkeley and Los Angeles: University of California Press, 1980.

Butel, Paul. "Les Amériques et l'Europe." In Pierre Leon, ed., *Histoire économique et sociale du monde.* 6 vols. Paris: A. Colin, 1978.

Cain, P. J., and A. G. Hopkins, eds. *British Imperialism: Innovation and Expansion, 1688–1914.* London: Longman, 1993.

Cambranes, J. C. *Coffee and Peasants in Guatemala: The Origins of the Modern Plantation Economy in Guatemala, 1853–1897.* Stockholm: Institute of Latin American Studies, 1985.

Cano, Wilson. *Raizes da concentração industrial em São Paulo.* São Paulo: DIFEL, 1977.

Cantón, Rodulfo G. *Proyecto sobre la formación de una sociedad y banco agrícola. Varias indicaciones relativas al henequén.* Mérida: Imprenta de la Librería Meridana de Cantón, 1876.

Cardoso, Ciro F. S. "The Formation of the Coffee Estate in Nineteenth-Century Costa Rica." In Kenneth Duncan and Ian Rutledge, eds., *Land and Labour in Latin America.: Essays on the Development of Agrarian Capitalism in the Nineteenth and Twentieth Centuries.* New York: Cambridge University Press, 1977, 165–202.

———. "Historia económica del café en Centroamérica." *Estudios Sociales Centroamericanos* 10:3 (1975): 9–55.

Cardoso, Ciro F. S., and Héctor Pérez Brignoli. *Historia económica de América Latina.* 2 vols. Barcelona: Editorial Crítica, 1979.

Cardoso, Fernando Henrique, and Enzo Faletto. *Dependency and Development in Latin America.* Trans. Marjory Mattingly Urquidi. Berkeley and Los Angeles: University of California Press, 1979.

Cardozo Galué, Germán. "El circuito agroexportador marabino a mediados del siglo XIX." *Boletín Americanista* 33:42–43 (1992–1993): 367–393.

Carr, Barry. *El movimiento obrero y la política en México, 1910–1929.* 2 vols. Mexico City: Secretaría de Educación Pública, 1976.

Carrillo Padilla, Ana Lorena. "Sufridas hijas del pueblo: La huelga de las escogedores de café de 1925 en Guatemala y Centro América." *Mesoamérica* 15:27 (June 1994): 157–173.

Carstensen, Fred V., and Diane Roazen-Parrillo. "Foreign Markets, Domestic

Initiative, and the Emergence of a Monocrop Economy: The Yucatecan Experience, 1825–1903." *Hispanic American Historical Review* 72:4 (1992): 555–592.

———. "International Harvester, Molina y Compañía and the Henequen Market: A Comment." *Latin American Research Review* 18:3 (Fall 1983): 197–203.

Castro, Juan Miguel. *El henequén de Yucatán y el monopolio.* Mérida: Imprenta del Comercio de Néstor Rubio Alpuche, 1876.

———. *Informe presentado en la sesión del 9 del mayo de 1878, Junta de Hacendados y Comerciantes.* Mérida: Imprenta del Comercio Ignacio L. Mena, 1878.

Cattapan-Renter, Elisabeth. "L'industrie à l'époque de 'l'Encilhamento' (1890–1892)." In Frédéric Mauro, ed., *La preindustrialization du Brésil: Essais sur une economie en transition, 1830/50–1930/50.* Paris: Editions de Centre National du Recherche Scientifique, 1984.

Caves, Richard E. "Export-Led Growth and the New Economic History." In Jagdish Bhagwati et al., eds., *Trade, Balance of Payments and Growth.* Amsterdam: North-Holland, 1971.

———. *Multinational Enterprise and Economic Analysis.* 2nd ed. Cambridge: Cambridge University Press, 1996.

Centro Industrial do Brasil. *O Brasil. Suas riquezas naturais, suas indústrias.* Rio de Janeiro: Imp. Orosco e Cia., 1908.

Chandler, Alfred. *The Visible Hand: The Managerial Revolution in American Business.* Cambridge, Mass.: Belknap Press of Harvard University Press, 1977.

Chapman, Stanley. "British Free-Standing Companies and Investment Groups in India and the Far East." In Mira Wilkins and Harm Schröter, eds., *The Free-Standing Company in the World Economy, 1830–1996.* Oxford: Oxford University Press, forthcoming.

———. *Merchant Enterprise in Britain: From the Industrial Revolution to World War I.* Cambridge: Cambridge University Press, 1992.

Chassen-López, Francie R. *Café y capitalismo: El proceso de transición, 1880–1930.* Mexico City: UNAM, 1982.

———. "'Cheaper than Machines': Women and Agriculture in Porfirian Yucatán, 1880–1911." In Heather Fowler Salamini and Mary Kay Vaughan, eds., *Women of the Mexican Countryside, 1850–1990: Creating Spaces, Shaping Transitions.* Tucson: University of Arizona Press, 1994, 27–50.

Chilcote, Ronald, and Joel Edelstein, eds. *The Struggle with Dependency and Beyond.* New York: John Wiley, 1983.

Chilcote, Ronald, and Dale Johnson, eds. *Theories of Development: Modes of Production or Dependency.* Beverly Hills, Calif.: Sage, 1983.

Cline, Howard. "The 'Aurora Yucateca' and the Spirit of Enterprise in Yucatán: 1821–1847." *Hispanic American Historical Review* 27:1 (1947): 30–60.

———. "The Henequen Episode in Yucatán." *Inter-American Economic Affairs* 2:2 (1948): 30–51.

Cobos López, Padre Alfonso. *Datos para la historia de Casigua El Cubo.* San Carlos de Zulia: Litografía El Colonés, 1974.

Collier, George. *Basta: Land and the Zapatista Rebellion in Chiapas.* Boston: Food First, 1995.

Colomo, José. *The Mexican Petroleum Law: Its Basis and Its Aims.* Mexico City, 1927.

Connelly, W. L. *The Oil Business as I Saw It: Half a Century with Sinclair.* Norman: University of Oklahoma Press, 1954.

Coomes, Oliver T., and Bradford L. Barham. "The Amazon Rubber Boom: Labor Control, Resistance, and Failed Plantation Development Revisited." *Hispanic American Historical Review* 74:2 (May 1994): 231–257.

Cooper, Frederick. "Africa and the World Economy." In Frederick Cooper et al., *Confronting Historical Paradigms: Peasants, Labor, and the Capitalist World System in Africa and Latin America.* Madison: University of Wisconsin Press, 1993, 84–201.

Cooper, Frederick, et al., *Confronting Historical Paradigms: Peasants, Labor, and the Capitalist World System in Africa and Latin America.* Madison: University of Wisconsin Press, 1993.

Córdova, Arnaldo. *La ideología de la Revolución mexicana: La formación del nuevo régimen.* Mexico City: Ediciones Era, 1973.

Cortés Conde, Roberto, and Shane J. Hunt, eds. *The Latin American Economies: Growth and the Export Sector, 1880–1930.* New York: Holmes and Meier, 1985.

Costa, Emília Viotti da. *Crowns of Glory, Tears of Blood.* New York: Oxford University Press, 1994.

Couvares, Francis G. *The Remaking of Pittsburgh: Class and Culture in an Industrializing City, 1877–1919.* Albany: State University of New York Press, 1984.

Crosby, Alfred W. , Jr. *America, Russia, Hemp and Napoleon: American Trade with Russia and the Baltic, 1783–1812.* Columbus: Ohio State University Press, 1965.

Cunill Grau, Pedro. *Geografía del poblamiento venezolano en el siglo XIX.* 3 vols. Caracas: Ediciones de la Presidencia de la República, 1987.

Curtin, Philip D. *The Atlantic Slave Trade: A Census.* Madison: University of Wisconsin Press, 1969.

———. *Cross-Cultural Trade in World History.* New York: Cambridge University Press, 1984.

Dafert, Franz. *Principes de culture rationnelle du café au Brèsil: Ètude sur les engrais à employer.* Paris: Augustin Challanuel, 1900.

———. *Über die Gegenwartige Lage des Kaffeebaus in Brasilien.* Amsterdam: J. H. de Bussy, 1898.

Davatz, Thomaz. *Memórias de un colono no Brasil (1850).* Trans. S. Buarque de Holanda. São Paulo: Editora Itatiaia and USSP, 1980.

Davenport, E. H., and Sidney Russell Cooke. *The Oil Trusts and Anglo-American Relations.* New York: Macmillan, 1924.

Davis, Clarence B., and Kenneth E. Wilburn, Jr., with Ronald Robinson, eds.

Railway Imperialism. New York: Greenwood Press, 1991.

Dean, Warren. *Brazil and the Struggle for Rubber: A Study in Environmental History*. New York: Cambridge University Press, 1987.

———. "The Green Wave of Coffee: Beginnings of Tropical Agricultural Research in Brazil (1885–1900)." *Hispanic American Historical Review* 69:1 (February 1989): 91–116.

———. *The Industrialization of São Paulo, 1880–1945*. Austin: University of Texas Press, 1969.

———. *Rio Claro: A Brazilian Plantation System, 1820–1920*. Stanford, Calif.: Stanford University Press, 1976.

Deas, Malcolm. "A Colombian Coffee Estate: Santa Bárbara, Cundinamarca, 1870–1912." In Kenneth Duncan and Ian Rutledge, eds., *Land and Labour in Latin America: Essays on the Development of Agrarian Capitalism in the Nineteenth and Twentieth Centuries*. New York: Cambridge University Press, 1977, 269–298.

Deerr, Noel. *The History of Sugar*. 2 vols. London: Chapman and Hall, 1949–1950.

Denis, Pierre. *Brazil*. London: T. F. Unwin, 1911.

Denny, Ludwell. *We Fight for Oil*. New York: Knopf, 1928.

Deterding, Henri. *An International Oilman*, as told to Stanley Naylor. London: Ivor Nicholson and Watson, 1934.

Dewey, Lyster H. *Fiber Production in the Western Hemisphere*. U.S. Department of Agriculture Miscellaneous Publication 518. Washington, D.C.: U.S. Government Printing Office, 1943.

Dewing, Arthur S. *A History of the National Cordage Company*. Cambridge, Mass.: Harvard University Press, 1913.

Díaz Alejandro, Carlos. *Essays on the Economic History of the Argentine Republic*. New Haven, Conn.: Yale University Press, 1970.

Dodge, Charles Richards. *A Descriptive Catalogue of Useful Fiber Plants of the World Including the Structural and Economic Classifications of Fibers*. Washington, D.C.: U.S. Government Printing Office, 1897.

———. *A Report on Flax, Hemp, Ramie, and Jute with Considerations upon Flax and Hemp Culture in Europe*. 2nd ed. Washington, D.C.: U.S. Government Printing Office, 1892.

Dolson, Hildegarde. *The Great Oildorado: The Gaudy and Turbulent Years of the First Oil Rush, Pennsylvania, 1859–1880*. New York: Random House, 1959.

Dos Santos, Theotonio. "Brazil, the Origins of a Crisis." In Ronald Chilcote and Joel Edelstein, eds., *Latin America: The Struggle with Dependency and Beyond*. New York: John Wiley and Sons, 1974, 409–490.

Durán de Seade, Esperanza. "Mexico's Relations with the Powers during the Great War." D. Phil. thesis, St. Antony's College, Oxford University, 1980.

El-Kareh, Almir Chaiban. *Filha branca de mae preta: A Companhia de Estrada de Ferro Dom Pedro II*. Petrópolis: Editora Vozes, 1980.

Engerman, Stanley. "Douglass C. North's *The Economic Growth of the United*

States, 1790–1860 Revisited." *Social Science History* 1:2 (1977): 248–257.

Ferguson, James. "Cultural Exchange: New Developments in the Anthropology of Commodities." *Cultural Anthropology* 3:1 (Feb 1988): 488–513.

Ferns, H. S. "The Baring Crisis Revisited." *Journal of Latin American Studies* 24 (1992): 241–273.

Ferrier, R. W. *The History of the British Petroleum Company.* 2 vols. New York: Cambridge University Press, 1982.

Ffrench-Davis, Ricardo, Oscar Muñoz, and José Gabriel Palma. "The Latin American Economies, 1950–1990." In Leslie Bethell, ed., *Cambridge History of Latin America*, vol. VI, pt. 1: New York: Cambridge University Press, 1994, 159–249.

Fick, Carolyn. *The Making of Haiti: The Saint Domingue Revolution from Below.* Knoxville: University of Tennessee Press, 1990.

Fieldhouse, D. K. "'Imperialism': An Historiographical Revision." In Kenneth E. Boulding and Tapan Mukurjee, eds., *Economic Imperialism: A Book of Readings.* Ann Arbor: University of Michigan Press, 1972, 95–123.

FitzGerald, E. V. K. "Restructuring through the Depression: The State and Capital Accumulation in Mexico, 1925–1940." In Rosemary Thorp, ed., *Latin America in the 1930s: The Role of the Periphery in World Crisis.* New York: St. Martin's Press, 1984, 242–278.

Fleming, William G. *Regional Development and Transportation in Argentina: Mendoza and the Gran Oeste Argentino Railroad, 1885–1914.* New York: Garland Press, 1987.

Font, Mauricio. "Coffee Planters, Politics and Development in Brazil." *Latin American Research Review* 22:3 (1987): 69–90.

Food and Agriculture Organization of the United Nations. *Trade: 1990.* FAO Statistics Series no. 102. Rome: FAO, 1991.

Forbes-Lindsay, C. H. *The Philippines: Under Spanish and American Rule.* Philadelphia, Penn.: John C. Winston, 1906.

Foreman, John. *The Philippine Islands: A Political, Geographical, Ethnographical, Social and Commercial History of the Philippine Archipelago.* 2nd ed. New York: Scribner, 1899.

Fowler-Salamini, Heather. "Gender, Work, and Coffee in Córdoba, Veracruz, 1850–1910." In Heather Fowler Salamini and Mary Kay Vaughan, eds., *Women of the Mexican Countryside, 1850–1990: Creating Spaces, Shaping Transitions.* Tucson: University of Arizona Press, 1994, 51–73.

Frank, André Gunder. *Capitalism and Underdevelopment in Latin America.* New York: Monthly Review Press, 1967.

———. *Dependent Accumulation and Underdevelopment.* London: Macmillan, 1978.

Frankel, Benjamin Adam. "Venezuela and the United States, 1810–1888." Ph.D. diss., University of California, Berkeley, 1964.

Fritsch, Winston. *External Constraints on Economic Policy in Brazil, 1889–1930.* Pittsburgh, Penn.: University of Pittsburgh Press, 1989.

Frondizi, Arturo. *Petróleo y política.* 2nd ed. Buenos Aires: Raigal, 1955.

Furtado, Celso. *The Economic Growth of Brazil: A Survey from Colonial to Modern Times.* Trans. Ricardo Aguiar and Eric Drysdale. Berkeley and Los Angeles: University of California Press, 1965.

————. *A fantasia organizada*. Rio de Janeiro: Paz e Terra, 1985.

————. *Obstacles to Development in Latin America*. New York: Anchor Books, 1970.

Galarza Zavala, Jaime. *El festín del petróleo*. 2nd ed. Caracas: Universidad Central de Venezuela, 1974.

Gallagher, John, and Ronald Robinson. "The Imperialism of Free Trade." *Economic History Review*, 2nd series, 6:1 (1953): 1–15.

Garay, Graciela de, and María Esther Pérez-Salas C. "El café en el Soconusco: Un comercio regional." In Virginia Guedea and Jaime Rodríguez O., eds., *Five Centuries of Mexican History*. 2 vols. Mexico City: Instituto José María Luis Mora, 1992, 168–192.

Geertz, Clifford. *Agricultural Involution: The Process of Agricultural Change in Indonesia*. Berkeley and Los Angeles: University of California Press, 1971.

Gereffi, Gary, and Miguel Korzeniewicz, eds. *Commodity Chains and Global Capitalism*. Westport, Conn.: Praeger, 1994.

Gerretson, F. C. *History of the Royal Dutch*. 4 vols. Leiden: Brill, 1953–1957.

Gerschenkron, Alexander. "Economic Backwardness in Historical Perspective." In idem, *Economic Backwardness in Historical Perspective: A Book of Essays*. Cambridge, Mass.: Belknap Press of Harvard University Press, 1962, 5–30.

Gerstl, Otto. *Memorias e historias*. 2nd ed. Caracas: Ediciones de la Fundación John Boulton, 1977.

Gibb, George Sweet, and Evelyn H. Knowlton. *The Resurgent Years, 1911–1927*. Vol. II of *The History of Standard Oil*. New York: Harper & Row, 1956.

Giddens, Paul H. *The Beginnings of the Petroleum Industry: Sources and Bibliography*. Harrisburg: Pennsylvania Historical Commission, 1941.

————. *Early Days of Oil: A Pictorial History of the Beginnings of the Industry in Pennsylvania*. Princeton, N.J.: Princeton University Press, 1948.

Gill, Christopher. "Campesino Patriarchy in the Times of Slavery: The Henequen Plantation Society of Yucatán, 1860–1915." Master's thesis, University of Texas–Austin, 1991.

Godio, Julio. *El movimiento obrero venezolano, 1850–1944*. Caracas: Editorial Ateneo de Caracas, ILDIS, 1980.

González Navarro, Moisés. *El porfiriato: La vida social*. In Daniel Cosío Villegas, gen. ed., *Historia moderna de México*. 10 vols. in 9. Mexico City: Editorial Hermes, 1955–1974.

————. "Tipología del liberalismo mexicano." *Historia Mexicana* 32:2 (1982): 198–225.

Goodman, David, and Michael Redclift. *From Peasant to Proletarian: Capitalist Development and Agrarian Transitions*. New York: St. Martin's Press, 1982.

Goodwin, Paul B., Jr. "The Central Argentine Railway and the Economic Development of Argentina, 1854–1881. *Hispanic American Historical Review* 57:4 (November 1977): 613–632.

Gootenberg, Paul E. *Between Silver and Guano: Commercial Policy and the State in Post-Independence Peru*. Princeton, N.J.: Princeton University Press, 1989.

————. *Imagining Development: Economic Ideas in Peru's "Fictitious Prosperity" of Guano, 1840–1880.* Berkeley and Los Angeles: University of California Press, 1993.

Gorender, Jacob. *A burguesia brasileira.* São Paulo: Brasiliense, 1981.

Gould, Jeffrey. "El café, el trabajo, y la comunidad indígena de Matagalpa, 1880–1925." In Héctor Pérez Brignoli and Mario Samper, eds., *Tierra, café y sociedad.* San José, Costa Rica: FLACSO, 1994, 279–376.

Graham, Richard. "Sepoys and Imperialists: Techniques of British Power in Nineteenth-Century Brazil." *Inter-American Economic Affairs* 23:2 (Autumn 1969): 23–37.

Greenhill, Robert. "The Brazilian Coffee Trade." In D. C. M. Platt, ed., *Business Imperialism, 1840–1930.* Oxford: Oxford University Press, 1977, 198–230.

————. "Investment Group, Free-Standing Company or Multinational? Brazilian Warrant, 1909–1952." *Business History* 37 (January 1995): 86–111.

————. "The Nitrate and Iodine Trades, 1880–1914." In D. C. M. Platt, ed., *Business Imperialism, 1840–1930.* Oxford: Oxford University Press, 1977, 231–283.

Haber, Stephen H. *Industry and Underdevelopment: The Industrialization of Mexico, 1890–1940.* Stanford, Calif.: Stanford University Press, 1989.

————, ed. *How Latin America Fell Behind: Essays on the Economic Histories of Brazil and Mexico, 1800–1914.* Stanford, Calif.: Stanford University Press, 1997.

Hahn, Stephen. "Class and State in Postemancipation Societies—Southern Planters in Comparative Perspective." *American Historical Review* 95:1 (February 1990): 75–98.

Hale, Charles. *Mexican Liberalism in the Age of Mora, 1821–1853.* New Haven, Conn.: Yale University Press, 1968.

————. *The Transformation of Liberalism in Late Nineteenth-Century Mexico.* Princeton, N.J.: Princeton University Press, 1989.

Hamilton, Nora. *The Limits of State Autonomy: Post Revolutionary Mexico.* Princeton, N.J.: Princeton University Press, 1982.

Hannicotte, R. G. *La vérité sur le Brésil.* Paris: Imp. Encyclopédie Nationale, 1909.

Harris, John, Janet Hunter, and Colin M. Lewis, eds. *The New Institutional Economics and Third World Development.* London: Routledge, 1995.

Hart, John M. *Anarchism and the Working Class in Mexico, 1860–1931.* Austin: University of Texas Press, 1978.

Harvey, Charles, and Jon Press. "The City and International Mining, 1870–1914." *Business History* 32 (July 1990): 98–119.

Harwitch Vallenilla, Nikita, ed. *Asfalto y revolución: La New York & Bermúdez Company.* Caracas: Monte Ávila Editores, 1992.

————. *Inversiones extranjeras en Venezuela, siglo XIX.* 2 vols. Caracas: Academia Nacional de Ciencias Económicas, 1992.

Heikkonen, Esko. *Reaping the Bounty: McCormick Harvesting Company Turns Abroad, 1878–1902.* Helsinki: Finnish Historical Society, 1996.

Herrera Canales, Inés. *Estadística del comercio exterior del México (1821–1875).* Mexico City: Instituto Nacional de Antropología e Historia, 1980.

Hidy, Ralph W., and Muriel E. Hidy. *Pioneering in Big Business, 1882–1911:*

History of the Standard Oil Company (New Jersey). New York: Harper & Row, 1955.

Hilferding, Rudolf. *Finance Capital: A Study of the Latest Phase of Capitalist Development.* Trans. Morris Watnick and Sam Gordon. London: Routledge and Kegan Paul, 1981 [1911].

Hilliard D'Auberteure, Michel-René. *Betrachtungen über den gegenwartigen Zustand der Französischen Colonie zu San Domingo.* Leipzig: Johann Friedrich Zunius, 1779.

Hirschman, Albert. "A Generalized Linkage Approach to Development with Special Reference to Staples." *Economic and Cultural Change* 25 (1977): 67–98.

———. "Ideologies of Economic Development in Latin America." In idem, ed., *Latin American Issues: Essays and Comments.* New York: Twentieth Century Fund, 1961.

———. *Journeys toward Progress: Studies of Economic Policy-Making in Latin America.* Westport, Conn.: Greenwood, 1965.

Hobsbawm, Eric. *The Age of Capital.* New York: Scribner's, 1975.

———. *The Age of Empire, 1875–1914.* New York: Pantheon Books, 1987.

Hobson, John A. *Imperialism: A Study.* London: Allen & Unwin, 1938 [1902].

Holden, Robert H. *Mexico and the Survey of Public Lands: The Management of Modernization, 1876–1911.* DeKalb: Northern Illinois University Press, 1993.

Hollander, Frederick A. "Oligarchy and the Politics of Petroleum in Argentina." Ph.D diss., UCLA, 1976.

Holloway, Thomas. *Immigrants on the Land: Coffee and Society in São Paulo, 1886–1934.* Chapel Hill: University of North Carolina Press, 1980.

———. "Migration and Mobility: Immigrants as Laborers and Landowners in the Coffee Zone of São Paulo, Brazil, 1886–1934." Ph.D. diss., University of Wisconsin, 1974.

Hope, Stanton. *The Battle for Oil.* London: R. Hale, 1958.

Hopkins, A. G. "Informal Empire in Argentina." *Journal of Latin American Studies* 26 (May 1994): 469–484.

Hopkins, James F. *A History of the Hemp Industry in Kentucky.* Lexington: University of Kentucky Press, 1951.

Horst, Thomas. *At Home Abroad.* Cambridge, Mass.: Ballinger, 1974.

Huber, Evelyn, and Frank Safford, eds. *Agrarian Structure and Political Power: Landlord and Peasant in the Making of Latin America.* Pittsburgh, Penn.: University of Pittsburgh Press, 1995.

Illiffe, John. *A Modern History of Tanganyika.* Cambridge: Cambridge University Press, 1979.

Innis, Harold A. *Essays in Canadian Economic History.* Toronto: University of Toronto Press, 1957.

Instituto Brasileiro de Geografia e Estatística. *Estatísticas históricas do Brasil.* Rio de Janeiro: IBGE, 1987.

Irigoyen, Renán. "La revolución agrícola-industrial henequenera del siglo XIX." In idem, ed., *Ensayos henequeneros.* Mérida: Ediciones del Cordemex, 1975, 114–128.

Jacobsen, Nils. *Mirages of Transition: The Peruvian Altiplano, 1780–1930.*

Berkeley and Los Angeles: University of California Press, 1993.

James, Marquis. *The Texaco Story: The First Fifty Years, 1902–1952.* New York: The Texas Company, 1953.

Jiménez, Michael. "Class, Gender and Peasant Resistance in Central Colombia, 1900–1930." In Forrest D. Colburn, ed., *Everyday Forms of Peasant Resistance.* Armonk, N.Y.: M. E. Sharp, 1989, 122–150.

———. "Traveling Far in Grandfather's Car: The Life Cycle of Central Colombian Coffee Estates. The Case of Viota, Cundinamarca (1900–1930)." *Hispanic American Historical Review* 69:2 (May 1989): 185–219.

Jones, Charles. "British Overseas Banks as Free-Standing Companies." In Mira Wilkins and Harm Schröter, eds., *The Free-Standing Company in the World Economy, 1830–1996.* Oxford: Oxford University Press, forthcoming.

———. "The Origins of Modern Multinational Corporations: British Firms in Latin America, 1850–1930." In Carlos Marichal, ed., *Foreign Investment in Latin America: Impact on Economic Development, 1850–1930.* Milan: Università Bocconi, 1994.

Jones, Geoffrey. *The Evolution of International Business.* London: Routledge, 1996.

———. *British Multinational Banking 1830–1990.* Oxford: Oxford University Press, 1993.

———. *The State and the Emergence of the British Oil Industry.* London: Macmillan, 1981.

Joseph, Gilbert M., Catherine C. LeGrand, and Ricardo D. Salvatore, eds. *Close Encounters of the Imperial Kind: Writing the Cultural History of U.S.–Latin American Relations.* Durham, N.C.: Duke University Press, forthcoming.

Joseph, Gilbert M., and Daniel Nugent, eds. *Everyday Forms of State Formation: Revolution and the Negotiation of Rule in Modern Mexico.* Durham, N.C.: Duke University Press, 1994.

Joseph, Gilbert M., and Allen Wells. "Collaboration and Informal Empire: The Case for Political Economy." *Latin American Research Review* 18:3 (Fall 1983): 204–218.

———. "Corporate Control of a Monocrop Economy: International Harvester and Yucatán's Henequen Industry during the Porfiriato." *Latin American Research Review* 17:1 (Spring 1982): 69–99.

———. "El monocultivo henequenero y sus contradicciones: Estructura de dominación y formas de resistencia en las haciendas yucatecas a fines del Porfiriato." *Siglo XIX* 3:6 (1988): 215–287.

Kaerger, Karl. *Landwirtschaft und Kolonisation in Spanischen Amerika.* 2 vols. Leipzig: Duncker & Humblot, 1901.

Karlsson, Weine. *Manufacturing in Venezuela: Studies on Development and Location.* Stockholm: Almqvist & Wiksell International, 1975.

Katz, Friedrich. "Labor Conditions on Haciendas in Porfirian Mexico: Some Trends and Tendencies." *Hispanic American Historical Review* 54 (February 1974), 1–47.

————. *The Secret War in Mexico: Europe, the United States, and the Mexican Revolution.* Chicago: University of Chicago Press, 1981.

Kay, Cristóbal. *Latin American Theories of Development and Underdevelopment.* London: Routledge, 1989.

Keightley, David N., ed. *The Origins of Chinese Civilization.* Berkeley and Los Angeles: University of California Press, 1983.

Kennedy, James Harrison. *A History of the City of Cleveland.* Cleveland: Imperial Press, 1896.

Kenwood, A. G., and A. L. Lougheed. *The Growth of the International Economy, 1820–1960.* London: Allen & Unwin, 1983.

Kepner, C. David, and Jay Soothill. *The Banana Empire: A Case Study of Economic Imperialism.* New York: Vanguard, 1967 [1935].

Klarén, Peter F., and Thomas J. Bossert, eds. *Promise of Development: Theories of Change in Latin America.* Boulder, Colo.: Westview Press, 1986.

Klein, Herbert S. "American Oil Companies in Latin America: The Bolivian Experience." *Inter-American Economic Affairs* 18:2 (Autumn 1964): 47–72.

Knight, Alan. "El liberalismo mexicano desde la Reforma hasta la Revolución (una interpretación)." *Historia Mexicana* 35:1 (1985): 59–91.

————. *The Mexican Revolution.* 2 vols. New York: Cambridge University Press, 1986.

————. "The Peculiarities of Mexican History: Mexico Compared to Latin America, 1821–1992." *Journal of Latin American Studies Supplement* 35–53 (1992): 99–144.

————. "The Political Economy of Revolutionary Mexico, 1900–1940." In Christopher Abel and Colin M. Lewis, eds., *Latin America, Economic Imperialism, and the State: The Political Economy of the External Connection from Independence to the Present.* London: Athlone, 1985, 288–317.

————. *U.S.–Mexican Relations, 1910–1940: An Interpretation.* San Diego, Calif.: Center for U.S.-Mexican Studies, University of California–San Diego, 1987.

Kolko, Gabriel. *Railroads and Regulation, 1877–1916.* Princeton, N.J.: Princeton University Press, 1965.

Kondratiev, Nicolai. *The Long Wave Cycle.* New York: Richardson and Snyder, 1984 [1927].

Kopytoff, Igor. "The Cultural Biography of Things: Commoditization as Process." In Arjun Appadurai, *The Social Life of Things: Commodities in Cultural Perspective.* New York: Cambridge University Press, 1986, 64–91.

Lambert, Jacques. *Le Brèsil: Structure social et institutions politiques.* Paris: A. Colin, 1953.

Landa, Diego de. *Relación de las cosas de Yucatán.* Trans. Charles P. Bowditch, ed. Alfred M. Tozzer, *Papers of the Peabody Museum of Archeology and Ethnology,* vol. 18 (1941).

Lapa, José Roberto do Amaral. *A economia cafeeira.* São Paulo: Brasiliense, 1983.

Larson, Henrietta M., Evelyn H. Knowlton, and Charles S. Popple. *New Horizons, 1927–1950.* Vol 3. of *History of Standard Oil Company (New Jersey).* New York: Harper, 1971.

Leclerc, Max. *Cartas do Brasil.* São Paulo: Companhia Editora Nacional, 1942 [1891].

Leff, Nathaniel H. *Underdevelopment and Development in Brazil.* 2 vols. London: Allen & Unwin, 1982.

Lenin, Vladimir I. *Imperialism, the Highest Stage of Capitalism.* Moscow: Progress Publishers, 1966 [1916].

Levy, Darrel. *The Prados of Brazil.* Athens: University of Georgia Press, 1987.

Levy, Maria Bárbara. "The Banking System and Foreign Capital in Brazil." In Rondo Cameron and V. I. Boykin, eds., *International Banking 1870–1914.* New York: Oxford University Press, 1991.

Lewallen, Kenneth A. "Economic Inequality in the Upper South: The Concentration of Wealth in Lafayette County, Missouri, 1850–1960." Ph.D. diss., Kansas State University, 1980.

Lewis, W. Arthur. *Growth and Fluctuations, 1870–1914.* Boston: Allen & Unwin, 1978.

Liehr, Reinhard, and Mariano E. Torres Bautista. "British Free-Standing Companies in Porfirian Mexico, 1884–1911." In Mira Wilkins and Harm Schröter, eds., *The Free-Standing Company in the World Economy, 1830–1996.* Oxford: Oxford University Press, forthcoming.

Lieuwen, Edwin. *Petroleum in Venezuela: A History.* Berkeley and Los Angeles: University of California Press, 1955.

———. "The Politics of Energy in Venezuela." In John D. Wirth, ed., *Latin American Oil Companies and the Politics of Energy.* Lincoln: University of Nebraska Press, 1985, 189–225.

Lima, João Heraldo. *Cafe e indústria em Minas Gerais, 1870–1920.* Petrópolis: Editora Vozes, 1981.

Linder, Peter S. "Coerced Labor in Venezuela, 1880–1936." *The Historian* 57:1 (Autumn 1994): 43–58.

Lindo-Fuentes, Héctor. "La economía de Centroamérica en las reformas borbónicas a las reformas liberales." Unpublished, n.d.

———.*Weak Foundations: The Economy of El Salvador in the Nineteenth Century, 1821–1898.* Berkeley and Los Angeles: University of California Press, 1990.

Louis, William Roger, ed. *Imperialism: The Robinson and Gallagher Controversy.* New York: New Viewpoints, 1976.

———. "Robinson and Gallagher and Their Critics." In idem, *Imperialism: The Robinson and Gallagher Controversy.* New York: New Viewpoints, 1976, 2–51.

Love, Joseph L. *Crafting the Third World: Theorizing Underdevelopment in Romania and Brazil.* Stanford, Calif.: Stanford University Press, 1996.

———. "Economic Ideas and Ideologies in Latin America since 1930." In Leslie Bethell, ed., *Cambridge History of Latin America,* vol. VI, pt. 1. New York: Cambridge University Press, 1994, 393–460.

———. *São Paulo in the Brazilian Federation, 1889–1937.* Stanford, Calif.: Stanford University Press, 1980.

————. "Structural Change and Conceptual Response in Latin America and Romania, 1860–1950." In idem and Nils Jacobsen, eds., *Guiding the Invisible Hand: Economic Liberalism and the State in Latin American History*. New York: Praeger, 1988, 1–33.

Love, Joseph L., and Bert J. Barickman. "Rulers and Owners: A Brazilian Case Study in Comparative Perspective." *Hispanic American Historical Review* 66:4 (1986): 743–765.

Love, Joseph L., and Nils Jacobsen, eds. *Guiding the Invisible Hand: Economic Liberalism and the State in Latin American History*. New York: Praeger, 1988.

Lucier, Richard L. *The International Political Economy of Coffee: From Juan Valdez to Yank's Diner*. New York: Praeger, 1988.

Lundell, Cyrus L. "Preliminary Sketch of the Phytogeography of the Yucatán Peninsula." *Contributions in American Archeology* 2:12 (October 1934): 255–321.

Luxemburg, Rosa. *The Accumulation of Capital*. Trans. Agnes Schwazschild. London: Routledge and Kegan Paul, 1951.

Lynch, Gerald. *Roughnecks, Drillers, and Tool Pushers: Thirty-Three Years in the Oil Fields*. Austin: University of Texas Press, 1987.

McBeth, B. S. *Juan Vicente Gómez and the Oil Companies in Venezuela, 1908–1935*. New York: Cambridge University Press, 1983.

McCreery, David. "Wage Labor, Free Labor and Vagrancy Laws: The Transition to Capitalism in Guatemala, 1920–1945." In William Roseberry, Lowell Gudmundson, and Mario Samper Kutschbach, eds., *Coffee, Society and Power in Latin America*. Baltimore, Md.: Johns Hopkins University Press, 1995, 206–231.

McCreery, M. G., And Mary L. Bynum. *The Coffee Industry in Brazil*. Report no. 92. Washington, D.C.: U.S. Department of Commerce, 1930.

McGreevey, William P. *An Economic History of Colombia, 1845–1930*. New York: Cambridge University Press, 1971.

McMahon, William. *Two Strikes and Out*. Garden City, N.Y.: Country Life Press, 1939.

Mallon, Florencia. *The Defense of Community in Peru's Central Highlands: Peasant Struggle and Capitalist Transition, 1860–1940*. Princeton, N.J.: Princeton University Press, 1983.

————. *Peasant and Nation: The Making of Postcolonial Mexico and Peru*. Berkeley and Los Angeles: University of California Press, 1994.

Marchant, Anyda. *Viscount Maua and the Empire of Brazil*. Berkeley and Los Angeles: University of California Press, 1965.

Marichal, Carlos. *A Century of Debt Crises in Latin America: From Independence to the Great Depression, 1820–1930*. Princeton, N.J.: Princeton University Press, 1989.

Martí, Obispo Mariano. *Documentos relativos a su visita pastoral de la diocesis de Caracas (1771–1784)*. 7 vols. Caracas: Biblioteca de la Academia Nacional de la Historia, 1969.

Martínez Suárez, Juan de Dios. *Las Barbúas: Mitos y leyendas de orígen africano presentes en el sur del Lago de Maracaibo*. Maracaibo: Colección Afrovenezolana, no. 2, 1986.

————. *Chimbangueles: Antecedentes y orígenes*. Maracaibo: Coleccíon Afrovenezolana, no. 1, 1983.

Mata, Celestino. *Historia sindical de Venezuela, 1813–1985*. Caracas: Urbina y Fuentes, 1985.

Mejía Fernández, Miguel. *Política agraria en México en el siglo XIX*. Mexico City: Siglo XXI, 1979.

Mello, Joāo Manuel Cardoso de. *O capitalismo tardio: Contribuição à revisão crítica da formação e do desenvolvimento da economia brasileira*. São Paulo: Editora Brasiliense, 1982.

Mello, Joāo Manuel Cardoso de, and María de Conceição Tavares. "The Capitalist Export Economy in Brazil." In Roberto Cortés Conde and Shane J. Hunt, eds., *The Latin American Economies: Growth and the Export Sector, 1880–1930*. New York: Holmes and Meier, 1985, 83–132.

Mello, Zélia Maria Cardoso de. *O metamorfose da riqueza: São Paulo, 1845–1895*. São Paulo: HUCITEC and Prefeitura do Município de São Paulo, Secretaria Municipal de Cultura, 1985.

Melo, Hildete Pereira de. "O café e a economia fluminense: 1889–1920." Paper presented at the First Brazilian Conference of International Economic History, São Paulo, 1993.

Melosi, Martin V. *Coping with Abundance: Energy and Environment in Industrial America*. Philadelphia, Penn.: Temple University Press, 1985.

Merchant, Carolyn. *Ecological Revolutions: Nature, Gender and Science in New England*. Chapel Hill: University of North Carolina Press, 1989.

Meyer, Jean. "Los Estados Unidos y el petróleo mexicano: Estado de la cuestión." *Historia Mexicana* 18:1 (1968): 79–96.

Meyer, Lorenzo. *Mexico and the United States in the Oil Controversy, 1916–1942*. Austin: University of Texas Press, 1977.

Miller, Rory. "British Firms and the Peruvian Government, 1885–1930." In D. C. M. Platt, *Business Imperialism, 1840–1930*. Oxford: Oxford University Press, 1977, 371–394.

————. "British Free-Standing Companies on the West Coast of South America." In Mira Wilkins and Harm Schröter, eds., *The Free-Standing Company in the World Economy, 1830–1996*. Oxford: Oxford University Press, forthcoming.

Mintz, Sidney. "Comments on Articles by Tomich, McMichael and Roseberry." *Theory and Society* 20:3 (June 1991): 383–392.

————. *Sweetness and Power: The Place of Sugar in Modern History*. New York: Penguin, 1985.

Mohr, Anton. *The Oil Wars*. New York: Harcourt, Brace & Company, 1926.

Molina Enríquez, Andrés. *Los grandes problemas nacionales*. Mexico City: A. Carranza e Hijos, 1909.

Moore, Barrington, Jr. *Social Origins of Dictatorship and Democracy: Land and Peasant in the Making of the Modern World*. Boston: Beacon Press, 1966.

Moreno Fraginals, Manuel. *El ingenio. Complejo económico social cubano del azúcar*. 3 vols. Havana: Editorial Ciencias Sociales, 1978.

Morgan, Dan. *Merchants of Grain*. New York: Viking Press, 1979.

Morgan, Edmund G. *American Slavery, American Freedom: The Ordeal of Colonial Virginia.* New York: Norton, 1975.

Morgan, Hal. *Symbols of America.* New York: Penguin Books, 1986.

Morison, Samuel E. *The Ropemakers of Plymouth: A History of the Plymouth Cordage Company, 1824–1949.* Boston: Houghton Mifflin, 1950.

Mosconi, Enrique. *La batalla del petróleo.* Buenos Aires: Ediciones Problemas Nacionales, 1957.

———. *El petróleo argentino, 1922–1930, y la ruptura de los trusts petrolíferos inglés y norteamericanos.* Buenos Aires: Talleres Gráficos Ferrari Hermanos, 1936.

Mulhall, Michael G. *The Dictionary of Statistics.* London: George Routledge and Sons, 1899.

Nabuco, Joaquim. *O abolicionismo.* London: Kingdon, 1883.

Nevins, Allan. *John D. Rockefeller: The Heroic Age of American Enterprise.* New York: Scribner, 1940.

Newbold, J. T. Walton. "The Beginnings of the World Crisis, 1873–1896." *Economic History* 2:8 (January 1932): 425–441.

Niemeyer, Waldyr. *Brasil e seu comércio interno.* Rio de Janeiro: A. Coelho Branco, 1948.

Nieto Arteta, Luis Eduardo. *El café en la sociedad colombiana.* Bogotá: La Soga del Cuello, 1971.

North, Douglass C. "Location Theory and Regional Economic Growth." *Journal of Political Economy* 63:3 (1955): 243–258.

Novais, Fernando. *Portugal e Brasil na crises do antigo sistema colonial, 1777–1808.* São Paulo: Editora HUCITEC, 1979.

Odell, Peter R. "The Oil Industry in Latin America." In Edith T. Penrose, ed., *The Large International Firm in Developing Countries: The International Petroleum Industry.* London: Allen & Unwin, 1968, 274–300.

Oliveira, José Teixeira de. *História do café no Brasil e no mundo.* Rio de Janeiro: Livraria Kosmos, 1984.

Olvera, Alberto J. "The Rise and Fall of Union Democracy at Poza Rica, 1932–1940." In Jonathan C. Brown and Alan Knight, eds., *The Mexican Petroleum Industry in the Twentieth Century.* Austin: University of Texas Press, 1992, 63–89.

Ortiz Fernández, Fernando. *Cuban Counterpoint: Tobacco and Sugar.* Trans. Bronislaw Malinowski. New York: Knopf, 1947.

Owen, Norman G. "Americans in the Abaca Trade: Peele, Hubbell & Co., 1856–1875." In Peter W. Stanley, ed., *Reappraising an Empire: New Perspectives on Philippine-American History.* Cambridge, Mass.: Harvard University Press, 1989, 95–114.

———. *Prosperity without Progress: Manila Hemp and Material Life in the Colonial Philippines.* Berkeley and Los Angeles: University of California Press, 1984.

———. "Subsistence in the Slump: Agricultural Adjustment in the Provincial Philippines." In Ian Brown, ed., *The Economies of Africa and Asia in the Inter-War Depression.* London and New York: Routledge, 1989, 95–114.

254

The Second Conquest of Latin America

Paige, Jeffrey M. *Agrarian Revolution: Social Movements and Export Agriculture in the Underdeveloped World.* New York: Free Press, 1975.

Palacios, Marco. *El café en Colombia, 1850–1970.* Mexico City: El Colegio de México, 1983; originally published as *Coffee in Colombia, 1850–1970,* Cambridge University Press, 1980.

Pang, Eul–Soo. *In Pursuit of Honor and Power: Noblemen of the Southern Cross in the Nineteenth Century in Brazil.* Tuscaloosa: University of Alabama Press, 1988.

Paredes Huggins, Nelson. *Vialidad y comercio en el occidente venezolano: Principios del siglo XX.* Caracas: Fondo Editorial Tropykos, 1984.

Parsons, James J. *Antioqueño Colonization in Western Colombia.* Berkeley and Los Angeles: University of California Press, 1949.

Patch, Robert. "A Colonial Regime: Maya and Spaniard in Yucatán." Ph.D. diss., Princeton University, 1979.

Patterson, Orlando. *Slavery and Social Death: A Comparative Study.* Cambridge, Mass.: Harvard University Press, 1982.

Peniche Rivero, Piedad. "Gender, Bridewealth, and Marriage: Social Reproduction of Peons on Henequen Haciendas in Yucatán, 1870–1901." In Heather Fowler Salamini and Mary Kay Vaughan, eds., *Women of the Mexican Countryside, 1850–1990: Creating Spaces, Shaping Transitions.* Tucson: University of Arizona Press, 1994, 74–89.

Penrose, Edith T., ed. *The Large International Firm in Developing Countries: The International Petroleum Industry.* London: Allen & Unwin, 1968.

Perales Frigols, Pablo. *Geografía económica del estado Zulia.* 2 vols. Maracaibo: Imprenta del Estado, 1957.

Pérez Brignoli, Héctor. *A Brief History of Central America.* Trans. Ricardo Sawrey A. and Susana Stettri de Sawrey. Berkeley and Los Angeles: University of California Press, 1989.

———. "Indians, Communists, and Peasants: The 1932 Rebellion in El Salvador." In William Roseberry, Lowell Gudmundson, and Mario Samper Kutschbach, eds., *Coffee, Society and Power in Latin America.* Baltimore, Md.: Johns Hopkins University Press, 1995, 232–261.

Philip, George. *Oil and Politics in Latin America: Nationalist Movements and the State Oil Companies.* New York: Cambridge University Press, 1982.

Pinelo, Adalberto. *The Multinational Corporation as a Force in Latin American Politics: A Case Study of the International Petroleum Company in Peru.* New York: Praeger, 1973.

Pratt, Joseph A. *The Growth of a Refining Region.* Greenwich, Conn.: Jai Press, 1980.

Rabe, Stephen G. *The Road to OPEC: United States Relations with Venezuela, 1919–1976.* Austin: University of Texas Press, 1982.

Radell, David. *Coffee and Transportation in Nicaragua.* Berkeley and Los Angeles: University of California Press, 1964.

Ramos, Augusto. *A crise do café: Parecer apresentado à sociedade rural brasileira.* São Paulo: Revista dos Tribunais, 1930.

Ramos, F. Ferreira. *The Valorization of Coffee in Brazil.* Antwerp: J. E. Buschmann, 1907.

Randall, Laura. *The Political Economy of Venezuelan Oil.* New York: Praeger, 1987.

Raymond, André. *Artisans et commerçants au Caire au XVIII siècle.* Damas: Institute Français de Damas, 1973–1974.

Reed, Nelson. *The Caste War of Yucatán.* Stanford, Calif.: Stanford University Press, 1964.

Remmers, Lawrence J. "Henequen, the Caste War and Economy of Yucatán, 1846–1883: The Roots of Dependence in a Mexican Region." 2 vols. Ph.D. diss., UCLA, 1981.

Rezende, Padua. *Defesa do Café exposição de 1922 e frigoríficos.* Rio de Janeiro: Imprensa Nacional, 1927.

Richards, John. "The Staples Debates." In Cameron Duncan, ed., *Explorations in Canadian Economic History: Essays in Honour of Irene Spry.* Ottowa: University of Ottowa Press, 1985, 45–72.

Rippy, Merrill. *Oil and the Mexican Revolution.* Leiden: Brill, 1972.

Roazen-Parrillo, Diane. "U.S. Business Interests and the Sisal Industry of Yucatán, Mexico, 1876–1926." Ph.D. diss., University of Chicago, 1984.

Robinson, Ronald. "Non-European Foundations of Economic Imperialism: Sketch for a Theory of Collaboration." In Roger Owen and Bob Sutcliffe, eds., *Studies in the Theory of Imperialism.* London: Longman, 1972, 117–142.

Roseberry, William. *Coffee and Capitalism in the Venezuelan Andes.* Austin: University of Texas Press, 1983.

———. "*La falta de brazos*: Land and Labor in the Coffee Economies of Nineteenth-Century Latin America." *Theory and Society* 20:3 (June 1991): 351–381.

Roseberry, William, Lowell Gudmundson, and Mario Samper Kutschbach, eds. *Coffee, Society and Power in Latin America.* Baltimore, Md.: Johns Hopkins University Press, 1995.

Rostow, Walt W. *The Stages of Economic Growth.* Cambridge: Cambridge University Press, 1960.

———. *The World Economy: History and Prospect.* Austin: University of Texas Press, 1978.

Rothstein, Morton. "America in the International Rivalry for the British Wheat Market, 1860–1914." In Harry N. Scheiber, ed., *U.S. Economic History: Selected Readings.* New York: Knopf, 1964, 290–308.

Rouaix, Pastor. *Génesis de los artículos 27 y 123 de la constitución política de 1917.* 2nd ed. Mexico City: Biblioteca del Instituto Nacional de Estudios Históricos de la Revolución Mexicana, 1959.

Rout, Leslie B., Jr. *Politics of the Chaco Peace Conference, 1935–1939.* Austin: University of Texas Press, 1970.

Rowe, J. W. F. *Primary Commodities in International Trade.* Cambridge: Cambridge University Press, 1965.

———. *Studies in the Artificial Control of Raw Material Supplies: Brazilian Coffee.* London: London and Cambridge Economic Service, 1932.

Rowe, Melodia B. *Captain Jones—the Biography of a Builder.* Hamilton, Ohio, 1942.

Roxborough, Ian. *Theories of Underdevelopment.* London: Macmillan, 1991.

Rueschmeyer, Dietrich, Evelyn Huber Stephens, and John D. Stephens. *Capitalist Development and Democracy.* Cambridge, Mass.: Polity, 1992.

Ruiz, Ramón Eduardo. *Labor and the Ambivalent Revolutionaries: Mexico, 1911–1923.* Baltimore, Md.: Johns Hopkins University Press, 1976.

Rus, Jan. "The 'Comunidad Revolucionaria Institucional': The Subversion of Native Government in Highland Chiapas, 1936–1938." In Gilbert M. Joseph and Daniel Nugent, eds., *Everyday Forms of State Formation: Revolution and the Negotiation of Rule in Modern Mexico.* Durham, N.C.: Duke University Press, 1994, 265–300.

Sábato, Hilda. "Citizenship, Political Participation, and the Formation of the Public Sphere in Buenos Aires, 1850s–1880s." *Past and Present* 136 (August 1989): 139–163.

Salazar-Carrillo, Jorge. *Oil and Development in Venezuela during the Twentieth Century.* Westport, Conn.: Praeger, 1994.

Sampson, Anthony. *The Seven Sisters: The Great Oil Companies and the World They Made.* New York: Viking, 1975.

Sánchez-Albornoz, Nicolás. *The Population of Latin America: A History.* Trans. W. A. R. Richardson. Berkeley and Los Angeles: University of California Press, 1974.

Sarmiento, Domingo F. *Life in the Argentine Republic in the Days of the Tyrants.* Trans. Mrs. Horace Mann. New York: Collier Books, 1961 [1868].

Schivelbusch, Wolfgang. *Tastes of Paradise: A Social History of Spices, Stimulants, and Intoxicants.* Trans. D. Jacobson. New York: Vintage, 1993.

Schmidt, Arthur. *The Social and Economic Effects of the Railroad in Puebla and Veracruz, Mexico, 1867–1911.* New York: Garland Press, 1987.

Scott, Rebecca. "Defining the Boundaries of Freedom in the World of Cane: Cuba, Brazil and Louisiana after Emancipation." *American Historical Review* 99:1 (February 1994): 70–102.

Seligson, Mitchell A. *Peasants of Costa Rica and the Development of Agrarian Capitalism.* Madison: University of Wisconsin Press, 1980.

Shafer, Michael D. *Winners and Losers: How Sectors Shape the Developmental Prospects of States.* Ithaca, N.Y.: Cornell University Press, 1994.

Shattuck, George C. *The Peninsula of Yucatán: Medical, Biological, Meteorological and Sociological Studies.* Washington, D.C.: Carnegie Institution, 1933.

Sheahan, John. *Patterns of Development in Latin America: Poverty, Repression and Economic Strategy.* Princeton, N.J.: Princeton University Press, 1987.

Silva, Eduardo. *Baroes e escravidão.* Rio de Janeiro: Editora Nova Fronteira, 1984.

Silva, Sérgio. *Expansão cafeeira e origens da indústria no Brasil.* São Paulo: Editora Alfa-Omega, 1981.

Silva Herzog, Jesús. *El petróleo de México.* Mexico City, 1940.

Singh, Kelvin. "Oil Politics in Venezuela during the López Contreras Administration (1936–1941)." *Journal of Latin American Studies* 21:1 (February 1989): 89–104.

Smith, Peter S. *Oil and Politics in Modern Brazil.* Toronto: Macmillan, 1976.

Soares, Luiz Carlos. "A manufatura na sociedade escravista: O surto manufatureiro no Rio de Janeiro e nas suas circunvizinhang as (1840–1870)." In Frédéric Mauro, ed., *La preindustrialization du Brésil: Essais sur une economie en transition, 1830/50–1930/50.* Paris: Editions de Centre National du Recherche Scientifique, 1984.

Solberg, Carl. E. "Entrepreneurship in Public Enterprise: General Enrique Mosconi and the Argentine Petroleum Industry." *Business History Review* 61 (1982): 380–399.

———. *Oil and Nationalism in Argentina: A History.* Stanford, Calif.: Stanford University Press, 1982.

———. "YPF: The Formative Years of Latin America's Pioneer State Oil Company, 1922–1939." In John D. Wirth, ed., *Latin American Oil Companies and the Politics of Energy.* Lincoln: University of Nebraska Press, 1985, 51–102.

Southworth, John Reginald. *El estado de Veracruz-Llave.* Liverpool: Blake & MacKenzie, 1900.

Spenser, Daniela. "Soconusco: The Formation of a Coffee Economy in Chiapas." In Thomas Benjamin and William McNellie, eds., *Other Mexicos: Essays on Regional Mexican History, 1876–1911.* Albuquerque: University of New Mexico Press, 1984, 123–143.

Staley, Eugene. *Raw Materials in Peace and War.* New York: Council on Foreign Relations, 1937.

Stallings, Barbara. *Banker to the Third World: U.S. Portfolio Investment in Latin America, 1900–1986.* Berkeley and Los Angeles: University of California Press, 1987.

Stein, Stanley. *Vassouras: A Brazilian Coffee County.* Cambridge, Mass: Harvard University Press, 1956.

Stern, Steve J. "Africa, Latin America and the Splintering of Historical Knowledge: From Fragmentation to Reverberation." In Frederick Cooper et al., *Confronting Historical Paradigms: Peasants, Labor, and the Capitalist World System in Africa and Latin America.* Madison: University of Wisconsin Press, 1993, 3–20.

———. "Feudalism, Capitalism and the World-System in the Perspective of Latin America and the Caribbean." In Frederick Cooper et al., *Confronting Historical Paradigms: Peasants, Labor, and the Capitalist World System in Africa and Latin America.* Madison: University of Wisconsin Press, 1993, 23–83.

Stewart, Randal G. *Coffee: The Political Economy of an Export Industry in Papua New Guinea.* Boulder, Colo.: Westview, 1992.

Stolcke, Verena. *Cafeicultura, homens, mulheres e capital (1850–1980).* Trans. Denise Bottmann and João R. Martins Filho. São Paulo: Brasiliense, 1986.

———. "The Labors of Coffee in Latin America: The Hidden Charm of Family Labor and Self-Provisioning." In William Roseberry, Lowell Gudmundson, and Mario Samper Kutschbach, eds., *Coffee, Society and Power in Latin America.* Baltimore, Md.: Johns Hopkins University Press, 1995, 65–94.

Stone, Samuel Z. *The Heritage of the Conquistadors: Ruling Classes in Central*

America from the Conquest to the Sandinistas. Lincoln: University of Nebraska Press, 1990.

The Story of Twine in Agriculture. Chicago: International Harvester Company, n.d.

Stover, Charles C. "Tropical Exports." In W. Arthur Lewis, ed., *Tropical Development, 1880–1913.* Evanston, Ill.: Northwestern University Press, 1970, 46–63.

Sweigart, Joseph. *Coffee Factorage and the Emergence of a Brazilian Coffee Market.* New York: Garland Press, 1987.

Taunay, Affonso de Escragnolle. *História do café no Brasil,* vol. XIII. Rio de Janeiro: Departamento Nacional de Café, 1943.

Taylor, Frank J., and Earl M. Welty. *Sign of the 76: The Fabulous Life and Times of the Union Oil Company of California.* Los Angeles: The Company, 1976.

Taylor, John G. *From Modernization to Modes of Production: A Critique of the Sociologies of Development and Underdevelopment.* London: Macmillan, 1979.

Tennassee, Paul Nehru. *Venezuela, los obreros petroleros y la lucha por la democracia.* Madrid: Editorial Popular, 1979.

Thompson, Andrew. "Informal Empire? An Exploration in the History of Anglo-Argentine Relations, 1810–1914." *Journal of Latin American Studies* 24 (1992): 419–436.

Thorp, Rosemary. "Latin America and the International Economy from the First World War to the World Depression." In Leslie Bethell, ed., *Cambridge History of Latin America,* vol. VI, pt. 1. New York: Cambridge University Press, 1994, 57–81.

———. *Latin America in the 1930s: The Role of the Periphery in World Crises.* New York: St. Martin's Press, 1984.

———. "The Latin American Economies, 1939–c. 1950." In Leslie Bethell, ed., *Cambridge History of Latin America,* vol. VI, pt. 1. New York: Cambridge University Press, 1994, 117–158.

Thorp, Rosemary, and Geoffrey Bertram. *Peru, 1890–1977: Growth and Policy in an Open Economy.* London: Macmillan, 1978.

Thurber, Francis B. *Coffee: From Plantation to Cup.* New York: American Grocer Publishing Association, 1886.

Tipps, Dean. "Modernization Theory and the Comparative Study of Societies: A Critical Perspective." *Comparative Studies in Society and History* 15:2 (1973): 200–211.

Topik, Steven. "Coffee." In *Cambridge History and Culture of Food and Nutrition,* forthcoming.

———. "The Economic Role of the State in Liberal Regimes: Brazil and Mexico Compared, 1888–1910." In Joseph L. Love and Nils Jacobsen, eds., *Guiding the Invisible Hand: Economic Liberalism and the State in Latin American History.* New York: Praeger, 1988, 117–144.

———. "L'état sur le marché: Approche comparative du café brésilien et du henequen mexicain." *Annales Economies, Sociétés, Civilisations* 46:2 (March–April 1991): 429–458.

———. *The Political Economy of the Brazilian State, 1889–1930.* Austin: University of Texas Press, 1987.

———. *Trade and Gunboats: The United States and Brazil in the Age of Empire.* Stanford, Calif.: Stanford University Press, 1996.

Trouillot, Michel–Rolph. "Motion in the System: Coffee, Color and Slavery in Eighteenth-Century Saint-Domingue." *Review* 5:3 (Winter 1982): 331–388.

Ukers, William H. *All about Coffee.* New York: The Tea and Coffee Trade Journal, 1935.

U.S. Department of Commerce. *Sisal Production: Prices, and Marketing. Trade Information Bulletin 200.* Washington, D.C.: U.S. Government Printing Office, 1924.

U.S. Department of Commerce and Labor, Bureau of Corporations. *The International Harvester Company.* Washington, D.C.: U.S. Government Printing Office, 1913.

Vallenilla, Luis. *Oil: The Making of a New Economic Order: Venezuelan Oil and OPEC.* New York: McGraw-Hill, 1975.

Villars, Jorge Dumont. *O café e sua produção e exportação.* São Paulo: Instituto de Café do Estado de São Paulo, 1927.

Wagner, Regina. "Actividades empresariales de los alemanes en Guatemala, 1850–1920." *Mesoamérica* 13 (June 1987): 98–107.

Wall, Bennett H. *Growth in a Changing Environment: A History of Standard Oil Company (New Jersey), Exxon Corporation, 1950–1975.* New York: McGraw-Hill,1988.

Wallerstein, Immanuel. *The Modern World System: Capitalist Agriculture and the Origins of the European World-Economy in the Sixteenth Century.* New York: Academic Press, 1974.

———. "The Rise and Future Demise of the World Capitalist System: Concepts for Comparative Analysis." *Comparative Studies in Society and History* 15:4 (September 1974): 387–415.

Wasserstrom, Robert. *Class and Society in Central Chiapas.* Berkeley and Los Angeles: University of California Press, 1983.

Watkins, Melville H. "A Staple Theory of Economic Growth." *Canadian Journal of Economics and Political Science* 29 (May 1963): 141–158.

Weiner, Richard. "Discourses on the Market in Porfirian Mexico." *Latin American Perspectives,* forthcoming.

Weinstein, Barbara. *The Amazon Rubber Boom, 1850–1920.* Stanford, Calif.: Stanford University Press, 1983.

Wells, Allen. "All in the Family: Railroads and Henequen Monoculture in Porfirian Yucatán." *Hispanic American Historical Review* 72:2 (May 1992): 159–209.

———. "From Hacienda to Plantation: The Transformation of Santo Domingo Xcuyum." In Jeffery T. Brannon and Gilbert M. Joseph, eds., *Land, Labor and Capital in Modern Yucatán: Essays in Regional History and Political Economy.* Tuscaloosa: University of Alabama Press, 1991, 112–142.

———. *Yucatán's Gilded Age: Haciendas, Henequen and International Harvester, 1860–1915.* Albuquerque: University of New Mexico Press, 1985.

Wells, Allen, and Gilbert M. Joseph. *Summer of Discontent, Seasons of Upheaval: Elite Politics and Rural Insurgency in Yucatán, 1876–1915.* Stanford, Calif.: Stanford University Press, 1996.

Wheelock R., Jaime. *Imperialismo y dictadura: Crisis de una formación social.* Mexico City: Siglo XXI, 1975.

White, Gerald T. *Formative Years in the Far West: A History of Standard Oil Company of California and Predecessors through 1919.* New York: Appleton-Century-Crofts, 1962.

Wickizer, V. D. *Coffee, Tea and Cocoa.* Stanford, Calif.: Food Research Center, 1959.

———. *The World Coffee Economy with Special Reference to Control Schemes.* Stanford, Calif.: Food Research Center, 1943.

Wilkins, Mira. *The Emergence of Multinational Enterprise: American Business Abroad from the Colonial Era to 1914.* Cambridge, Mass.: Harvard University Press, 1970.

———. "The Free-Standing Company, 1870–1914: An Important Type of British Foreign Direct Investment." *Economic History Review* 2nd ser., 41 (May 1988): 259–282.

———. "The Free-Standing Company Revisited." In Mira Wilkins and Harm Schröter, eds., *The Free-Standing Company in the World Economy, 1830–1996.* Oxford: Oxford University Press, forthcoming.

———. *The Growth of Multinational Enterprise.* Aldershot, England: E. Elgar, 1991.

———. *The History of Foreign Investment in the United States to 1914.* Cambridge, Mass.: Harvard University Press, 1989.

———. *The History of Foreign Investment in the United States after 1914.* Forthcoming.

———. *The Maturing Enterprise: American Business Abroad from 1914–1970.* Cambridge, Mass.: Harvard University Press, 1974.

———. "Multinational Corporations: An Historical Account." In Robert Rowthorn and Richard Kozul-Wright, eds., *Transnational Corporations and the Global Economy.* London: Macmillan, forthcoming.

———. "Multinational Oil Companies in South America in the 1920s: In Argentina, Bolivia, Brazil, Chile, Colombia, Ecuador, Peru." *Business History Review* 48 (Autumn 1974): 414–446.

Williams, Eric. *Slavery and Capitalism.* New York: Capricorn Books, 1966.

Williams, Robert G. *States and Social Evolution: Coffee and the Rise of National Governments in Central America.* Chapel Hill: University of North Carolina Press, 1994.

Williamson, Harold F., and Arnold R. Daum. *The American Petroleum Industry.* 2 vols. Evanston, Ill.: Northwestern University Press, 1959–1963.

Wilson, Eugene M. "Physical Geography of the Yucatán Peninsula." In Edward H. Moseley and Edward D. Terry, eds., *Yucatán: A World Apart.* Tuscaloosa: University of Alabama Press, 1980, 5–40.

Winks, Robin. "On Decolonization and Informal Empire." *American Historical Review* 81:3 (1976): 540–556.

Winson, Anthony. *Coffee and Democracy in Modern Latin America.* London: Macmillan, 1989.

Wirth, John D. *Politics of Brazilian Development, 1930–1954.* Stanford, Calif.: Stanford University Press, 1970.

———. "Setting the Brazilian Agenda, 1936–1953." In John D. Wirth, ed., *Latin American Oil Companies and the Politics of Energy.* Lincoln: University of Nebraska Press, 1985, 103–144.

Wolf, Eric, and Sidney Mintz. "Haciendas and Plantations in Middle America and the Antilles." *Social and Economic Studies* 6:3 (September 1957): 380–422.

Womack, John, Jr. "The Mexican Economy during the Revolution, 1910–1920." *Marxist Perspectives* 1:4 (1978): 80–123.

Wright, Winthrop R. *Café con leche: Race, Class, and National Image in Venezuela.* Austin: University of Texas Press, 1990.

Zimmerman, Siegried. *Theodor Wille.* Hamburg: N.p., 1969.

Contributors

Jonathan C. Brown teaches Latin American history at the University of Texas at Austin, where he is Professor of History. He is author of *Oil and Revolution in Mexico* (University of California Press, 1993) and the prizewinning *A Socioeconomic History of Argentina* (Cambridge University Press, 1979) and editor of *Workers' Control in Latin America, 1930–1979* (University of North Carolina Press, 1997). He is currently completing a book on the social history of colonial Latin America.

Peter Linder, a specialist in the history of nineteenth and twentieth century Venezuela, received his Ph.D. in Latin American history from the University of Texas in 1992. Having taught in recent years at Bates College and the University of Maine at Machias, he is currently Assistant Professor of Latin American and borderlands history at New Mexico Highlands University in Las Vegas.

Steven Topik is Professor and Chair of History at the University of California, Irvine. He is author of *The Political Economy of the Brazilian State (1889–1930)* (University of Texas Press, 1987) and *Trade and Gunboats: The United States and Brazil in the Age of Empire* (Stanford University Press, 1996).

Allen Wells is Associate Dean for Academic Affairs and Professor of History at Bowdoin College, Brunswick, Maine. The history of modern Yucatán has been the focus of much of his scholarly work. His most recent publication, with Gilbert M. Joseph (Yale University), is *Summer of Discontent, Seasons of Upheaval: Elite Politics and Rural Insurgency in Yucatán, 1876–1915* (Stanford University Press, 1996).

Mira Wilkins is Professor of Economics at Florida International University in Miami. Her major work has been in the field of business history, where she has focused on the history of multinational enterprise. She has published numerous articles and books, including: *The Emergence of Multinational Enterprise: American Business Abroad from the Colonial Period to 1914* (1970); *The Maturing of Multinational Enterprise: American Business Abroad from 1914 to 1970* (1974); and *The History of Foreign Investment in the United States to 1914* (1989), all published by Harvard University Press. A coedited volume, *The Free-Standing Company in the World Economy, 1830–1996,* will be published by Oxford University Press in 1998.

Index